The Evaluation of Transportation Investment Projects

Routledge Advances in Management and Business Studies

For a full list of title in this series, please visit www.routledge.com

The Evaluation of Transportation Investment Projects

Joseph Berechman

Routledge
Taylor & Francis Group
New York   London

First published 2009
by Routledge
711 Third Avenue, New York, NY 10017

Simultaneously published in the UK
by Routledge
2 Park Square, Milton Park, Abingdon, Oxfordshire OX14 4RN

First issued in paperback 2014

Routledge is an imprint of the Taylor and Francis Group, an informa company

Typeset in Sabon by IBT Global.

Library of Congress Cataloging in Publication Data

Berechman, Joseph.
The evaluation of transportation investment projects / by Joseph Berechman.
p. cm. -- (Routledge advances in management and business studies ; 42)
Includes bibliographical references and index.
1. Transportation--Finance.   2. Construction projects--Evaluation.   I. Title.

HE196.5.B47 2009
388'.049--dc22   2009004664

ISBN13: 978-0-415-77715-5 (hbk)
ISBN13: 978-0-415-75446-0 (pbk)

I dedicate this book to my newborn grandson, Ely.
May his world be just and peaceful.

Contents

Figures

Tables

Preface

I keep six honest serving-men
(They taught me all I knew);
Their names are What and Why and When
And How and Where and Who.
I send them over land and sea,
I send them east and west;
But after they have worked for me,
I give them all a rest.

I let them rest from nine till five,
For I am busy then,
As well as breakfast, lunch, and tea,
For they are hungry men.
But different folk have different views.
I know a person small—
She keeps ten million serving-men,
Who get no rest at all!

She sends 'em abroad on her own affairs,
From the second she opens her eyes—
One million Hows, two million Wheres,
And seven million Whys!

—Rudyard Kipling
From *"The Elephant's Child"*

In a previous book written by Prof. David Banister and myself, we raised the question of whether transportation investment projects generate economic growth benefits and, if so, what is their nature and how significant are they (Banister and Berechman, 2000). Our motivation in exploring these questions grew from our concern that in many cases, when transportation investment projects cannot be fully or even partly justified on the basis of their direct transportation benefits, their advocates tend to argue that the project will nonetheless engender substantial economic benefits. We showed that, by and large, for a given transportation investment, economic development benefits are difficult to establish and substantiate. In general, the economic development benefits growing out of such investments are poorly defined, with attempts to appraise them often double-counting the benefits. Rationalization of projects mainly on the basis of economic development benefits is consequently erroneous and likely to conclude in the implementation of inferior projects.

In recent years I have been engaged in several studies designed to analyze and evaluate transportation investment projects. In one recent major study, the objective was to prioritize a set of large-scale rail and transit hub investments in New York for the purpose of recommending which should be carried out (Berechman and Paaswell, 2005). In the course of carrying out this study, the most striking observation was the tenuous evaluation process that key stakeholders used to rationalize their positions on the various projects. These stakeholders neither saw the need for a systematic and well-founded evaluation procedure nor worried much about the modest value of the anticipated transportation benefits. Ambiguous catch phrases such as "the project's potential for urban development," "promoting regional needs," "strengthening the vitality of the city's economy," or "the critical importance of rapid transit services to business and economic development" were used prima facie to justify their favorite project. Yet, from transportation, economic, and even social perspectives, these projects made little sense. As a transportation economist and planner, I was deeply troubled by the staggering capital costs of these projects—running into billions of dollars—which could have been invested in public infrastructure either in transportation or in other domains, such as the environment, health, and education.

This situation, however, is not unique to New York City or, for that matter, to any specific urban area or country. A growing body of literature has documented the colossal failure of many transportation mega-projects worldwide to meet projected budgets, travel volumes, and timetables (Flyvbjerg et al., 2003; Winston and Maheshri, 2007). The absence of a well-founded, comprehensive, and ongoing evaluation process at a core stage in decision making is commonly cited as one of the main causes of the failures (US Government Accountability Office, 2005).

Explanations for this phenomenon encompass a wide range of reasons. They include the politics of public infrastructure decision making; state and federal capital subsidization of local projects, which encourage non-systematic project evaluation; or the downplay of transportation impacts by placing excessive weight on claims that the investment will automatically engender regional economic growth. Not less glaring, however, is the impression that many transportation professionals are not well acquainted with the literature on transportation project evaluation, and especially of its recent developments. This might be due to the fact that no currently available topical book on the subject is sufficiently comprehensive to cover all the relevant aspects of transportation investment decision making, or adequately up-to-date to offer the most recent analytical and empirical advances in the germane areas.

To be sure, most countries use some formal transportation project evaluation procedures. Yet, these are, by and large, partial, ad hoc, and applied only at the initial phases of the planning process, when vital information (mainly, cost and demand projections) is largely missing. Many of these procedures neglect to consider key issues such as project risks, methods of capital funding, latent demand, market imperfections, and incompatibilities between trip rates, travel costs, and activity location. As a result, projects that would not have been accepted had a comprehensive and effective evaluation process been applied are judged viable under deficient and sometimes faulty evaluation schemes.

This state of affairs motivated the writing of this book. Its main objective: to present a comprehensive and methodical transportation investment evaluation scheme. To be viable, such a scheme should rest on four major principles: well-established theoretical principles; comprehensiveness with respect to all the relevant evaluation issues; applicability to a wide range of transportation investment projects; and amenability to sensitivity analysis relative to decision-making preferences and future scenarios.

The first principle is embedded in normative theories and models of micro and welfare economics, financial and risk analysis, transportation planning and traffic flow, and urban activity location. Compliance with the second principle is accomplished through the use of a public policy analysis approach based on detailed definition of planning objectives and design alternatives, the identification of stakeholders and their preferences, and specification of germane decision criteria. The third principle is the result of the development, as presented in this book, of operational measures and methods that can be used to evaluate a broad range of transportation investment projects. Application of these methods to several real-world case studies will demonstrate their effectiveness as evaluation tools. Finally, the decision framework developed in this book allows realization of the fourth principle: the explicit expression of stakeholders' preferences at the project selection and choice phases of the evaluation in addition to the testing of alternative planning and economic scenarios.

A well-established body of knowledge containing normative models and rules for transportation cost-benefit assessment and project evaluation is already in place. Yet, this knowledge is not well organized, nor readily accessible to economists and planners having only basic knowledge of transportation economics, transportation planning, and quantitative methods. This observation applies to students as well as practitioners. As a result, the book's potential audiences are graduate students in the areas of transportation and urban economics, geography, urban planning, and transportation engineering. Professionals such as traffic engineers, transportation planners, urban planners, practicing economists, and consultants directly involved with the evaluation of transportation infrastructure investments will also find it useful.

While this is not a book on policy analysis, it nevertheless devotes considerable space to the role of policymaking in influencing project evaluation and selection. Western democracies are marked by complex public decision-making institutions that are predisposed to interest group pressure, conflicting concerns over major social and economic issues, opposing ideologies, and, at times, even unethical behavior. Thus, understanding the motivations of decision makers and how they think about public investments is an important ingredient in constructing a decision-making paradigm conducive to rational transportation infrastructure investment and development.

In sum, my basic objective in writing this book is to help inform present and future generations of transportation specialists on the tools available for carrying out project evaluation, the theoretical foundations of those tools, and how they should be applied. The book will hopefully prove valuable to those intent on improving transportation investment evaluation and rationalization.

Acknowledgments

Several institutions were very instrumental in carrying out the necessary research and writings for this book. I wish to acknowledge the generous financial support for editorial assistance that I have received from Tel Aviv University, Israel and for the financial research support that I have received from the University Transportation Research Center Region 2, and The City College of New York (CUNY). Technical support for data collection was received from the Sauder Business School, The University of British Columbia in Vancouver, Canada.

Many of my academic colleagues and friends were kind enough to read versions of the manuscript and provide me with invaluable comments on specific chapters. While their contributions have, undoubtedly, improved the manuscript significantly, the responsibility for the views expressed in this book, its analysis and conclusions, is solely mine. In alphabetic order I wish to thank David Banister, Dan Chatman, Genevieve Giuliano, David Gillen, Patricia Mokhtarian, Robert (Buz) Paaswell, Yoram Shiftan, Martin Wachs, Itzhak Zilcha, Rachel Weinberger. Many others have provided helpful comments on models that have been presented at conferences and seminars. My thanks are warmly extended to all these colleagues.

I would also like to thank Mrs. Nina Reshef and Ms. Bailey Schroeder for their painstaking editing and proof reading of the manuscript and the staff of Routledge Books for their highly professional help during the preparation of the book.

Joseph Berechman
New York, April 2009

1 Objectives, Scope, and Structure

Not everything in the world that can be counted counts,
and not everything that counts can be counted.

—Albert Einstein

1. PERSPECTIVE

Countries across the globe routinely invest massive resources in transportation infrastructure in the form of new facilities, expansion of existing ones, or maintenance and repair of the network in place. What is common to all of these investments is that they are products of public sector decision making at the local, regional, national, and, at times, international level. Despite their strong technical and economic dimensions, transportation investments represent partial political statements regarding objectives, funding priorities, and targeted service recipients. Viewed from this perspective, transportation investments are similar to other public sector projects. Given this reality, the key questions that this book sets out to explore are normative in nature: What should the objectives and purposes of transportation investments cover? What should their scope be relative to population and space? How should they be analyzed in terms of available analytical tools and the attendant decision making?

Of these, the first question is often the most problematic. The difficulty arises from the fact that like the case of beauty as an objective of art, the purpose of a transportation investment is in the eye of the beholder. Some will argue for transportation-related objectives such as reducing congestion, increasing accessibility, or improving highway safety. Others may argue that equity concerns related to job market access, improved reachability of rural areas, and general spatial mobility should be a project's leading objectives. Still other arguments pertain to the mitigation of environmental externalities, the impact on urban structure, and the generation of economic growth. Only rarely are political motives cited as the underlying raison d'être for a specific project, although these may very often be the true incentives impelling political decision makers to allocate huge amounts of financial resources to projects that might not have been constructed otherwise. According to this somewhat cynical view, the costs of a project are in effect political benefits to be distributed among constituents, supporters, and functionaries.[1]

Policy analysts using the tools of their trade might study transportation projects in terms of the key players, their social and economic viewpoints and political agendas, including coalition-building and distributive goals. They might also investigate other stakeholders, such as rent seekers, the administrative bureaucracy, and relationships with other political institutions (e.g., local and federal governments).

While this may be a valid approach to the understanding of how public decision making is conducted, it does not provide a genuine guide—in a normative sense—to which transportation investment alternatives best enhance social welfare. Moreover, several transportation projects are often considered concurrently and under budget constraints that require rationalization, prioritization, and selection. To that end, transportation planning and economic literature provides a set of models and techniques for the analysis of transportation investment projects. The common denominator underlying all of these tools is their goal: ascertaining which alternative investment will yield the highest social return, defined as a combination of transportation, economic, environmental, and social benefits. In following this course, this book regards the enhancement of social welfare, broadly defined, as the prime objective that should guide transportation infrastructure investments policies. (An economically based working definition of social welfare is given in Chapter 3.)

A key distinction should be made here between the concepts *project evaluation* and *project assessment*. The former refers to the *overall process* by which investment alternatives are conceptualized, generated, assessed, ranked, and finally chosen, with economic and noneconomic criteria employed in decision making. The latter concept, (i.e., project assessment), refers to the structured procedure by which the transportation-economic worthiness of each planning alternative is determined. Such assessments are indeed part of project evaluation, which also refers to investment policy together with other decision-making components. While a significant part of this book is devoted to the transportation-economic underpinnings of project assessment, it should be clearly understood that this facet is not an end in itself. Rather, we consider the overall process of project evaluation to be the crucial mechanism for selecting a project, sources of funding, and final implementation (Chapter 2 formally examines these issues). Furthermore, since we vigorously believe in transparency and accountability as inherent features of public decision making, we also maintain that the entire process of project evaluation should be based on acceptable rational, systematic, and justifiable principles. These issues are dealt with in Part E of the book.

Returning to project assessment, this book takes the view that the objective of social welfare maximization is best served by the selection of the "best" project from an array of possible transportation investment alternatives. A related tenet is that an assessment's results should be conveyed to decision makers by highlighting the fundamental issue of optimal allocation of scarce societal resources, namely, the opportunity costs associated with the forgone investment alternatives. Therefore, with respect to project assessment, the book's focus is on methods, techniques, and their underlying theories, all aimed at identifying the project that will yield the greatest welfare contribution.

As to project evaluation, the perspective taken in this book states that decisions on the selection and implementation of transportation investment projects are ultimately based on myriad considerations, including economic, planning, engineering, social, environmental, legal, institutional, and political interests. While each of these factors is important in itself and requires a focused analysis, as is the case when deciding other policy matters, the "whole is more than the sum of its parts". Hence, it would be wrong to assume that project choice decisions are based only on one or a subset of these key considerations. We argue here that all these factors should enter the overall decision process, subject to the fundamental requirement that they be transparent. The structure of decision making, which represents a crucial part of the overall evaluation process, should therefore be transparent as well.

2. APPROACHES TO TRANSPORTATION PROJECT EVALUATION

We can study the process of infrastructure project evaluation from several alternative viewpoints. For instance, the process can be examined from a "positive" perspective, implying that we study how the process actually unfolds. Alternatively, we can study it from a "normative" perspective, where theoretically derived rules are utilized to establish how the process should be carried out. Still another approach entails employment of "policy analysis" tools in order to portray the decision-making process that led to a specific project's selection.

The distinction between positive and normative analysis, two seemingly polar approaches, is somewhat contrived. A normative analysis aimed at developing guiding principles for project assessment cannot be carried out independently of the parameters set by a positive analysis. That is, a project's spatial and institutional boundaries provide the framework for its normative analysis regarding the range and distribution of its transportation and nontransportation impacts. Similarly, the required discount rate, the value of time-by-trip type, or the time span of a particular project's implementation provides inputs for the normative analysis. Alternatively, a positive analysis must employ methodologies that are based on theoretical assumptions guiding the users' behavior and objectives (e.g., utility maximization) and market structure (e.g., equilibrium market share of various travel modes).

The policy analysis approach is applied to project evaluation in order to characterize the decision making behind project prioritization. To do so, various inputs must be obtained from positive and normative analyses: benefit-to-cost ratios, sources of funding, and the distribution of benefits and costs among socioeconomic groups. A corollary to this observation states that a positive or normative analysis cannot provide relevant information if it does not consider elements of policy analysis such as the weights that various stakeholders and decision makers attach to each type of project impact.

Recognizing these critical interdependencies, this book delves into the key elements from the three major approaches. Part B therefore provides a normative welfare-maximization approach to project assessment. Parts B, C, and D employ a mix of positive and normative approaches to examine assessment principles and techniques of transportation investment projects. Based on these results, Part E develops a policy analysis evaluation approach to the ranking and selection of projects from a large set of alternatives.

3. TRANSPORTATION PROJECT EVALUATION: WHAT INTERESTS US?

The term "transportation project evaluation" is commonly used to describe a formal procedure for ascertaining the net societal welfare contribution found among several specific investment alternatives that may differ in nature (e.g., mode), goals, and incidence of benefits and costs. While societal welfare gains need to be formally defined (see Part B), here we will deal with the application of project evaluation at four levels of transportation planning.

A. Comprehensive Transportation Plan

Sometimes called "a transportation master plan," its main function is to map the full range of transportation issues and needs located within a given geographical area and to subsequently propose a range of transportation developmental options. As such, this plan should be part of a larger comprehensive land-use plan that defines urban and regional objectives as well as articulates the planners' and community's views about the region's future spatial structure. Both plans must be compatible with land-use and population policies as well as harmonized in a dynamic way so that the recommended transportation investments will support larger regional growth and social objectives. The land-use segment of the plan should also facilitate execution of the transportation plan with respect to eminent domain rights-of-way and generation of the critical demand necessary to rationalize the transportation investment. In brief, the comprehensive transportation plan acts as a guidebook from which more specified plans could be derived.

Given the nature of the comprehensive transportation plan, the evaluation process focuses on its compatibility with the comprehensive land-use plan and how well the region's economic, social and environmental objectives are supported by the plan. From a normative perspective, comprehensive transportation plans should be rationalized and updated periodically even if not statutorily required. This recommendation is rarely complied with. In practice, the most appropriate time to do so is the period following a national census, when new population and travel data and trends can be extrapolated.

B. Transportation Development Plan

A transportation development plan's declared aim is to provide the legal, economic, and planning guidelines for implementing the transportation options derived from the comprehensive plan. Of special concern are statutory issues, planning components such as phasing and readiness for implementation, and acquisition of right-of-way. Evaluations of transportation development plans focus mainly on their ability to promote project implementation within 10–15 years time horizon.

C. Transportation Investment Plan

Also called a "strategic plan" or a "comprehensive investment plan," it represents a package or set of projects that are likely to be implemented in the medium- to long-term. The key objective of a strategic plan is to provide a framework for measuring and prioritizing a set of specific transportation investment projects for the purpose of determining an adequate schedule or implementation sequence. Since transportation projects can be technically and spatially interdependent within a region, it is necessary to determine the optimal set of plans that will maximize social welfare given expected budget, statutory, and planning constraints. A strategic plan likewise needs to show the value of an alternative set of projects in light of strategic policy options as well as a range of future travel growth rates (Nash, 1993). Evaluations of such plans are suitable for only 4 to 5 years because beyond this period, key conditions—primarily financial resources availabilities—are likely to change.

D. Specific Investment Projects

The key objective of plan evaluation is to determine the welfare contribution of a specific project relative to a set of planning alternatives, including the so-called "do-nothing" or "do-minimum" alternative. Economic measures, such as benefit-to-cost ratios, are the key criteria applied to these plans provided that statutory, planning, and right-of-way conditions will be met.

This book deals mainly with evaluation of specific transportation investment projects even though analyses of specific plans and strategic plans are highly related due to their common use of the "positive net social welfare" criterion as the key decision principle. Therefore, while issues related to the evaluation of comprehensive or transportation investment plans will be discussed, evaluation of specific investments and their selection from a set of planning alternatives will remain the focus of our attention.

4. STRUCTURE OF BOOK

The overall structure of the book is shown in Figure 1.1.

Part A of the book, *Objectives, Scope, and Policy Framework*, contains two chapters. Chapter 1 presents the book's overall objectives and scope with respect to project evaluation and choice. Its fundamental canons begin with the view that decision making on transportation investments is, first and foremost, a political statement made within the political arena regarding the allocation of societal resources. The political arena is peopled by multiple interest groups and stakeholders, each with its own agendas, and each vying for the same public resources. Moreover, the decision-making process is carried out within the public sphere, a domain ruled by legal, institutional, bureaucratic, economic, environmental, social, and cultural factors.

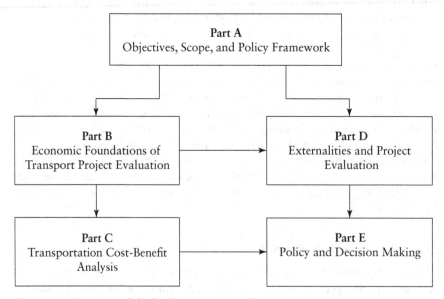

Figure 1.1 Structure of the book.

Notwithstanding these constraints, the second tenet states that since public decision making is about obtaining the "best" allocation of resources, the respective debate should necessarily center on the transportation-economic value of the specific project. Applying a term taken from the welfare economics lexicon, the issue is that of the investment's *social rate of return*, relative to its alternatives. To arrive at this rate of return, a technical analysis of the benefits and costs of an investment and of its alternatives is required. While this kind of analysis is a necessary condition, it is certainly not a sufficient one for sound decision making. Chapter 2, therefore, examines the political economy framework of project evaluation, while emphasizing the use of rational and formal project evaluation tools. This approach advocates, in essence, the use of a normative approach to transportation planning and project assessment, while recognizing the grim reality of informal, inefficient, and unfounded evaluations that characterize transportation decision making in general and mega-projects in particular.

Subsequent to accepting the rational approach to project evaluation, **Part B** of the book focuses on the economic underpinnings of public project assessment. Chapter 3 examines the welfare foundations of public investment. Chapter 4 examines components of those users' benefits engendered by transport supply improvements. Similarly, Chapter 5 analyzes the societal cost components involved in transportation infrastructure investments. Using the constructs developed in Chapters 3, 4, and 5 as inputs, Chapter 6 formally analyzes benefit-cost methods and measures.

In turning our attention to the specific attributes of transportation infrastructure investments, **Part C** focuses on four major features. Chapter 7 explores traffic flow and congestion conditions following capacity expansion. Chapter 8 then analyzes several key difficulties associated with the actual computation of benefits from a transportation investment under conditions of a fully loaded network with fixed demand and with capacity expansion-induced demand. Chapter 9 discusses the risk components of these investments, including financial risk, cost overruns, overestimation of benefits and the risk entailed in nonuniform distribution of benefits and costs. It further examines how risk can be included in project assessment. The issue of funding and its impact on transport project evaluation and ranking is examined in Chapter 10, which also discusses financing in public-private partnerships in addition to the related issue of risk sharing. Chapter 11 dwells on the equity issues raised by transportation investments especially when investments result in disproportionate accessibility to labor markets.

The subject of **Part D** is externalities, negative and positive, resulting from transportation investments and their impact on project appraisal. As indicated by Figure 1.1, the theoretical outcomes from Part B underlie the modeling and measurement of these impacts. Chapter 12 examines environmental externalities like noise and pollution as well as the safety consequences of transport improvements. Chapter 13 examines the issue of transportation investment and economic growth with respect to their underlying causes, magnitude, spatial incidence, and land-use patterns.

Part E focuses on transportation investment policy and decision making. As indicated by Figure 1.1, we accept the argument that decision making recognizes transportation cost-benefit evaluations (Part C) as major inputs for such decisions. Chapter 14 thus examines alternative methods of project ranking and selection, such as goal achievement matrix, multicriteria analysis and performance measures. The chapter then compares evaluation regimes followed in different countries. Chapter 15 explores the question of why wasteful transportation investments are so often made. Several contentions are examined and applied to three mega-projects.

To summarize, this book examines transportation investment evaluation from normative and positive viewpoints. Its major proposition is that evaluation approaches need to be grounded in sound economic and planning theory and practice, while simultaneously considering political, social, environmental, and institutional issues. The structure of the book, outlined above, reflects this principle.

2 The Policy Framework of Project Evaluation

... the ideas of economists and political philosophers, both when they are right and when they are wrong, are more powerful than is commonly understood. Indeed the world is ruled by little else. Practical men, who believe themselves to be quite exempt from any intellectual influences, are usually the slaves of some defunct economist. Madmen in authority, who hear voices in the air, are distilling their frenzy from some academic scribbler of a few years back. I am sure that the power of vested interests is vastly exaggerated compared with the gradual encroachment of ideas ... for in the field of economic and political philosophy there are not many who are influenced by new theories after they are twenty-five or thirty years of age, so that the ideas which civil servants and politicians and even agitators apply to current events are not likely to be the newest. But, soon or late, it is ideas, not vested interests, which are dangerous for good or evil.

John Maynard Keynes, *The General Theory of Employment, Interest and Money*, 1936, Chapter 24, "Concluding Notes on the Social Philosophy Towards Which the General Theory Might Lead."

1. INTRODUCTION

Transportation investments are generally declared to be projects meant to solve or ameliorate transportation problems such as traffic congestion, or to make alternative modes of travel available. At times, other objectives, for instance, road safety and environmental improvement, are said to motivate these projects. Frequently left unstated, however, are the political considerations, including funding availability, job creation and equity effects, which are oftentimes the main forces stimulating the investment. We can therefore plausibly argue that in the public sphere, any debate over efficiency improvements flowing from public investments in transportation is rather secondary to distributional differences and control over funding.

Despite this reality, from a normative point of view it remains useful to reassert the primary goal of public investment—maximization of social welfare—together with its equity and distributional impacts. In the context of transportation, social welfare can be defined in terms of travel time savings, increased mobility, improved safety, and reduced negative externalities such as air pollution and release of greenhouse gasses. Yet, welfare maximization must be carried out under conditions of restricted resources, mainly of capital and space (e.g., land), as well as considerable uncertainty about the future value of key variables: transportation behavior, prices, interest rates, and demographics. We are therefore faced with a quite complex decision problem, where the main methodological task is to define the proper objective function, pertinent constraints, and distribution of transportation determinants—travel times and volumes—over time and space.

This characterization of welfare maximization nonetheless lacks one major ingredient, namely, political considerations, defined as the distribution of benefits among user groups relative to income, location, political inclination, and other socioeconomic attributes. As noted previously, public decision makers are rather partial to this issue, which tends to dominate most other factors (Wachs, 1995). Accounting for such qualitative considerations has become a daunting task in normative project evaluation due to the difficulty of measurement and specification of those values to be used as inputs in a decision model. Various project selection techniques have been developed to overcome these obstacles (see Chapter 14).

In most cases, legislation dictates that several options must be proposed for a given project's implementation. We are therefore required to rank and prioritize them all in order to identify the project that best meets plan objectives. And, because a transportation investment's costs and benefits disproportionately affect different population segments and areas, project selection must also take the special characteristics of these populations and locations into account. To this end we need to apply a selection procedure that is rational, systematic, and, most importantly, honest and transparent. We should be aware, however, that complicating achievement of this goal is a large number of stakeholders exhibiting conflicting interests and agendas. Where public funds are involved, investments are determined at the political level; their evaluation and selection is inherently influenced by value-based political considerations that frequently overlook the significance of other criteria.

The fact is that the political features of transportation project selection manifest themselves in various ways, ranging from ill-defined objectives to irrational and unsystematic evaluations and on to ambiguous decision-making.[1] This reality often reflects the nature of democracy and legitimate democratic processes, where conflicting objectives and interests are constantly vying for public recognition and support.

How, then, are we to carry out the evaluation of transportation investment projects? To answer this question the chapter first examines several policy analysis approaches to project evaluation and then highlights key planning features of transportation project evaluation. Section 2 proposes a conceptual framework for project evaluation that reflects the general structure of this book. Section 3 examines key planning factors that affect the overall evaluation process. Section 4 further examines the rationale and motivation underlying transportation investments in metropolitan areas. A summary and conclusions are presented in Section 5.

2. CONCEPTUAL FRAMEWORK OF PROJECT EVALUATION

Transportation investment project valuation entails four primary analytic components, as shown in Figure 2.1:

What this figure indicates is the elaborate interaction between technology, markets, funding, and decision making affecting evaluation. The relative impact of each of these factors on final choices may vary, depending on the nature of the project and on local conditions. But all inevitably influence the evaluation and ranking of alternatives.

For an evaluation to be properly conducted, we further require that all publicly funded transportation systems meet several criteria. First, they must be *available and open* to all users (or to all ticket-holders), as in the case of public mass transit. Second, they must provide *rapid services* at *reasonable costs* to prevent underuse, a euphemism for abandonment in favor of faster modes of travel. Third, they must be *technically and economically efficient* relative to the cost of resources. Fourth, they must be *reliable, safe and secure* with respect to service delivery. Present realties also demand that they be *safe and secure* from the execution of hostile acts.[2]

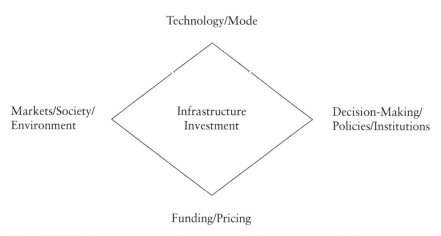

Figure 2.1 Critical components of transportation investment evaluation.

2.1 Evaluation Framework

When constructing an evaluation framework, three types of paradigms are available. A *positive* or *descriptive model*, which outlines how public decision makers actually make investment decisions; a *normative model*, which defines how authorities should make a decision in order to maximize social welfare; and a *prescriptive model* defining the rules applied when attempting to attain a set of goals that may not necessarily maximize social welfare (e.g., improved accessibility to a particular group such as employees in the Central Business District or CBD). Maximization of social welfare inherently calls for a normative evaluation model, whose primary benefit is captured in its production of benchmarks (i.e., a welfare-improving investment criteria) against which projects can be compared. For instance, the costs and benefits of a highway capacity expansion project can be compared with those of a transit capacity expansion project.

Figure 2.2 outlines the formal process for evaluation and selection of an "optimal" alternative among several transportation investment projects. It explicitly assumes that given the objectives, each project has at least two alternatives, one of which is the "do not implement" or the "status quo" option. Simon (1957) first suggested this type of paradigm as a standard for rational, systematic, and well-defined decision-making.

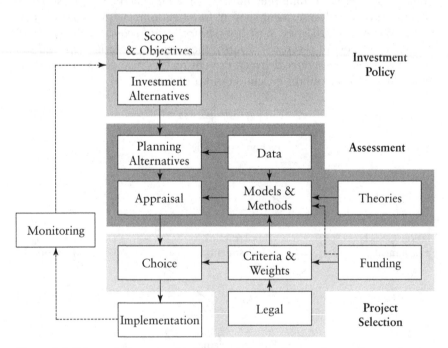

Figure 2.2 Schematic framework of a normative transportation project evaluation process.

This evaluation framework contains three major modules. The first is an *investment policy* module in which the project's objectives are defined along with its potential investment alternatives. This is the phase where decision makers (e.g., the overseeing agency or elected officials) stipulate the project's overall goals and boundaries and suggest alternative (e.g., Bus Rapid Transit vs. Light Rail). Next is an *assessment* module where each alternative's design aspects (e.g., alignment) are specified together with their relative contributions to social welfare. A significant proportion of this book focuses on this module. The third module refers to *project selection*, where final decision making regarding the alternatives takes place. Part E of this book elaborates on this module's elements.

Looking at Figure 2.2 we notice the broken line between Funding and still another module, Models & Methods. This arrow indicates that funding, although a key choice criterion (and thus integral to the Criteria & Weights phase as well) is seldom included as a feature of the Models & Methods module (see Chapter 10 for a discussion). This reality implies that most appraisal models, such as benefit-cost analysis, normally do not explicitly consider funding. Also notice the broken line between the Implementation module and the Monitoring and Objectives modules, indicating that rarely is any attempt made to ascertain whether the project actually meets its specified objectives. Once a publicly funded project is implemented, public agencies are unlikely to monitor its performance for various reasons (e.g., a leadership change), hence the paucity of *ex post* studies of transportation investments.

Within this framework, a transportation cost-benefit analysis can be characterized as a well-defined paradigm for comparing relevant and properly discounted future streams of transportation benefits against the future stream of project costs for the purpose of determining the project's present economic value. The same type of analysis is also used to rank projects in response to resource constraints.

Long ago, Lindblom (1959) suggested that a normative paradigm cannot describe what actually happens in the real world, that this model is antithetical to facts in the field. Years of documented experience in public policy analysis, including transportation, have confirmed that the evaluation and selection of an "optimal project" lacks internal logic, is rather unsystematic, incremental, and, more often than not, complicated by bureaucratic and political hurdles (Altshuler, 1965).

Although it is beyond the scope of this book to examine this and the related issues to the necessary depth, in the opinion of this author, some major phases of project evaluation—primarily those conducted by transportation and economic professionals—actually do follow a process similar to that described in Figure 2.2. For instance, the quantification of benefits and costs and the preparation of an Environmental Impact Statement (EIS) adhere, by and large, to a general formal framework put forward by state or national agencies and organizations.[3] Yet, significant details, such as the identification and measurement of key variables and parameters, are often left for local agencies to decide. This does not in any way deny that other parts of the evaluation process are concluded with less formality, mainly due to attempts to construct a consensus at the expense of so-called "scientific truth." We therefore find cloudy specification of objectives, unsystematic generation of alternatives and the use of unclear and even elusive selection criteria. These issues are examined more closely next.

2.2 Political Project Decision Making and Project Evaluation

Large-scale transportation investments typically generate numerous effects that are given to categorization in various ways, ranging from the fully quantifiable (e.g., travel time saving and ridership) to the totally qualitative (e.g., lifestyle or aesthetic; see Wright et al., 1998, Chapter 10). Yet, public decision makers often regard political gains and coalition building to be as crucial to their decisions as are welfare-maximizing impacts such as accessibility improvements. While these considerations may be legitimate from the decision makers' viewpoint, normative evaluation rejects them. Moreover, their use as key decision criteria often leads to the adoption of unworthy projects among other disastrous results (see for example, Flyvburg et al., 2003, for a database on failed projects).

An interesting exercise would be to identify the sources of this phenomenon, which epitomizes decision making regarding transportation investments, particularly large-scale projects (also called "mega-projects"). After all, these decisions entail the spending of billions of taxpayers' dollars by elected officials who are presumed to be responsible and accountable. Many sources have indeed been located, ranging from political expediency and inefficient fiscal federalism, to hidden agendas and fraud (Kain, 1990; Wachs, 1995). Here we briefly comment on three additional but major sources: history, vision, and bounded rationality.

In a significant number of cases, historical context is the principal force propelling initiation of mega-projects. A case in a point is New York's Second Avenue Subway (SAS)—a project valued at over $17 billion, Phase 1 of which is currently under construction. In the mid 1950s, the Third Avenue Elevated Rail Line (the El) in Manhattan came down against the assumption that the SAS would soon be built to replace it. This act left the entire East Side of Manhattan served by only one subway line (the Lexington Avenue line). At the time, civic groups and politicians had raised concerns about congestion and accessibility to the downtown area. By 1960, the additional line had become an issue in the mayoral race run that year. Subway overcrowding and the new subway line's necessity remained a popular fixation, soon to evolve into an accepted truism among political decision makers, planners, and the public. In 1972, with the limited funding available, three segments of the required tunnel were built, but the decade's fiscal crisis soon shelved the project. The idea, however, retained its appeal, with various civic and professional groups keeping the idea of the project alive despite the major physical, demographic, economic, and social changes experienced throughout the city. Even today, relatively little transportation-economic research has been conducted on such a massive project's rationale in 21st-century New York. Put briefly, this project cannot be understood outside its historical context, which may explain its continued popularity and generally unquestioned acceptance.

In many cases, politicians and other public opinion leaders regard themselves as "far-sighted" or "visionary" with respect to a region's future spatial and socioeconomic structure, including the role of transport. Transportation projects may evolve from these sweeping visions into technocratic projections of future investments and use (Wachs, 2004). What is interesting about such "visions" is that they tend to get locked into public awareness. As a result, the life expectancy of a vision can exceed that of its creators. The planned railroad from Central Israel to the city of Eilat, located on the southern tip of the country, can serve as an example of this phenomenon. The railroad is regarded as the cornerstone of a five-decade-old grand vision, the transformation of a large, sparsely populated, and arid region into a flowering garden with a thriving economic center. All conventional benefit-cost studies completed to date have not supported the project's transportation-economic rationality. This fact, however, has not deterred generations of political leaders from commissioning new studies and actively seeking funding for the project. These comments do not mean to suggest that vision is superfluous or harmful for transportation planning. A vision outlining a region's long-term development can become the catalyst for placing transportation investments high on the public agenda. However, the practice of substituting an uncorroborated vision for a formal evaluation process can drive the implementation of disastrous projects, as examples scattered throughout this book show.

A third interesting source for the draw of some projects can be found in the literature on bounded rationality (see Kahneman, 2003, for an overview). According to this explanation, "people rely on a limited number of heuristic principles which reduce the complex tasks of assessing probabilities and predicting values to simple judgmental operations. In general, these heuristics are quite useful, but sometimes they lead to severe and systematic errors" (Kahneman and Tversky, 1979). Decision makers operate under substantial uncertainty in the field of transportation. They often make grave judgmental errors by ignoring information that does not correspond with their habitual heuristic guidelines. Preconceived ideas, reluctance to review new information, favorable attributes embraced as decisive judgmental criteria together with elimination of unfavorable ones represent just some of the conceptual devises that can lead to gross errors. Such behavior helps explain the observation that when making decisions about large-scale transportation investments, political decision makers seem predisposed to prefer projects with presumably high economic development benefits and modest transportation benefits over projects with the opposite features.

Bounded rationality is obviously not confined to politicians. The public, unaware of the real social costs of transportation projects, frequently supports a large-scale project as a quick fix to perceived problems without understanding the implications of the investment. At the core of this attitude is a pervasive optimism that views all problems as solvable without the introduction of behavioral changes attuned to mode choice, time of departure, or shopping destination. Public support of such investments in turn motivates politicians to propose and support wasteful investments.

Given that politicians are supposedly responsive to public opinion, the relevant question becomes how do people form opinions and why are they myopic when it comes to mega-projects? Can ideology be a factor "bounding" or limiting rationality? Blinder and Krueger (2004) have conducted a survey on people's views on economic policy and how these views are formed. Based on the survey's results, the authors concluded that ideology rather than detailed knowledge affects the public's stand on issues and that, moreover, ideological positions are situational. Blinder and Krueger argue that individuals often find it difficult to educate themselves on specific policy issues either because obtaining the relevant information is costly or because they lack the necessary background to comprehend the issues. Under these constraints, ideology serves as a rational basis for opinion formation. This is not to say that people should not form opinions on policies that may not benefit them directly or at all, let alone those that affect them negatively (e.g., increasing direct taxation or a decline in real estate values). The point is that they regularly do so by using ideology as a substitute for hard facts and informed opinions. Politicians, responsive as they are to voter views, act accordingly, even if they are aware of the ideological basis of those views.

What can economic theory suggest with respect to this tendency of promoting costly, noneconomical transportation projects? Brueckner and Selod (2006) have developed a stylized model of the political economy of transport system choice. Their model is based on the "voting model" rationale, namely, that the distribution of voters by skills or income influences the provision of public goods such as transport systems.[4] The authors show that when a city is heterogeneous with respect to labor skills and the distribution of skills is even moderately skewed in the direction of high-level skills, more expensive and faster systems (e.g., subways) will be chosen in place of less expensive and slower but optimal systems. This result holds regardless of land ownership patterns although under residential land ownership, overinvestment in transportation will be more evident. While the model is somewhat restrictive in its assumptions, especially about a city's spatial structure, it does suggest an economic explanation for the observed practice of investing in expensive but nonoptimal transport projects.

3. FACTORS AFFECTING TRANSPORTATION PROJECT PLANNING AND EVALUATION[5]

A key module in the project evaluation paradigm shown in Figure 2.2 is investment policy, which is the phase where the project is initiated, its objectives defined and planning alternatives proposed for assessment. What are the main factors that affect this module?

3.1 Project Initiation

How is a given transportation investment project initiated, how does it enter the public agenda, and how is it then transformed from an option to an actual capital budget item?[6] Two related sets of factors, political and institutional, best explain transportation project initiation. In major metropolitan areas, several agencies are responsible for transportation policy (see Table 2.1). In the majority of cases, no one agency has the inclusive authority as well as sufficient resources to plan and administer regional transportation policy; in consequence, no one agency can rank and prioritize projects. Moreover, elected officials (e.g., the mayor, the governor, and councilpersons) lack ubiquitous legal and political control. This institutional structure creates a governance vacuum motivating competition over resources between elected leaders and administrative agencies, a competition that manifests itself in uncoordinated and often conflicting investment proposals. These proposals are, by and large, the brainchildren of politicians or the products of political pacts. Politicians who want to show that they have a "transportation policy" often elaborate proposals for the large-scale transportation projects that they believe will meet the approval of their constituents and selected interest groups. Alternatively, the project may address a politician's preconceived ideas of what the city needs, a vision that often becomes his or her idée fixe, the focus for forceful attempts at creating a supportive coalition in addition to funding. The desire to depart politics as a legend is apparently a very powerful political motive.

To demonstrate the overlap between politics and institutional structure consider the following case. The mayor of New York City wanted to develop housing, commercial, and office real estate with the addition of recreational facilities (mainly a sports stadium) on Manhattan's West side, whereas the governor of New York State wanted to rebuild Lower Manhattan—mainly the site of the World Trade Center.[7] The two projects' rationalizations expressed distinctive political needs, shared constituencies, an eye to history, but also the structure of government. While the mayor and the governor were far from political allies, each found it expedient to avoid neutralizing the other's development plans. The agreement reached covered major transportation investments requiring the political, legal, planning, and financial support of these two elected leaders. A major ingredient in the mayor's development plan was extension of the number 7 subway line (from Times Square to the Upper West Side), at an estimated capital cost of $1.7 billion. Included in the governor's plan was a different major project, viewed as a key to the development of Lower Manhattan—the direct rail connection to JFK airport—at a capital cost of about $2.5 billion, depending on the exact alignment.

This example serves to illustrate how major transportation investment projects often represent byproducts or derivatives of nontransportation development (or other) interests. In cases like these, the projects are relegated to supporting roles within the framework of other, often much more ambitious initiatives. The core question for us here, however, is whether this fact influences how project appraisal will be carried out? Might we demand, for example, removal of the condition that aggregate transportation benefits exceed the project's total costs in such cases?

Generating grandiose ideas is relatively easy, as all experienced heads of transportation agencies know; obtaining funding and executing them is quite anther matter. As we will show, the ability to secure funding frequently represents the underlying rationale for initiating a specific transportation project. This economic (and political) reality may explain some of the major political and bureaucratic battles surrounding projects that, even if incompatible, nonetheless vie for the same public monies.

3.2 Government and Governance

Government agencies at all levels—local, regional, state, and federal—are involved in building transportation infrastructure (Wachs, 2006). The more complicated the project in terms of its physical, geographical, and capital outlay features, the more intricate is this involvement. To illustrate this point, consider decision making in the state of New York as shown in Tables 2.1 and 2.2.

In addition to these agencies, several organizations may be set up to build and manage a sole project.[8] The Federal Government's role should obviously be considered throughout because for most large-scale projects, a sizeable portion of the needed capital funds comes from federal coffers.

3.3 Generation of Project Alternatives

As mentioned previously, there are always several alternatives to a project, including the "do-nothing" or "do-minimum" option (also referred to as the "benchmark" or the "zero" alternative). This particular alternative takes two forms. First, it may represent the status quo or present-day travel conditions if no action is taken. Second, it may represent travel conditions at a future period if travel demand keeps rising but investment is kept at present-day levels. The idea behind this alternative is that after assessing a proposed project benefit—such as travel time savings—the results obtained

Table 2.1 New York Regional Transportation Decision Makers

Decision Maker	Powers
Governor	Suggests projects; appoints boards of major public authorities—including MTA and PANYNJ; has budget veto power; appoints NYS DOT commissioners; structures MPO
State Legislature	Develops state budgets and decides allocations; must have adequate majority to override a gubernatorial veto
Mayor, City of NY	Suggests budget; suggests programs and projects; appoints the transportation commissioner and some members of the MTA board
US Congress	Can introduce local projects into federal budgets

Legend: MTA = Metropolitan Transportation Authority; PANYNJ = Port Authority of New York and New Jersey; DOT = Department of Transportation; MPO = Metropolitan Planning Organization.
Source: Paaswell and Berechman (2007).

Table 2.2 Regional Agencies Affecting Transportation Investment in New York City

Agency	Responsibilities	Source of Capital Funds
MTA	Operates rapid rail and bus service within NYC; commuter rail from suburbs to Manhattan's core; some toll facilities	Federal, state, local government issue debt, tax revenues
PANYNJ	Operates commuter rail (PATH) from adjacent New Jersey to Manhattan's core; operates toll facilities between NYC and NJ; operates major regional airports and the Port of NY/NJ	Issues debt; cross subsidies from bridge and tunnel tolls
NYSDOT/ NJDOT	Maintains selected roadways within region	Federal and state government
NJT	Operates commuter rail and bus from NJ to Manhattan	Federal and state government; debt issues
AMTRAK	Intercity rail through heart of the North-East Corridor; operates from Penn Station in Manhattan, the busiest railway station in the nation	Fares; federal and state subsidies

Legend: PATH = Port Authority Trans Hudson; NYSDOT = New York State Department of Transportation; NJDOT = New Jersey Department of Transportation; NJT = New Jersey Transit; NYMTC = New York Metropolitan Transportation Commission (MPO)
Source: Paaswell and Berechman (2007).

will be measured against the benchmark, that is, current conditions, or current conditions extrapolated into the future.

In general, project alternatives can be specified along a set of dimensions including physical properties, route alignment, level of service, market attributes, and regulation. Alternatives can also reflect various levels of capacity improvement (e.g., adding one, two, or three highway lanes), or different modal solutions to congestion (e.g., rail vs. bus). Another source of variation refers to how the alternatives correspond to the different policy packages they were designed to implement, for instance, improved access to the CBD. The relevant policies may embrace infrastructure investment, road pricing, Travel Demand Management (TDM), or any combination of the three. As transportation is a networked delivery system, an alternative should be specified according to the affected components.[9]

Whether there are only a very few or a large number of alternatives, each needs to be assessed, ranked, and prioritized in order to make a prudent policy choice. The underlying rationale for establishing priorities is that each decision made entails opportunity costs in terms of forgone net social welfare or the rate of return earned with other alternatives.

3.4 Typology of Factors Used in the Evaluation Process

The set of factors used in the overall project evaluation process can be divided into three sets. The first includes variables that are endogenous to the process and derived from data estimation or simulation. Examples are traffic volumes, travel times, modal shares, or future ridership rates. The second set contains policy variables with values determined solely by policy (read political) considerations. Examples are the financial incentives offered by the state to Public–Private Partnership projects or the weights assigned to benefits in the final evaluation scheme. The third set contains variables that reflect market conditions but carry values set by regulatory agencies. Key examples are the project's discount rate, the Value Of Time (VOT) by trip purpose, and public transit fare structure.

By transforming market-determined variables into policy variables, oversight agencies can effectively manipulate the overall transportation-economic value of the project. For example, setting the VOT at a certain level is a powerful administrative tool for achieving the desired benefit-to-cost ratio. It is therefore of utmost importance that analysts verify the actual economic value of these variables before using them to determine the range of welfare-improving benefits the project indeed provides. The difference in the results obtained when project variables are assessed according to their politically assigned values as opposed to their correct economic values represents the social cost of policy intervention in project evaluation. A good example is the use of an administrative versus the social discount rate in cost-benefit analysis. Subsequent chapters further elaborate on each of these factors that enter the overall evaluation process.

4. RATIONAL TRANSPORTATION PLANNING

The project initiation process described above, while common in many large metropolitan areas, is certainly not the only one possible. We next outline several other options, often providing sounder guidelines when initiating the planning of transportation investments.

4.1 Compliance with Local, State, or Federal Legislation

In many countries, local authorities are required by law to prepare long-term transportation plans. In the US, for example, federal law requires local Metropolitan Planning Organizations (MPOs) to prepare and update a long-term Regional Transportation Plan (RTP) and a shorter-term Transportation Improvement Plan (TIP). The RTP provides guidelines for the region's transportation development over a period of 25 years. The RTP must be updated every three years on the basis of projected growth in population, economic activity, traffic, and other urban activities (e.g., housing and commercial development). As to the TIP, it must be updated annually or biannually, depending on state law, because it is comprised of a fiscally constrained list of projects that the region has committed to execute. To be included in the TIP, a project must be specified in the RTP and obtain committed funding from regional government. Although the RTP is, in theory, an effective tool for developing rational transportation plans, how well it actually works in assessing and subsequently selecting optimal transportation projects remains cloudy. Conflicting regional interests, uncertain sources of income and underestimated capital costs often render this long-term evaluation process rather inefficient (Wachs, 2006).[10]

4.2 Responses to Critical Transportation Needs

1. *Acute Transportation Problems*

Much of the work of transportation planners is devoted to identifying acute transportation needs requiring capital investments (e.g., upgrading existing facilities or constructing new ones). Jammed highway intersections, insufficient rail capacity, congested bridges, and overcrowded passenger terminals are examples of critical needs. In these cases, projects are evaluated and selected on the basis of how well they promise to respond to these needs, given their costs.

2. *Critical Network*

The term *critical network* refers to that part of the regional network essential for the functioning of the overall transportation system. Stated differently, it is the part of the regional network that, if seriously damaged, will incapacitate the entire system. Planners apply this approach to determining which system components require upgrading or additional capacity rather than referring to transportation problems at specific locations in isolation. Projects are then evaluated on the basis of their impact on the critical part of the network. The direct implication of this approach is that benefits from such projects are measured at the network rather than at the facility level. For example, if the closing down of a critical bridge, tunnel, or a set of intersections will halt the operation of a substantial part of the network, the benefits from a project designed to keep these facilities functioning are calculated in terms of traffic flow over the entire relevant network.

4.3 Acceptable Levels of Service

1. Maintaining an Acceptable Level of Service

Often, the primary objective of a transportation investment is to maintain an acceptable Level of Service (LOS) rather than substantially upgrading the overall system. LOS is generally defined in terms of a desired balance between demand and capacity. For example, it can be defined as a tolerable level of crowding in public transit or as highway traffic speed and reliability. Current "acceptable LOS" is likely to become "unacceptable LOS" in the future because travel conditions have worsened or, perhaps, our present tolerance of congestion has declined. In either case, new investments are continuously needed. The main result of this piecemeal approach is that the existing transportation system is rarely overhauled.

2. Maintaining and/or Upgrading of Fixed and Rolling Stock

In practice, large segments of the transportation budget are devoted to maintaining and upgrading existing fixed facilities and rolling stock. Keeping transportation capital stock in a "state of good repair" cannot be side-stepped for long or the entire system's effectiveness will begin to crumble. Often, replacement of rolling stock is paid for by federal funds, which tends to influence the allocation of funds among other types of investment projects local transit authorities (Berechman, 1993). Yet, whatever the funding method, project evaluation of maintenance and upgrading projects aims at finding the best investment alternative for meeting engineering standards at least cost.

4.4 Normative Objective Functions

Conceptually, transportation planning should begin with the normative question: "What is the best transportation system for the region given a set of future socioeconomic, demographic, and spatial objectives?" Since such objectives are difficult to define and hotly debated, this question is rarely asked; at best, planning agencies consider narrower and much more focused normative objectives.

1. Effect on Specific Sectors

At times, agencies wish to affect the transportation status of targeted populations (e.g., the mobility impaired), or economic sectors (e.g., manufacturing). To that end, they design projects aimed at achieving agency goals for these populations. Projects are then evaluated on the basis of their relative contribution to the transportation needs of the targeted groups.[11]

2. Effect on Specific Locations

Similar to the first case, agencies may wish to influence trends in specific locations, such as the CBD or a port area, which are presently judged as undersupplied in terms of transportation. Projects are then evaluated relative to their impact on public accessibility to these areas.

3. Future Regional Transportation Needs

Rapidly growing areas are likely to experience severe accessibility declines due to expanding car and truck traffic. In such cases, projections of present travel trends are made and compared with the network's existing capacity. The planning objective in this case is to maintain accessibility at levels that are considered favorable to the overall regional economic and population growth. The difficult question is how to define such supportive accessibility levels, given the region's complex land use and economic structure.

4.4 Project Availability and Funding

1. Projects Available for Implementation

In many instances, initial engineering feasibility studies are made prior to any transportation-economic assessment. When budgets later become available through the legislative process, assuming engineering practicability and compliance with environmental standards, such projects are often submitted for immediate implementation irrespective of the missing economic evaluation. Concerns over the consequences of not using available budgets have therefore been found to be the decisive criterion in many transportation decision events.

2. Funding Availability

In practice, budgeting and legislative processes sometimes make funding available for a transportation project even before comprehensive economic evaluation studies have been completed. In cases like these, evaluation is limited to mainly design or alignment alternatives. What matters most for us is that under these conditions, the only projects considered for implementation are those with secured funding, irrespective of true regional needs.

4.6 Nontransportation Objectives

1. Promoting Economic Development

Frequently, transportation projects are planned on the basis of their anticipated ability to promote regional and local economic growth. In such cases, transportation impacts (e.g., reduced congestion) are secondary to the economic growth impacts assessed during the evaluation. At times, this motive remains implicit for fear of upsetting interest groups. Vague explanations such as "the project provides a vital transportation need" are then attached to the project to mask its true goal: land and real estate development, among others (more on this issue in Chapter 13).

2. Altering Urban Form

The relationship between transportation and land use has been quite thoroughly researched (see, for example, Berechman et al., 1996, for a collection of articles on this subject). Transportation planners frequently attempt to use transportation-targeted capital investments to alter the location and intensity of land-use activities within a region. The promotion of activity concentrations is just such a purpose. Under these constraints, projects are evaluated accordingly.[12]

3. Safety and Environmental Objectives

Many purportedly "small-scale" projects in financial terms are aimed at improving safety and reducing automobile accidents, the direct and social costs of which have a substantial effect on the national economy (see Chapter 12). In rural areas in particular, where traffic is light and traffic patterns are relatively erratic and therefore dangerous, the key objective of road improvements is safety enhancement. Even in crowded metropolitan areas, a sizeable proportion of the total cost of capital-intensive projects is safety-related. Environmental concerns, especially air quality improvement and emission abatement, also constitute key transportation investments goals. From a planning perspective, however, it is the mandatory Environmental Impact Statement (EIS) required in the US by all federally funded projects that effectively shift environmental issues to the level of necessary conditions rather than planning objectives.

4. Transportation as a Complementary Investment

From a conceptual perspective, transportation can be regarded as an intermediary input in the production of final outputs. That is, a trip can be treated as an economic activity enabling trip takers to obtain final outputs (e.g., shopping) at a destination location (e.g., a shopping mall), given their location origin (e.g., home).[13] Hence, the term "derived demand" is used in the context of transportation to characterize the demand for travel in relation to the demand for final outputs. Although transportation system expansion is commonly carried out independently of any specific trip type or Origin-Destination pair, these investments are sometimes made for the sole purpose of improving accessibility to the sites of specific activities.

To illustrate this point, consider the major debate that took place in New York in 2005 regarding the location of a new $1.4 billion sports stadium, allegedly planned to improve New York's chances to be designated as the site for the 2012 Summer Olympics (London has since "won" the competition). The discussion focused on two site alternatives: Manhattan's West Side (near the Jacob Javits Convention Center) and the Flushing Meadows-Corona Park area in Queens. The first alternative entailed extension of the number 7 subway line at an estimated cost of $1.7 billion, whereas the Queens alternative, which was already being served by this line as well as by the Long Island Railroad, required only highway improvements, at a significantly lower cost. Irrespective of the underlying business, real estate, and planning objectives put forth by the powerful interest groups championing one or another site alternatives, the transportation investments that each entailed were byproducts of the decision to invest in a sports facility. Stated simply, while the proposed subway investment would provide an efficient link between Queens and Manhattan's West Side, public transportation benefits were tangential to the project's primary objective.

For project evaluation purposes, transportation investments which complements other, nontransportation investments, raise several analytical questions. First, what benefits should be included in the cost-benefit analysis: travel benefits only or the combined benefits of travel and final output (e.g., increased commercial sales)? Second, if the latter is the case, aren't we in effect double-counting benefits since the final outputs may actually represent capitalized transportation benefits? Third, in selecting among the alternatives that have passed the cost-benefit test, what weight should be given to transportation benefits relative to the final outputs that motivated the transportation investment in the first place? Mentioning these issues will suffice here because Part E of the book explores them in greater detail.

5. SUMMARY AND CONCLUSIONS

This chapter examined two principal approaches to carrying out transportation planning and investment decisions. A positive approach, which focuses on how transportation decisions are made, and a normative approach, which establishes a systematic and logical framework for the estimation of welfare maximization associated with investment decisions. It argues that a mix of these two can best describe the way transportation planning and infrastructure decisions are actually made.

It should not come as a surprise to any student of transportation that power politics plays a major role in shaping the respective decisions. If politics are considered as a mechanism for the distribution of public resources, the alternative to power politics is a market-based mechanism whose aim it is to identify projects promising to yield the highest economic return given the invested resources. With all of its limitations (see Chapter 6), cost-benefits analysis, which uses market prices or imputed shadow prices, is one such mechanism.

Transportation investment projects do not suddenly appear on the public agenda. Project initiation and the generation of alternatives are intricate processes, governed mainly by political and institutional forces. Yet, more rational planning procedures are occasionally applied, especially when mandated by law, or when local needs become blatant, or in order to maintain a tolerable level of service and state of good repair. Quite often, though, projects are suggested in order to achieve nontransportation objectives such as promoting economic development or changing urban form. Funding availability also plays a major role even though it subordinates the concept of rational planning to funding formulae. Transportation needs, we have to conclude, too frequently play second role to other project objectives and conditions.

The fact that the power politics plays such a decisive role in transportation decision making raises several interesting questions. From the viewpoint of economic analysis, if the projects eventually implemented are not optimal (occasionally not even remotely so), what does this imply for measurement of trip makers' behavior (e.g., mode choice and facilities use)? Stated differently, because the data used in travel analysis reflect the behavior of users who are faced with inefficient infrastructure, the implications of such analyses may be implausible. This observation helps explain why the evolution of cities and regions is to some extent the outcome of the supply of inefficient or even wasteful transportation facilities. Measuring the welfare contribution of additional infrastructure investments consequently becomes problematic, with second- or third-best type analyses performed instead.

Finally, from a policy analysis perspective, the penetration of politics into transportation supply raises several difficult ethical issues. These include dishonesty and inadequate transparency, irrational public decision making, inferior information on alternative uses of resources, and unwarranted competition for public funds. We will return to some of these weighty issues in Part E.

3 Welfare Foundations of Project Appraisal

1. INTRODUCTION

In Chapters 1 and 2, we distinguished between project evaluation and project assessment, with the former concept referring to the entire project evaluation and choice process whereas the latter is limited to the measurement of a project's net economic value. Here we focus on project assessment (or project appraisal) and examine the key concepts and principles to be applied in this type of analysis. Technically, project assessment is carried out by using Cost-Benefit Analysis (COBA). This chapter, therefore, also examines the theoretical foundations of COBA, which are based on the principles of welfare economics. Given that the key assumption underlying COBA is that a project should be accepted only if it generates positive net welfare gains, we discuss how this type of analysis accounts for various welfare conditions.

The germane literature provides two main views of COBA as an economic discipline. As to the first, the main purpose of COBA as an application of welfare economics is to use normative rules to determine the welfare contribution of a given public program or investment. Put differently, viewed from this perspective, COBA provides a set of welfare-based rules that determine the degree to which social welfare is enhanced by a public project subsequent to the reallocation of societal resources.

The second view defines COBA as a set of systematic and transparent rules, based on the economic rationale of markets and individual behavior, constructed for the purpose of ranking projects relative to various decision criteria. From this perspective, COBA's primary aim is to provide constructive information, in a concise and unambiguous way, to the stakeholders who decide a project's fate.

Considering the complexity and value judgments intrinsic to COBA (see Chapters 2 and 6), most applications of its rules seem to comply with the second view. Yet, in the opinion of this author, the application of COBA rules should clearly explicate why, and by how much, society would be better off if it goes through with the proposed project. This is especially true when considering the opportunity costs incurred when forgoing alternatives. In brief, while COBA must provide practical, instructive information on the investment's various features, we maintain that it must also inform decision makers on the extent to which the project complies with welfare criteria.

A key question related to the conduct of cost-benefit analysis of public investments is: "What types of benefits should be examined?" The literature advocates three such categories: (a) *direct benefits*, which in the case of transportation focus on travel time and cost savings; (b) *indirect effects*, including negative and positive externalities such as air pollution, or economic development; and (c) *social and urban effects* such as changes in equity and urban form. The discussion in this chapter focuses mainly on category (a), while leaving the treatment of (b) and (c) to Parts C and D of this volume.

It should be noted, though, that this classification of effects is not common to all public agencies dealing with transportation. Consider, for example, a recent status report submitted to the US Congress on the conditions and performance of the nation's transportation infrastructure (US DOT, 2003). This report accepts category (a), direct effects, modifies category (b), and omits category (c). The "new" category (b) is defined as social benefits, which the report identifies as environmental externalities, roadway wear and tear, and transportation system administration. The report includes an additional category, defined as agency benefits resulting from increased revenues from increased ridership and reductions in operating and maintenance costs. In contrast, in another report (US DOT, 2000), the Federal Transit Administration considers changes in real estate values and urban agglomeration (included in category (b), above) as direct benefits issuing from transit investments.

The design of this chapter is as follows. Section 2 reviews the welfare foundations underlying COBA. Section 3 examines the concept *welfare function*, its components and uses when measuring a project's net benefits. Section 4 analyzes welfare changes in imperfect markets. Formulation and measurement of net welfare gains in the context of market imperfections is investigated in Section 5. A summary and conclusions are offered in Section 6.

2. THE WELFARE FOUNDATIONS OF TRANSPORTATION COBA[1]

2.1 Welfare Principles

Individual preferences, hence utility, are regarded as the fundamental building block of traditional welfare economics. However, the use of preferences to appraise welfare improvements rests on several key postulates such as the constancy and consistency of preferences. Dissenting views of these concepts, which question the meaning and nature of "welfare" or "well-being" (e.g., Sen, 1992), are products of experimental approaches to human decision making and the study of economics as a philosophical discipline.

Additional critiques are rooted in the perception that human preferences are conditional, depending on the framework and reference point from which people make economic decisions and choices. This implies that the prevalent use of revealed (or stated) preferences as means to elicit consumers' attitude towards a public investment can lead to erroneous or biased results if the project's context is not properly defined.[2]

A related criticism refers to the intrinsic need in welfare economics to aggregate over individuals' preferences or utilities prior to deriving a project's welfare outcomes. The economic literature has raised a host of difficult questions regarding such aggregation when the subjects are individuals with diverse socioeconomic profiles and preferences. The key problem, whatever the aggregation procedure applied, centers on the need for making interpersonal comparisons, relative to preferences and the marginal utility of income.[3] As a rigorous examination of these and related issues lies beyond the scope of this chapter, readers interested in the theoretical underpinnings of welfare economics are referred to the writings of earlier scholars such as Marshall (1920, p. 811), Hicks (1940), Samuelson (1947), and Friedman (1949) or more contemporary ones such as Arrow and Kurtz (1970), Willig (1976), Auerbach (1986), Mishan (1988), and Tirole (1988).

These issues notwithstanding, the main objective of project appraisal remains constant: To make an informed decision regarding the acceptance or rejection of a public investment given its impacts and alternatives. This decision rests—at least in part—on the economic benefits that the investment is expected to yield net of the costs incurred (all properly discounted).[4]

In what follows we accept COBA's conventional welfare foundations, which are based on the common observation that in competitive markets, consumers display their preferences by purchasing goods and services assumed to confer benefits that are expressed in monetary terms.[5] For example, people willingly pay a given amount of money in exchange for the opportunity to travel faster and thereby save some amount of time. Similarly, users are willing to pay for a more expensive transport mode if it confers quantifiable door-to-door travel time savings and other amenities. The use of monetary values likewise facilitates summation over individuals when deriving a service's aggregate utility; this method consequently does away with the complexities of interpersonal comparisons.[6]

To be sure, we make no claims here that COBA takes all of the important issues that enter—or should enter—the public debate over a given transportation investment into account. Other potential impacts, such as equity and urban structure, should be analyzed separately, although not independently of primary travel effects. What COBA does, then, is provide a welfare-based rationale for the systematic analysis of changes in aggregate utility pursuant to a project's implementation. Viewed in this light, use of COBA can significantly alleviate the crucial quandaries—lack of transparency, accountability, openness, and differences of opinion, to name a few—that stain public policy making.

2.2 Pareto Optimum

Since public investment essentially entails the allocation of economic resources, it raises the question of how efficient an allocation may be. For a set of alternative allocations, if a shift from one to another can make at least one individual better off without making any other individual worse off, it is defined as a *Pareto improvement allocation*. An allocation is defined as *Pareto optimum* (often, *Pareto efficient*) when no further Pareto improvements can be made.[7] Economic theory suggests several conditions that, if met, configure an allocation as Pareto optimal (for a detailed analysis see Friedman, 1985; Mas-Colell et al., 1995; Sen, 1992). For instance, if an allocation (e.g., a public investment in a new transportation facility) can be shown to be Pareto inefficient, economic theory suggests that there is room for further improvement through reallocation of resources, for example, by changing features of the project or investing in a different project. To become Pareto efficient, the revised option would improve the welfare of at least one individual without reducing the welfare accruing to anyone else.

Suppose that a reallocation of resources has reduced the welfare of some individuals but improved the welfare of others. If the gainers compensate the losers for their welfare losses, the allocation would also be Pareto optimal. This conclusion would hold even if the gainers would *potentially* compensate the losers. That is, compensation need not be direct. This concept, advanced by two early theoreticians, Kaldor (1939) and Hicks (1940), is known as the Kaldor–Hicks compensation criterion (also known as the Scitovsky criterion). It simply states that a more efficient allocation overall can nonetheless result in some individuals being worse off.

Now think of a new road that is to be constructed. If the road's *net benefits* are judged to be positive (and higher than those yielded by any alternative), the project should be implemented. This measure—*positive net benefits*—is, in essence, an adaptation of the Kaldor–Hicks criterion. It is equivalent to requiring that a project's benefits be sufficient for those who gain from its implementation to compensate in some form those whose welfare has been reduced by it. Use of the criterion is based on the argument that a project can be justified for society as a whole if its total gains outweigh its losses, leading to Pareto improvement for society as a whole. The Kaldor–Hicks criterion is used to determine whether an activity is moving the economy towards Pareto efficiency and thus provides the fundamental rationale for COBA.

3. THE SOCIAL WELFARE FUNCTION

In the context of public project welfare evaluation, the Social Welfare function (SW) is commonly used to calculate an investment's total economic effect on society after its new or improved services have been delivered.[8]

That is, measures of the overall welfare effect of a transportation investment project are conceived in terms of total future changes in welfare, defined as:

$$\Delta SW = \Delta CS + \Delta PS + \Delta E \tag{1}$$

where, ΔSW denotes the net change in total welfare, ΔCS the net change in total consumer surplus, ΔPS the net change in total producer surplus, and ΔE the change in total external costs, which can be negative.[9] In what follows, equation (1) is used to develop a project's welfare contribution, considered as the key COBA measure.

3.1 Willingness to Pay, Willingness to Accept, and Consumers' Surplus

The first term on the right-hand side of equation (1) represents *change in consumer surplus*, the measure most commonly used to assess individuals' welfare gains from economic investments such as improved transportation infrastructure. Analytically, this term represents the area under the aggregate private demand curve bounded by the prices of services before and after the improvement is introduced. Figure 3.1 illustrates this measure.

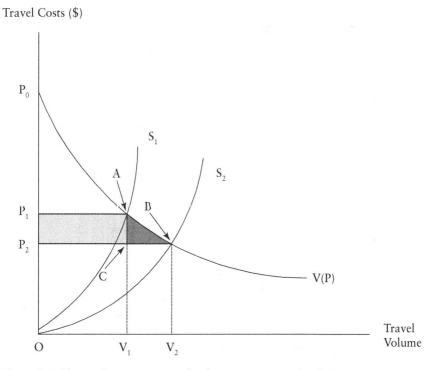

Figure 3.1 Change in consumer surplus from a transportation improvement.

At the root of assessments of *consumer surplus* is the concept *willingness to pay* (WTP), which refers to the maximum amount of money an informed consumer would be willing to pay to receive the new or improved service—such as a travel time savings of 10 minutes—offered by the project. A consumer surplus is produced when a consumer receives a service while paying less than he/she is willing to pay. Thus, under reasonable conditions, changes in the consumer surplus resulting from an improvement correctly measure the WTP associated with this improvement (Bradford and Hildebrandt, 1977; Sudgen, 2003).

A complementary concept is *willingness to accept* (WTA), which indicates the minimum amount of money an informed consumer is willing to accept in compensation for incurring certain costs associated with a new project, such as increased noise from additional traffic. In this case, a consumer surplus is generated if the consumer receives some form of compensation that exceeds his/her WTA.[10]

Theoretically, WTP and WTA estimates produce similar results if certain assumptions about consumers' preference structures and consistency are maintained. Yet, it is well known that the two are not symmetrical. Part of this discrepancy is explained by the Slutsky effect,[11] although part is also due to the fact that consumer preferences are conditional on the context or the reference point from which they make their decisions (Sudgen, 2003); importantly, these may differ between WTP and WTA. In general, if no significant distortions are identified in the relevant markets, the WTP adequately indicates the gross economic benefits accruing to consumers from a project's implementation.

There have been several attempts in the transportation literature to empirically estimate another measure—the marginal willingness to pay (MWP)—for reduced commuting time. For example, based on a job market search model, van Ommeren et al. (2000) were able to estimate MWP: about $0.20 per kilometer per day using Dutch data. If the average commuting distance is 20 kilometers, the overall average MWP for reduced commuting time of one hour is $4 for an 8-hour workday, which translates into about half the average hourly wage rate.

3.2 Measurement of Changes in Consumer Surplus

With the help of the above welfare concepts, changes in consumer surplus are commonly used to measure benefits from improvements such as the construction of a new road.[12] Figure 3.1 depicts the change in consumer surplus from a project that increases road capacity between two locations—and consequently lowering travel costs—given the demand for travel between the two respective locations.

In Figure 3.1, the curve $V(P)$ represents the demand (traffic volume) for travel on this facility as a function of price.[13] A supply function, S_1,[14] intersects the demand function at point A, resulting in travel cost P_1 and travel volume V_1. Following a capacity investment, the supply function shifts downward to S_2 and intersects the demand function at point B, with travel price P_2 and travel volume V_2. Total change in consumer surplus is therefore the area P_1ABP_2, covering the change in consumer surplus for present users (the shaded area P_1ACP_2) and for new users (the shaded area ACB).

Analytically, consumer surplus before the change is given by (2):

$$CS = \int_{P_1}^{P_0} V(z)dz \tag{2}$$

where P_0 is the point where the demand curve V intersects the price axis. Similarly, consumer surplus after the change is given by:

$$CS = \int_{P_2}^{P_0} V(z)dz \tag{3}$$

The *change* in consumer surplus (ΔCS) is, therefore:

$$\Delta CS = \int_{P_2}^{P_0} V(z)dz - \int_{P_1}^{P_0} V(z)dz$$

or

$$\Delta CS = \int_{P_1}^{P_2} V(z)dz \tag{4}$$

An alternative way of computing CS requires integrating over the inverse demand function $P(V)$ $(=V^{-1}(P))$, where P is travel price as a function of travel volume V. In terms of Figure 3.1, total consumer surplus could be computed as the area under $P(V)$ between 0 and V_1 (i.e., the area $0V_1AP_0$), minus the area $0V_1AP_1$, which represents total users' costs of travel. Thus,

$$CS_1 = \int_0^{V_1} P(v)dv - V_1 \cdot P_1 \tag{5}$$

CS, after capacity expansion $(S_1 \rightarrow S_2)$, is

$$CS_2 = \int_0^{V_2} P(v)dv - V_2 \cdot P_2 \tag{6}$$

The change in consumer surplus from this capacity investment is, therefore,

$\Delta CS = CS_2 - CS_1$, or:

$$\Delta CS = \left[\int_0^{V_2} P(v)dv - V_2 \cdot P_2 \right] - \left[\int_0^{V_1} P(v)dv - V_1 \cdot P_1 \right] \tag{7}$$

If the demand function can be assumed to be almost linear between points A and B, the triangular area ABC covers roughly half the number of new users, times the reduction in total travel costs (from P_1 to P_2). In the transportation literature, this is known as the *rule of half*, implying that we need not estimate the entire demand function, only the number of new users and the change in total costs, in order to arrive at an estimate of the change in consumer surplus (Small, 1992a).

Let ΔP represent the generalized cost savings per ride from a capacity improvement project, requiring users to switch from an alternative mode or route. If ΔV is the estimated change in the number of users, then the change in consumer surplus can be approximated by:

$$\Delta CS = \Delta P \cdot \Delta V \tag{8}$$

Under the rule of half, the change in consumer surplus ΔCS is:

$$\Delta CS = V_1(P_1 - P_2) + \frac{1}{2}(V_2 - V_1)(P_1 - P_2)$$

or

$$\Delta CS = \frac{1}{2}(P_1 - P_2)(V_1 + V_2) \tag{9}$$

Equation (9) is the common expression used for the rule of half, where the subscripts 1 and 2 denote "before" and "after" the investment, respectively.

Before proceeding, it is important to observe that this analysis assumes no distortions in the economy (i.e., divergence of prices and marginal costs), so that the opportunity costs of the resources used to increase supply from S_1 to S_2 equal the benefits (willingness to pay) forgone elsewhere in the economy. Section 5 examines welfare changes when market imperfections make it impossible for these conditions to hold.

3.3 Producer Surplus

Producer surplus represents the difference between the opportunity costs of adding another unit of service (e.g., transportation) to the market, captured by the supply curve S, and the revenues earned by selling that additional unit. The concept reflects the producers' total gain from increased demand, reduced average (and marginal) costs or both, as produced by external and internal factors. External factors include direct public subsidies (to users and/or producers), or public investments that increase capacity and thus supply. Internal factors primarily entail technological improvements that increase efficiency in service production.

To measure producer surplus, we make use of the observation that the supply curve S represents the industry's marginal costs curve.[15] If production takes place at the point where the aggregate demand curve $V(P)$ intersects the supply curve at a point where $MC > AC$, the transportation firm will cover all its costs, including its capital costs.[16] To illustrate this principle we next examine two cases. In the first, at zero output, the transportation firm incurs no variable costs so that the supply curve starts at point O, as

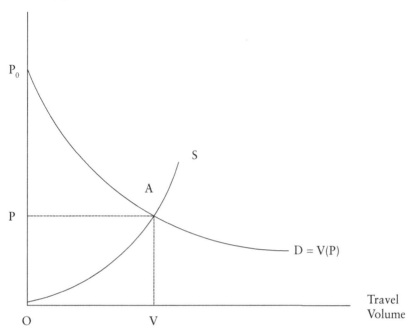

Travel Costs ($)

Figure 3.2 Measure of producer surplus.

in Figure 3.2; in the second, the firm's variable costs also include a cost of capital component, meaning that the supply curve intersects the price curve above point O, as in Figure 3.3.

In Figure 3.2, the area OAP represents the producer surplus (PS), which can be computed by subtracting the area OVA, or total cost, from the area $OVAP$, which represents total revenues:

$$PS = P \cdot V - V \cdot C(V) \tag{10}$$

where $P \cdot V$ is total revenue and $VC(V)$ is the firm's variable cost as a function of traffic volume V. Expression (10) can thus be written as:

$$PS = P \cdot V - \int_0^V MC(v)dv \tag{11}$$

In cases where the firm's variable costs also include the cost of capital (e.g., debt service), we regard the firm's supply curve as the firm's total variable cost (TVC) curve. In that case, the TVC curve would intersect the price axis at point B, as in Figure 3.3.

Expression (10) then becomes:

$$PS = P \cdot V - TVC(V) \tag{12}$$

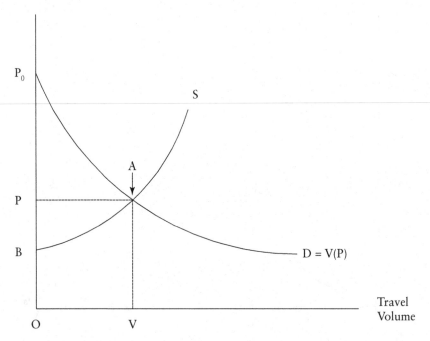

Travel Costs ($)

Figure 3.3 Measure of producer surplus with capital costs included.

Or, in terms of expression (11),

$$PS = P \cdot V - \int_0^V TVC(v)dv \tag{13}$$

Given these definitions, how can we estimate the *change* in producer surplus (ΔPS) resulting from a capital investment? Figure 3.4 illustrates this change assuming, for simplicity, linear demand and supply functions.

As shown in Figure 3.4, the supply curve S shifts downward to the right ($S_1 \rightarrow S_2$) following an investment in highway capacity so that the change in producer surplus is the difference between area P_1AB and area P_2CB. Notice that a visual inspection alone cannot determine whether $\Delta PS > 0$. This value depends on the elasticity of the demand and supply functions in the vicinity of P_1 and P_2, which requires precise computation. Using (13), the change in producer surplus from the investment is:

$$\Delta PS = \left[P_2 \cdot V_2 - \int_0^{V_2} TVC_2(v)dv \right] - \left[P_1 \cdot V_1 - \int_0^{V_1} TVC_1(v)dv \right] \tag{14}$$

Where, TVC_1 and TVC_2 represent S_1 and S_2, respectively.

Travel Costs

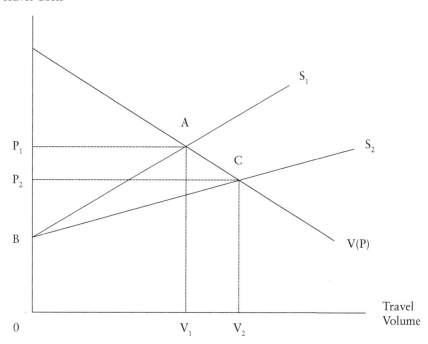

Figure 3.4 Change in producer surplus.

From expression (14), an approximation of the change in producer surplus (see Figure 3.4), we derive expression (15):

$$\Delta PS = \left[(P_2 \cdot V_2) - (P_1 \cdot V_1)\right] + \left[(C_2(V_2) - C_1(V_1))\right] \tag{15}$$

where $C_1(V_1)$ and $C_2(V_2)$ are total variable costs with and without investment in the project, respectively.

3.4 Net Welfare Change

Based on expressions (7) and (14), we can now compute the net change in social welfare (ΔSW) from the project: $\Delta SW = \Delta CS + \Delta PS$. Thus,

$$\Delta SW = \left[\int_0^{V_2} P(v)dv - V_2 \cdot P_2\right] - \left[\int_0^{V_1} P(v)dv - V_1 \cdot P_1\right]$$
$$+ \left[V_2 \cdot P_2 - \int_0^{V_2} TVC_2(v)dv\right] - \left[V_1 \cdot P_1 - \int_0^{V_1} TVC_1(v)dv\right] \tag{16}$$

Since total revenue appears on both sides of (16) but with different signs, we obtain:

$$\Delta SW = \left[\int_0^{V_2} P(v)dv - \int_0^{V_1} P(v)dv \right] + \left[\int_0^{V_2} TVC_2(v)dv - \int_0^{V_1} TVC_1(v)dv \right] \qquad (17)$$

As before, the subscripts 1 and 2 indicate "before" and "after" the change in capacity, respectively. In general notation, equation (17) can be written as:

$$\Delta SW = \Delta CS + \Delta TVC \qquad (18)$$

In (18), ΔTVC is the change in total variable costs arising from the investment, which include the annual debt service payment incurred by the investment. Appendix A in Chapter 8 demonstrates the use of these expressions in numerical computations.

3.5 First- and Second-Best Equilibrium Solutions

When conducting a transportation network analysis we commonly distinguish between the concepts *user equilibrium* (sometimes called *market equilibrium*) and *system equilibrium* (sometimes called *social equilibrium*). The former refers to the case where users who make travel choices (e.g., route selection) only consider their private average travel costs (time) and ignore the externality costs they impose on others. A user equilibrium solution is thus computed at the point where the demand curve intersects the *average private cost curve*. This solution is suboptimal because users do not pay for the marginal social costs of their travel decisions.

In contrast, social equilibrium implies that travel price and volume are set where the demand curve intersects the *marginal social costs* of the travel curve, implying that the externality has been internalized. This result can be achieved through the imposition of externality tax, such as a congestion toll, on network users. Any solution that does not equate marginal social costs with travel demand is Pareto Optimum inferior relative to the social equilibrium solution. Figure 3.5 shows these two types of equilibrium solutions.

In Figure 3.5, the demand curve $V(P)$ intersects the average cost curve $S = AC$ (the users' private cost curve) at point B, resulting in travel volume V_1 and travel cost P_1, respectively. Social equilibrium is achieved at point E, where $V(P)$ intersects the social marginal cost curve SMC, with V^* and P^* being equilibrium travel volume and travel costs, respectively. The deviation between the private (users') equilibrium and the social equilibrium is due to the (noninternalized) congestion externality. At volume V^*, the line segment EF (or $P^* - P'$) gives the per-trip size of this externality.

For the purpose of correctly measuring the net social benefits obtained from a transportation improvement, the computations need to be carried out at the social equilibrium solution E, which is also referred to as the *first-best solution*.[17] This solution, however, requires the introduction of a Pigouvian tax[18] in the form of a congestion toll ($P^* - P'$), meant to internalize the congestion externality. However, due mainly to political constraints, congestions tolls are rarely used so that traffic decisions tend to be taken at

Travel Costs

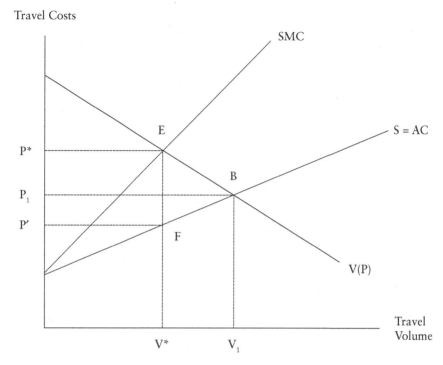

Figure 3.5 User equilibrium vs. social equilibrium.

the users' equilibrium point, *B*, which is therefore referred to as a *second-best solution*. Adoption of second-best solutions imply that the difference between the actual prices paid by consumers (trip makers) and the social marginal cost pricing that should be applied by producers (e.g., transportation agencies) have not been narrowed by any corrective measures, that is, no Pigouvian-type congestion toll has been imposed.[19]

First- and second-best solutions are not limited to the presence or absence of congestion tolls. If a roadway is efficiently tolled but parallel roads and roads downstream or upstream of the tolled road are not, a second-best solution emerges. Alternatively, if a congestion toll is imposed under a profit constraint (including a breakeven constraint), we continue to face a second-best solution. Under second-best conditions, a welfare gain from an investment in increased capacity is generally not Pareto optimal in that it may result in nonoptimal capacity expansion (Wheaton, 1973).

4. WELFARE EFFECTS OF MARKET IMPERFECTIONS

Most transportation markets are rather noncompetitive due to factors such as allocative externalities (e.g., traffic congestion), price regulation (e.g., a transit property controlling fares in an area), the availability of public goods (e.g., the road network), and distortionary taxation (e.g., gasoline tax). The common denominator in all these forms of market imperfections or *market failures*, as they are usually called, is the mismatch between observed market prices and the true social value of the resources used in the production and consumption of the respective services. Under conditions of market failure, the allocation of societal resources becomes inefficient, a condition that can result in overinvestment in highway facilities, to name just one outcome.

4.1 Sources of Market Imperfections

We generally define market failures as instances where consumers and producers face different sets of prices for the same goods and services. The classic public finance literature cites several major sources of market failure: provision of public goods, production under conditions of declining average costs, consumption or production with externalities, absent markets, asymmetric information, and price regulation. In transportation, externalities are the most common cause of market failures. In addition, public transit is often treated as a natural monopoly at the same time that parts of the uncongested highway network are considered a public good (MC = 0).

Two types of market externalities should be distinguished due to their distinctive effects on the appraisal of transportation projects: *allocative* or *technical externalities* and *pecuniary externalities*. As the name implies, externalities of the first type arise from factors pertaining to consumption and production technologies. That is, in the process of consuming or producing transportation services, individuals and firms generate byproducts. These, in turn, involuntarily affect the utility or profit level of other individuals and firms. A necessary condition for the presence of technological externalities is the absence of market mechanisms to compensate the affected parties for their loss of welfare or profits. A classic example is the emission of toxic fumes and noise from automobile driving, which affects the welfare (i.e., the health) of residents living in the vicinity of roads and highways. Obviously, we can also observe positive externalities, which confer positive utility to third parties. In transportation, the opening of a new link to reduce network-wide travel times is known as a network externality.[20] As a rule, negative and positive technological externalities result in nonoptimal resource allocation in the form of under- or overproduction of economic activities, such as automobile trips.

Government can employ several mechanisms to internalize technological externalities and thus achieve optimal allocation of resources. These range from regulation (e.g., restricted entry into transit markets) to the imposition of standards (e.g., permitted emission levels) to Pigouvian taxes or subsidies (e.g., congestion tolls). Given the voluminous literature on these subjects, they will not be discussed here. Chapter 12 explores the effect of environmental and safety externalities on COBA. In addition, the reader is referred to Vickrey (1960) for a valuable analysis of the subject.

Turning to *pecuniary externalities*, these arise when transactions made by economic agents are capitalized in imperfect markets.[21] In events of this type, market prices do not correctly measure the marginal costs and benefits—and thus the true social value—of the transacting agents' actions. Monopoly pricing is an obvious example. In many metropolitan areas, transit firms are public monopolies that set the transit fare structure in ways that do not reflect the true market value of the transit services provided. For instance, fares may be invariant with distance, time of day, type of vehicle, or location. They may also rarely change over long periods of time despite evidence that people are placing increasingly higher value on travel.

In transportation, pecuniary externalities can also occur when reduced transportation costs following a project's implementation alter relative prices in other markets. Such price changes in turn generate benefits and costs for the third parties active in the same markets. Economic development arising from transport improvements constitutes an important case of pecuniary externalities. Such externalities are observed when the transportation benefits accrued at specific locations are capitalized in local land markets without reflecting true market values from the perspective of society. The importance of these externalities for project evaluation arises from the fact that their market results (e.g., enhanced property value) often provide a political rationale for investing in transportation irrespective of the project's direct transportation effects (e.g., time savings). Chapter 13 further discusses these issues.

Venables and Gasiorek (1999) argue that the joint presence of allocative and pecuniary externalities may result in a cumulative effect, meaning that the impacts of a transportation project may be amplified as they spread through the economy. For instance, intersector and spatial spillover effects may not, as is frequently assumed, decline monotonically when rippling through the economy (Pred, 1966); they may in fact increase. These impacts can easily be either positive as negative. Thus, a transportation investment that improves accessibility may induce a firm to relocate to a nearby site. This allocative externality may, in turn, attract other firms, resulting in a cumulative agglomeration effect. The concentration of pharmaceutical firms in one area of New Jersey (US) that is highly accessible by highway and rail is a case in a point. Another example is network economies. In a given section of the network, construction of two links frequently confers more than twice the benefits that would be obtained from construction of one link, given the costs.

Mohring and Williamson (1969) have identified another form of externality, which they labeled *industrial reorganization benefits*. According to their model, the reduced travel time resulting from a transportation project can affect production and shipment logistics. Reduced inventories, just-in-time production, consolidation of truckloads and overnight guaranteed delivery are examples of these benefits. As important as these effects may be, demonstration of how they can be capitalized in a firm's costs relative to its use of all other resources remains vital. The issue is whether the changes can now be considered *additional benefits*, not merely benefits captured by reduced transportation costs. Double-counting of benefits is discussed in Chapter 13.

In addition to distorting the true societal costs of transport service provision, externalities also generate nonlinear impacts: Congestion tends to increase exponentially with traffic, housing values abate at an increasing rate with distance from the transportation facility (e.g., train stations), and level of firm agglomeration does not vary linearly by spatial proximity. Measurement of these phenomena thus requires the use of quite complicated models and techniques, which we discuss further in Chapters 8 and 13.

4.2 Welfare Changes from Market Imperfections

Transportation is a derived demand or intermediate good in the consumption of final goods (e.g., purchase of groceries). Should this fact have any bearing on the magnitude and measurement of imperfections in transportation markets? More generally, should intermediate good markets be treated differently than final good markets in the context of market imperfections? The answer, in general, is "no" so long as consumers can continue to purchase an alternative good that varies by alternative transportation features such as time of departure, mode, or route.

Table 3.1 shows distortions in transportation markets rooted in the relationship between Private and Social Marginal Costs (PMC and SMC, respectively), in addition to Private and Social Marginal Benefits (PMB and SMB, respectively).

Table 3.1's first cell shows a case where people pay a bus fare (PMC) that is below the social marginal cost of transit (SMC) while they derive a marginal benefit (PMB) that is greater than the social marginal benefit (SMB).[22] In cases where: PMC < SMC and PMB > SMB, we can expect excessive

Table 3.1 Relationship between Private and Social Marginal Costs

	PMB > SMB	*PMB = SMB*	*PMB < SMB*
PMC < SMC	Subsidy to transit users	Environmental congestion	Amount of distortion unknown
PMC = SMC	Subsidy to highway users	Competitive market	Monopoly
PMC > SMC	Amount of distortion unknown	Taxation	Automobile taxation

Source: Venables and Gasiorek, (1999).

amounts of travel. On the other hand, when PMC > SMC and PMB < SMB, there will be less than socially desired amounts of travel. In all other cases, a detailed analysis is required to ascertain the impact of the distortion on the amount of trips taken.

How should the welfare impact of these imperfections in transportation markets be formulated? Assuming externalities as the source of the market failure, the social welfare function is defined as the sum of total consumer and producer surplus minus the externality costs, that is,

$$SW = CS + PS + E \qquad (19)$$

where E represents externality costs, or benefits (if the externality produces positive utility). The change in welfare resulting from the transportation improvement is thus:

$$\Delta SW = \Delta CS + \Delta PS + \Delta E \qquad (20)$$

Figure 3.5 illustrates the case of a congestion externality. The social marginal cost curve is given by:

$$SMC(V) = S + V \cdot \frac{\partial S}{\partial V} \qquad (21)$$

The term $V \cdot \frac{\partial S}{\partial V}$ represents the nontolled externality as a function of travel volume V.[23] According to Figure 3.5, the private price of making a trip P_1 under these conditions is below the optimal price P^*, resulting in V_1, the number of actual trips taken, which exceeds the socially optimal volume V^*. This situation leads to a suboptimal level of social welfare since the gain in benefits at the lower price, V^*EBV_1, comes at an opportunity cost of V^*FBV_1, resulting in a welfare loss of EFB.

Another example of the market imperfections prevalent in transportation is price regulation, such as that observed in public transit. As shown in Figure 3.6, the state regulates the price of transit, setting it at regulated price P_R, below the equilibrium price P^*. Regulation requires the transit firm to meet all demand at P_R, namely, V_R. At this price, however, the transit firm would like to supply V_S. Under these conditions, total benefits (consumer and producer surplus) are represented by the area $OAXV_R$. Total opportunity costs are represented by $OCYV_R$, associated with revenue TR and equal to $TR = P_R \cdot V_R$. Can we therefore conclude that price regulation is a welfare-improving policy?

To answer this question we note that the increase in benefits is given by the area V_SBXV_R, while the change in opportunity costs is area V_SBYV_R. Because the increase in benefits is smaller than the increase in opportunity costs, the net effect is a welfare loss equal to the area BXY. Hence, this specific transfer of income to consumers from producers in the form of price reductions does not have a zero net effect on social welfare but, rather, a negative effect. That is, producer surplus decreases more than consumer surplus increases when the price of travel is reduced through regulation.[24]

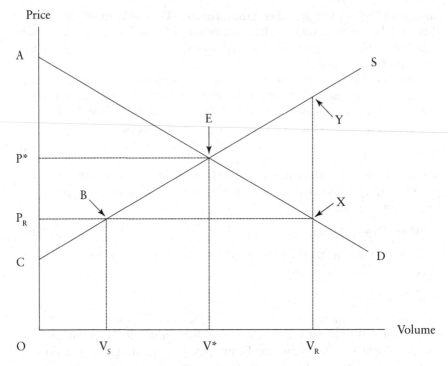

Figure 3.6 Consumer and producer surplus under price regulation.

5. FORMULATION OF NET WELFARE CHANGES UNDER MARKET IMPERFECTIONS

We have already noted that ignoring congestion externalities in the appraisal of net benefits from a capacity change can lead to nonoptimal investments. This section takes a formal look at the effects of externalities and of changes in the measurement of net benefits prompted by exogenous changes such as capacity improvements.

5.1 Externality Effects

Expression (20) defined the change in social welfare ΔSW as the sum of changes in consumer and producer surplus together with externality costs ΔE. Following equation (3), consumer surplus CS can be written as:

$$CS = \int_0^{V^*} D(z)dz - P^*V^* \tag{22}$$

In (22), P^* and V^* are equilibrium market price and quantity of travel, respectively: D denotes the demand curve and CS the difference between what a consumer receives from the consumption of a commodity in terms of benefits and her total expenditures on that commodity.

Referring to Figure 3.3, producer surplus *PS* is the difference between the opportunity cost of introducing an additional unit of transportation into the market, shown by supply curve S, and the revenue earned by the producer from selling that additional unit, shown by demand curve D. Following equation (13), at equilibrium, *PS* can be written as:

$$PS = P^*V^* - \int_0^{V^*} S(z)dz \tag{23}$$

If an externality exists, it is the difference between the private and the social cost of a good, which may be positive or negative, depending on whether it adds or detracts from total social welfare. Hence, the impact on social welfare *W* of a negative externality *E* can be written as:

$$E = \int_0^{V^*} SMC(z)dz - \int_0^{V^*} S(z)dz \tag{24}$$

where *SMC* is social opportunity cost. Combining (22), (23), and (24) we obtain:

$$W = \left[\int_0^{V^*} D(z)dz - P^*V^* \right] + \left[P^*V^* - \int_0^{V^*} S(z)dz \right] - \left[\int_0^{V^*} SMC(z)dz - \int_0^{V^*} S(z)dz \right] \tag{25}$$

In the absence of (negative) externalities, $\int_0^{V^*} SMC(z)dz = \int_0^{V^*} S(z)dz$ and

$$W = \int_0^{V^*} D(z)dz - \int_0^{V^*} S(z)dz \tag{26}$$

However, if externalities do exist:

$$W = \int_0^{V^*} D(z)dz - \int_0^{V^*} SMC(z)dz^{25} \tag{27}$$

Since a negative externality implies that $\int_0^{V^*} SMC(z)dz > \int_0^{V^*} S(z)dz$, its presence reduces social welfare in comparison with cases where no negative externality is present. Note that the sign of (27) can be negative, depending on the elasticities of the demand (*D*) and social marginal cost (*SMC*) functions.

5.2 Deadweight Welfare Loss from User Charges

Another important welfare concept is that of welfare loss, known as *deadweight loss*, which occurs whenever consumers and producers face different sets of prices when carrying out their economic decisions. Consider the case where a user charge (e.g., a flat toll) is introduced on vehicle travel over a facility (e.g., a bridge) in the absence of congestion. What welfare implications can be associated with the charge?

Using lower-case letters, the inverse demand function is: $p = f^{-1}(v)$, where p is the generalized cost of travel per (vehicle) trip and v is travel volume. Total consumer gross benefit (or consumer surplus) is given by:

$$\int_0^v f^{-1}(v)dv \tag{28}$$

Prior to introduction of the user charge, the equilibrium price of travel was p^* and travel volume was v^*. Therefore, net consumer surplus was:

$$\int_0^{v^*} f^{-1}(v)dv - p^* \cdot v^* \tag{29}$$

After the charge ρ per (vehicle) trip is imposed, the total cost of travel increases to $p'(p' = p^* + \rho)$, and travel volume declines to $v'(v' < v^*)$.[26] Net benefits are now:

$$\int_0^{v'} f^{-1}(v)dv - p'v' \tag{30}$$

Since the amount $\rho \cdot v'$ is a pure transfer from users to the public authorities, the real change in net benefits is:

$$\int_0^{v'} f^{-1}(v)dv - (p'v' - \rho \cdot v') \tag{31}$$

Subtracting (29) from (31) ("before" minus "after") shows the change in Net Benefits (NB) resulting from the introduction of charge ρ to be:

$$\Delta NB = \left(\int_0^{v^*} f^{-1}(v)dv - p^* \cdot v^*\right) - \left(\int_0^{v'} f^{-1}(v)dv - v'(p' - \rho)\right) \tag{32}$$

or

$$\Delta NB = \left(\int_{v'}^{v^*} f^{-1}(v)dv - p^*(v^* - v')\right) \tag{33}$$

Expression (33) is the deadweight loss from the introduction of the user charge, whose exact magnitude depends on demand elasticity and the size of the charge. From (33), if $\rho = 0$, $p^* = p'$, $v^* = v'$, and $\Delta NB = 0$. This is a welfare loss because it was calculated from an exogenous increase in price over a "normal" demand function. The factor explaining this loss is the gap between the prices faced by users (p') and those faced by producers (the authorities) $(p' - \rho)$, created by the charge. As a result of this divergence in price, each party's economic decisions regarding the quantities consumed and produced also diverge (v' vs. v^*), which results in a welfare loss.

The key point behind this abstract example is that use of a user charge, whose level is independent of traffic level, is usually accompanied by a welfare loss, a result worth considering when assessing the overall net benefits of charges. This conclusion also applies when the source of the gap between the prices faced by consumers and producers is caused by an externality such as congestion, a situation where social marginal cost deviates from users' actual cost. In such a case, however, an efficient congestion charge (toll) can bridge this gap in prices, resulting in a Pareto optimal allocation of resources.

6. SUMMARY AND CONCLUSIONS

The aim of this chapter was to present the welfare foundations of transportation project evaluation. It outlined the key principles for welfare measurement as well as the welfare distortions that can arise in the presence of market imperfections. Under welfare maximization, a project should be accepted if and only if the present discount value of the net social benefits generated is positive. To carry out a correct analysis of an investment project's welfare contribution, we therefore need to determine whether the calculations are carried out under first- or second-best conditions and whether externalities are present in the germane markets.

Because only second-best conditions can be observed in most true-to-life cases, it is necessary to show how COBA, as used in project assessment, actually considers these distortions. Moreover, the presence of deadweight losses from charges or externalities is also to be taken into account. The chapters immediately following deal with the benefits and costs of transportation investments (Chapters 4 and 5). Chapter 6 in particular examines which COBA methods are intrinsically based on the welfare principles analyzed in the current chapter. Finally, this chapter has not dealt with equity issues that often constitute the grounds for undertaking a new transportation investment project. These are examined in Chapter 11.

4 Transportation Benefits from Infrastructure Improvements

1. INTRODUCTION

The declared objective of investing in transportation is to enhance social welfare by generating benefits for the economy. In this chapter we inquire into the nature and magnitude of these benefits by focusing on two major questions: First, what effects should be regarded as actual benefits rather than merely income transfers between parties? Second, how are we to convert these benefits into monetary values for the purpose of the investment's comparative assessment? The latter question, regarding incorporation of the estimated benefits into the project appraisal process, is dealt with in Chapter 6. Here we deal with the prior question.

In general, we can distinguish between two major categories of benefits flowing from transportation investments: Benefits accruing directly to present and future users of the transportation system have been termed *direct benefits*, whereas benefits representing nonuser effects, accruing to non-transportation activities in the local, regional, or national economy, have been given the label *indirect or secondary benefits*. This chapter examines the various direct transportation benefits. Analysis of the indirect benefits is carried out in Chapter 13.

As pointed out in Chapter 3, real benefits from transportation improvements are actually net changes in social welfare. In real-world analyses, however, we need to define what specific benefit components need to be measured "before" and "after" the improvement to ascertain the net change. Section 2 discusses those components that, because they are readily measured as reductions in commuters' direct costs, do not require further conversion into monetary units.

Since some benefit components, most noticeably Travel Time Savings (TTS), are specified in physical units (i.e., time), we need to convert them into monetary units for purposes of project appraisal. This conversion is essential because it enables clear economic valuation of the overall investment. However, the transformation of real benefits into monetary values requires the use of conversion factors, in this case, the monetary value of time.

Sections 3 and 4 deal with the theoretical and empirical issues associated with deriving the respective conversion factors.

Transit system improvements affect transit users in ways different from those that general transport or highway improvements impose on auto users. Benefits to highway users are observed mainly in the form of reduced travel times and costs. In contrast, transit users benefit mainly from reduced wait time, increased service reliability, and reduced in-vehicle overcrowding; Section 5 examines these benefits. Transport demand elasticities, used to assess changes in demand flowing from changes in price and service attributes, are reviewed in Section 6. A summary and conclusions are to be found in Section 7.

2. COMPONENTS OF USERS' BENEFITS FROM TRANSPORTATION IMPROVEMENTS

It was shown in Chapter 3 that total benefits from transportation investments entail a net change in consumer surplus (CS) and producer surplus (PS) alike. CS can be approximated by the rule of half, especially in highway projects, whereas PS can be estimated as total revenue (for the economy) minus total costs. Travel quantities are normally measured in units of car trips for highway projects, or in passenger trips for transit projects.[1] Travel prices are measured in terms of generalized cost of travel, which includes monetary expenses and travel time. Because traffic is comprised of vehicles of various sizes, it is customary to convert all vehicles into Private Car Equivalent (PCE) units. For example, an eighteen-wheel truck is usually taken as equivalent to 3 PCEs.

Travel implies costs (or disutility[2]) to users and operators; hence, improved transportation necessarily implies reduction in these costs, direct and indirect. Hence, in evaluating transportation improvements, cost reductions are usually regarded as the prime direct benefits to trip makers and—in the absence of externalities—to society as a whole.

In their study on the full marginal costs to society of highway investment, Ozbay et al. (2001) found that congestion costs—which are the time costs motorists incur from the additional time spent in traffic above free-flow travel conditions—constitute the largest single component among all societal costs (users' costs and externalities). In Chapter 12 we discuss these results and their derivation at greater length. For the purposes of this chapter, we should note that from the users' perspective, the key direct costs are travel time followed by auto operating costs and related expenses. Cost reductions from a transportation investment therefore capture the benefits emanating from that investment. Herein lies the importance of properly measuring the respective cost factors.

With respect to direct costs, transport investments can introduce auto operating cost savings, O-D travel time savings, changes in parking fees, reduced transit fares, and decreasing traffic accident rates. Of these, the first two items (auto costs, including tolls, and travel time) are most sensitive to transportation developments designed to increase speed and improve travel flow. Users' monetary costs of auto travel include primarily depreciation, vehicle operating costs, and insurance. Section 2.1 deals with the estimation and percent distribution of these costs.

2.1 Vehicle Operating Costs

Vehicle depreciation, fuel, oil, tire wear, insurance, parking fees, and tolls, in addition to regular and unexpected maintenance, are the items covered by the category of vehicle operating costs. In a study on the full marginal costs of transportation development, Ozbay et al. (2001) estimated a general function for estimating vehicle operating cost:

$$C_{opr} = f(C_d, C_g, C_o, C_t, C_m, C_I, C_{pt}) \tag{1}$$

where, C_{opr} is vehicle operating cost (\$/vehicle), C_d is vehicle depreciation, C_g is gasoline (\$/mile), C_o is oil (\$/mile), C_t is tires (\$/mile), C_m is maintenance (\$/mile), C_I is insurance (\$/year), C_{pt} is parking and tolls (\$/mile), which for daily commuters are fixed sums. Both C_{opr} and C_d are defined over a period of time (e.g., 10 years). The following model was estimated:

$$C_{opr} = 6240.36 + 0.104 \cdot \frac{m}{a} + 2027.73 \cdot a + 0.1227 \cdot m \tag{2}$$

where m denotes mileage and a denotes the vehicle's age. Table 4.1 shows these operating cost components in \$ per mile (excluding insurance, which is a yearly cost).

Among these cost components, only gasoline and oil consumption vary with travel time, or speed and distance. Hence, if travel time declines in the wake of a transportation improvement, we can expect primarily gasoline

Table 4.1 Operating Costs (in 2000 dollar value, net of tax)

Operating Expenses	Costs
Gasoline & oil	0.061 (\$/mile)
Maintenance	0.029 (\$/mile)
Tires	0.0145 (\$/mile)
Insurance cost	1,350 (\$/year)
Parking and tolls	0.0182 (\$/mile)

Source: AAMA, (1996); US DOT, (1991).

and oil cost savings to the extent that traveled distance is invariant with travel speed; all other vehicle operating costs will remain unaffected. However, if a transportation improvement allows higher speeds and increases in miles traveled, the above expressions can be used to assess these subsequent impacts on operating costs.

Estimation is also based on the percentage distribution of operating cost components by vehicle age. For annual mileage of 13,000 miles, the typical percentage distribution of: (a) depreciation, gasoline, oil, and tires; (b) parking and tolls; and (c) insurance for a new car is: 74%, 14%, and 12%, respectively. After 5 years, it is 43%, 31%, and 26%; after 10 years it is 36%, 33%, and 31%. These figures can be used to compute vehicle cost savings from transportation improvements for a traffic fleet of average age (about 5 years).

3. VALUE OF TRAVEL TIME SAVINGS (TTS)

Among all travel cost variables, the key one is undoubtedly travel time, a component directly affected by transportation improvements. Unlike vehicle operating costs, travel time is estimated and measured in units of time; it therefore needs to be converted into monetary values for use in COBA. This conversion is achieved through the use of Value of Time (VOT) parameters, expressed as $ per hour. This section examines the theoretical underpinnings of the VOT derivation, followed by a presentation of the empirical VOT parameters used for various trip types in different countries.

3.1 Key Questions in VOT Analysis

In general, we distinguish between at least two types of trips: work and non-work. The first category is sometimes further divided into work and work-related, whereas the second category is always disaggregated into purposes such as shopping, education, recreation, and leisure. Should the time saved in carrying out all these trip types be assigned the same monetary value? In theory, when faced with no physical, economic, or institutional constraints and complete information, an individual can allocate her daily time allotment (24 hours) so that the marginal value of the time saved on all trips is equal. In reality, however, several institutional and fiscal constraints introduce variance into the VOT for different trips. Among these we can list work rules (such as fixed initiation and conclusion of work shifts), marginal tax on earned income (which is above the average tax rate), household arrangements (which require trip chaining), and insufficient information on travel conditions. The key argument, therefore, is that due to these constraints, the time saved in travel to work is more valuable to the economy—as opposed to the individual—than the same amount of time saved for other types of trips.

A second question concerns the difference between *measured* travel time saved and *perceived* travel time saved. Trip makers generally cannot measure travel time accurately, even for daily commuting trips. This is due to perceptual issues as well as the wide distribution of travel times by trip segment, day of the week, and trip length. In particular, individuals tend to overestimate time saved mainly as a result of perceptual biases; that is, frequent users of an infrastructure facility tend to overestimate time savings relative to *measured* time savings. As an illustration of this phenomenon, we cite Segonne (1998), who reports that users of new infrastructure have estimated time savings of 23 minutes while, in fact, measurement showed only 8 minutes of time saved. Another issue pertains to valuation: For trip makers, does the value of 1 minute saved equal one-tenth of a bloc of 10 minutes saved? Is there a threshold below which individuals are unable to value TTS? Alternatively, does a user's utility from TTS exhibit declining marginal utility relative to the total amount of time saved?

Given trip purpose, the common practice is to treat units of time equally, mainly because attempts to view travel time savings as nonlinear is bound to raise insoluble computational problems even when the differences are rather minor (Small, 1992a).

Because of these and related issues, average travel times by trip purpose are used for COBA. However, because these averages are derived from a broad range of travel times–which are unlikely to be normally distributed— the use of averages (or sometimes the median) can be quite misleading.[3] This observation raises a third question: What is the proper TTS to be used to avoid biases in actual applications? Still another important question relates to the VOT for nonwork activities such as leisure-time activities. Do time savings in lieu of such activities yield measurable economic benefits? If so, what are they?

As explained in Chapter 7, door-to-door travel time is comprised of various factors: access and egress time and travel time on various road types (e.g., collector, arterial, or freeway). In public transit, wait time, in-vehicle time, transfer time, and reliability of service are the salient variables. What values should be assigned to these factors? A 5-minute savings in in-vehicle time may have lower utility for users than does five minutes saved in wait time.

We next examine the general methodology used for estimating VOT parameters and subsequently review VOT data reported from various studies conducted in different countries.

3.2 A Model of Time Allocation

The value of time is defined as the marginal rate of substitution between time and cost or price of travel, that is,

$$\frac{\partial U}{\partial t} \Big/ \frac{\partial U}{\partial p}$$

where U denotes utility; t and p are time and price, respectively. A fundamental tenet of value of time analysis is that people allocate their time amongst different activities in ways that maximize their utility, subject to income and time constraints. Given this approach, almost all the theoretical models used to derive the value of time are outgrowths of Becker's original formulation (Becker, 1965). Examples are: DeSerpa (1971, 1973), Mohring (1976), Bruzelius (1979), Hensher and Truong (1985) and Small (1992a). These models maximize the utility of a representative consumer with respect to time-consuming activities, subject to time and budget constraints. To illustrate this idea, Appendix A presents a formal time allocation model containing two time categories, time spent at work and time spent in leisure activities (see also MVA, 1997).

For our purposes, the key result from this model is that if an individual is unconstrained by the number of hours he can allocate to work, he will do so until the utility from the last unit of time spent at work approximately equals his wage rate. This result helps to explain why the VOT figures used in empirical studies of benefits from infrastructure investments are regularly specified in terms of hourly wages (average, median, or some other statistic). Tables 4.3 and 4.4 provide some examples. A second result from the model is that if minimum work hours and minimum leisure time constraints are not binding, the total reward for an additional unit of work time, at equilibrium, equals the utility of the last unit of foregone leisure time. Thus, at equilibrium, the utility from an additional unit of leisure time represents the opportunity costs of time worked.

The formulation in Appendix A does not include travel time as a separate component of time. We could claim that travel time is just another type of time, spent on activities similar to, say, shopping. Yet, it can be argued that travel time differs from other types of time in several important ways. First of all, it confers negative utility, whereas the utility from time spent in all other activities is, arguably, positive. Second, in the short- and medium-term, travel time—unlike other activities—is not fully controllable by individuals because it is subject to the influence of exogenous conditions such as congestion or level of service. Thus, given each activity's location (e.g., residential or employment), the question is how to treat travel time from within a utility maximization framework.[4]

McFadden and Train (1978) were the first to take up this question in the random utility literature. Their goal was to examine how price and income can enter a direct utility function of mode choice. Truong and Hensher (1985) further investigated this issue within the framework of DeSerpa's (1971) model. Their objective was to derive a simple form to capture the deterministic element of the random utility model as applied to choice between travel alternatives (see also MVA, 1997). The main result obtained from these inquiries is that the ratio of the shadow price of the income constraint, which includes travel costs, to that of the shadow price of the travel time constraint associated with a transportation alternative (e.g., a mode or a route) equals the value of time saved when using that alternative.

As the second part of the model shown in Appendix A demonstrates, an individual can alter her valuation of a unit of travel time saved in response to the work and travel environments that she faces. For example, flexible working hours, or the ability to depart home at will, can influence derived VOT parameters. Therein lies the importance of understanding the work and travel markets in which transportation investments are made.

3.3 VOT from Discrete Choice Models

The value of time can also be calculated from discrete choice models, especially Multinomial Logit Models (MNL). In these models, VOT is calculated as the ratio between the time coefficient in the utility function and the total cost of the travel coefficient. That is,

$$VOT = \frac{\beta_1}{\beta_2} = \frac{utils / hour}{utils / \$} = \frac{\$}{hour},$$

where β_1 is the coefficient of the time component and β_2 is the coefficient of travel cost. Units should be adjusted for correct measurements (i.e., \$/hour).

New studies exploring the implications of random coefficient mixed logit models for the valuation of Travel Time Savings (TTS) have come up with some surprising results. First, some proportion of the population may assign a zero—if not actually negative—value to TTS, that is, a positive coefficient for Travel Time (TT), which implies increased utility from additional travel (Cirillo and Axhausen, 2006; Hensher and Rose, 2005; Hess et al., 2005).[5] These studies also show that valuation of TTS can vary considerably, depending on the assumptions made about the distribution of random TT coefficients in a mixed logit model. In any case, while the range of TTS does cover negative values, sample means of \$ per person-hour are normally used for project evaluation purposes and do have a positive value.

Given these theoretical constructs, how are travel time values derived? What are the empirical values associated with various trip types and modes?

4. MEASUREMENT OF VALUE OF TRAVEL TIME

The literature on the empirical estimation of VOT is quite voluminous. Results have been estimated by travel mode, socioeconomic characteristics of trip makers, trip purpose, component of travel time, travel conditions, time of day, and location. These results notwithstanding, many countries actually direct transportation analysts as to which VOT parameters they are to use in various contexts. In fact, VOT values are often used as policy variables for COBAs of transportation investment projects (see for example US DOT, 1997; UK Department of Transport, 2004). The conventional arguments for this widespread practice claim that it prevents intentional bias from entering the evaluation of specific projects and that it provides a common yardstick for ranking projects irrespective of the analysts' views. However, it is useful to decide which VOT is appropriate for COBA of a specific project. A case can then be made, for example, that different VOT should be used when comparing a freight corridor versus a highway project.

4.1 Methodological Questions in Measuring VOT

Two alternative approaches are available for the estimation of VOT values. First, we can observe (directly or indirectly) the amount of money a trip maker actually spends in order to save one unit of travel time. For example, data from toll roads have been used as indicators of how much users are actually willing to pay to drive on a fast tolled lane when the alternative is travel on more congested, slower but toll-free lanes (Brownstone and Small, 2005; Von Wartburg and Waters, 2004). A second approach is to survey people's preferences relative to their willingness to pay for a unit of time saved. These two approaches are commonly referred to as the Revealed Preference (RP) and the Stated Preferences (SP) approaches, respectively. Some studies have used a mixed database, composed of RP and SP observations (Small et al., 2005).

Considerable differences in time savings are obtained from SP as opposed to RP studies. Using French data, Segonne (1998) estimated a median VOT of €5.34/hour from a SP study and €7.8/hour from a RP study. Hensher (1997), using Australian data, likewise reports significant differences between VOT results from models using SP data relative to the opportunity costs of time. In another study, Calfee and Winston (1998), using SP data, concluded that the marginal VOT savings for highway commuters is rather low, about 15%–25% of the gross wage rate. They explain their findings in terms of commuters' perceptual adjustments relative to mode, locations, and times of departure.

Another issue is the value of travel reliability. Does a commuter's overall VOT also contain a premium for reliability? And if so, what is the relationship between the VOT and the Value of Reliability (VOR)? In Section 4.3, we provide data on estimated VOR, whereas in Chapter 7 we conduct a detailed examination of traffic flow reliability and its implications.

Given these comments, what can we conclude are the key problems to be considered when assessing the value of travel time from empirical sources in the course of a COBA analysis? The key issues are listed below under five headers: What VOT statistic to use, treatment of various trip types, treatment of various travel time components, measurement of travel time saved, and whether travel time savings are linearly additive.

1. Use of a VOT Statistic

Since the hourly wage rate providing the basis for VOT figures is in fact derived from a distribution, should VOT be measured on the basis of a simple average, which is subject to extreme values, a weighted average, or any other statistic? The common practice is to use the mean as a good representative statistic. Yet, in some European countries, value of personal car use is reported as a range (e.g., Finland, from €1.5/hour to €2.5/hour, EURET, 1994). The question is, then, should a range of VOT or a single statistic be used for assessing a project's total benefits?

A related difficulty is that for computational purposes, travel times are measured as averages, while disregarding the variance. This practice introduces bias into the computation of travel time saving, whose magnitude, although unknown, could be quite large if the project has extensive network-wide effects.

2. Treatment of Various Trip Types

Benefits from travel improvements accrue to all trip types but at a disproportionate rate. Since home-to-work trips are performed mostly at peak time, when roads and transit systems are highly congested, these stand to benefit most from congestion relief measures. Other trip types, such as shopping, occur at other times: hence, they will be much less affected by such measures. What, then, should the VOT be for work as opposed to nonwork trips? Within each work trip category, should commuting have the same VOT as other work-related trips (e.g., trips in lieu of work or for business purposes)? Finally, should we assign different VOTs for commuters traveling by different modes?

3. Treatment of Travel Time Components

How should we treat the VOT of time components such as access, egress, waiting, transfer, and parking, which users regard as part of their overall travel time? In general, trip makers value these factors differentially, mainly due to the degree of uncertainty embedded in each. Nonetheless, a single VOT parameter is normally used for a given transportation project, a practice that may lead to underestimating its benefits. For example, an investment, which increases mainly headways will reduce wait time but have little impact on actual in-vehicle time. It may also reduce overcrowding and wait time on parallel transit lines. To the extent that commuters value wait time more than in-vehicle time, the use of a single VOT parameter can bias estimation of the project's true benefits.

4. Level of Measurement of Time Saved

Should travel time changes resulting from a project be measured at the project, the facility, or the network level? In transit projects especially, the tendency is to measure travel time savings at the line—rail or bus—level, thus disregarding network effects such as trip diversion from other lines. Furthermore, induced travel demand may render travel time savings at the facility level quite inaccurate as other parts of the network may become congested. Hence, the investment project's network-wide effects require consideration.

5. Treating Travel Time Savings as a Linearly Additive

Can we treat travel time as a linear additive so that 3 minutes saved by each of 10,000 daily commuters equals 500 hours of time saved or, in turn, 30 minutes saved by each of 1,000 commuters? The importance of this question cannot be emphasized enough because this is the way that total travel time saved by a project is computed in COBA studies. To the extent that we believe that each minute of travel time saved is productive and confers the same utility as does the previous minute, this practice is sensible. However, if 5 minutes saved by each of 6 commuters are less productive than 30 minutes saved by one commuter, we need to regard the *distribution* of travel time saved as well as the distribution—rather than the average—of VOT in order to obtain a correct measure of this travel feature's economic value. In that case, the distribution's moments (mainly its mean and variance) would provide better measures of the value of total time saving. As Table 4.7 shows, it makes sense to examine the project by using lower and upper values of VOT in addition to its average or median. A more elaborate approach would be to consider the upper bounds on cases falling within one, two, or more standard deviations from the mean.

4.2 Empirical Results from Value of Time Studies

The literature provides plenty of information on VOT, either as a percentage of wage rates or in monetary units per hour. Table 4.2 shows results obtained from various studies by country, trip purpose, type of market, and method of analysis.

As can be seen from Table 4.2, the results vary considerably, depending mainly on the estimation model and database used. Comparisons are also problematic: It is difficult to compare results from a regression model with those from a logit model; it is also difficult to compare between studies that use the same model but different databases relative to their sources, the years covered and method of collection. To partly overcome this complexity, Table 4.3 provides estimates of VOT savings values for work and nonwork trips from different countries relative to GDP per capita.

Like Table 4.2 this table shows the wide diversity of results to be obtained between countries and between studies in same country. However, it also shows that trips to work are assigned much higher values than are nonwork trips. If we accept the averages as reflecting some common values, it seems that the VOT for travel to work is about three times the GDP per capita for nonwork trips.

Table 4.2 Survey of Studies of Value of Time Savings

Study	Country	Trip Purpose	Choice Market	Method of Analysis	VOT (% of Wage Rate, or $/hour)
Atkins (1983)	UK	Commuting	Route	Logit	38%–61%[a,c]
Bates and Roberts (1986)	UK	Commuting	Route	SP, market segmentation	43%[a]
Beesley (1965)	UK	Commuting	Car, transit	SP	33%–50%[b]
Beggs et al. (1981)	Australia	Recreation	Car	Demand for site	Aus$79.60/day
Chui and McFarland (1987)	US	Commuting (interurban, rural)	Car (speed)	Regression (actual and perceived costs)	82% ($7.75/hour)
Cole (1990)	Canada	Commuting, leisure, work	Auto, rail, bus, air	SP, comparison, logit	Commute: 170%[d] Leisure: 165%[d]
Dawson and Everall (1972)	Italy	Intercity	Car		60%–89%
Deacon and Sonstelie (1985)	US	Leisure	Car	SP, Regression	52%–254%[e]

Study	Country	Purpose	Mode	Method	Result
Edmonds (1983)	Japan	Commuting (inferred from location)	Car, bus, rail	Hedonic regression	42%–49% US$3.58–$4.18 (1983 prices)
Forsyth (1980)	Australia US UK	Tradeoffs: leisure, work	Unstated	Utility maximization model	Aus$4.75—1976 US$5.19—1976 UK£1.56—1976
Fowkes (1986)	UK	Commuting	Rail, bus	Logit, SP	27%–59%
Ghosh, Lees, and Seal (1975)	UK	Commuting (interurban)	Car	Regression (speed choice)	73%–89%
Gunn (1991)	Netherlands	Commuting business	Car Car	SP SP	Dfl12.7/hour Dfl19.8/hour
Lam and Small (2001)	US	Commuting (SR-91)	Car	Regression	$23–$24/hour (median VOT)
Steimetz and Brownstone (2005)	US	Commuting (I-15 express lane)	Car	Conditional logit[f]	$30/hour (median VOT); $7–$65 by motorists' characteristics

Legend: SP = Stated Preferences; RP = Revealed Preferences.
Notes: [a]Varies with income; [b]Approximation; [c]Estimates sensitive to sample composition and size; [d]Logit Model, car travel; [e]Varies with income; [f]In response to tolls and trip makers characteristics.

Table 4.3 Value of Time (VOT) Relative to GDP per Capita in Different Countries[a,b]

Country	VOT for Work and Work-Related Trips Relative to GDP Per Capita	VOT for Nonwork-Related Trips Relative to GDP Per Capita	Ratio of VOT for Nonwork to Work Trips
US (state of Indiana)	0.84	0.421	0.501
Austria	1.47	0.434	0.295
Belgium	2.36		
Denmark	1.64		
Denmark	2.48	0.622	0.251
Finland	1.31		
Finland	2.05		
Finland	1.85	0.248	0.134
France	0.94		
Germany	1.75		
Germany	1.67	1.052	0.631
Germany	4.68	1.638	0.350
Ireland	2.61		
Israel	2.18	0.212	0.097
Italy	2.37		
Luxemburg	2.19		
The Netherlands	2.22		
The Netherlands	2.09	0.634	0.303
The Netherlands	2.03	0.501	0.246
Average	2.04	0.64	0.31

Source: de Jong, (1999).
Notes: [a]Empty cells mean information is unavailable; [b]More than one set of results for the same country indicates that they were taken from different studies.

4.3 Recommended VOT Savings Values

As mentioned, many countries regard VOT savings as policy variables that should be determined by the authorities and adhered to when performing transportation COBA. Tables 4.4 and 4.5 show recommended US values as a percentage of the hourly wage rate, and in $/hour.

Table 4.5 provides VOT savings in dollars per average hour of work.

The data from Table 4.5 raise a further question: What hourly wage rate should be used for VOT calculations? This rate changes, of course, from place to place as well as by occupation. Hence, similar projects at different places will require different VOT saving values.[6]

For illustration purposes, Table 4.6 shows French VOT savings by trip type.

The need to use very few VOT figures for the COBA of a given project has led to the generalization of VOT statistics. Thus, based on a large number of studies, Von Wartburg and Waters (2004) have recommended that all non-work-related trips, *irrespective* of their purpose, should be valued at 50% of the average after-tax hourly wage. For business trips, they recommend setting VOT at 100% of the before-tax hourly wage rate plus the fringe benefits paid to employees.

The above results do not pertain to the value of travel reliability that, as mentioned above, is highly valued by trip makers. This phenomenon is

Table 4.4 US VOT Savings as a Percentage of Hourly Wage Rate (2000)[a]

Trip Type	Surface Modes[b,c]	Truck Drivers
Local Travel		
In-vehicle personal	35%–60% (50%)	
In-vehicle business	80%–120% (100%)	100%
Excess (wait, walking, transfer) personal	100%[d]	
Excess (wait, walking, transfer) business	100%[d]	
Intercity		
In-vehicle personal	60%–90% (70%)	
In-vehicle business	80%–120% (100%)	100%

Source: US DOT (1997); US DOT (2001).
Notes: [a]Percentages in brackets are recommended values; [b]Apply to all combinations of in-vehicle and other transit time; [c]Walk, wait and transfer times should be evaluated at 100% of the wage rate when improvements affect only these elements of transit time; [d]Obtained from US DOT (1997).

Table 4.5 US Recommended VOT Savings $/Average Hour of Work (2000 Prices)[a]

Trip Type	Surface Modes	Truck Drivers
Local Travel		
Personal	$7.40–$12.70 ($10.60)	
Business	$17.00–$25.40 ($21.20)	$18.10
All purposes	$7.90–$13.40 ($11.20)	
Intercity		
Personal	$12.70–$19.00 ($14.80)	
Business	$17.00–$25.40 ($21.20)	$18.10
All purposes	$13.20–$19.80 ($15.60)	

Source: US DOT (2001).
Note: [a]Figures in brackets are recommended values.

reflected in findings showing that commuters ascribe much higher value to avoiding late arrivals than to early arrivals. De Palma and Rochat (1998), using data from Geneva, Switzerland, estimated the cost of late arrival as more than 8 times the cost of early arrival (2.69% of VOT vs. 0.327% of VOT, respectively). Using US data, Small (1992a) reports similar results (2.39% for late arrival against 0.64% of VOT for early arrival). Wardman (2001), who used British data, has reported that the value of avoiding late arrival, on average, is 7.4 times greater than the value of in-vehicle time.

Table 4.6 French VOT Savings by Trip Type (1998 prices)

Trip Purpose[a]	Percent of Gross Salary[b]	Percent of Wage Costs[c]	France (€)	Ile de France (Paris Region) (€)[d]
Business	85%	61%	10.5	13.0
Home-to-work	77%	55%	9.5	11.6
Nonwork[e]	42%	30%	5.2	6.4
Mean value if trip purpose unknown	59%	42%	7.2	8.8

Source: Boiteux, (2000); Quinet and Vickerman, (2004).
Notes: [a]Under the assumption that 10% of all trips are business trips, 35% home-to-work trips, and 55% all other purposes; [b]Based on 1998 average monthly gross salary, assuming a 39-hour work week; [c]On average, wage costs are about 70% of gross salary; [d]In Ile de France salaries were about 23% above the national average; [e]Shopping, leisure, etc.

Thus, investments that also increase the reliability of transport systems actually generate benefits significantly above and beyond mere travel time savings. We return to this issue in Chapter 7.

5. ESTIMATING BENEFITS FROM TRANSIT IMPROVEMENTS

Direct transit benefits can be divided into a time component, a price component, and an option value component.[7] The first category, which is the more conventional, is overvalued in many cases, especially in rail transit, because it is estimated at the project level, irrespective of network effects. Diversions from other transit modes, mainly buses, or from substitute rail lines, or from off-peak periods, actually tend to substantially reduce the benefits measured at the project level.

A key problem in transit analysis has emerged from the unit of demand used—the number of passengers or passenger-trips—while treating the cost of service provision as a function of vehicle-trips or vehicle-miles (Berechman, 1993). It is therefore necessary to convert demand and cost units into a common measure when carrying out COBA. Vehicle occupancy rates can be used to convert vehicle-trips into passenger-trips. However, since occupancy rates vary considerably by time period, it is necessary to establish their distribution to correctly convert vehicle-trips to passengers-trips.[8]

5.1 Transit's Direct Benefits

It has already been observed that door-to-door travel time is comprised of different time components, including access and egress, wait, transfer, and in-vehicle time. Thus, whereas highway improvements affect mainly in-vehicle travel time, most transit improvements affect wait and transfer time. This especially applies to rail transit's fixed-route technology and, to a large extent, to bus transit as well, which must stop at short intervals. With given station locations and platform sizes, it becomes clear why increased headways or adding more cars primarily reduce the wait and transfer time variables. In-vehicle travel time is affected by transit only when new rail lines or exclusive bus-ways are constructed, which rarely take place in well-developed urban areas. Reduced overcrowding is also cited on occasion as an important transit benefit. Yet, while users undoubtedly benefit from lessened crowding, there is no clear data to indicate how much they would pay for this benefit.

Turning now to the price component in Chapter 3 (expression 10), we observed at the time that revenues to producers represent costs to users, culminating in a zero net social welfare-change. The same conclusion also applies to transit—so long as transit users actually pay the true costs of services provision. However, most transit services, particularly rail, are heavily subsidized, at times more than 100% of the fare paid by passengers (Berechman, 1993). Without subsidies, total farebox revenue, at equilibrium, represents income transferred from consumers to producers, where the actual fare represents the marginal value of the service to paying passengers. With subsidies, however, we face a different welfare situation as the marginal value of taxpayers' income differs from the marginal value of the transit services produced.

Since subsidies lower the price that passengers pay—relative to the equilibrium price and given demand elasticity—more passengers are expected to use subsidized as opposed to nonsubsidized travel. Without subsidies, the transit market clearing price and quantity, at equilibrium, are P^* and Q^*. With subsidies, actual fare is F, $(F < P^*)$, and actual demand is Q, $(Q > Q^*)$; total farebox revenue is, then, $F \cdot Q$. Suppose that the subsidy scheme requires the transit provider to receive $\$(1 + \alpha)$ for each $1 fare, where $0 < \alpha$ is the subsidy rate. Total income is then $F(1 + \alpha)Q$, of which $F \cdot Q$ is income transferred from passengers to the transit provider. The difference, $\alpha \cdot F \cdot Q$, which is nontransferable income, should be included within the producer surplus. Thus, when carrying out COBA of a transit investment, subsidies should be included as revenues to the service producer (see also Chapter 10, which examines the impact of transport financing methods on COBA).

When a transit firm receives significant subsidies, its pricing scheme may undercut competitors' prices. For example, many intercity, regional, and suburban rail providers compete directly with bus as well as with aviation services (e.g., the Northeast corridor in the US). Due to heavy subsidies, rail can offer deep discounts that its rivals cannot match.[9] Were it to charge market prices, the number of its passengers might decline significantly, which would in turn imply lower benefits. Obviously, then, a meaningful analysis of benefits should take into account the effect of subsidization on market conditions and modal shares.

5.2 Transit VOT for Time Savings

Due to the distinct time savings components applicable to transit improvements, VOT figures used in transit tend to deviate from the comparable figures used for highway projects. Table 4.7 shows Transport Canada's VOT figures for use in COBA of transit projects.

In Table 4.7, wait time, time in crowded conditions, and time in unsecured conditions are linear transformations of in-vehicle time. Hence, the VOT of wait time is twice that of the VOT of in-vehicle trip time, the VOT of crowded conditions is three times higher, and the VOT of unsecured conditions is one and a half times higher. These differences result from the greater disutility of the time spent in crowded and unsecured conditions, in comparison to in-vehicle time. Another point requiring attention is that the distribution of VOT around the median is skewed to the right (10.5 – 9 <

Table 4.7 Canada's Range of VOT Estimates for Transit (Can$/Hour)

Commuter-Trip Time Component	Range		
	10% Lower Limit	*Median*	*10% Upper Limit*
In-vehicle	9.0	10.5	12.8
Walking	11.2	13.1	15.9
Wait	18.0	21.0	25.5
Crowded conditions[a]	27.0	31.5	38.3
Unsecured conditions[a,b]	13.5	15.8	19.1

Source: Transport Canada, 1999a, (http://www.tc.gc.ca/programs/environment/utsp/transit studies/docs/Cost-Benefit.pdf).
Note: [a]Time spent in these conditions; [b]when passengers are unprotected by police or surveillance devices.

12.8 – 10.5). This implies that more commuters assign higher than lower VOT to the same time savings.

A final note on VOT is that the value of TTS varies with income and with distance. Income elasticity of 0.75 and a positive distance elasticity of 0.3 are common, acceptable estimates. Travel demand elasticities and their importance for cost and benefit analysis are discussed below, in Section 6.

5.3 Transit Option Value Benefits

In addition to the direct benefits that transit users derive from improved services, nonusers may derive an additional benefit from the sheer availability of transit in a region. Transportation diversity is generally regarded as a benefit because it provides ubiquitous availability, affordability, and connectivity of travel options. This benefit is known in the literature as *option value*.[10] The argument states that auto users who are unlikely to use transit nevertheless derive benefits from the presence of public transit services in their area that, under some unforeseen conditions, might serve them as "mobility insurance." It has likewise been argued that option value also influences public decision making on transit services' provision, which is largely affected by intangibles such as community pride, potential for urban redevelopment and equity (Dunn, 1998).

Underlying the notion of option value benefits is the concept of users' present willingness-to-pay for reduction of mobility uncertainty or for potential benefits of transit contingency. The uncertainty relates not only to actual availability of transit services but also to future levels of service and price. This argument raises questions about the importance of option value relative to the overall benefits gained from transit supply and its measurement in monetary terms.

Boardman et al. (2001) define Option Value (OV) as: $OV = OP - E(S)$, where OP is option price and $E(S)$ is expected surplus.[11] Defined this way, option price is the amount that individuals are willing to pay for service availability, while option value is the amount that should be added to their expected surplus, $E(S)$, to make it equal to option price. In other words, option value can be viewed as an adjustment to conventional benefit measures, relative to availability uncertainties. Smith (1984) has suggested that for services having less-perfect substitutes, the relative size of option value to expected surplus is large. This result would certainly hold if there were very few mobility alternatives for a large population segment.[12]

How can option value be measured in practice? It has been suggested that subsidies to public transport indicate society's willingness-to-pay for transport diversity (ECONorthwest and PBQD, 2002). Thus, in suburban areas, which tend to be dominated by automobile use, such subsidies are justified mainly for their equity and option value benefits. Based on the notion that transit subsidies can be used to estimate the monetary price of transit option value, the TDM Encyclopedia (VTPI, 2005) suggests an approach that allocates total transit subsidy to key benefit categories. Accordingly, two-thirds of transit subsidies are justified on the basis of transportation equity and option value that, under further assumptions about society's willingness-to-pay for more transit, amounts to $0.5¢$ per vehicle mile. The major problem with this approach is that the amount of subsidy paid to transit is *not* necessarily a direct function of transit availability and level of service but of market imperfections in transit supply, for example, the monopolistic power of transport worker unions.[13]

In summary, the concept of option value has potential economic implications especially for investments in areas with limited public transportation supply. Yet, in mature metropolitan areas where the existing transit system is quite well developed, it is doubtful that a new investment, even if extensive (e.g., a new subway line), will confer tangible option values. But if such benefits can be clearly demonstrated and measured, they ought to be added to the investment's direct benefits (mainly time-saving benefits) for the purpose of calculating of the project's net welfare contribution.

6. TRAVEL DEMAND ELASTICITIES

We have so far regarded a transportation project as an investment aimed at increasing the capacity of an existing network or constructing a new system. However, many transportation projects essentially involve changes in the level or price of service of an existing system. In such a case, the issue is how to measure changes in the demanded quantity of service. If demand functions were readily available, the analyst could easily compute the effect of a change on that quantity and its welfare value. However, demand functions for highway and transit are rarely obtainable, which requires us to use estimated demand elasticities to compute the necessary quantities. For example, transit price elasticities are used to assess ridership and revenues from changes in transit fares that are, in turn, employed to estimate the economic value of the change.

The literature reports numerous estimates of highway and transit demand elasticity with respect to various demand factors (see, for example, Litman, 2004a; Oum et al. 1992). Table 4.8 shows how changes in fuel price affect direct elasticity of demand for highway travel and the corresponding transit cross-elasticity.

As this table shows, a 10% increase in fuel prices result in a 1.1% decline in the number of commuting trips with a corresponding 2.2% increase in public transit trips.

Table 4.9 provides bus fare elasticities for peak and off-peak demand, based on US data. It shows that peak-period fare elasticity is much more inelastic than is the comparable off-peak-period elasticity. Thus, a 10% increase in bus fare results in 1.8% decline in the number of peak-hour bus trips but a 3.9% decline in the number of off-peak trips. This result can

Table 4.8 Fuel Price Demand Elasticities

Trip Type	Car Driver	Public Transit (Cross-Elasticities)
Number of Trips		
Commuting	–0.11	+0.20
Business	–0.04	+0.24
Education	–0.18	+0.01
Other	–0.25	+0.15
Total	–0.19	+0.13
Kilometers Traveled		
Commuting	–0.20	+0.22
Business	–0.22	+0.05
Education	–0.32	+0.00
Other	–0.44	+0.18
Total	–0.29	+0.14

Source: TRACE (1999, Tables 8 and 9).

Table 4.9 Bus Fare Elasticities (US data)

	Large Cities[a]	Smaller Cities
Average for All Hours	−0.36	−0.43
Peak Period	−0.18	−0.27
Off-Peak Period	−0.39	−0.46
Peak Hour Average	−0.23	
Off-Peak Average	−0.42	

Source: Pham and Linsalata (1991).
Notes: [a]More than 1 million residents.

Table 4.10 European Car Travel Elasticities[a]

Term/Purpose	Car Trips WRT[b] Fuel Price	Car-Kms WRT Fuel Price	Car Trips WRT Travel Time	Car-Kms WRT Travel Time
Short-term:				
Commuting	−0.20	−0.12	−0.62	
HB[c] Business	−0.06	−0.02		
NHB[d] Business	−0.06	−0.02		
Education	−0.22	−0.09		
Other	−0.20	−0.20	−0.52	
Total	−0.16	−0.16	−0.60	−0.20
Long-term:				
Commuting	−0.14	−0.23	−0.41	−0.63
HB Business	−0.07	−0.20	−0.30	−0.61
NHB Business	−0.17	−0.26	−0.12	−0.53
Education	−0.40	−0.41	−0.57	−0.76
Other	−0.15	−0.29	−0.52	−0.85
Total	−0.19	−0.26	−0.29	−0.74

Sources: de Jong and Gunn (2001).
Notes: [a]Figures in absolute values, i.e., elasticity of −0.3 is greater than −0.2; [b]WRT = With Respect To; [c]HB=Home Based; [d]NHB=Nonhome Based.

be explained by the fact that a large proportion of peak-period riders are mode-captive, low-income passengers.

Table 4.10 shows European short- and long-term car travel demand elasticities with respect to fuel price and travel time, by trip type.

It is evident from Table 4.10 that car travel demand elasticity with respect to travel time is much higher than the fuel price elasticity. However, this result might not hold if the prices of fuel escalate considerably as has been happening in recent years.

Table 4.11 shows short- and long-term transit demand elasticities with respect to income, fare and vehicle-kilometer (VKM) traveled for the UK and France, estimated from log-log (constant elasticity) and semi-log (non-constant elasticity) models.

As evident from Table 4.11, car and transit long-term elasticities are, by and large, greater (in absolute terms) than are the short-term elasticities. Similar results were obtained from a climate change study conducted in Canada where gasoline price elasticities for cars and light trucks were estimated to be in the range of –0.1 to –0.2 in the short-term, and –0.4 to –0.8 in the long-term (Transport Canada, 1999a). It evidently requires time for car and transit users to adjust their travel behavior to changes in income, prices, or level of service.

Table 4.11 Income, Fare, and VKM Transit Elasticities

	England		France	
	Log-Log	*Semi-Log*	*Log-Log*	*Semi-Log*
Income				
Short-term	–0.67	–0.69	–0.05	–0.04
Long-term	–0.90	–0.95	–0.09	–0.07
Fare				
Short-term	–0.51	–0.54	–0.32	–0.30
Long-term	–0.69	–0.75	–0.61	–0.59
Transit VKM				
Short-term	0.57	0.54	0.29	0.29
Long-term	0.77	0.74	0.57	0.57
Annual fare elasticity growth rate		1.59%		0.66%

Source: Dargay, et al. (1999, Table 4).

7. SUMMARY AND CONCLUSIONS

This chapter examined the various benefit components flowing from transportation improvements. Major distinctions were made between highway and public transit transportation, relative to type of benefits, magnitude, and method of measurement. Several key conclusions emerge from the discussion in this chapter.

Travel Time Savings (TTS) constitute the prime direct benefit from transportation improvements of all types. While the costs of using an automobile or transit are also affected by such improvements, they represent only a small fraction of total benefits. For this reason, it is extremely important that TTS is accurately measured.

Conversion of travel time savings into monetary units requires the use of Value Of Time (VOT) parameters. Theory suggests that when faced with no time constraints, individuals will allocate their time in a way that equalizes their marginal utility from all their activities, a utility that equals the net wage rate they earn. However, due to various labor market and other constraints, such allocations are not feasible. In practice, many countries therefore regard the value of time as a policy variable. This they do by specifying mandatory values for specific travel activities. As a result, leisure time receives a relatively low value, probably an underestimate of the true value that individuals assign to time spent in leisure activities.

For public transit, travel time savings occur primarily in the form of reduced wait time, access and egress time, transfer time, and time spent in crowded conditions. Monetary values for these time components tend to exceed the value of TTS for in-vehicle travel time by a magnitude of 200%–300%.

In general, VOT parameters are set as a percentage of the average hourly wage rate for non-self-employed workers. This practice can, however, seriously bias the true welfare value of time saved. First, business travel should reflect the value of time for these trip makers, which exceeds the value of the average hourly wage rate by far. Moreover, from an economic perspective, VOT in lieu of work and business trips should reflect the return of an hour worked, defined as total GDP divided per hour worked. Thus, time saved in these trip types should be valued above the average wage rate. In addition, travel for educational purposes reflects returns on human capital investments that, in a competitive economy, are equivalent to the returns of an hour worked by skilled labor. Lastly, given the increasing proportion of leisure time activities, which constitute an important economic sector, travel to such activities can no longer be valued as a small portion (about 20%–30%) of the average hourly wage rate.

Treating the value of time saved as a constant over time and space is a gross mistake. First, VOT varies with income, which tends to grow over time, income elasticity being about 0.70 to 0.80 (higher incomes imply higher VOT values). Second, VOT varies with distance, with a positive distance elasticity of 0.3 (Litman, 2004a). VOT for travel time savings, by trip type, should thus be considered a range and *not* a single average number. Moreover, in assessing the value of travel time savings, trips should be further categorized by distance traveled. VOT values for suburban to city-center work trips should therefore be higher than for intra-urban work trips.

Because the utility (or productivity) of time saved is unlikely to be linear for different units of travel time, with small amounts of time saved (e.g., 1–5 minutes) conferring little if any measurable benefits to commuters, it is essential that we examine the distribution of VOT. Using the moments of such a distribution can provide good proxies on the actual amount of benefits obtained from an improvement.

Travel time reliability is another major factor affecting VOT values. Reliability is directly related to travel flow conditions; hence, VOT of work trips in congested traffic should be about twice the VOT in uncongested traffic.

It has been argued that transit benefits should include an additional, separate benefit category—the "option value of public transit"—that reflects uncertainties about future travel needs and availability. In practice, it is quite difficult to estimate the magnitude of option value, especially in areas with well-developed transit systems, although it has been suggested that the amount of subsidy given to transit can be used as an approximation.

Lastly, changes in the supply or price of transportation induce changes in the amount of travel demanded. Given that demand functions are largely unknown, demand elasticities have been derived for various demand attributes such as peak and off-peak travel, fuel costs and transit fare. Depending on the model used, elasticities can vary considerably, requiring that care be exercised when applying models to specific situations.

APPENDIX A: DERIVATION OF TRAVEL TIME VALUE

Assume a utility maximizing individual who allocates his time budget (e.g., 24 hours) between a consumption good, z_i, whose price is p_{z_i}, time spent at work t_w, and time spent on nonwork activities, t_l.

$$\max. U(t_w, t_l, z)$$
$$t_w, t_l, z$$

subject to:
$$\sum_i z_i \cdot p_{z_i} = y + w \cdot t_w \quad [\lambda]$$

$$t_w + t_l = \bar{t} \quad [\mu]$$

$$t_w \geq \bar{t_w} \quad [\theta] \tag{A1}$$

$$t_l \geq \bar{t_l} \quad [\eta]$$

$$z, t_w, t_l > 0$$

where w is the wage rate, net of taxes. Hence the term $w \cdot t_w$ is earned income.[14] Let $\bar{t}$ denote the total time endowment of individuals (normally, 24 hours, net of essential requirements such as sleeping and eating[15]), and y, unearned income. Let $\bar{t}_w$ and $\bar{t}_l$ be the minimum amount of time that must be allotted to work and to leisure activities, respectively. Further assume that the level of consumption is independent of the cost of travel, which is exogenously defined. The parameters λ, μ, θ, η are the shadow prices of the constraints.

The first constraint in (A1) is the monetary budget whereas the second is the time budget. The constraints $t_w \geq \bar{t}_w$ and $t_l \geq \bar{t}_l$ imply that each time component requires a minimum duration (which may, of course, be zero[16]). In this model, a consumer essentially makes three simultaneous decisions. He decides about the allocation of income between consumption goods, the utility maximization quantity of each good, and the allocation of time between work and leisure activities. The Lagrangian of the model is given by (A2):

$$L = U(t_w, t_l, z) + \lambda(y + w \cdot t_w - \sum_i z_i \cdot P_{z_i}) + \mu(\bar{t} - t_w - t_l)$$
$$+ \theta(t_w - \bar{t}_w) + \eta(t_l - \bar{t}_l) \tag{A2}$$

The Lagrangian multipliers λ, μ, θ and η reflect the marginal utility of income (earned and unearned), the marginal utility of total time available $\bar{t}$, the marginal utility of the minimum working hours constraint and the marginal utility of additional leisure time, respectively. The first order conditions are:

$$\frac{\partial U}{\partial t_w} = -\lambda \cdot w - \mu + \theta \tag{A3}$$

$$\frac{\partial U}{\partial t_l} = -\mu + \eta \tag{A4}$$

$$\frac{\partial U}{\partial Z} = -\lambda \cdot p_z \tag{A5}$$

By using the consumption good as a numeraire and setting its price equal to 1 ($p_z = 1$), we obtain:

$$\frac{1}{\lambda}\left(\frac{\partial U}{\partial t_l}\right) = \frac{\mu}{\lambda} - \frac{\eta}{\lambda} \tag{A6}$$

The left-hand side of (A4) is the value of time when undertaking a leisure activity. If the leisure time constraint is not binding (i.e., $\eta = 0$), then this *marginal valuation* of time $1/\lambda(\partial U/\partial t_l)$ equals μ/λ, known as the *resource value of time* (MVA, 1997). If it is binding, that is, $(\eta > 0)$, the difference η/λ is referred to as the *value of time savings* in an activity (DeSerpa, 1971). It is also commonly referred to as the *value of time*, which is used to appraise transportation projects. From (A6), the value of time saving, η/λ , equals the resource value of time, μ/λ, minus the marginal valuation of time spent for leisure activity.

Dividing (A3) by (A5) and assuming that the work-hours constraint is not binding $(\theta = 0)$, the marginal utility of time used for work is given by (A7).

$$(\frac{\partial U}{\partial t_w}) / (\frac{\partial U}{\partial z}) = w - \frac{\mu}{\lambda} \tag{A7}$$

Expression (A7) implies that if an individual is unconstrained by the number of hours he can allocate to work, he will do so until the last unit of time spent at work approximately equals this wage rate.[17] From the above first-order conditions we further obtain:

$$(\frac{\partial U}{\partial t_w}) / (\frac{\partial U}{\partial z}) + w - (\frac{\theta}{\lambda} + \frac{\eta}{\lambda}) = -(\frac{\partial U}{\partial t_l}) / (\frac{\partial U}{\partial t_z}) \tag{A8}$$

If the minimum work hours and minimum leisure time constraints are not binding (i.e., $\theta = 0$, $\eta = 0$), then the left-hand side of equation (A8) is the total reward for an additional unit of work time that, at equilibrium, equals the utility value from the last unit of forgone leisure time (the right-hand side). This value is, in essence, the opportunity cost of work time.

The above formulation does not treat travel time and costs as separate components of travel costs. As argued in the text, this issue can be quite important in the short and medium term, when travelers are unable to change locations. Thus, we further need to inquire how to treat travel time and costs in a utility maximization framework. Reformulating problem (A1) gives us,

$$\max_{t_w,t_l,z} .U(t_w,t_l,z,t(d))$$

subject to: $\quad F(d) + \sum_i z_i \cdot p_{z_i} = y + w \cdot t_w \quad [\lambda]$

$$t_w + t_l + t(d) = \bar{t} \qquad\qquad [\mu]$$

$$t_w \geq \overline{t_w} \qquad\qquad\qquad [\theta] \tag{A9}$$

$$t_l \geq \overline{t_l} \qquad\qquad\qquad [\eta]$$

$$z,t_w,t_l,t(d) > 0$$

In this model, $t(d)$ and $F(d)$ are the time and costs of traveling distance d, respectively. Notice that the money cost of travel, $F(d)$, is introduced directly into the budget constraint (see also Mohring, 1976). Following the same analysis as above, we obtain:

$$(\frac{\partial U}{\partial t(d)}) = -\mu - \lambda \cdot (\frac{\partial t(d)}{\partial d})^{-1}(\frac{\partial F(d)}{\partial d}) \qquad\qquad (A10)$$

Expression (A10) indicates that the marginal utility of travel time equals the (negative) ratio of the shadow price of the income constraint λ, weighted by the shadow price of the time constraint μ. The weight equals the change in the marginal cost of travel resulting from a marginal change in travel time, the latter regarded as an accessibility change.

Assuming that the minimum leisure time constraint is not binding, we get:

$$(\frac{\partial U}{\partial t(d)}) / (\frac{\partial U}{\partial z}) + (\frac{\partial t(d)}{\partial d})^{-1}(\frac{\partial F(d)}{\partial d}) = -(\frac{\partial U}{\partial t_l}) / (\frac{\partial U}{\partial z}) \qquad\qquad (A11)$$

The left-hand side of (A11) represents the total value gained from additional travel time or additional distance. It is composed of the change in utility from travel time plus the accessibility change introduced during that time period. As in (A7), the total value of the last unit of travel equals the value of the last unit of foregone leisure time.

Note that internal or external conditions can affect an individual's subjective valuation of time. Examples of internal conditions are preference structures, level of earned and unearned income, and proximity to work location. On the other hand, the wage rate, the money cost of travel, the price of the consumption good, and traffic conditions are external factors. Hence, the same individual—depending on her work and travel environment—might change her valuation of a unit of travel time saved.

5 Measuring the Costs of Transportation Investment Projects

1. INTRODUCTION

Transportation infrastructure investment projects are costly undertakings that can easily run into the hundreds of millions or billions of dollars. Given this level of expenditure, the key questions examined in this chapter are: What are the cost components of such investments, how should they be measured, and how should they enter the COBA process?

Later in this book (Chapter 9) we examine the issue of costs overruns, which seem to be the rule rather than the exception in transportation infrastructure investments, primarily rail. Costs overruns are partially the result of deliberate underestimation of costs, made early for the purpose of securing a political commitment to the project. But such overruns are also due to failure to include major cost items and incorrect measurement of input factor prices. Section 2 of this chapter discusses the most crucial cost components and their magnitude.

An important distinction to be made in this regard is that between the economic value of input factors and their accounting values, which enter the project's budget at the very outset. For example, the right-of-way already owned by the government is unlikely to appear as a budget item. Yet, the opportunity price of land is a real cost to society. It must be accounted for when doing the project's COBA to establish the project's true economic value and subsequently rank that project correctly relative to its alternatives. Section 3 deals with the overall issue of measuring the true opportunity costs of input factors and the implications of disregarding those costs.

Engineering cost estimates are routinely used in assessing the overall project costs. There is little doubt that such estimates are vital for the computations of the quantities of material and labor needed for construction. They are also essential for estimating the financial implications of various changes in the structure's alignment and physical design. Engineers, however, tend to assess costs using rules of thumb that are all too often unfounded. Section 4 discusses these problems. A summary and conclusions are found in Section 5.

2. COST COMPONENTS OF TRANSPORTATION INVESTMENTS

2.1 Capital Costs

Infrastructure costs include all the project's short- and long-term expenditures, such as land acquisition, facility construction, material, labor, and administration as well as regular and unexpected maintenance expenses. Debt service costs, which reflect the opportunity costs of invested capital, are likewise part of the investment's overall costs.

One approach to categorizing infrastructure costs is to consider them as new construction, maintenance and operating costs, together with improvement and right-of-way (land acquisition) expenses, spent over the project's life span. Construction and maintenance costs should be further divided into subcategories due to the considerable variety of the work required (Ozbay et al., 2000). Estimates of these costs can vary greatly at different stages of the project's design. We therefore distinguish between the order-of-magnitude estimates made at the conceptual development stage, estimates made at the preliminary design stage, estimates done at the final design stage, and estimates made at the postaward stage.[1]

In the case of highway construction, specific cost functions can be estimated for each type of construction, maintenance, and improvement project. For example, road projects may include: (a) major reconstruction with/without roadway widening; (b) roadway widening with/without resurfacing; and (c) resurfacing with/without minor roadway widening. In addition, these functions are project-dependent as prevailing travel conditions, traffic makeup, pavement characteristics, and location render each project unique.

Table 5.1 Distribution of Roadway Expenditures (US Data)

Expenditure	*Percent of Total*
Maintenance and operation	26
Capacity expansion	23
Reconstruction, rehabilitation, and restoration	19
Administration	9
Patrol and safety	8
Local road capital improvement	8
Interest on debt	4
Other	3

Source: Goldberg (1996).

Established methods are available for estimating resurfacing cycles (Small et al., 1989) although there seem to be no practical methods for estimating the other work cycles. In general, the first two maintenance and improvement categories are undertaken when a highway segment becomes inadequate for carrying its traffic load. Table 5.1 shows the distribution of roadway costs in the US, across various activities.

Specific cost figures per lane-mile of roadway construction and maintenance projects in the US are given in Table 5.2.

The data shown in Table 5.2 highlight the significant impact of the area where construction and maintenance activities take place. For instance, the cost of intersection construction per lane-mile are 50% higher in built areas than in outlying areas. It further shows that freeways (limited access highways) are by far more expensive to construct and maintain than are other divided and undivided highways.

Table 5.2 Roadway Project Costs (US$1000 per lane-mile, 2000)

	Freeways		Other Divided Highways		Undivided Highways	
	Built-Up Areas	Outlying Areas	Built-Up Areas	Outlying Areas	Built-Up Areas	Outlying Areas
Right-of-way for new lanes	$632	$253	$570	$229	$514	$209
Construction of new lanes	$2,541	$2,138	$2,288	$1,922	$2,057	$1,728
Reconstruction with new lanes	$3,173	$2,391	$2,858	$2,152	$2,572	$1,936
Reconstruction with wider lanes	$2,330	$1,682	$2,099	$1,514	$1,889	$1,362
Intersections	$15,000	$10,000	$2,000	$4,000	$500	$100
Pavement reconstruction	$1,628	$1,466	$1,471	$1,321	$1,326	$1,190
Major widening	$1,300	$1,043	$1,170	$940	$1,052	$845
Minor widening	$940	$721	$845	$648	$760	$584
Resurfacing with shoulders	$443	$388	$400	$350	$361	$314
Resurfacing	$193	$178	$175	$158	$157	$145

Source: VTPI (2000).

The above discussion pertains mainly to roadway construction, but what about the costs associated with rail investments, including subway, light and heavy rail? Unfortunately, no established methods are available to determine these costs. Sometimes costs are established on a per-mile basis but these seem to be distributed over too wide range to allow use of a single acceptable measure (Flyvbjerg, et al., 2002). For example, total construction costs for one mile of subway in New York City can range from $500 million to $1.2 billion (Berechman and Paaswell, 2005). Targeted cost analyses need to be done for such projects (VTPI, 1994). We next examine one type of cost that arises from actual construction, namely, disruption costs, which in urbanized areas are common to all road and rail projects.

2.2 Costs of Work Zone Disruptions

Construction of a major transportation facility, whether a new subway line or the rehabilitation of an existing freeway, implies significant costs of disruption to current trip makers in addition to current residents and business owners. Also called "work zone costs" (Highway Research Board, 1965), these disruptions constitute about 10% of total delay costs for road projects (see Chapter 7, Figure 7.1).

Specifically, work zone costs include costs to users resulting from construction, maintenance, or rehabilitation of the facility, as the following list shows:

1. Traffic costs from serious delays to the normal traffic flow
2. Safety-related costs (traffic accidents)
3. Slowdowns from disproportional truck movements in the work zone area
4. Diversion of traffic to other routes for extended periods of time.

In addition, externality costs are to be considered, such as:

1. Economic costs due to loss of retail and commercial revenues from declining demand in the surrounding areas, and
2. Environmental costs—such as air and noise pollution—to local residents.

Work zone costs largely depend on the nature of the location where the construction or maintenance activities take place. That is, construction in a densely populated urban area will yield significantly higher costs than will the same construction activities performed in a sparsely settled area. Rehabilitation of a freeway in an intensively used corridor will result in higher work zone costs than will the same work done on a low-volume freeway. Given the area's characteristics, work zone costs are a function of:

1. Size (lane-miles) of the work zone
2. Number and capacity of lanes remaining open
3. Duration of lane closures
6. Timing (hours of the day and days of the week) of lane closures
5. Posted speed
7. Availability of alternative routes and their traffic characteristics.

For interurban projects, the major disruption costs are manifested in reduced capacity, speed, and safety. These effects induce additional user costs and increased safety costs, which then become part of the project's overall investment costs. In intra-urban areas, compensation for land-use activity modifications is an additional outlay that should be carefully assessed and factored into the project's capital expenditures.

Two main approaches to the assessment of disruption costs are currently in use, the American and the European. The American approach calls for additional investment to prevent or at least mitigate the costs of disruption triggered by the project. It also stipulates compensation for the harm done to land uses with respect to its extent and spatial incidence. The European approach, in contrast, calls for direct estimation of the negative effects from work zone activity, namely, the costs of disruption using a full-scale traffic model.[2] Some optimization models have been proposed to minimize work zone disruption costs (e.g., Jiang and Adeli, 2003) although by and large, calculations are based on per-kilometer unit costs, which vary according to traffic levels, road type, and location.

2.3 Debt Service Costs

Public investments in transportation, like private investments, entail opportunity costs in the form of forgone returns from alternative investments. In principle, the rate used for discounting future streams of benefits and costs should reflect the rate of return on these investments, although an arbitrary discount rate is very often mandated (see Chapter 6). Such investments are financed through various mechanisms, including taxation and user charges, borrowing, and franchising (see Chapter 10 for a detailed discussion). How, then, should we incorporate the associated financial costs into a project's COBA? For instance, if a project is financed through public borrowing, its annual debt-service payment becomes a public expenditure for the project's life span and should therefore be counted in the project's overall investment costs. To illustrate this principle, consider a $1 billion investment, financed through a bond issue with an annual interest rate of 5% (or $50 million annual debt service). Discounted at, say, 7% over the project's 20-year life span, total debt service costs will equal about $530 million, without doubt a considerable public expense.[3] In Chapter 6 we argue that if the discount rate does not represent an efficient cost of capital, annual debt service expenditures should enter the COBA formulation. In any case, prudent financial accounting requires debt service costs to be computed in order to correctly assess the investing agency's annual financial obligations.

2.4 Maintenance and Operating Costs

Annual highway maintenance costs reflect those expenditures necessary to maintain the facility in a state of good repair. As such they must be distinguished from reconstruction costs, which occur after several years of use, and from operating costs, which are allocated to managing the facility for the purpose of ensuring safety and efficient traffic flow. Table 5.3 summarizes these cost items.

Different types of operating and maintenance costs characterize rail operations. These cost items are presented in Table 5.4.

In general, maintenance and operating costs can reach 20% of total capital costs, depending on the project and location; they are normally higher for rail than for highway investments.[4]

2.5 Planning, Management, and Construction Supervision Costs

Every large-scale project, especially if it involves complicated construction—such as tunneling and bridges—requires sophisticated technical (i.e., engineering) planning, detailed project management and tight construction

Table 5.3 Highway Maintenance and Operating Cost Items

Maintenance Costs	*Operating Costs*
Organization and general information	Organization and general information
Pavement delineation maintenance	Safety plan
Drainage maintenance and slope repair	Equipment plan
Landscape and roadside maintenance	Toll collection and operations plan
Bridge and structure maintenance	Snow and ice control plan
Third-party damages and emergency maintenance	Facilities' operations plan
Roadway safety features and system maintenance	Traffic and travel management plan
Sign and signal system maintenance	Customer service plan
Lighting and electrical system maintenance	Emergency management plan
Maintenance of toll booth and plaza	

Table 5.4 Rail Maintenance and Operating Cost Items

Maintenance Costs	Operating Costs
Track maintenance	Service supervision
Vehicle maintenance	Vehicle operators
Facility maintenance	Fuel and energy
Station maintenance	Security
	Rail traffic control
	Property tax
	Insurance

Source: Leclair, (2004).

supervision. And these activities are quite costly, at times amounting to 15%–20% of total capital costs. While these costs are indispensable for the successful project completion, their magnitude nevertheless sharply contrasts with the level of costs invested in socioeconomic data collection, assessment of the transportation-economic rationale of the project, and development of sound comprehensive transportation as well as land-use policies capable of supporting the project's objectives. As the examples in Chapter 15 indicate, in most cases, the cost of demographic and economic feasibility studies, in addition to transportation planning, amount to a fraction of total costs, (significantly less than 1% of total capital costs). As a result, transportation projects that are usually well designed and planned from an engineering standpoint are often poorly defined, assessed, and planned from transportation, economic, social, and policy viewpoints. Thus, one way to increase the likelihood of selecting worthy transportation investment projects for implementation is to allot a minimum level of resources to project analysis, assessment, and planning.

3. THE MEASUREMENT OF INPUT FACTOR PRICES

In order to accurately calculate the costs of a transportation investment, we first need to decide on a pricing principle for computing the values of input factors such as labor, land, fixed assets, and rolling stock. Economic theory suggests that the opportunity cost of a resource, measured by the area under the MC curve, represents its correct value. It is not always clear, however, what this cost should be if government activities affect market demand and supply or if an input market is noncompetitive. Furthermore, the issue of which monetary values should be used when measuring input costs continues to be vague. Should we use market prices or input factor prices in consideration of the fact that the difference between these prices represents taxes and other government charges? Budget allocations may not always provide the correct answer if government purchase prices exclude taxes and tariffs, or if they affect market prices. In addition, if market prices are to be used in noncompetitive markets, should they represent market prices before or after the investment was made? These are the main issues discussed in this section.

3.1 Defining Opportunity Costs

The correct monetary value of a resource is measured by its opportunity cost, which can be defined as the budget expenditure for the resource plus the net change (positive or negative) in social welfare (consumer and producer surplus) resulting from its purchase. For example, in the case of a publicly owned parcel of land, if it could be sold in the open market for a unit price of P, this would be its opportunity cost, entered into the COBA together with the other project's investment costs. Alternatively, if the only designated alternative use for this tract of land is, say, a public park, the value of the benefits from the park should be entered as the land's opportunity cost. If the government acts as a monopolist in the land market so that its purchases of land affect prices and induce a loss of consumer surplus among private landowners, adjustments need to be introduced before assessing the land's opportunity costs. In any case, evaluating expenditures on land at a zero price after contending that the public already owns it and has paid for it in the past is a fallacious course to take because this approach can lead to acceptance of socially inferior projects.

The key question that we need to ask, then, is under what conditions do allocations for an input factor represent that factor's true social opportunity cost? As we shall see, the answer to this question depends on the degree to which government actions affect input markets. In some cases, the deviation of social costs from a budget allocation is sufficiently small to warrant the latter's use as the correct measure of factor prices.

3.2 Market Prices versus Factor Prices

In factor markets, buyers assess the utility of the services and goods purchased by their market prices, that is, final sale prices. Sellers, on the other hand, assess the value of the inputs they sell by the price they obtain, net of tax. For example, individuals free to sell their labor skills in the marketplace decide on the amount of labor to supply after calculating the net pay they stand to collect. Buyers of labor look at the total price they pay, including taxes, when purchasing skills. In the absence of taxes—at competitive market equilibrium—these two sets of prices are identical. However, faced with an average income tax rate of t levied on labor, for each \$1 purchase of labor, buyers (potential employers) will pay $(1 + t)$, of which sellers (the potential employees) will receive only \$1 of the seller's outlay, with $t later going to government coffers as tax revenue.[5]

This is not to mean that resources have different values when they are in the hands of the government as opposed to the hands of private consumers. When the government spends \$1, it does so in terms of the unit factor cost while the cost to consumers of spending the same \$1 in terms of disposable income is $(1 + t)$, which is the unit market price. That is, each unit factor cost converts into $(1 + t)$ market price units, with the conversion rate being the tax correction factor.

This argument also applies to nontradable goods sold in the market place. Consider an example in which the government invests \$1 million (in factor cost terms) on a road improvement whose major benefits are time savings. Suppose these benefits have a value of "V" when measured in terms of individuals' willingness-to-pay. It is obvious, then, that from a social viewpoint, the magnitude of V must be $V(1 + t)$ in order for the investment to be worthwhile. Thus, when carrying out a COBA in which costs are measured in unit factor costs, the benefits must be deflated by the tax rate since, from the consumers' viewpoint, they reflect the unit market price. Put differently, a person's willingness to pay up to \$1 to save one extra unit of travel time reflects his willingness to forgo consumption goods worth \$1 *at market prices*. In terms of *unit factor prices*, the same person is willing to forgo consumption goods worth $1(1 + t)$.

Finally, in Chapter 3 we have explained the concept of a *deadweight loss*, which arises whenever consumers and producers face different sets of prices. The magnitude of this welfare loss depends on the level of charges and taxes (or subsidies), as well as on demand and supply elasticities. Therefore, if a transportation investment is financed, for example, by a wage tax, the resulting welfare loss to the economy should be accounted for when calculating the overall net social-welfare contribution of this project (more on this in Chapter 10).

3.3 Budget Expenditures as a Measure of Project Costs

A common practice in project appraisal is to treat budget expenditures for inputs as investment costs. As explained above, the correct price of inputs should be their opportunity costs or, in the case of competitive markets, their marginal costs. In general, opportunity costs include total budgetary expenditures *plus* the net gain or loss in social welfare (consumer and producer surplus). Net social-welfare changes can be positive or negative if, for example, inputs are subsidized or taxed, respectively. Similar effects occur when markets are imperfect, as in the presence of government monopolies.[6] We next examine two hypothetical yet common cases where budgeted expenditures underestimated the true opportunity costs of a resource to be used in an investment project.

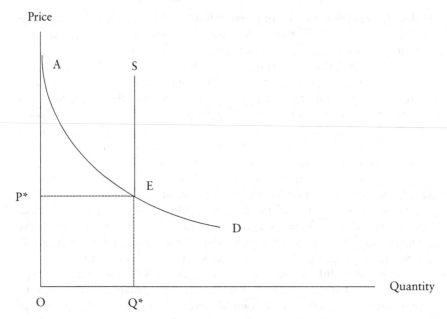

Figure 5.1 Welfare loss from government market power.

The first case occurs when the supply curve is totally inelastic, as in the market for land, which is a fixed quantity (see Figure 5.1). Say that the government uses its power of eminent domain to acquire a large parcel of land. What is the correct social price of land?

In Figure 5.1, S denotes the inelastic supply curve for land and D is the elastic demand curve for land, with equilibrium at E. If, through its eminent domain power, the government obtains Q^* units of land at the price P^*, the area AEP^* represents total consumer surplus and the area P^*EQ^*O represents total government's expenditures. Yet, these expenditures underestimate the true social value of this resource under the given conditions. This happens because the total social-welfare value of land as an input, represented by the area AEQ^*O, includes the consumer surplus of private landowners who, in the absence of government market power, could have sold their land in small units and thereby increased their revenues, that is, their welfare.

Consider a second situation where the demand for an input shifts upward due to government purchasing power despite the supply curve's elasticity. This demand shift serves to alter relative prices, as shown in Figure 5.2.

In Figure 5.2, demand rises from D_1 to D_2 following procurement of a resource at a quantity large enough—relative to market size—to shift equilibrium from E_1 to E_2. For example, in the US, prices for heavy and light rail cars have escalated substantially since the mid 1990s, partly due to large

Price

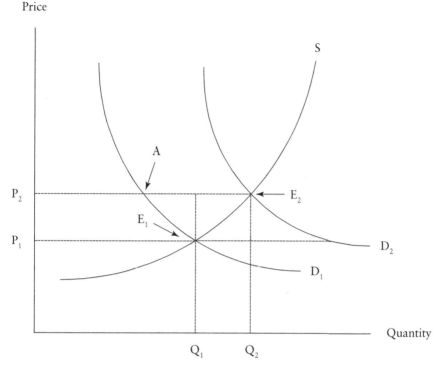

Figure 5.2 Welfare implications from government purchasing power.

government purchases.[7] As shown in Figure 5.2, the government's purchase of $Q_2 - Q_1$ rail cars caused prices to rise from P_1 to P_2. Total government expenditures are thus $P_2(Q_2 - Q_1)$. Under these conditions, government demand has increased the producer surplus by an amount represented by the area $P_1E_1E_2P_2$ while decreasing the consumer surplus of previous consumers by an amount represented by the area $P_1E_1AP_2$. The situation implies a transfer of welfare from consumers to producers, with the net gain in social surplus given by the area: AE_1E_2 (= $P_1E_1E_2P_2 - P_1E_1AP_2$). Hence, the budget allocation is larger than the net social costs of government acquisition of these resources.

What, then, is the correct opportunity cost of the government purchase of $Q_2 - Q_1$ input factors? In this case, it would be total expenditures, $P_2(Q_2 - Q_1)$, *less* the net gain in producers' surplus of AE_1E_2. The magnitude of this area depends on the magnitude of the rise in the input price from P_1 to P_2, which in turn depends on the size of the government purchase and the elasticities exhibited by the demand and supply curves.[8]

A key conclusion to be reached is that an analysis of the opportunity costs of inputs used in transportation investments requires the inclusion of a thorough account of the net changes in social welfare during the period in question. Failure to consider such changes, especially in markets for inelastic inputs such as land, can lead to biased estimates of the social value of the resources to be used.

If government market transactions can so drastically affect the price of one resource, as in the above example, what, then is the rule for setting the price of land to be used for computing project costs when government is the major buyer?

3.4 PRICING INPUT FACTORS IN NONCOMPETITIVE MARKETS

Land and structures are probably the more costly input factors used in transportation projects, especially in populated urban areas. Since local and national governments can act as monopolists in these markets, they obviously can affect the prices of these inputs. We thus need to ask what price—current land price or the posttake price—should be used for conducting a COBA.

Studies of congestionable public goods such as roads, when using production function models, have by and large indicated increasing returns to scale (e.g., Kraus, 1981). Under such conditions, use of a marginal cost pricing rule for setting the price of land will yield a loss to government. Small (1999b) has argued that if a cost function model is used to estimate scale economies, increasing returns might be offset by increases in the supply price of land following its acquisition for road construction, thereby yielding a balanced government budget under marginal cost pricing. Using such a model, Small has derived self-financing rules, with and without price discrimination, which incorporate the after-take land price and the actual supply elasticities faced by the government.

Small's results directly contrast with those obtained by Berechman and Pines (1991). Using a production function model, these authors showed that land should be priced at a nonmonopolistic market price that reflects the alternative use of land prior to its public acquisition. Their conclusion accords with the Strotz (1965) analysis, which advocates the use of market clearing rents to price land for road construction. The disagreement can be explained by the kind of question asked: Which first-best pricing and investment rules should be applied (Berechman and Pines, 1991), or will the official authority encounter losses in pricing land at the postproject price (Small, 1999).

In real-world applications, government authorities often use the "fair price of land" for calculating their costs. This price is determined by the alternative use of the respective parcel, based on the prevailing land-use plan or zoning regulations as assessed by an official appraiser. This price includes additional costs for severance damage emanating from partial take of residential or commercial land.[9]

3.5 Market or Factor Prices in an Actual Analysis

The previous theoretical analysis must now come to terms with reality, where just how to calculate input factor prices, even when markets are reasonably competitive, may not be obvious. Taxes and charges on inputs, which are collected by more than one public agency or jurisdiction, are deductible at various government levels. Taxes paid to the city can be used, in part, to defray taxes paid to the state or to the federal government (when applicable). Moreover, taxes and charges vary considerably across localities and regions as well as over time. In countries where value added taxes are imposed, it takes considerable effort to correctly assess the precise tax paid at each level. In addition, transaction costs mask the true resource costs considered when imposing taxes.

For most projects, the complexity of correctly breaking down factor market prices into resource costs as well as taxes, levies, and charges renders it impractical to assess factor prices at their genuine resource costs. A further complication, crucial when input markets are noncompetitive, is the constraint of unknown demand and supply elasticities. Since these elasticities are necessary for the computation of net social gains or losses, social costs accounting becomes intractable.

In the light of these practical hurdles, the prevailing practice followed by transportation agencies in Western countries is to measure input costs at their observed market price, reflected in budgetary allocations. However, when there is an obvious bias in the market, this approach should not absolve the analyst from attempting to approximate the input's correct opportunity cost. We return to the market for land to illustrate this point.

It should also be recognized that this practice can conflict with the way benefits are computed for transportation COBA calculations. That is, the value of time is ordinarily computed on the basis of the hourly wage rate, net of taxes, to reflect the way trip makers arrive at their travel decisions. If factor costs are based on observed market prices, which include taxes, the two sides of the COBA equation may not balance. It is therefore imperative for the project analyst to pay attention to these issues and that she explains how factor prices were actually computed in her COBA report.

4. SUNK COSTS, JOINT COSTS, AND PROJECT IRREVERSIBILITY

4.1 Sunk Costs

The concept *sunk costs* refers to those costs that have been incurred and which cannot be recovered or reversed. Sunk costs can be money spent or irrevocably committed, such as legal fees or the costs of a tendering process. The question is, then, should sunk costs be considered in carrying out project appraisals? Following the standard economic approach, the criterion applied is the opportunity costs of these past commitments. If the opportunity costs of sunk costs are zero after being calculated, they can be ignored. However, if it can be shown that a resource purchased in the past currently carries opportunity costs, sunk costs must be considered. For example, land already owned and paid for by the public sector should *not* be considered at its original acquisition price but at its current asset value, which is determined by its present alternative use. Failure to account for these costs in carrying out the project's COBA will result in significant overestimation of its net benefits.

While past actions can certainly influence the magnitude of costs and benefits from future projects, the relevant costs to be considered are those effective in the present and future. Unfortunately, the common reality in transportation is that past commitments to a particular technology, such as rail, often make it politically thorny to objectively consider alternative technologies in the present. Consider studies aimed at extending transportation services to suburbs: These studies too frequently consider only options that involve extensions of the existing light rail technology. In this case, the costs sunk in the existing rail system inappropriately constrain future investment options. While there may be some costs and operational advantages to extending existing rail services, other technologies, such as bus rapid transit, should be considered since there is no reason, a priori, to assume that rail is the better investment.

Other significant sunk costs, typical for transportation and resulting from technological factors, make transportation investments largely irreversible. These are manifested along two dimensions. The first is an investment that cannot be used for any other purpose, such as a tunnel dug for a new subway line.[10] Chapter 9 addresses this irreversibility in the context of risk assessment of a project. The second form of irreversibility is political. Once a political decision has been made, the likelihood that new information on the true costs or benefits of a project will result in its reassessment—let alone an altered decision—is nil even before the initial sum has been spent. Considerable evidence has been gathered demonstrating that projects are rarely reappraised and relinquished despite new information demonstrating their inferiority (see Chapter 15). This variety of sunk cost is rarely brought before the public when decisions are being made.

4.2 Joint Costs

The economic concept *joint costs* refers to those costs incurred when multiple activities share a common input factor. When this occurs, the question becomes how to allocate these costs among the various uses so that the true value of each use can be assessed. In transportation, shared use of the same right-of-way is a common case of joint costs. For example, a proposed new highway includes a wide median reserved for a future light rail transit system. If the two modes, motor and rail, were each designed in isolation of the other, the right-of-way costs could be fairly easily separated into those parts attributable to the highway and those to the rail line. But having them both sharing the same right-of-way makes such assessments impossible. In a similar manner, the costs of drainage or overpasses in highway construction will not be the same, depending on whether the projects are built together or individually.

In such circumstances, the key issue is how to decide on a proper scheme for cost-sharing. The economic literature on joint costs provides some rules for proper cost allocation between multiple uses. These rules mainly involve econometric estimation of multiproduct cost functions using cross-sectional or longitudinal observations (see Berechman, 1993, for such studies). Engineering studies likewise often distinguish between costs that are separable and those that are nonseparable or "joint" (Newnan et al., 2000). Once identified, ad hoc rules are set on how to reasonably allocate these costs. For example, joint costs are often allocated in proportion to other costs, in proportion to benefits, or to some combination of both. A sensitivity analysis conducted on these allocation rules can indicate the degree to which joint costs affect the ranking and selection of alternative projects. Finally, a common approach to joint cost allocation is the use of output-based formulae. When several operators use the same infrastructure, the costs of the shared facility are allocated to each user on the basis of its respective output.[11]

A mistake frequently made is to assign all or a significant portion of the joint costs to one project, generally the one most likely to generate substantial benefits. Doing so amounts to subsidizing the other project, which might not be economically justifiable in the absence of subsidization. As we might anticipate, such practices tend to support economically poor decisions regarding the "weaker" project.

5. SUMMARY AND CONCLUSIONS

This chapter has focused on the identification and correct measurement of the investment costs associated with transportation infrastructure projects. Based on this discussion, we can derive several conclusions regarding the cost components to be included in a COBA scheme.

The first conclusion is that capital costs largely depend on the nature of the transportation project under study. New construction, maintenance, and improvement imply different types of costs, whose magnitudes depend on the project's location and scale and its established life cycle of maintenance and improvement.

Of particular importance are the costs of disruption, which for megaprojects can be quite substantial, especially if carried out in densely populated urban areas. Irrespective of the approach used to assess the magnitude of these costs, they all recognize the need to include disruption costs among the project's overall capital costs.

All input factors should be evaluated by their social opportunity costs. If the markets for input factors—right-of-way, land, labor, fixed, and rolling stock—were efficient, project expenditures based on observed market prices would correctly reflect the factors' opportunity costs. However, factor markets seldom operate at or near competitive conditions, making the question of the correct social opportunity costs rather crucial. A key conclusion is, therefore, that any analysis of the opportunity costs of the inputs used in transportation investments requires a thorough accounting of net changes in social welfare. Failure to consider such changes can culminate in biased estimates of the true social value of the resources used.

Due to taxes levied and subsidies provided, buyers of inputs (in our case, the government or a public agency) and sellers of services face disparate sets of prices that cause revenues to sellers and costs to the government to differ by the magnitude of the tax or the subsidy. This, in turn, requires that when performing COBA calculations, government spending and sellers' revenues as well as users' benefits are to be specified in comparable before—or after-tax terms.

Sunk costs and joint costs are characteristic of transportation investment projects. It is nonetheless incorrect to argue that an asset already owned and paid for by the public sector represents sunk costs and, therefore, that those costs are irrelevant for present-day decision making. Such an asset ought to be considered at its current value, measured by its present opportunity costs, rather than by its straightforward book value. In general, however, the only costs considered relevant are those occurring in the present and future; commitments made to past investments should not determine future investment decisions. Relatedly, joint costs should be carefully assigned to technically related projects to avoid acceptance of otherwise noneconomical projects.

Finally, in real-world applications, budget allocations are most commonly used as measures of costs. While this approach conflicts with the theoretical arguments made in this chapter, it can be justified on grounds of practicality and the lack of necessary data. Still, some cases do require the analyst to consider the true competitiveness of input markets and whether, like acquisition of right-of-way, social accounting is necessary to determine the correct opportunity costs of the respective inputs.

6 Methods of Project Cost-Benefit Analysis

1. INTRODUCTION

Cost-Benefit Analysis (COBA) is essentially an economic accounting framework for appraising the net social welfare contributed by a public investment. It enables calculation of the total monetary value of a project's benefits relative to the total monetary value of the resources used. The purpose of COBA is to establish how much the former exceeds the latter. As we always face competing uses for available resources, we need to evaluate each in order to identify the alternative providing the highest net contribution to social welfare. COBA is therefore used mainly to rate and prioritize project alternatives although, as we shall see, its application is sometimes limited.

Underlying COBA is the tenet that opportunity costs are associated with the use of resources. That is, from a social welfare viewpoint, because resources can be invested in alternative projects, the economic returns from these projects serve as benchmarks for project selection. COBA's major advantage regarding this goal lies in its ability to produce a single monetary net value for each alternative that is comparable with the monetary net value assigned to others.

Despite this advantage, the COBA approach has been widely criticized. First, not all benefits and costs can be quantified and measured in monetary values. Second, the distribution of costs and benefits across socioeconomic groups and geographic space is nonuniform, often rewarding some at the expense of others. Third, market failures, regulation, taxation, subsidization or institutional arrangements may render the results obtained as nonoptimal. Fourth, considerable uncertainty surrounds the future benefits and costs of most projects, which have life cycles typically spanning 30–50 years. These issues notwithstanding, COBA is still the most commonly used approach in transportation project evaluation. As shown in this and subsequent chapters, advanced COBA methods can account for various market imperfections, risk and equity concerns, making it a valuable resource in itself.

Historically, COBA evolved as a form of social accounting first introduced in 1844 by the French engineer Jules Dupuit for the purpose of determining the net economic value of public improvements (Dupuit, 1844).

The US Federal Flood Control Act of 1936 actually mandated that the US Corps of Engineers carry out waterway improvement projects only when it could be shown that the total benefits to be obtained from the project, regardless of the party to which they accrued, surpassed its total costs. The act basically stimulated further development of the COBA approach currently used.[1] As a result of the act's passage, the Corps of Engineers developed sets of rules and methods to measure the various benefit and cost components of infrastructure projects. Yet, it was only in the early 1950s that economists established the theoretical, economic underpinnings of COBA by providing the approach with rigorous and coherent methods as well as decision rules. Net contribution to social welfare, as defined in Chapter 3, has since become the key criterion for project evaluation.

The main objectives of this chapter are, then, to examine the analytical components of COBA and, subsequently, to present the different COBA measures used to ascertain a project's net economic worth. Section 2 of this chapter presents the fundamental principles at the heart of COBA while Section 3 describes the Net Present Value (NPV) method and its applications. Considerations applied when selecting the discount rate of future benefit and cost streams are presented in Section 4. Section 5 discusses the Internal Rate of Return method, which is often used when ranking projects. Section 6 presents other criteria used to rank projects, assuming no technical or financial constraints, whereas Section 7 discusses project selection under those constraints. Section 8 examines COBA computations under conditions of market imperfections. A summary and conclusions appear in Section 9.

2. BENEFITS, BENCHMARKS, AND THE VALUE OF FUTURE BENEFITS AND COSTS

As discussed in Chapter 4, the transportation benefits flowing from an investment are usually regarded as improvements in travel conditions such as travel time and safety. To assess these improvements we first need to establish a baseline—or benchmark—against which the project's transportation effects can be measured. As an investment's benefits—as well as its costs—accrue over a long period of time, a common denominator for their values is required. This section deals with these issues.

2.1 The "Do Nothing" Benchmark

The most common approach for establishing a benchmark when estimating a project's benefits is to define a basic alternative, frequently referred to as the "do not invest," "do nothing," the "base-case," or the "zero alternative."[2] The idea is to ask what the region's travel conditions would be if no new capital investments were made (save for routine maintenance) at the same time that travel demand from population growth and economic expansion kept increasing. Benefits from the project under consideration are then measured against these *future* travel conditions, *not* present-day conditions.[3]

A key problem with this approach is that future conditions are frequently computed on the basis of increased travel and economic activity at *existing locations*, meaning that preset and invariable activity patterns are implicitly assumed. In reality, land uses and Origin-Destination (O-D) patterns tend to respond in the medium- and long-run to changing travel conditions through relocation and modified travel behavior. Common manifestations of these phenomena are the continuous dispersion of activities in the metropolitan area, modal switching as well as changing times of departure and travel destinations. In addition, the "do nothing" approach assumes the consistency of the relevant land-use and transportation policies. For example, congestion tolls have become more acceptable in recent years as a policy-motivated means of travel control. If the use of congestion tolls becomes more prevalent, a "do nothing" alternative that ignores potential policy changes would be quite misleading. Unfortunately, many project evaluation studies that use the "do-nothing" alternative tend to ignore potential changes in land use, travel behavior, and transportation policy, thereby producing inappropriate travel benchmarks that are subsequently used to compute benefits from planned investments (see for example, New Jersey Transit, 2001).

2.2 Time Value of Future Streams of Benefits and Costs

At the very minimum, we require that for each project alternative, the total value of its benefits (B) exceed the total value of its costs (C). This rule implies that for an alternative to be acceptable, its Net Welfare (NW) contribution should be positive. That is: $NW = (B - C) > 0$; or $B/C > 1$.

Since the benefits as well as the costs of a transportation project accumulate over time, we need to provide a common denominator for their measurement. Assuming that benefits and costs are known with certainty, we can present their longitudinal distribution in a way similar to that shown in Table 6.1.

Table 6.1 Schematic Distribution of Costs and Benefits over the Project's Life Span[a]

Year	1	2	3	4	5	6	....	10	11	....	20	21	....	30
Costs														
Capital	+	+	+	+	+	0	0	0	0	0	+	+	0	0
Operating & Maintenance	0	0	0	0	0	+	+	+	+	+	0	0	+	+
Benefits	0	0	0	0	0	+	+	+	+	+	0	0	+	+

Note: [a]The "+" and "0" indicate positive or zero expenditures or benefits, respectively.

What this table represents is a hypothetical bridge construction project whose life span is 30 years, with an investment period (capital cost outlays) extending over the first 5 years only. Afterwards, benefits begin to accrue, as do operating (O) and maintenance (M) costs. At year 20, there is a major capital outlay (for example, renovating the bridge) covering 2 years, during which there are no benefits (the bridge is shut down) but also no operating or maintenance costs. Afterwards, from year 22 until year 30, benefits reappear. It should be understood that the "+" does not imply *equal* amounts of expenditures or benefits, just positive ones.

In order to measure the streams of future costs and benefits using one common denominator, we use the concept "time value of money." It implies that an alternative's cost of money equals the return that the respective amount would yield if it was put to another use. To illustrate, $100 received this year, if invested at the market interest rate r, would be worth $100 \cdot (1 + r)^2$ after two years. The Present Value (PV) of the $100 received at the end of year 2, therefore, is $100/(1 + r)^2$. More generally, $PV = \$100/(1 + r)^t$, where t indicates the number of years in the time period required. Below we discuss the nature of the discount rate r. If present value of benefits is computed continuously (not on an annual basis), $PV = \int^T e^{-rt}(B_t)dt$, where T is the life span of the investment, r the discount rate, and B_t the benefits.

3. THE NET PRESENT VALUE METHOD

In the ensuing analysis we explicitly assume that transportation investment projects are implemented, first and foremost, to increase transportation benefits and reduce transportation costs (see Chapters 4 and 5). Transportation projects aimed at reducing environmental externalities or creating jobs are discussed in Chapters 12 and 13.

3.1 Net Present Value and the Consumer/Producer Surplus

As explained in Chapter 3, changes in consumer surplus (ΔCS) and producer surplus (ΔPS) underlie the evaluation of net social-welfare improvements from a project. The Net Present Value (NPV) of an improvement can be expressed as:

$$NPV = -PV(C) + \sum_{t=1}^{T}(\Delta CS_t + \Delta PS_t)(1+r)^{-t} \tag{1}$$

In (1), $PV(C)$ is the present value of the investment's capital costs, t denotes a year and r the discount rate.[4] Using the "rule of half" (see Chapter 3), the change in consumer surplus is approximated using:

$$\Delta CS_t \cong Q_{t0}(P_{t0} - P_{t1}) + \frac{1}{2}(P_{t0} - P_{t1})(Q_{t1} - Q_{t0}) = \frac{1}{2}(P_{t0} - P_{t1})(Q_{t0} + Q_{t1}) \tag{2}$$

where P and Q denote the price and number of trips, respectively. The subscripts "0" and "1" denote the "before" and "after" (or "with" and "without") investment, respectively. Producer surplus is given as:

$$\Delta PS_t = (P_{t1} \cdot Q_{t1} - P_{t0} \cdot Q_{t0}) + (C_{to}(Q_{t0}) - C_{t1}(Q_{t1})) \tag{3}$$

In (3), $C_{to}(Q_{t0})$ and $C_{t1}(Q_{t1})$ are total variable costs with and without investment, respectively. Given these concepts, next we discuss NPV measures.

3.2 Formulation of NPV Measures

Let C_t be capital costs, B_t benefits (e.g., value of time saved), R_t revenues (see next section), M_t maintenance costs, O_t operating costs, all on an annual basis. The symbol T_C denotes the construction (or investment) period, T is the project's life span, and r the discount rate (see Section 4). Thus,

$$NPV = \left[-\sum_{t=1}^{T_C} \frac{C_t}{(1+r)^t} \right] + \sum_{t=T_C+1}^{T+T_C} \frac{B_t + R_t - M_t - O_t}{(1+r)^t} \tag{4}$$

While cost outlays are made throughout the fiscal year and user benefits are received continuously over time, for computation purposes it is generally assumed that all costs and all benefits accrue at the end of each calendar or fiscal year. We thus set the time index t to $t = 1,2, \ldots ,T$. Alternatively, NPV can be computed assuming that costs and benefits are made and received at the beginning of the fiscal year; in that case, the time counter is set as $t = 0,1,2, \ldots ,(T-1)$.

It is obvious from expression (4) that the higher the discount rate, the lower the NPV, holding all other variables constant. Note also that benefits accruing at distant periods add relatively very little to the computed NPV. For projects with long life spans, say 30–50 years, this can be an acute problem. In such cases, benefits will be received by generations not born yet. A high r would then imply that the welfare of these generations is of low priority among present-day decision-makers. To partially compensate for this effect, it has been suggested that the discount rate decline over time (Harvey, 1994). We return to this issue in Chapter 12, where we discuss transportation externalities.

3.3 The Opportunity Costs of Capital

Some agencies report a project's total capital costs without specifying how these costs are to be distributed over the investment period. They may also not report whether those costs include debt service costs, which are interest payments on the investment and can be quite substantial over the project's life span. In principle, debt service represents the opportunity costs earned had the capital been invested elsewhere. For example, $1 billion invested in a rail project could have earned a higher rate if invested, for example, in a health care facility or if returned to taxpayers who could have placed their shares of the money in long-term savings deposit accounts.

It might be argued that the size of the initial capital outlay C is irrelevant for an NPV analysis since only the size of the debt service matters. That is, as long as debt service can be paid (along an infinite time horizon), the repayment of capital is of no interest. The flaw in such an argument is that it disregards the *opportunity costs* of C. If liquidation of the assets financed by C is costly then C can, in essence, be spent only once. This being the case, the rate of return on other possible investments that could be financed by C becomes important. It follows that if alternative projects offer higher rates of return than does the current project, they should be undertaken instead.

Another argument has to do with the efficiency (or inefficiency) of the cost of capital. If r, the rate used to discount the future streams of benefits and costs, are assumed efficient (i.e., if r is the correct shadow price of capital), then debt service payments are already accounted for and need not be included in a COBA.[5] They need to be considered, however, when computing the project's annual expenses (see equation 18). This reasoning explains the formulation of NPV in equation (4).

If r is an inefficient rate, especially if it falls below the correct market price of capital, adjustments need to be made to reflect the available social-welfare alternatives for the invested resources. In that case, the COBA formulation should include a cost component indicating the additional costs to society emanating from use of that capital for the selected project. If we can assume that the debt's interest rate reflects the market's cost of capital, the project's NPV is:

$$NPV = \left[-\sum_{t=1}^{T_C} \frac{C_t + \rho \cdot C}{(1+r)^t} \right] + \sum_{t=T_C+1}^{T+T_C} \frac{B_t + (R_t - M_t - O_t) - \rho \cdot C}{(1+r)^t} \tag{5}$$

In (5), $\rho \cdot C$ is the annual debt service cost (ρ is the debt's interest rate). The term $(R_t - M_t - O_t)$ represents net variable costs, which include maintenance (M_t) and operating (O_t) costs. In transit investments, the aggregate fare that users pay make up the transit agency's farebox revenues, and thus can be regarded as a pure transfer payment, which need *not* be included in the NPV calculation. However, most local transit agencies also receive a direct annual subsidy, S_t, from state and federal (central) government's coffers. Since benefits from this subsidy accrue to the local population only, it would be incorrect to regard it as a transfer payment. Therefore, this subsidy should be included as part of the producer's surplus (Mishan, 1971).[6] If data on subsidies are unavailable, farebox revenues, R_t, can be used as a proxy.[7]

In many cases, capital may still have a "terminal value" (sometimes referred to as "salvage value") at the end of the project's life span. For instance, tunnels may retain some of their value long beyond T years. Hence, the terminal value should reflect the stream of benefits that the project can generate beyond year T. In such cases, NPV becomes:

$$NPV = \left[-\sum_{t=1}^{T_C} \frac{C_t}{(1+r)^t} \right] + \sum_{t=T_C+1}^{T+T_C} \frac{B_t + R_t - M_t - O_t}{(1+r)^t} + V_{(T+T_C)} \tag{6}$$

The term $V_{(T+T_C)}$ is the terminal value at the end of the project's total life span.

3.4 Benefits and Costs: In Nominal or Real Values?

A calculation problem can arise if benefits and costs are expressed in nominal values when the discount rate r is expressed in real terms (Hanke et al., 1975). That is,

$$NPV = \left[-\sum_{t=1}^{T_C} \frac{C_t(1+f)^t}{(1+r)^t} \right] + \sum_{t=T_C+1}^{T+T_C} \frac{(B_t + R_t - M_t - O_t)(1+f)^t}{(1+r)^t} \tag{7}$$

where f is the inflation rate. The correct approach would be to express benefits, costs, *and* the discount rate in nominal terms. That is,

$$NPV = \left[-\sum_{t=1}^{T_C} \frac{C_t(1+f)^t}{[(1+r)(1+f)]^t} \right] + \sum_{t=T_C+1}^{T+T_C} \frac{(B_t + R_t - M_t - O_t)(1+f)^t}{[(1+r)(1+f)]^t} \tag{8}$$

Equation (8) implies that consistent use of nominal or real values for the benefits and the costs as well as the discount rate will result in identical NPVs.[8]

What if inflation affects the nominal value of benefits *differently* than it does the nominal value of costs? For example, the price index of labor and materials often rises faster than does income, which affects the nominal value of time and hence of benefits. In such cases, use of either nominal or real terms to compute NPV does matter. Moreover, under these conditions, there is no intrinsic reason why the same discount rate should be used for both (Harvey, 1994). If we further consider the fact that the inflation rate is normally stated as the annual percent change in the Consumer Price Index (CPI), we can begin to understand the seriousness of this problem. That is, the basket of goods and services used to calculate CPI normally does not contain cost items that are typical for transportation investments, such as heavy construction labor and materials. Thus, the inflation rate, specified in terms of CPI, may over- or understate price changes in the construction sector, with the consequent results for computation of the correct NPV of an infrastructure project. In addition, the funding commitments of various agencies and jurisdictions, which in many cases are based on their ability to raise taxes, are unlikely to be pegged directly to the CPI. In such a financial structure, the risk of underfunding—even if all the components are stated in nominal terms—grows.[9]

3.5 Treatment of Expected Growth in Benefits and Revenues

In Chapter 4 we saw that the direct benefits from a transportation investment project are a combination of the time and cost savings, ridership, and reliability, all of which are likely to grow over time; these benefits will be realized mainly in responses to increasing income, thus VOT, population, and motorization rates. Hence, for appraisal purposes, we need to account for such potential growth in benefits and introduce this factor into NPV formulae (Nash, 1993).

Methods meant to derive the growth rates of transportation project benefits are generally based on fitting curves to the longitudinal data reflecting changes in automobile ownership, driver's licenses held, Vehicles Miles Traveled (VMT), income, population size, household formation rates, and employment. Since most of these variables are highly correlated with one another, care must be exercised to avoid overestimation of their growth rates.

To illustrate, let g denote the annual rate of growth in benefits. Inserting this element into the basic NPV formula we obtain:

$$NPV = \left[-\sum_{t=1}^{T_C} \frac{C_t}{(1+r)^t} \right] + \sum_{t=T_C+1}^{T+T_C} \frac{B_t(1+g)^t + R_t - M_t - O_t}{(1+r)^t} \tag{9}$$

It is unlikely that benefits will grow unabated during the project's entire life span since there are upper bounds on the number of auto or transit users expected to benefit from a project. For example, the population within a rail project's corridor may reach saturation. We may therefore want to use decreasing growth rate configurations such as:

$$g(t) = \frac{g_0}{1 + \alpha(t - T_C)}, \, t > T_C \tag{10}$$

In (10), $g(t)$ is growth rate at time t, α is the attenuation rate, g_0 is the growth rate at the beginning of the period, T is the project's life span, and T_C is the construction period.[10]

As previously explained with respect to rail and bus projects, annual farebox revenue can be used as a proxy for subsidies. Since farebox revenue is a function of ridership and fares (R_t), the revenue term should also be augmented to reflect annual growth in ridership. To the extent that ridership also affects maintenance and operating costs, using equation (5) so long as we account for debt service costs. We thus obtain:

$$NPV = \left[-\sum_{t=1}^{T_C} \frac{C_t + \rho \cdot C}{(1+r)^t} \right] + \sum_{t=T_C+1}^{T+T_C} \frac{(B_t + R_t - M_t - O_t) \cdot (1+g)^t - \rho \cdot C}{(1+r)^t} \tag{11}$$

For some projects, especially rail, maintenance costs tend to grow at a rate much steeper than the increase in ridership. The reasons for this result are mainly deterioration in the state of repair of fixed and rolling stock as well as the need to introduce new technologies (e.g., communication and signaling).[11] A careful analysis of maintenance trends is therefore mandatory if we are to accurately determine the future impact of factors such as rising maintenance costs on the true economic value of the project in addition to the oversight agency's ability to meet its long-term financial obligations.

3.6 Problems Intrinsic to Use of the NPV Method

In theory, if the discount rate is properly selected, if all benefits and costs germane to the project are correctly defined and measured, and if markets function reasonably efficiently, the NPV is the correct measure for evaluating and thus ranking projects. This does not deny that the method is still subject to several intrinsic limitations, consideration of which is necessary when evaluating a specific project.

1. Monetary Scale

When used for ranking projects, NPV is susceptible to the project's monetary scale. That is, projects with benefits and costs measured in hundreds of millions of dollars are likely to show smaller NPV than are projects measured in billions. Since the benefit-to-cost ratio is insensitive to project scale, this method is to be preferred as a ranking criterion in many cases (see Section 7 for more on this method).

2. Time Horizon (Short vs. Long Term)

NPV use is biased in favor of short-term projects. For some project types, benefits accrue in the far future; due to discounting, their NPVs may be quite small when compared with shorter period projects.[12] NPV outcomes are therefore liable to indicate subway and high-speed rail, for instance, as inferior to highway projects. The earlier projects typically require many years for investments to reach fruition but exhibit benefits lasting many years forward, whereas the latter projects enjoy much shorter investment period and fairly rapid accrual of benefits. If rail projects are regarded as preferable to highway projects from the perspective of transportation, urban and environmental criteria, weighting methods can be used to neutralize the bias introduced by time (see Chapter 14 for weighting methods).

3. Rate of Reinvestment of Interim Proceeds

Use of the NPV method intrinsically assumes that annual benefits will be reinvested at a rate that equals the investment's discount rate. This can be seen from equation (4), where net benefits at time t are added to the benefits accumulated thus far (i.e., from period 1 through period $t - 1$) at rate r. If net benefits are negative for some periods, equation (4) implies a "loan" made at rate r. It follows that if the discount rate, used for discounting a given project, is different than the market's efficient rate, the NPV calculations will generate incorrect results. Hence the importance of correct specification of the discount rate by project (see Sections 4 and 5).

4. Disregard of Large-Scale Investment Risk

The types and levels of risks associated with large investments are generally disregarded when using NPV methods. As shown by Flyvbjerg et al. (2003), the larger the investment, the more likely it is that actual benefits and costs will deviate from projected ones. Chapter 9 explores this issue in detail.

5. Intergenerational Comparisons

A fundamental issue associated with transportation projects is that two projects with different life spans may benefit different generations. For instance, a subway project with a construction period of 10–15 years and a productive life of 30–50 years will benefit future generations more than it will the present generation. The question is, then, can we compare the present generation's welfare with that of future generations? This problem could be mollified if a *social discount rate* were used to discount future benefits and costs. Regrettably, market imperfections, which tend to distort the marginal rates of return on alternative investments, present the main obstacles to employment of such a rate. This issue is elaborated next.

4. SELECTING THE PROPER DISCOUNT RATE

We have so far emphasized the decisive impact of the discount rate on a project's NPV. It is pertinent to ask, therefore, what should this rate be and how should it be determined? The literature on these subjects is quite voluminous and their in-depth examination is beyond the scope of this book. Nevertheless, because of its importance, we present here a brief discussion of some of the methods proposed for selecting an appropriate discount rate for assessing public investments.[13]

It should be noted at the outset that by and large, state and federal treasury departments and national ministries of finance impose a single and obligatory rate for discounting *all* the transportation projects initiated by *all* oversight agencies. However, this rate does not necessarily reflect an economic or business rationale, for it is used predominantly as a regulatory policy variable. This practice is generally rooted in one of two arguments. First, application of any of the methods examined below requires extensive information on market interest rates and investment yields. Thus, for practical reasons and to maintain uniformity in the evaluation of alternative projects, a single discount rate is to be preferred. The second argument rests on political expediency and central government's distrust of local authorities, especially when funding comes from national coffers.[14] Appendix C shows the discount rates used in various countries.

4.1 Methods for Selecting the Discount Rate

In general, we can distinguish between several broad approaches to the selection of a discount factor.[15] What is common to all of these approaches is their stress on the *opportunity costs* of government's funds as the correct discount rate for calculating a project's NPV. Here we briefly examine three of the most frequently used approaches.

1. The Opportunity Costs of Public Funds in Private Markets

This approach treats public and private investments as competing for the same resources and, therefore, requires that the discount rate of public investments reflects the opportunity costs of the same funds if used for private investments. Most transportation investments are financed from tax revenues, either by a dedicated tax (e.g., the US Highway Trust Fund is financed by gasoline taxes) or from general tax revenues. Under such conditions, public-sector investments are said to displace private investments by siphoning away resources that could otherwise have earned private sector rates of return. The argument is that public investments should be at least as profitable as private sector investments are; the discount rate for public investments, r, should therefore equal the private sector's rate of return, r_l.

Yet, adoption of this method for selection of the discount rate raises several problems. First, technical problems impede identification of a single private sector rate of return since financial markets yield many rates of return, depending on the particular investment's magnitude and risk level. Second, private investors pay various taxes on their earnings that tend to distort observed market yields. Third, private sector investments most often do not account for the externalities (e.g., environmental impacts) introduced by these investments; hence, their returns may be socially inefficient. Fourth, through regulation, taxation, and borrowing, the public sector affects yields in private capital markets;[16] it also affects the rate of savings—and thus of private investment—through compulsory savings plans such as social security. In brief, using the before-tax rate of return on private investments as the proper discount rate for public investments may result in a number of suboptimal projects.

Still another problem emanating from this approach is that funds raised by taxation are, in reality, diverted mainly from consumption, *not* from savings. In fact, many households are "negative savers" as they use consumption credit to spend more than their income would allow. To regard all tax revenues as displacing private investment is consequently incorrect since the social opportunity costs of public investments include private savings *and* consumption. To alleviate this problem, it has been recommended that a weighted average rate of return on private investment, r_I, and private consumption, r_C, be used as the proper discount rate for public projects.[17] Let s be the proportion of public investment originating in private investment (e.g., saving accounts), and $(1 - s)$ be the proportion originating in private consumption. The weighted average rate of discount, $\bar{r}$, then becomes $\bar{r} = s \cdot r_I + (1 - s) \cdot r_C \cdot (1 - t)$, where t is the average income tax rate (Gramlich, 2000).[18]

In the real world, however, s can be close to zero (many households do not save at all) so that in effect, $r = r_C \cdot (1 - t)$. Since $r_C \cdot (1 - t)$ is a product of the tax regime and regulation of the interest rates that consumers face, it is difficult to argue that this should be *the* discount rate applied to public investments.

2. The Marginal Cost of Recruiting Funds

This approach posits that the discount rate for public funds should reflect the shadow price of limited public resources, interpreted as the marginal cost of recruiting public funds. This most often characterizes the policies of small economies where governments are forced to raise capital in international markets. Thus, r is set to equal the weighted sum of the various factors that impact on the cost of recruiting an additional dollar, including prime rates in international financial markets, risk premiums reflecting the country's credit status, as well as another reflecting local political and economic risks. In small open economies, these risk premiums can be quite substantial.[19] Often, the marginal deadweight loss from taxation is also factored in. To illustrate the consequences of these factors, Appendix A shows the computation of the cost of capital for UK airports.

3. The Social Time-Preference Rate

This approach treats public investment as a mechanism for distributing intergenerational social benefits and costs; therefore, the discount rate is set to reflect the rate at which society prefers to achieve this distribution over time (see Appendix B for a formal analysis). Since returns from transportation projects can accrue many years forward, a characteristic that benefits future rather than current generations, any investment decision made at present necessarily reveals today's preferences regarding the allocation of resources between periods. This approach raises two fundamental questions. First, is it correct, in principle, to use the discount rate for intergenerational transfers of resources? Can other mechanisms, such as taxation, income policies, or investments in human capital, do a better job with respect to these resources? Second, how are we to decide on the rate appropriate for distributing benefits to future generations? Can returns on current investments be used as a guideline?

An answer to the first question necessarily involves a priori value judgments regarding social objectives, desired income distribution, and government's role in the economy. To answer the second question, we should reframe it as follows: If we wish future generations to be as well off as the present generation, measured, say, by income per capita, what proportion of present resources should be invested in long-term projects? A practical response to both can be obtained by employing demographic and macroeconomic models accounting for population as well as economic growth.

Theoretically, the social time preference rate is composed of two components: a pure time preference and an intergenerational wealth substitution factor. If today's preferences dictate that the well-being of future generations be considered as important as that of the present generation, then the discount rate should be "zero" since a positive rate would violate this stipulation. On the other hand, current trends in economic growth imply that the well-being of future generations will exceed that of the present generation so that consumption currently foregone actually transfers wealth from a contemporary "poorer" generation to a future "wealthier" one. For this reason, it is correct to use a positive discount rate.[20] In practice, this approach is rarely used because the welfare of future generations, while regarded as important, is not directly defined by today's decision makers.

4.2 Discount Rates Employed in Practice

Discount rate computations contain three major components: the inflation rate, a risk premium, and a "real" interest rate that reflects the marginal productivity of money, net of inflation. Governments typically use the rate at which they borrow money as a basis for calculating discount rates. For example, in 2005, the coupon rate of a risk-free US government 10-year treasury bill was 4.25%. With inflation, measured as the change in the Consumer Price Index (CPI) of 2.35%, the "real" discount rate was 1.9% (4.25% 2.35%).[21] As indicated by the data shown in Appendix C various countries use different discount rates, which, at least in part, reflect the use of different calculation methods.

What are the practical lessons to be learned from this analysis? First, if a bond issue is used to finance a project, the issue's coupon rate should serve as the minimum required rate of return on the investment. That is, the project's future benefits and costs should be discounted by a rate that is at least equal to the minimum rate of return obtained for this type of investment. Second, for projects funded from nonearmarked government coffers, the interest rate the government pays on its long-term debt (e.g., inflation-indexed treasury bonds) should serve as the *lower bound* for the discount rate. This guideline is based on the proposition that generally speaking—i.e., disregarding distributional considerations—it makes no sense for the government to undertake a project whose yield is below its cost of funding. Hence, to the extent that the government's cost of funding can be approximated it should be utilized as the lower bound of the discount rate.

The use of an inappropriate discount rate has several consequences, which ought to be made explicit. Given budget constraints, adoption of "too low" a rate will not only permit making unworthy investments, it will also prevent implementation of more profitable ones. Alternatively, given current trends in income distribution, the use of a low discount rate, especially for public transit projects, amounts to a transfer of resources from higher to lower income groups. If the latter is indeed true, income distribution rather than economic efficiency should provide the main reason for implementing some projects. While the use of a mandatory discount rate may render the above considerations superfluous, it certainly does not absolve analysts from considering the reasonableness of the rates they do employ when discounting benefits and costs. A sensitivity analysis of the project's NPV relative to alternative discount rates can potentially reveal the range of NPV over which a project can contribute to social welfare.

A final note on the proper discount rate is dedicated to the nonmonetary benefits and costs, such as health, fatalities, pain, and suffering. The use of any rate to discount future values of these flows inherently assumes that they have measurable opportunity costs. But since there are no markets for these "commodities," it is difficult to accept this notion. This applies even when transportation projects are aimed precisely at reducing fatalities and minimizing injuries. Chapter 12 deals with these issues.

5. INTERNAL RATE OF RETURN ANALYSIS

One method that is frequently used to rank alternative investments is the Internal Rate of Return (IRR). The IRR is defined as that value of the discount rate for which NPV is 0. That is, solve for i^*, for which $NPV(i^*) = 0$:

$$NPV(i^*) = \left[-\sum_t^{T_C} \frac{C_t}{(1+i^*)^t} \right] + \sum_{t=T_C+1}^{T+T_C} \frac{B_t + R_t - M_t - O_t}{(1+i^*)^t} = 0 \qquad (12)$$

What the IRR of a project actually implies is that discounting a project by any rate below the IRR will produce a positive NPV. That is, for any $i < i^*$ $NPV(i) > 0$, where i^* is the internal rate of return. As a ranking criterion, the IRR implies that a project with a high IRR is more "profitable" than a project with a low IRR.

Despite its popularity, the IRR method suffers from several analytical problems that render its usefulness for transportation project evaluation rather questionable. First, the computation of IRR requires a solution to a polynomial equation of the type "find i^* for which":

$$-C + \frac{B_1}{(1+i)^1} + \frac{B_2}{(1+i)^2} + \ldots \frac{B_T}{(1+i)^T} = 0 \tag{13}$$

Clearly, equation (13) can have multiple solutions and, consequently, there may be several—rather than a single—IRR values.[22] In general, a high-degree polynomial function (e.g., an investment scheme with 10 periods) will generate many roots, making the computation of a single IRR value rather problematic.[23]

Figure 6.1 depicts still another difficulty with the use of IRR to rank investments. It shows two investments I_1 and I_2 whose IRR values are i_1 and i_2, respectively, with $i_1 > i_2$.

Based on the IRR criterion, investment I_1 should be ranked higher than investment I_2. However, if the actual discount rate is r, investment I_2 yields a higher NPV. In fact, for every r that is smaller than r', investment I_2 is preferred. Thus, when faced with two or more alternatives to rank, indiscriminate use of IRR can yield incorrect results.

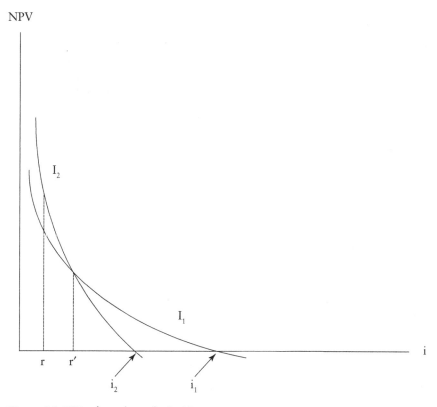

Figure 6.1 IRR of two hypothetical investments.

A further theoretical problem with the IRR measure is its embedded assumption about the rate at which intermediate net benefits are reinvested. As we have seen, one assumption built into the NPV method is that interim net benefits are reinvested at a rate equal to the discount rate. In contrast, the use of IRR assumes a reinvestment scheme at the IRR rate, which is an unsustainable assumption. Stated differently, the IRR of a given project (denoted by i), with an initial capital investment I and life span T, assumes an annual return of i percent of I for T years, which would ensure the entire return of I at the end of T.

When is it likely for the NPV and the IRR method to rank projects similarly? This could happen if there were no budget limitations, if projects were completely independent (building project A does not preclude or necessitate the building of project B), and if investment costs exceed the stream of benefits for the first year. In reality, these conditions are seldom met. We must therefore conclude that of the two, only the NPV method should be used to rank projects.

6. OTHER CRITERIA USED TO RANK PROJECTS

Several NPV-derived measures are commonly used as part of COBA for the purpose of ranking projects. We can distinguish between two main categories of cases: (a) when projects are independent and exhibit no financial constraints; and (b) when projects are technically dependent and their appraisal is conducted under resource constraints. The first case is examined next, the second in Section 7.

6.1 NPV-Related Measures

The measures presented below should be regarded as complementary to NPV as they provide additional information on an investment's economic attributes.

1. *The Benefit-Cost Ratio*

(BCR or B/C or "benefits per dollar invested") is defined as the present value of the project's total benefits divided by the present value of its total costs. In effect, B/C shows the benefits per dollar invested, which must be greater than one if the project is to be accepted:

$$\frac{B}{C} = \frac{\displaystyle\sum_{t=T_C+1}^{T+T_C} \frac{B_t}{(1+r)^t}}{\left[\displaystyle\sum_{t=1}^{T_C} \frac{C_t}{(1+r)^t}\right] + \displaystyle\sum_{t=T_C+1}^{T+T_C} \frac{-R_t + O_t + M_t}{(1+r)^t}} \tag{14}$$

Note that in (14), annual farebox revenues R_t, used as a proxy for subsidy amount, displays a minus sign when it appears in the denominator, because R_t is a component of producer surplus, which *reduces* total net costs.

Assuming $(B/C) > 1$, the larger this ratio, the higher the project will be ranked. When all of the alternatives considered have the same PV(C), this measure is also referred to as "cost-effectiveness," because it shows the benefits obtained per one dollar of investment. Unlike NPV, the B/C ratio is insensitive to the scale of the project. Hence, a project with an NPV larger than that of another project may have a B/C ratio lower than the second project. This point is further elaborated below.

2. The Investment's Rate of Return (ROR)

represents the percentage of NPV as a factor in the PV of the capital investment: $[NPV/PV(C)] \cdot 100$ or $[(B - C)/C] \cdot 100$. That is,

$$ROR = \left\{ \frac{\left[-\sum_{t=1}^{T_C} \dfrac{C_t}{(1+r)^t} \right] + \sum_{t=T_C+1}^{T+T_C} \dfrac{B_t + R_t - M_t - O_t}{(1+r)^t}}{\left[\sum_{t=1}^{T_C} \dfrac{C_t}{(1+r)^t} \right]} \right\} \cdot 100 \tag{15}$$

When using (15), the project obtaining the highest ROR is ranked as most preferable. The Benefit-Cost Ratio (BCR) and ROR are related as follows:

$$ROR = \frac{NPV}{C} = \frac{B-C}{C} = \frac{B}{C} - 1, \text{ or } \frac{B}{C} = ROR + 1.$$

Both measures produce equivalent ranks (see Table 6.2), although the ROR has a more direct economic interpretation.

3. First-Year Rate of Return (FYRR)

is computed by dividing the first year's net benefits by the PV of the cost of the investment. A low FYRR—when compared with market rates (e.g., government bond yields)—may indicate a poor investment.

4. Payback Period

is defined as the number of years necessary for recovery of capital costs. When conducting a comparison, we are required to arrive at the minimum number of years, denoted by T, for which the PV of each alternative's benefits, net of the annual maintenance and operating costs, equals the PV of its capital costs. Formally, find T for which:

$$\frac{\sum_{t=T_C+1}^{T+T_C} \dfrac{B_t + R_t - M_t - O_t}{\left(1+r^*\right)^t}}{\left[\sum_{t}^{T_C} \dfrac{C_t}{\left(1+r^*\right)^t}\right]} = 1 \tag{16}$$

The project with the smallest T is ranked as the "preferred project."

5. Annual Cash Flow

Irrespective of a project's high rate of return, prudent managerial practice requires that its annual net cash flow be considered over the project's life span. That is, following the investment period, the project's annual expenditures (maintenance, operating, and upgrading costs) must be covered either from farebox or toll revenue in addition to subsidies (S_t). Let F_t be the project's annual cash flow:

$$F_t = \left[R_t + S_t - (O_t + M_t + G_t + \rho \cdot C)\right] \tag{17}$$

In (17), G_t represents the periodic upgrading costs necessary to keep the system attuned to technological changes not covered by annual maintenance; $\rho \cdot C$ are annual debt service costs.[24] For any year t, if $F_t < 0$, a deficit occurs and the oversight authority will have to raise prices, find an alternative source of funding, or reduce the level of service. Successive years of negative F_t can force projects into insolvency or partial shutdown.[25] Note that the revenue and costs items in (17) are expressed in real terms. Hence, the inflation rate should be factored in to express a future year's cash flow in nominal terms.

6. Timing Rule

From an economic standpoint, it is quite appropriate to ask questions about the optimal timing for making investments. Disregarding uncertainties (see Chapter 9), the response should be: Invest when a project's annual net benefits exceed its annual debt service costs, $\rho \cdot C$, when ρ is the debt's interest rate. This rule is especially important when annual benefits are expected to grow over time (see FHWA, Conference on Benefit Cost Analysis 1996, p. 17).

To illustrate how alternative criteria conclude in different project rankings, consider the data shown in Table 6.2. The table is based on a preliminary analysis done to evaluate two rail alternatives for the city of Jerusalem, Israel: a low-cost investment (labeled HGB) and a high-cost investment (labeled LRT). The two sets of results are shown by alternative values of time (VOT).

It should be clear from this example that using NPV as the ranking criterion indicates that the high-cost LRT investment should be selected under

Table 6.2 Jerusalem Light Rail: Results of a COBA (in millions of NIS)

Criteria	High VOT		Low VOT	
	HGB	LRT	HGB	LRT
NPV	4,004	8,711	1,548	2,813
IRR	34%	30%	21%	18%
B/C	8.5	6.81	3.90	2.87
ROR	7.5	5.81	2.90	1.87
Payback Period	2	3	5	8

both high and low VOTs. However, the ranks would reverse if we used other criteria. For example, using rate of return (ROR), the lower-cost HGB alternative should be selected. What this example highlights is that projects of different magnitude are ranked differently when using alternative criteria.

In general, for a set of projects with comparable costs and no budget constraints, NPV is the correct criterion to utilize when ranking projects. It is the most direct and precise way available to arrive at the net total welfare contribution from a specific project's implementation relative to its alternatives. However, because of the effect of investment size, the Benefit-to-Cost ratio is the more advantageous measure. Appendix C, which shows the criteria used in various countries, highlights this observation.

6.2 Additional Ranking Criteria

Four additional criteria are occasionally used in project assessment. The first is the *incremental benefit-cost ratio*, which enables sequential comparison of the benefits and costs of each alternative with those of a base case. Mathematically, this approach is equivalent to the NPV method and provides the same results.

The second method, already mentioned, is *cost-effectiveness*, which computes the present value of benefits to be obtained from a given level of funding. The rule is: Select the alternative with the highest $PV(B)$ for a given level of investment.

The third criterion entails computation of the *critical values* of benefits and costs for which the NPV equals zero. That is, given a $PV(C)$, what would be the $PV(B)$ when $NPV = 0$. The rule would then be: Select the alternative that requires the least $PV(B)$. Similarly, for a given level of $PV(B)$, select the alternative with the lowest $PV(C)$ necessary for $NPV = 0$.

Finally, an approach supported by the US Federal Highway Administration is the *life-cycle method*. Its main objective is to compare alternative highway investment strategies by comparing user benefits with the project's life-cycle capital, operating, and maintenance costs under different investment scenarios. The approach is used to assess the tradeoffs between system expansion and system preservation as well as to evaluate the benefits of different overall levels of investment.

Life-cycle cost analysis requires annual capital, operations, and maintenance cost data. For highway projects, capital costs are averaged over the project's life span. When conducting such an assessment of light rail and bus rapid transit projects, capital costs include facilities and equipment with various life cycles. The total annualized life-cycle cost, then, is the aggregation of the annualized capital, operations, and maintenance costs.[26]

7. PROJECT APPRAISAL AND RANKING WITH TECHNICAL AND FINANCIAL CONSTRAINTS

When selecting among alternative projects, problems frequently arise as a result of the projects' potential dependence on one another. We can distinguish between two forms of dependence—technical and financial—with the latter prompted by binding budgets. Another common form of project dependence, excluded here, is political in nature: It occurs when, for instance, political support for one project is exchanged for implementation of another, a frequent event involved in the passage of what is known as "pork-barrel" legislation in the US and other countries.

This issue's salience has two sources. First, project evaluation is motivated by the wish to select those projects that yield the highest net social benefits. If these benefits are not created independently among the projects in the choice set, we may be more liable to select inferior projects. Second, when preparing a long-term transportation investment plan, it is necessary to identify potential interrelationships in order to define an optimal investment set.

7.1 Technical Relationships between Projects

We can distinguish three major types of technical interrelationships between projects. First, projects may be *technically neutral* so that the net benefits of carrying out projects x and y jointly equal the sum of the two projects' net benefits. That is: $B(x + y) = B(x) + B(y)$. Second, projects can be *substitutable* so that the net benefits of implementing them jointly are less than the sum of their stand-alone benefits, that is, $B(x + y) < B(x) + B(y)$. Obviously, there are differing degrees of substitution; at the extreme, projects are mutually exclusive, that is, $B(x + y) < \{B(x) \text{ or } B(y)\}$. The third type includes projects that are *technically complementary* so that the net total benefit of their joint implementation exceeds the sum of the net benefits of their separate implementation, that is, $B(x + y) > B(x) + B(y)$.

From an economic perspective, at the root of substitutability and complementarity relationships lies a common input factor that the projects use either competitively or jointly. For example, a certain right-of-way is a key input factor for either a rail line or a highway but not for both *simultaneously*. The projects can therefore be said to be mutually exclusive. On the other hand, surface rail and subway systems are said to be complementary projects because the users of each share the same terminal or hub. Building projects with shared facilities can yield net social benefits that are greater than the sum of each project's net benefits when each is built with its own terminal facility.

The question, then, is how are we to account for these technical interactions among projects when performing a COBA? Especially in the case of complementary projects, should they be assessed jointly or separately? If analyzed individually, each project may not pass the COBA test (i.e., $NPV < 0$) whereas as a joint project, the two may have a substantial positive NPV value. A ferryboat service with a low NPV value may engender much higher net benefits if linked to a bus project that provides ferry passengers with quick transportation to and from downtown destinations. Similarly, as a joint investment project, a new railway station *and* a car parking facility for daily commuters may yield substantial *scope economies*, implying that the total net benefits from *joint* implementation of the two projects substantially exceeds each project's net benefits when considered separately.

However, we should not overlook the computational difficulty of determining potential substitutability or complementarity within a set of N projects. First, the degree of substitutability or complementarity may vary with the size of the projects. Infrequent ferryboat and bus services may yield mild complementarities whereas high-frequency services may yield significant net benefits. Second, when N is large, the number of tests that need to be performed on all possible subsets of N can be exceedingly large and cumbersome. Third, transportation, being a network-type industry, produces multiple effects relative to travel conditions, network layout, mode choice, environmental impacts, and other externalities. Hence, the computation of potential technical interdependence may be quite difficult and open to inaccuracies.

A common pitfall in project evaluation is the independent appraisal of one of two interdependent projects while assuming the other project as given. Suppose a port expansion project is appraised under the assumption of sufficient rail capacity for hauling freight, or that an investment in a new rail line assumes ample available terminal space and warehousing capacity. When appraised independently, each may be appear to be profitable. However, joint appraisal of the investment in port *and* rail capacity might yield a low NPV, especially if large-scale diseconomies are associated with the joint investment. One approach to overcoming these contingencies is the introduction of a risk factor into the assessment of each individual investment in order to account for the likelihood that the other project may not be built as assumed. Chapter 9 deals with these risk issues in greater depth.

7.2 Project Dependence under Budgetary (Financial) Constraints

One problem distinguishing the ranking of projects under budgetary constraints is the possibility that the projects exhibiting the highest NPV may yield inferior welfare contributions. That is, if a budgetary constraint is binding, not all projects having a positive NPV can be funded. In that case, one subset of these projects may confer higher total net benefits than will another subset, constructed of projects with the highest NPV. Consider the hypothetical data on four projects, presented in Table 6.3.

Suppose that the budgetary constraint is 100. Under the NPV criterion, project A is selected. However, we can also maximize net welfare gains by selecting projects B, C, and D, whose total capital investment is likewise 100. By doing so we generate a total NPV of 23 (10 + 8 + 5), which exceeds project A's NPV (20). If, however, all these projects are mutually exclusive so that only one can be implemented, project A, with the highest NPV, should be selected.

From an economic perspective, this phenomenon is explained by the fact that under budgetary constraints, the rate used to discount the set of projects is too low, as it does not reflect the true opportunity costs of the limited resources available. The proper approach should be to first compute the discount rate that equates the *combined* funding requirements of all the projects whose NPV > 0 with the available budget. After arriving at this rate, projects should be ranked on the basis of the NPV criterion.[27] In such instances, a simulation-search model can be used in which the discount rate is raised systematically for all projects until equilibrium conditions are met.[28] Obviously, the NPV of each project changes with the different discount rates, as do the projects, subsets.[29] As noted, most countries dictate the discount rate for public projects, a practice that precludes investigations like those described here. For this reason, as we have explained, suboptimal sets of projects are often selected by these same governments.

Table 6.3 Ranking Projects under Budgetary Constraints

Project	PVB[a]	PVC[b]	NPV	ROR[c]	B/C[d]	Rank by ROR or B/C
A	120	100	20	0.2	1.20	3
B	70	60	10	0.16	1.16	4
C	38	30	8	0.26	1.26	2
D	15	10	5	0.5	1.50	1

Notes: [a]PVB = Present Value of Benefits; [b]PVC = Present Value of Capital Costs; [c]ROR=NPV/PVC; [d]B/C = PVB/PVC.

Table 6.4 Costs and Benefits Compared to Baseline Year, 2020

	Bush Administration's "Clear Skies" Plan	Sen. Carper's Plan	Sen. Jeffords's Plan
PV of costs to industry (billions)	$6.2	$9.3	$34.0
PV of health benefits (billions)	$113.8	$130.4	$175.5
NPV	$107.6	$121.1	$141.5
Benefits per dollar invested (B/C)	$18.35	$14.02	$5.16
Annual reduction in deaths	14,000	16,000	22,000

Source: Abt Associates for Clear the Air (2004).

To further illustrate the problematics that budgetary constraints introduce into project selection, consider a study on the cost of reducing emissions from coal-fired power plants in the US (Abt Associates, 2004). The key pollutants are sulfur dioxide, nitrogen oxide, mercury, and carbon dioxide. It has been estimated that almost 24,000 people die prematurely each year as a result of power plant emissions, largely in Pennsylvania, Ohio, and Florida. Three proposals to curtail emissions and thus reduce death and other related health problems were put before the US Senate. The first, by the Bush Administration, addressed the first three pollutants but not the fourth (carbon dioxide), whereas the other two proposals addressed all four types. Table 6.4 summarizes the key forecasted outcomes for the year 2020, the first year when all emission curtailment plans would be fully implemented.

In the absence of a budgetary constraint, the proposal by Senator Jeffords has the highest NPV and thus should be ranked as the top alternative. However, once a budgetary constraint is introduced, the picture may change, depending on the size of the constraint. The "per dollar invested" rule might provide a more appropriate selection criterion in such circumstances, which would conclude in a clear preference for the administration's plan

8. COBA WITH MARKET IMPERFECTIONS

In Chapter 3, I examined the issue of measuring welfare changes from transportation improvements under market imperfections. To briefly review, many transportation markets are subject to various types of market distortions due to regulation, monopoly, unpriced externalities, and lumpy investments, among other factors. As a result, the welfare changes measured from a transportation improvement that would lower only the marginal costs of service provision tend to distort the true value of the project's welfare contribution. How does this observation impact on COBA?

COBA, which is based on the calculation of changes in consumer and producer surpluses resulting from a project, generally produces incorrect estimations of the project's total benefits when the market for the project's output is imperfect. The same applies to assessments of net gains from transportation investments if the markets that use transportation as an input are also imperfect. Furthermore, whenever COBA calculations require analysis of a second-best option—which is commonly the case—the process will misestimate the option's true social benefits when compared with a competitive market case. The exact level of estimation bias will depend on various elasticities, including the elasticity of firm output with respect to transportation inputs, travel demand elasticity, and degree of market imperfection.

If these elasticities are unknown—as seems to be the case with respect to most real-world transportation investment cases—extensive simulations may be the only feasible way to obtain estimates of the true range of benefits to be reaped from a project. Venables and Gasiorek (1999) have carried out a large number of COBA simulations to ascertain the welfare gains emerging from a reduction in a regional monopolist's transportation costs. Their results show underestimation of total benefits in the range of 10%–40%, depending on the level of cost reduction as well as the demand and supply elasticities. As pointed out by Lakshmanan and Anderson (2002), these results imply that underestimation of benefits under imperfect competition might be the rule. Moreover, in order to capture the full benefits stream we would need to calculate a variety of parameters that are normally beyond the scope of most COBA studies.

9. SUMMARY AND CONCLUSIONS

This chapter examined the most common methods used to appraise a transportation project's welfare contribution as well as to rank and prioritize alternative investments. More particularly, it focused on three subjects: the analytical underpinnings and formulation of these COBA methods; the proper rate for discounting future benefit and cost flows; and the problems arising from technical and financial interdependence between projects.

The principal conclusion derived in this chapter is that despite its shortcomings, the Net Present Value (NPV) method—or its derivative, the Benefit-Cost Ratio (BCR)—is the preferred method for correctly assessing the economic contribution to be gained from a transportation project. However, when considering technical interrelationships between projects, simple application of the NPV method is likely to produce incorrect results with respect to project selection. Under financial constraints, NPV use requires care inasmuch as a subset of projects, each with lower NPV than that of the "best" project, may yield a higher welfare contribution.

In theory, the discount rate's value should reflect the opportunity costs associated with using a given project's resources. However, for various technical and economic reasons, calculation of this rate is quite complex. Transportation analysts must therefore take on the responsibility of ascertaining how well the rate used approximates the market's true opportunity costs. For projects with life spans of 25–30 years or more, the yield on long-term government bonds can serve as the lower bounds of the correct discount rate at least until some more accurate measure is constructed. In practice, though, a state ministry or agency dictates the rate used to discount future streams of benefits and costs in most countries.

APPENDIX A: COMPUTATION OF THE COST OF CAPITAL FOR AIRPORTS—THE UK CASE

The objective of this example, based on a report by the Civil Aeronautics Administration (CAA) (2001), is to demonstrate how capital costs, used as the discount rate, can be computed using a method called Weighted Averages Capital Cost (WACC). The variables used by the WACC technique are:

1. Return on risk-free assets: This variable is based on the yield on long-term CAA government bonds, the current rate being 3.0%.
2. Equity risk premium: The risk premium is the price paid to investors for bearing risk. It is computed as the *ex post* difference between yields on risk-free and risky assets. Based on several estimations, CAA used rates of 3.5% to 4.5%.
3. Airport company *beta*: *Beta* is a factor that measures the nondiversifiable risk of investment. Based on estimated *beta* values for industries associated with the airport industry, the CAA adopted a *beta* range of 0.7–0.9.
4. Debt premium: Financial markets demand a premium on corporate debt over risk-free assets to allow for the greater risk of default on debt. The CAA used rates of 1.5%–2.0%.
5. Gearing and treatment of tax: The tax paid on investment yields is part of capital cost. The effective tax rate depends on the firm's capital structure (the mix of debt and equity). Gearing is 0.2 and the corporate tax rate used is 0.3.

Based on these criteria, the computation results are shown in Table A6.1:

Table A6.1 Components and Results of
Cost-of-Capital Computations

	Low	High
Assets Beta	0.6	0.7
Gearing	0.2	0.3
Risk-free rate	2.75%	3.25%
Equity risk premium	3.5%	4.5%
Equity beta	0.7	0.9
Posttax cost of equity	5.2%	7.3%
Debt premium	0.3%	0.8%
Cost of debt	3.05%	4.05%
Corporate tax	30%	30%
Posttax WACC	4.28%	6.65%

Source: CAA (2001).

From this table, the cost of capital is estimated in the range of 4.28%–6.65%. The formula used to calculate the results is:

$$WACC = g(r_f + \rho)(1 - t) + (1 - g)(r_f + (ERP) \cdot \beta)$$

Where: g = gearing; r_f= risk-free rate; ρ = debt premium; t = corporate tax rate; ERP = equity risk premium; β = *beta*.

APPENDIX B: DERIVATION DISCOUNT RATE, WHICH EQUALS THE RATE OF TIME PREFERENCE

What should the discount rate be if society wishes to achieve a certain inter-generational social benefits and costs distribution? Let the utility function U be defined over the amount of consumption in two time periods, x_1 and x_2. The utility is maximized subject to a budget constraint Y, defined as:

$$Y = x_1 + \frac{x_2}{1+r},$$

where r is the market interest rate. The maximization problem is thus:

Max. $U(x_1, x_2)$

s.t.

$$Y = x_1 + \frac{x_2}{1+r} \tag{B1}$$

Forming the Lagrangian:

$$Z = U(x_1, x_2) + \lambda(Y - (x_1 + \frac{x_2}{1+r})) \tag{B2}$$

where λ is the Lagrangian multiplier. First-order conditions are:

$$\frac{\partial U}{\partial x_1} - \lambda = 0 \tag{B3}$$

$$\frac{\partial U}{\partial x_2} - \frac{\lambda}{1+r} = 0 \tag{B4}$$

The marginal rate of substitution between the two periods is defined as:

$$\frac{\partial U}{\partial x_1} / \frac{\partial U}{\partial x_2} \equiv (1 + \delta) \tag{B5}$$

where δ is the marginal rate of time preferences. Since:

$$\frac{\partial U}{\partial x_1} / \frac{\partial U}{\partial x_2} \equiv (1 + r)$$

expression (B5) implies that at the optimum, the market interest rate r should equal the marginal rate of time preferences δ.

APPENDIX C: TRANSPORTATION EVALUATION METHODS AND DISCOUNT RATES USED IN VARIOUS COUNTRIES

Table C6.1 Evaluation Methods and Discount Rates in Various Countries (1995)

Country	Evaluation Method	Evaluation Period (Years)	Discount Rate	Residual Value of Capital Calculated
Belgium	Multicriteria Analysis (MCA), NPV	Project's lifetime[a]	4%	No
Denmark[b]	1st Year Rate of Return	30	6%	N/A
Finland	Benefit-Cost Ratio	30	6%	Yes
France	1st Year Rate of Return	N/A	8%	N/A
Germany	Benefit-Cost Ratio	30	3%	No
Ireland	Benefit-Cost Ratio	30	Various[c]	N/A
Israel	NPV	15	7%	Yes
Italy	Benefit-Cost Ratio	N/A	N/A	N/A
Netherlands	MCA, NPV	30	4% (1998)[d]	No
Norway	Benefit Cost Ratio	25	7%	Yes
Portugal	NPV	20	8%	No
Spain	Benefit-Cost Ratio	30	6%	No
Sweden	Benefit-Cost Ratio	40	4%	No
United Kingdom	Benefit-Cost Ratio	30	8%	No
Australia	Benefit-Cost Ratio	30	7% (1996)[e]	No
Canada	NPV	30	10%	No
New Zealand	Benefit-Cost Ratio	25	10%	Yes
South Africa	Benefit-Cost Ratio	30	15%	No
United States	Benefit-Cost Ratio	40	7% (1992)[f]	Yes

Source: EURET/385/94, 1994, Report commissioned by the European Commission DG VII.
Notes: [a]The project's benefits are estimated for 30 years and assumed constant thereafter. Benefits and costs are discounted over an infinite lifetime; [b]Future discounted maintenance costs are added to the project's total first-year costs; [c]Various trial discount rates are used as a form of sensitivity analysis; [d]This is the official rate of return for risk-free projects; for risky projects, a higher discount rate is applied. This rate is based on the long-run net interest rate of government bonds; [e]Austroads, 1996; [f]U.S. Office of Management and Budget (OMB), 1992.

7 Traffic Flow, Congestion, and Infrastructure Investment

The real solution is not reducing traffic to fit capacity.
We must expand capacity to handle the growing traffic.

—DOT Secretary Norman Mineta, Feb. 28, 2006

1. INTRODUCTION

Traffic congestion is a widely accepted indicator of the Level of Service (LOS) provided by an existing transportation system. Congestion consequently provides the rationale for new infrastructure investments. That being said, every transportation analysis should nonetheless involve an examination of congestion's transportation-economic underpinnings, its dimensions and significance for the measurement of benefits from a particular infrastructure investment.

From an economic perspective, the production of transportation services—trips—requires consumers (trip makers) to provide a major input, namely, their time: The accumulated access and egress, wait, transfer, and in-vehicle time they spend traveling each day. Because the amount of time spent is a function of the rate of consumption per unit of output, LOS will decline (i.e., congestion will intensify) when consumption rises above a certain threshold and will keep declining at an increasing rate with each added level of consumption. In technical terms, congestion develops whenever traffic flow per unit of time approaches capacity, a level creating additional time delays, vehicle costs, as well as nontangible costs such as passengers or drivers' stress. While congestion will transpire even in the presence of congestion pricing, its magnitude will, of course, be affected by that price.

Key features of congestion are, therefore, its temporal and spatial distributions. Given road and transit networks' configuration in place, travel flow on some facilities will exceed capacity at specific hours, resulting in delays. A related major feature is congestion's sensitivity to small fluctuations in traffic flow. To illustrate, consider the Bureau of Public Road (BPR) volume-capacity function for a highway segment[1]:

Congested Speed = (Free-Flow Speed)/(1 + 0.15[Volume/Capacity]^4)

where free-flow speed refers to congestion-free maximum speed. This function indicates that speed-flow relationships are nonlinear, meaning that travel speed will be reduced more than proportionally for a given increase in traffic volume (see Figure 7.3).

From an analytical viewpoint, a plausible question requiring an answer is whether traffic congestion is a cause or symptom of deteriorating LOS. On the one hand, it can be argued that congestion is mainly a symptom of the concentration of trips in time and space, a phenomenon that reflects land-use patterns and densities, in turn, as well as travel behavior. As such, congestion can be interpreted as an indication of economic activity, whose magnitude is a direct function of a region's economic vitality. On the other hand, it is also true that congestion in specific key locations can affect location and travel decisions. Fundamentally, however, congestion is the outcome of aggregate decisions made by households and firms, given the region's geography and transportation network structure.

Public decision makers, however, tend to regard congestion as the sole major cause of declining LOS, manifested in excessive travel costs, lost productivity, and environmental nuisances. Considering the dual nature of congestion as both a cause and effect of transportation-related conditions, and given the tendency to make transportation capacity-increasing investments primarily in response to observed levels of congestion at specific locations, we need to ask whether such investments indeed reduce congestion or merely shift it elsewhere or to other time periods. If the answer to our question is positive, measurement of the direct benefits from capacity investments in terms of reduced congestion *at specific locations* may in fact produce biased results as it ignores congestion's spatial and temporal shifts.

We accept the notion that congestion is fundamentally a symptom and not a cause although, left untreated, it can engender resource misallocation. Congestion can thus be seen as an externality that, if not internalized through corrective taxes (congestion tolls), induces excess travel and over-investment in capacity.[2] As long as reduction of congestion remains a policy goal, an understanding of its attributes, however measured, the associated user and social costs as well as its development under various road conditions is mandatory. The objective in this chapter is, therefore, to contribute to our understanding of these issues.

Section 2 examines sources of congestion and its key spatial and temporal attributes. Section 3 looks into various user and social costs of congestion. The analytical structure of the travel supply functions that underlie measurement of congestion is discussed in Section 4. Various ways to model and measure congestion are discussed in Section 5. Section 6 examines travel time and flow reliability, both of which are known to affect travel behavior and patterns. Key conclusions are found in Section 7.

2. ATTRIBUTES OF CONGESTION

2.1 Sources of Congestion

The US Federal Highway Administration (FHWA) provides the following statistics on the sources of congestion[3]:

Figure 7.1 shows that only 40% of congestion results from "ordinary" bottlenecks. Unexpected incidences such as stalled trucks or buses in a major intersection, oil spills, or automobile accidents are responsible for another 25% of all traffic delays. Other causes of traffic congestion are blocked work zones, bad weather, and special sport events. These events are predictable to some extent and can be taken into account by motorists when making their travel decisions, including their time of departure.

2.2 Temporal, Spatial, and Modal Attributes of Congestion

Traffic congestion, then, has strong temporal, spatial, and modal attributes. It concentrates within well-defined times, commonly referred to as "peak period" or "peak hour," it transpires on some facilities more than on others, and it is subject to modal capacity and availability.

We begin with the temporal aspect. Is it correct to say that congestion, as we commonly hear, is worsening over time? Using US highway-based data, collected from selected highway segments, it was shown that travel

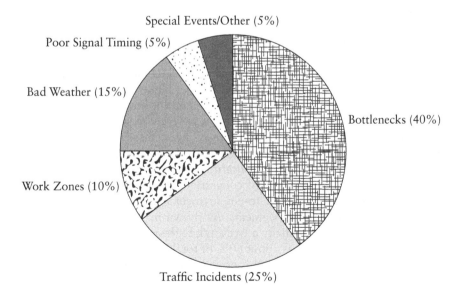

Figure 7.1 Sources of congestion, national summary (US).

Source: FHWA (http://www.ops.fhwa.dot.gov/aboutus/opstory.htm).

times have indeed consistently increased over time (Urban Mobility Report, 2001). Whereas average congestion travel time in cities with populations over 3 million was 20% above free-flow conditions in 1982, it reached 50% more in 2002. Similarly, while average weekday peak-period trips took about 13% longer than the same trip in the middle of the day in 1982, those trips were 40% longer in 2002. Furthermore, in 1982, 34% of major highway systems were congested during peak hours; in 2002, the corresponding figure was 59%. In general, total daily trip times have kept growing, in many metropolitan areas by over 3% per annum; travel during the midday period (9:30 a.m. to 3:30 p.m.) has also grown significantly and can now account for more than one-third of all daily trips. In addition, these temporal trip patterns have become more dispersed across the region, mainly outside the urban core.

All of this may indicate more congestion and longer hours spent traveling. However, if congestion is measured as door-to-door or entire trip travel time, the congestion picture is not that unequivocal. US National Household Travel Survey (*NHTS*, 2001) data, collected periodically since 1969, suggest that commute travel times have not increased nearly as fast as the highway data cited indicate (Schrank and Lomax, 2002). From 1980 to 1990, the US added 18 million workers, with mean travel time to work growing by 40 seconds to 22.4 minutes. From 1990 to 2000, 13 million workers were added and mean travel time to work grew by about 3 minutes to 25.5 minutes.

One major explanation for this increase in travel time is the spatial dispersion of both residential and employment locations that, taken together, have significantly slowed down the increase in mean travel times (Gordon et al., 2004). These trends do not, of course, negate the marked increase in congestion on specific segments of the highway network. They do, however, indicate that on the average, commuters have greater choice between routes and destinations, factors enabling them to offset highway congestion.

How does congestion distribute over the relevant hours of the day? The data shown in Figure 7.2, as collected from the New Jersey Turnpike, highlight this issue. While this turnpike is quite congested for most hours of the day, the figure demonstrates a typical picture of morning and afternoon peak periods with midday and late afternoon off-peak periods.

Turning to the spatial aspect of congestion, Taylor (2002) provides an example of how a typical home-to-employment daily commute is actually distributed over various trip segments. As shown in Table 7.1, travel time over a congested facility (usually a freeway), represents about 40% of total travel time, while its length is about 60% of total travel distance. Moreover, the speed on the congested facility is often higher than speeds on other segments of the trip.

As to the modal aspect of congestion, Table 7.2 provides aggregate US data on average travel distance, travel time, and speed by car and by transit for various years.

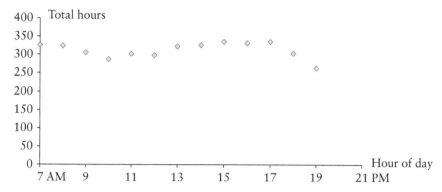

Figure 7.2 Total hours of travel time in New Jersey Turnpike over 12 consecutive hours.

Source: Ozbay et al., (2001).

In itself, the "all modes" category shown in Table 7.2 conveys little information because we are not told of the relative weight of each mode and how it has changed over time. For comparative purposes, however, these data show that while average travel time for all modes went up between 1983 and 2001 by about 28.7%, average car travel time increased by about 30% while average transit travel time increased by 65.2%. Congestion evidently affects transit more than it does cars. To the degree that these data represent

Table 7.1 A Sample of a Drive-Alone Commute Trip

Trip Segment	Distance (miles)	Time (minutes)	Speed (mph)
Walk to car	0.01	0.2	3
Drive to collector	0.25	1.3	12
Drive to arterial	0.50	1.9	16
Drive to freeway	2.00	6.0	20
Drive on congested freeway	6.00	14.4	25
Drive in arterial	1.50	4.5	20
Drive on parking structure	0.25	1.9	8
Walk to office	0.10	6.0	1
Total/Average	10.61	36.1	18

Source: Taylor (2002).

Table 7.2 Average Commute Length, Time, and Speed, US 1983–2001, MSA Data

	All modes[a]				Privately Operated Vehicles (POV)				Transit[b]			
	1983	1990	1995	2001	1983	1990	1995	2001	1983	1990	1995	2001
Length (miles)	8.6	10.6	11.7	11.9	8.8	10.9	11.9	11.8	11.8	13.2	12.9	12.4
Time (minutes)	18.8	20.2	21.5	24.2	17.9	19.5	20.8	22.9	33.9	41.3	42.1	56.0
Speed (mph)	27.2	32.3	33.7	31.1	29.3	33.6	34.2	31.0	17.8	17.9	19.2	19.4

Notes: [a]"All modes" includes all other transportation modes, such as airplane, taxi, school bus, bicycle, and walking in addition to HOV and transit; [b]Transit includes bus, Amtrak, commuter train, streetcar/trolley, and elevated rail/subway.
Source: Gordon et al. (2004, Table 2.1), based on the authors' calculations.

equilibrium conditions, transportation improvements are expected to bring about a new market equilibrium in terms of travel times and speeds, modal use, specific facilities used, and trip timing, what Downs (2004) calls the "principal of the triple convergence." We return to this issue in Chapter 8, where we examine the measurement of benefits from improvements with induced demand.

3. COSTS OF CONGESTION

When speaking of the *costs of congestion* that provide the rationale for transportation infrastructure investment, we generally distinguish between costs borne directly by the trip maker and costs borne by other motorists, also called *average private users costs* and *marginal social costs*, respectively. Both types appear as delay and auto-use costs, above the costs associated with free-flow conditions. In public transit, these costs express themselves mainly in the form of excess wait time, in-vehicle time, and overcrowding. Figure 7.3 demonstrates the relationships between the private users cost curve (labeled as AC_1 and AC_2) and the social costs curve (labeled FMC_1 and FMC_2, respectively). The figure shows that for given traffic volume (e.g., Q^0), the vertical difference between these curves represents the *congestion externality* costs. In the absence of congestion pricing, this externality is not internalized, resulting in excess travel.

In a study conducted by the Dutch Ministry of Transport, researchers estimated that marginal congestion costs per kilometer fall between €0.2 and €2 for private cars. Myers et al. (1996) and De Borger and Proost (1997), using Belgian data, estimated marginal costs for urban travel, which they found to be in the range of €1.0 to €1.5 per kilometer for private cars and €2.95 for buses. For interregional travel, the respective figures were €0.83 per kilometer for private cars and €1.66 for trucks.

As the European studies indicate, congestion is not confined to city centers. A large proportion of congestion occurs at bridge crossings, tunnels, and major intersections. Dutch data show that for major cities about 90% of daily congestion takes place at a location 25 kilometers away from city center.

Another issue needing clarification is the percentage of daily commuters actually affected by congestion. In the Netherlands, this figure equals about 5%, a rather small proportion of the total commuting population. The majority of commuters live or work in uncongested areas, use rail transit systems, or travel at off-peak hours. But those who are subject to congestion experience very high costs, estimated at about €800 million per year in the Netherlands alone.

Based on BPR-type speed-flow relationships, Levinson (1995) estimated that marginal peak-period congestion costs for urban highways average $.06–$.09 when travel speed is 50 miles/hour, and increase to $.37 when

Full Cost
($/trip)

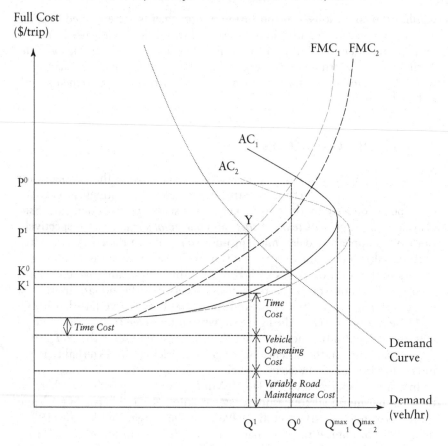

Figure 7.3 Private average costs and full marginal social costs functions.

speed drops to 40 miles/hour. Ozbay et al. (2001) calculated the marginal cost categories for an average trip distance of 9–15 miles, using New Jersey Highway data (see Table 12.4, chapter 12).

The figures in Table 12.4 indicate that users' private costs exceed by far all other cost items and that private costs are larger than congestion externality costs by a factor of 6. Estimates of marginal congestion costs (private and social) by vehicle type, for rural and urban highways, are shown in Table 7.3.

As can be expected, marginal congestion costs vary significantly by vehicle type and area (highway category). This is mainly due to differences in road alignment and capacity, driving conditions, and traffic composition. Note that the estimate of total congestion costs per mile obtained by Ozbay et al. (2001)—$0.44 ($3.78 + $0.63)/10)—comes very close to the median cost for all highways and all vehicles: $.047.

Table 7.3 Marginal Highway Congestion Costs (Cents per Vehicle-Mile)

	Rural Highways			Urban Highways			All Highways		
	High	Med.	Low	High	Med.	Low	High	Med.	Low
Auto	3.76	1.28	0.34	18.27	6.21	1.64	13.17	4.48	1.19
Pickup and van	3.80	1.29	0.34	17.78	6.04	1.60	11.75	4.00	1.06
Buses	6.96	2.37	0.63	37.59	12.78	3.38	24.79	8.43	2.23
Single unit truck	7.43	2.53	0.67	42.65	14.50	3.84	26.81	9.11	2.41
Combination truck	10.87	3.70	0.98	49.34	16.78	4.44	25.81	8.78	2.32
All vehicles	4.40	1.50	0.40	19.72	6.71	1.78	13.81	4.70	1.24

Source: USDOT, FHWA (1997).

The Texas Transportation Institute (TTI) uses a congestion index to calculate the congestion costs for major US cities (Schrank and Lomax, 2001). In 1999, their estimated congestion costs for 68 major metropolitan areas amounted to a total of $78 billion. Litman (2004b) translated this figure (after taking into account congestion not covered by the TTI report) to 20¢ per urban-peak vehicle-mile.

Estimates for Australia's major cities show that whereas marginal congestion costs on freeways equal about 14¢ (Australian) per kilometer, they are about 2.8–4.7 times higher on the country's Central Business District streets (BTCE, 1996, Table 5.1). British data indicate that while the marginal external costs of congestion on motorways averaged 26 pence per vehicle-kilometer in 1990, they reached 36.37 pence at peak time and 29.23 at off-peak time in central urban areas (Maddison et al., 1996, Tables 5.5–11).

Finally, an interesting question is how congestion grows with the increase in Vehicle Miles Traveled (VMT), which is strongly influenced by urban sprawl. Using US data, Zupan (2001) reports that whereas a 1% rise in VMT was associated with a 3.5% increase in congestion in the 1980s, this connection disappeared in the 1990s. Based on 2000 census data and the 2001 National Household Travel Survey, Gordon et al. (2004) portray a much more complicated picture. Their analysis shows that nationwide average commute time (for all modes) rose to 25.5 minutes in 2000 from 22.4 minutes in 1990, a 14.1% increase. Moreover, data on distributions show a decrease in the proportion of workers having short commutes (less than 20 minutes) together with an increase in the proportions of workers having long commutes. In general, however, 59.7% of all commutes in 2000 fell within the range of 5 to 24 minutes actual travel time (not including walking to and from the transportation site).

4. THE STRUCTURE OF TRAVEL SUPPLY FUNCTIONS

The term *Private Average Costs* (AC) indicates the monetary value of what an individual trip maker considers the average time she expects it will take her to reach her destination given the current level of traffic on her chosen transportation facility. The concept *Marginal Social Costs*, on the other hand, indicates the monetary value of additional costs to society of an additional trip, taking into account the congestion externalities produced by this trip. If, in addition to the congestion externality, we also consider other social costs, such as pollution, we apply the term *Full Marginal Costs* (FMC) to the additional travel (see Chapter 12 for a discussion of FMC). Figure 7.3 graphically illustrates the theoretical relationships between AC and FMC (see Varaiya, 2005, for empirically derived relationships).

It is evident from Figure 7.3 that at low levels of traffic, AC = FMC and that the gap between the two functions increases exponentially with intensifying traffic. The shape of the AC function further reflects the phenomenon known as *backward bending* (at Q^{max}), indicating that costs grow when traffic flow decreases below a binding capacity constraint. Figure 7.3 shows that social equilibrium should have been at point Y, where the demand curve intersects FMC_1 with travel flow Q^1; however, for lack of congestion pricing, equilibrium occurs at point Q^0, where demand intersects the AC_1 curve. We next examine some key properties of travel supply functions.

4.1 Properties of Travel Supply Functions

According to convention, travel supply functions are equated with Volume-Capacity (VC) functions, which are defined as upward sloping, continuous exponential functions (see AC_1 in Figure 7.3). Here we define capacity as the maximum travel flow on a certain facility at a given Level of Service (LOS). That is, at a given time of day, capacity is the maximum number of vehicles that can traverse a unit of distance at a minimum speed and at a given headway level. A typical VC function is the BPR mentioned above, even though these functions have changed considerably during the last couple of decades.[4] Regardless of their specific empirical structure, however, volume-capacity functions have a finite capacity, which by definition implies that volume-capacity ratios cannot exceed 1, that is, $((V/\overline{C}) \leq 1)$, where V denotes traffic volume and $\overline{C}$ denotes maximum capacity. Thus,

$$S(V) = \begin{cases} S(V) & \text{for } 0 \leq V \leq \overline{C} \\ \overline{C} & \text{otherwise} \end{cases} \tag{1}$$

where $S(V)$ is the flow (supply) function (or the AC function in Figure 7.3). When traffic flow exceeds $\overline{C}$, congestion or delay time will grow exponentially, with a possible decline in flow (the backward-banding phenomenon),

Travel Costs

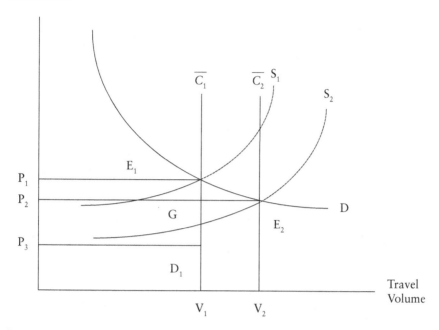

Figure 7.4 Capacity constrained continuous travel supply functions.

as shown in Figure 7.3 at the low point of Q^{max}. Figure 7.4 shows a simplified version of this phenomenon, where the supply function is undefined beyond the range $(V/\overline{C}) \leq 1$.

The representation of transportation supply functions as volume-capacity functions with finite capacity introduces a major difficulty into the estimation of benefits from capacity improvements because the impact of an increase in demand has no direct economic interpretation. Moreover, if we further introduce the case of fixed demand (see Chapter 8), welfare improvements from capacity expansion cannot be estimated. We thus need to reinterpret the transportation supply function in order to account for the observed increase in travel time as a function of increased demand for the cases where V > C.

Disregarding for now the question of empirical estimation, one approach is to define travel supply functions as trip makers' marginal cost functions that reflect incremental changes in total costs of travel between an Origin-Destination (O-D) pair as travel volume increases during a given time period. From this perspective the problem of volume exceeding capacity does not arise.

A second approach is to derive the AC or MC functions from the link performance functions and let the trip assignment algorithm allocate traffic among links accordingly. That is, the static assignment procedure, commonly used in transportation planning, contains an upward-sloping link performance function in the form of a VC function, which allows $(V/C) > 1$.[5] However, since the penalty for $(V/C) > 1$ in terms of travel time will be quite large, the assignment algorithm will tend *not* to assign traffic to links exhibiting this level of traffic and will, instead, shift flow to other links, those that do exhibit $(V/C) < 1$. Thus, $(V/C) > 1$ should not be an issue for this function.[6]

Another approach is to use a bottleneck model. That is, in the presence of a traffic bottleneck, the flow behind the bottleneck (also called the demand upstream) may exceed the capacity of the specific highway segment for some time. When this happens, there will be a queue behind the bottleneck, resulting in delays for the queued vehicles. Dynamic traffic assignment models can be used to accurately describe this process and quantify the delay. Hence, while we cannot obtain data for the case where $(V/C) > 1$, adding the queue's delay time to the time spent traversing the capacitated road segment will constitute either the AC or MC functions. In this way, flow can exceed link capacity by capturing the queuing behind the bottleneck. Such a queuing model is demonstrated in Appendix A.

4.2 The Indivisible, Noncontinuous Structure of Travel Supply Functions

Another important feature of travel supply functions is their step-function shape, which stems from the fact that capacity—as a unit—is indivisible, meaning that it can be expanded only in fixed units (e.g., lane-km). From an economic perspective, the issue of capacity indivisibility implies the discontinuity of the supply function, which creates problems when determining the optimal level of infrastructure investment and the setting of optimal congestion prices. Here, however, the focus is on the traffic consequences of capacity supply lumpiness, which is depicted in Figure 7.5.

After comparing Figures 7.4 and 7.5, it should be obvious that the equilibrium solutions E_1 and E_2 imply different amounts of welfare improvement from capacity expansion $(\overline{C}_1 \rightarrow \overline{C}_2)$. Moreover, unlike the situation captured in the continuous supply function, any shift in total demand over a wide range of supply—for example, between 0 and V_1 along S_1—will not yield higher travel costs, the situation depicted in Figure 7.5.

While for individual links capacity expansion indeed is carried out in indivisible quantities, for the entire network capacity is expanded only at the margin; hence, continuous upward sloping supply functions can be used to characterize travel conditions. We adhere to this argument and concentrate on issues of measuring welfare changes at the network level from capacity expansion while assuming continuous supply functions as in Figure 3. Still, for the purpose of analyzing welfare changes from capacity investment in specific facilities—such as fixed rail—discontinuous supply functions should be used (see Oum and Zhang, 1990, for an extended analysis).

Travel Costs

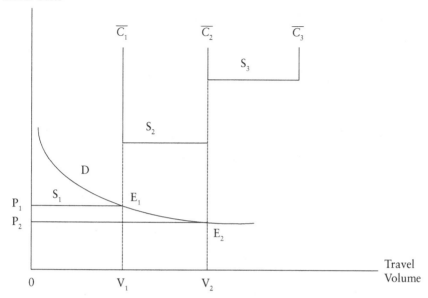

Figure 7.5 Travel supply function with lumpy capacity expansion.

5. MEASURING CONGESTION

Several indicators have been developed to measure congestion. These are:

a) *Traffic engineering LOS:* This measure defines several categories of LOS, by road type, as a function of speed, flow, and density. For example, LOS "A" implies speed over 60 miles/hour with a flow range of less than 700 vehicles per hour per lane, with road density of less than 12 vehicles per mile. The corresponding figures for LOS "F", the lowest level, are less than 30 miles/hour, over 2,000 vehicles per hour per lane and a maximum of 67 vehicles per mile (Homburger et al., 1992).

b) *Length of peak:* This measure refers to the length of the peak period during which congestion conditions exist. Thus, if we define congestion as the case when $V \approx C$, then the length of the period during which these conditions exist becomes a measure of congestion.

c) *Travel Rate Index (TRI):* TRI is defined as the ratio of peak period to free-flow travel times. Hence, a TRI of 1.5 indicates that an off-peak trip that takes 30 minutes would last 45 minutes during peak time. TRI provides the basis for calculating longitudinal changes in congestion or the total number of annual hours of delay caused by congestion.[7]

5.1 A Model of Travel Flow with Congestion

As previously noted, a key problem in assessing benefits from transportation improvements rests in the fact that the MC function equates with a volume-capacity function, which cannot be defined for the range: $(V/C) > 1$. Above, we mentioned the bottleneck model for deriving travel time functions in terms of queue formation and delays behind the bottleneck (Mun, 1994). Figure 7.6 illustrates the idea behind this model.

In Figure 7.6, $Q(t)$ is incoming traffic at time t, and C_b is the congested facility's capacity. The figure shows that if $Q_1(t) < C_b$, then incoming traffic volume will be equal to outgoing traffic volume, $Q_2(t)$. Otherwise, incoming traffic will accumulate at the bottleneck and form a queue. Within the queue, vehicles move at a speed equal to the speed of outgoing traffic. As soon as $Q_1(t)$ exceeds C_b, the queue propagates upstream, further reducing the speed. Appendix A presents the model's details.

To illustrate the derivation of the travel cost functions from this model, consider the following hypothetical numerical example (Ozbay et al., 2001). Suppose, as in Figure 7.6, the following values: $C_a = 2490$ vehicle/hour; $C_b = 2000$ vehicles/hour; road length, $L = 10$ miles; value of time, $v = \$10/$ hour; peak period = 30 minutes. Following the model in Appendix A, we can obtain total and marginal cost values for $Q(t)$. The speed function for the calculations chosen is as follows:

$$V_1 = \left(\frac{C_a - Q}{0.523}\right)^{1/2} + 35.34 \quad \text{speed in normal flow,}$$

$$V_2 = -\left(\frac{C_a - Q}{0.523}\right)^{1/2} + 35.34 \quad \text{speed in congested flow.}$$

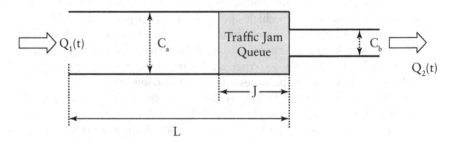

Figure 7.6 Structure of a bottleneck.

Source: Mun, (1994).

Using equation (A3) and (A4) in Appendix A, we can calculate total and marginal costs,

$$\frac{\partial V_1}{\partial Q} = -0.956\left(\frac{C_a - Q}{0.523}\right)^{-1/2}$$

Figure 7.7 depicts the curve $v \cdot Q \cdot \frac{dT}{dQ} - Q$, which is the time lost in the queue only.

For purposes of comparison, Figure 7.8 shows a plot of the cost functions used by Small (1992a) and by Mun (1994) for the same values of $Q(t)$. While Mun calculates the time spent both in the queue and on the rest of the trip, Small considers only the time lost due to congestion.

It is evident that Small's congestion costs underestimate the actual costs to users from the time they spend in the queue *together with* the time lost in the congested facility. Thus, even though volume on a facility cannot exceed its capacity ($V \leq C$), the very formation of the queue exerts additional travel time costs on users that, in turn, allow the use of continuous and increasing supply functions such as FMC_1 (see Figure 7.3). This last conclusion is

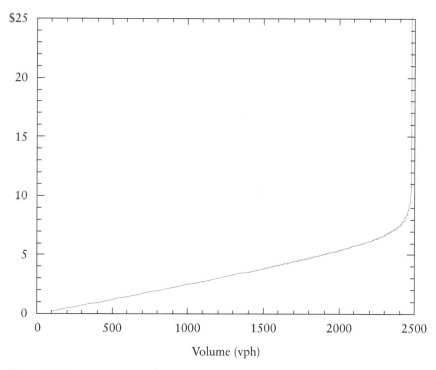

Figure 7.7 Congestion costs from a queue.

Cost imposed on the other users by an additional car

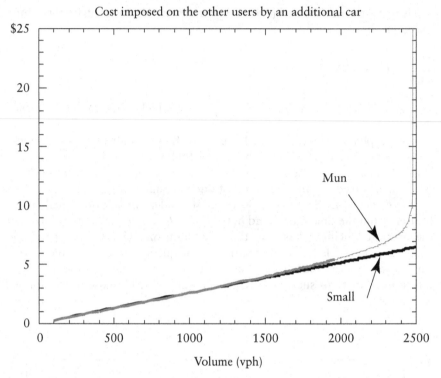

Figure 7.8 Comparison of two congestion models.

Sources: Mun (1994); Small, (1992).

of utmost importance for the calculation of welfare benefits from capacity investment projects.

6. TRAFFIC FLOW RELIABILITY

A key element of traffic flow, having major consequences for congestion analysis, is traffic flow reliability. There is a vast literature on public transit and highway travel reliability that focuses primarily on the mean-variance of travel times (see Noland and Polak, 2002, for a review). This litera-ture is indispensable for the trip scheduling literature as it has been shown theoretically and empirically that, when faced with high travel time uncer-tainty, commuters will choose to depart earlier than they actually would prefer in order to avoid late arrivals (Small, 1992b). In general, however, the uncertainty and scheduling literatures have paid only scant attention to the questions that lie at the heart of this book, namely, how to estimate the economic value of improved reliability from capacity investments and how it should be accounted for in the cost-benefit analysis of a capacity investment.

For motorists, the traffic flow variability of repetitive day-to-day travel time, especially in peak periods, is a perceptual rather than a statistical phenomenon. That is, since travelers are uncertain about their exact time of arrival, they tend to assign higher subjective costs to unpredictable delays in traffic. Lengthy but consistent and predictable home-to-work travel time is regarded as more tolerable than shorter trips having irregular and unexpected delays. Put simply, motorists appreciate the ability to predict time of travel with certainty. Hence, if capacity expansion can indeed improve travel time certainty, it will be regarded as an important benefit even if travel time itself has not been significantly shortened. What lies behind this attitude is the assumption that more predictable travel times enable better allocation of time, thereby reducing unproductive time. For example, having to leave early in order to make an important meeting implies wasted time, which reduces productivity.[8] The key hypothesis here is, therefore, that travel time variability has a greater effect on travel behavior than does the average or typical travel time. What, then, is the economic value of improved reliability?

As indicated in Figure 7.1, bottlenecks cause up to 40% of all traffic delays. These recurring disturbances, resulting from variations in day-to-day travel demand, are the principal generators of traffic unreliability. It is important to reemphasize that our objective is *not* to compare between free flow and congestion conditions; rather, our objective is to assess the impacts of random incidents on average or expected commute times and to subsequently assess their costs to motorists.

While subjective in nature, the reliability of travel times can be measured by the statistical variation of commute travel times around their means, which are measured by the standard deviation or the coefficient of variation (the variance divided by the mean) of travel time.[9] Alternatively, this variation can be measured by the percentage of times when travel delays rise above a given threshold. Using these statistical measures the following model was obtained (Cohen and Southworth, 1999; Noland et al., 1998[10]):

$$d = \alpha \cdot t + \beta \cdot v(t) + \gamma \cdot c \qquad (2)$$

In (2), d is the expected cost of the daily commute trip, t is commute time, $v(t)$ is a measure of trip variability, c is the monetary cost of travel, and α, β, and γ are parameters. The ratio β/α measures the relative magnitude of changes in travel time variability against changes in total trip travel time, while β/γ is the monetary cost of travel time variability. For empirical purposes, $v(t)$ is usually defined as the standard deviation of travel time.

As can be expected, empirical valuations of unexpected delays range significantly, depending on location, road type, and nature of the database.

Using a Stated Preference (SP) sample of morning commuters' route choice in Los Angeles, Abdel-Aty et al. (1997) estimated a ratio of $\beta/\alpha = 0.35$ (their model, however, did not include the monetary cost of commuting, as does expression (2)). At the other end of the range, using also a SP sample of morning peak-period commuters, Small et al. (1999), using expression (2), found that a 1 minute increase in the standard deviation of travel time was valued 1.31 times more than the value of a 1 minute addition to total travel time, a value estimated at 50% of the median wage rate earned by the participants in their sample. Another study (MVA, 1992) estimated a range for β/α of 1.1–2.2. Based on a review of various studies, the value of the standard deviation of trip time was found to range from 0.3 to 1.3 of the value of travel time in uncongested conditions (Cohen and Southworth, 1999, Table 1).

Another measure used to assess reliability is the *reliability ratio* defined as the value of reliability over the value of time (Noland and Polak, 2002). Essentially it indicates how trip makers are likely to respond to changes in travel reliability relative to changes in mean travel time. Using British data, Bates et al., (2001) found that for commuters using public transit, the reliability ratio ranged from 1.04 to 1.22, depending on the underlying distributional assumptions. These results indicate that commuters value reliability more than mean travel time by a factor of 0.04 to 0.22. A more recent study has questioned the use of mean-variance to measure the value of reliability. It found that monetizing Travel Time Variability (TTV) using the mean-variance approach could lead to substantial underestimation of TTV. The study thus showed that transit users attached similar penalties to mean travel time and to early arrival but a much higher penalty for late arrival (Hollander, 2006).

7. SUMMARY AND CONCLUSIONS

Congestion is usually regarded as the prime rationale for infrastructure improvements in public and private transportation modes. This chapter examined the nature of congestion relative to its sources, spatial and temporal distribution, and mode. While increasing demand for travel is the prime cause of congestion what also became evident was that random events such as traffic accidents, stalled vehicles, or bad weather, which are not amenable to congestion relief measures such as capacity expansion, are also major causes of a significant proportion of all congestion. The chapter further highlighted the nonlinear nature of congestion with respect to travel flow, and considered its impacts on the marginal costs of congestion.

To measure the benefits flowing from the added capacity introduced to relieve congestion, it is necessary to understand the analytical structure of travel supply functions. More particularly, it was shown that the assumption that flow (V) could not exceed capacity (C), implying that travel time would not change once $V = C$, is quite problematic for the assessment of the benefits to be gained from a capacity expansion project. To circumvent this assumption, it has been shown that in a capacitated network, congestion would develop in the form of time spent in a queue and that this time would grow exponentially with travel flow. Hence, the benefits of capacity improvements are concentrated in the form of queue reduction and thus total travel time.

Another benefit from congestion reduction is the increase in travel time reliability or the reduction of travel time uncertainty. While reliability is essentially a subjective phenomenon, statistical measures such as the coefficient of variation of travel time indicate that commuters tend to value a given reduction in uncertainty significantly higher than an equivalent reduction in mean travel time. Reliability, in addition to average travel time savings, is therefore a benefit that needs to be included in benefit-cost analyses of transportation improvements.

APPENDIX A: A BOTTLENECK QUEUING MODEL

In Figure 7.6, $Q(t)$ is incoming traffic at time t, and C_b is the congested facility's capacity. The figure shows that if $Q_1(t) < C_b$, then incoming traffic volume will be equal to outgoing traffic volume, $Q_2(t)$. The speed and density of traffic will then be $V_1(Q(t))$ and $K_1(Q(t))$, respectively. Otherwise, incoming traffic will accumulate at the bottleneck and form a queue. Within the queue, vehicles move at a speed equal to the speed of outgoing traffic, which is $V_2(C_b)$. (Here, V_2 stands for the speed under hypercongested conditions.) As soon as $Q(t)$ exceeds C_b, the queue propagates upstream, at a speed of $G(t)$, where,

$$G(t) = \frac{C_b - Q(t)}{K_2(C_b) - K_1(Q(t))} \tag{A1}$$

Note: This formula is valid only when $Q(t)$ is greater than C_b and propagation speed is negative. The queue's length can also be expressed as:

$$J(t) = \int_{ta}^{t} -G(u).du \tag{A2}$$

where t_a is the time when incoming traffic begins to exceed C_b. Travel time $T(t)$ through the bottleneck is presented as

$$T(t) = \frac{J(t)}{V_2(C_b)} + \frac{L - J(t)}{V_1(Q(t))} \tag{A3}$$

where L is the length of the road. Time spent in the traffic jam is divided into two stages. The first term on the right-hand side of equation (A3) defines the time elapsed in passing through the queue whereas the second term defines the time required to pass along the remaining road segment before reaching one's destination.

The total value of time lost in congestion during the time interval $[t_a, t]$ is calculated by multiplying the time by the Value of Time (VOT) (see Chapter 4 for detailed discussion).

The costs imposed on other users by an additional vehicle are the social marginal costs (see Section 4). It is calculated by taking the derivative of the time lost by one vehicle in congestion with respect to Q (demand is assumed to be constant) and multiplying the derivative by VOT. Thus,

$$MC = Q.(VOT).\left\{ -\frac{L - J(t)}{[V_1(Q)]^2} \cdot \frac{dV_1}{dQ} + \left[\frac{-1}{V_1(Q)} + \frac{1}{V_2(C_b)} \right] \cdot \frac{dJ(t)}{dQ} \right\} \qquad (A4)$$

(A4) is a positive and increasing function of the queue length, $J(t)$, as it propagates through upstream (traffic before the bottleneck).

Small (1992) also developed a congestion function that can be used in these analyses. This model, too, is a representation of traffic flow through a bottleneck and quite similar to the model presented above, although less tenable because Small (1992) represents only the time elapsed in the queue.

If we apply the same notation used in Mun (1994), the derivation of the time function is as follows:

$$Q_2(t) = \begin{cases} Q(t) & \text{if } Q(t) \leq Q_2(t) \text{ and } J(t) = 0 \\ C_b & \text{otherwise} \end{cases} \qquad (A5)$$

The difference in the length of the queue with respect to time is given by:[11]

$$J'(t) = Q(t) - Q_2(t) \qquad (A6)$$

$$J(t_q) = \int_{t_a}^{t_q} [Q(t) - C_b] dt = 0 \qquad (A7)$$

In equation (A7) t_a is the time when upstream volume exceeds downstream capacity. Equation (A7) shows that after the downstream capacity is exceeded and a queue begins to form, its length will continue to propagate. At some point, upstream volume decreases and falls below C_b. At time t_q the total rate of difference between the two capacities approaches zero. Total waiting time when a vehicle enters the queue at time u is given as follows:

$$T(t) = \frac{N(t)}{C_b} = \int_{t_a}^{t_q} \left[\frac{Q(u)}{C_b} - 1 \right] .du, \qquad t_a \leq t \leq u \qquad (A8)$$

We skip the required mathematical operations for the integration. Time elapsed in the queue is presented below, assuming incoming volume independent of t which is constant during the congestion period.

$$T(t) = \begin{cases} 0 & \text{if } Q(t) \leq C_b \\ (Q/C_b - 1).(t - t_a) & \text{if } Q(t) > C_b \end{cases} \tag{A9}$$

For the traffic flow Q, the cost imposed on the other vehicles by adding one more vehicle during congestion will be:

$$Q.v.\frac{dT(t)}{dQ} = Q.v.\frac{t - t_a}{C_b} \tag{A10}$$

8 Measurement of Benefits from Transportation Improvements
Computational Issues

1. INTRODUCTION

Transportation infrastructure investments are made—at least in theory—in order to improve travel conditions.[1] Chapter 7 examined various spatial and temporal facets of congestion, a key objective of infrastructure improvements. This chapter focuses on computational issues associated with the correct measurement of those improved travel conditions amenable to COBA.

It was shown in Chapter 3 that, under marginal cost pricing, the correct measure of net welfare gains from transportation investments equals total consumer and producer surplus. However, attempts to apply this principle to actual measurement of welfare gains from transportation investments raises several difficulties, due mainly to the special characteristics of transportation systems and the intricacies of transportation planning. Chief among these difficulties are the lack of information on demand elasticities at the facility level, the use of private rather than social marginal costs, the indivisibility of capacity, and the fluctuations in demand relative to mode, time of travel, route, and location. Hence, the key challenge for measurement is reconciliation of the welfare-economic principles of net welfare gains with common transportation planning practices and models. By and large, benefits are derived from user equilibrium conditions and *not* from social equilibrium conditions, that is, from equating travel demand with a marginal social cost function. The welfare gains referred to in this chapter should therefore be viewed as second best and deviating from Pareto Optimal solutions.

It is important to mention at the outset that conventional peak-period congestion reduction is regarded as the main objective of transportation capacity-improvement investment. This objective, however, often proves to be misleading because the added capacity can cause a shift in the transportation system's current equilibrium to a new equilibrium without alleviating the previous peak-period congestion levels. And so, the use of peak travel time savings as the principle measure of an investment's benefits can produce biased results. In this chapter we argue that in addition to time savings, the key benefits of a transportation project accrue in the form of an expanded set of opportunities available to motorists, expressed in terms of more flexible departure times, multiple route and mode choices, as well as greater traffic flow reliability.

In order to appraise transportation investments, the computation of future travel demand patterns, derived from land-use distributions and projections, is required. These future demand estimates are modeled in the form of Origin-Destination (O-D) travel demand matrices by mode, and subsequently assigned to the transportation network. The main outputs from these assignments are travel times, speeds and volumes, distributed by network segments, possibly by time of day or total Vehicle Miles Traveled (VMT). Comparison of these pre- and postinvestment values enables computation of cost savings from the project, which are used to assess its economic value.

A key issue in the evaluation of transportation capacity investments is the tendency to view the increased travel flow following capacity expansion as a benefit even though it may be associated with escalated externalities, such as emissions. The problem is aggravated by the failure to set travel prices that equate demand with social marginal cost. The approach adopted here is to first analyze the source of the increased traffic on the new or expanded facility, which often originates in trips diverted from other facilities, modes, or times of day. The *net* change in traffic is then regarded as a benefit. The social costs of negative externalities from changes in traffic are examined in Chapter 12 and incorporated into project COBA in Chapter 14.

Section 2 identifies the basic issue of gauging benefits from transportation improvements while Section 3 provides definitions of the key variables. Short- and long-term sources of changes in demand following transportation improvements are examined in Section 4. Section 5 reviews the measurement of benefits under conditions of elastic and inelastic demand. The problem of induced demand pursuant to capacity expansion and its implications for benefit assessment is taken up in Section 6. This issue is further examined in Section 7 within the framework of the land use-transportation planning process. Section 8 discusses partial solutions to the measurement problems identified using conventional transportation planning models. Other approaches to the estimation of benefits, including the use of random utility measures, are discussed in Section 9. The plausibility of the estimated benefits is examined in Section 10, followed by summary and major conclusions, presented in Section 11.

2. COMPUTATION OF ECONOMIC BENEFITS FROM CAPACITY INVESTMENTS

The following phenomenon is often observed. In order to alleviate traffic congestion on a certain facility (e.g., a highway), a capacity investment project is undertaken that, in terms of travel demand and supply, implies an increase in supply.[2] Yet, shortly after the project is completed, travel time and congestion are back to previous levels. This observation raises several key questions. First, what are the transportation-economic reasons for this phenomenon? Second, what are the economic benefits from the investment project obtained under these conditions? Third, how can we measure these benefits in transportation COBA framework?

Before investigating these questions, we should clarify the meaning of supply shifts from a capacity investment perspective. In general, motorists view transportation supply as their private marginal costs, associated with traversing a link.[3] These costs, denoted by t, are measured in terms of travel time as a function of traffic flow, given the link's capacity. Link capacity, denoted by $\bar{c}$, is defined as the maximum number of vehicles, $v_1(t)$, that can traverse link l, within a time period t at a given speed s. Given $\bar{c}$, $t = t(v/\bar{c})$ is the supply function, with $(\partial t/\partial v) > 0$. A shift in supply from capacity expansion thus means movement of the entire curve as $\bar{c}$ changes. Hence, for a given v, $(\partial t/\partial \bar{c}) < 0$.

Actual network capacity assignment analysis can be defined in terms of vehicle density (vehicles per km) and flow constraints. It follows that the number of vehicles on link l, $x_l(t)$, at time period t, is constrained by the maximal number of vehicles on this link, a figure defined above as link's l capacity.[4] Let d_l denote the length (in km) of link l. Let q_l^{max} denote the maximum traffic density that link l can accommodate. Hence, the maximal number of vehicles on this link, $d_l \times q_l^{max}$, is the effective constraining capacity of this link. At any time period t, the conservation constraint is $x_l(t) \leq d_l \times q_l^{max}$, $\forall l$. Similarly, it is possible to define the exit flow capacity constraint, v_l^{max}, with the capacity conservation constraint $v_l(t) \leq v_l^{max}$, $\forall l$. The use of these constraints in actual traffic assignment analysis provides effective definitions of link capacity. Hence, capacity expansion actually means raising maximal density and flow constraints.[5] Notice that practical application of this model requires specification of explicit vehicle density and flow functions such as the Bureau of Public Road (BPR) function.[6]

Figure 8.1 shows equilibrium travel demand and supply before and after a capacity investment.

In Figure 8.1 the price of travel (in time units) that users face and travel volumes are denoted by P and by V, respectively. Following capacity expansion, the present supply function S_1 shifts to S_2. Equilibrium consequently shifts from E_1 to E_2, which translates into a shift in travel costs and volume from P_1 to P_2 and from V_1 to V_2, respectively. In the context of transportation traffic analysis, this economic exposition implies that previous users (V_1) benefit from the reduction in costs from P_1 to P_2, represented by the area $P_1P_2FE_1$, whereas benefits to new users, ($V_2 - V_1$), are measured by the area enclosed by E_1FE_2.[7] Hence, the area $P_1E_1E_2P_2$ shows the total change in consumer surplus. Adding the change in producer surplus (the areas AP_1E_1 and BP_2E_2, respectively), the net economic change, ΔNB, equals:

Travel Cost

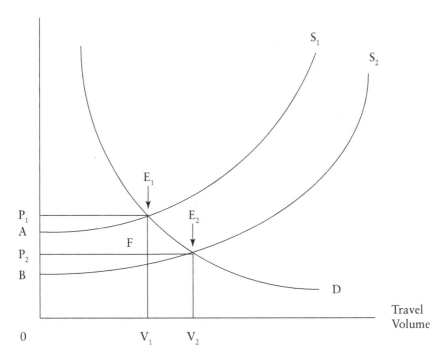

Figure 8.1 Change in equilibrium travel cost and volume from capacity expansion.

$$\Delta NB = \left[\int_0^{V_2} P(v)dv - \int_0^{V_1} P(v)dv \right] + \left[\int_0^{V_2} TVC_2(v)dv - \int_0^{V_1} TVC_1(v)dv \right] \quad (1)$$

In (1), $P(v)$ is the inverse demand function (i.e., travel volume as a function of travel price); and $TVC(v)$ denotes total producer's variable costs.

This common analysis raises two analytical questions. First, where does the additional demand $(V_2 - V_1)$ come from? And second, given the finite capacity of transportation facilities, do the upward rising supply functions S_1 and S_2 correctly represent reality? While these questions have been examined previously in the literature, we return to them in subsequent sections when trying to correctly measure the welfare changes from a transportation investment.

Two further issues regarding capacity expansion need to be dealt before commencing. The first issue is that of travel time reliability. As noted in previous chapters (Chapter 4, Section 4.3 and Chapter 7, Section 6.3), trip makers are more sensitive to improvements in the distribution of their travel time than to proportional improvements in their absolute travel time. Reducing the uncertainty associated with deviations from mean travel time for any given trip type is viewed as conferring greater benefits than actual reduction in travel time of a comparable magnitude. Hence, to the extent that capacity improvement actually improves travel time reliability, it—rather than the mere counting of travel time savings—should be included as a benefit.

The second issue regards measurement of the benefits from a specific transportation investment in isolation of other projects. In cases where an investment is part of a strategic transportation improvement plan, the measurement of its benefits should be contingent on the other investments planned relative to base case, time frame, synergies between investments, and level of detail. (The subject of strategic plans was discussed in Chapter 2.)

A final comment concerns the use of "travel volume" as the quantity variable. For travel analysis, what matters is *traffic flow*, defined in terms of number of vehicles per time unit that traverse a given facility (e.g., 1 km of road). Hence, in the analysis that follows, when the term *volume* is used to mark travel quantity, it explicitly refers to mean *traffic flow*.

3. THE MEASUREMENT OF TRAVEL VOLUME AND PRICE

In the ensuing analysis, we define *trip* as a vehicular movement between a pair of Origin-Destination (O-D) locations, at a given time of day, over a network link or a facility, using a given mode.[8] Accordingly, we define *capacity increase* as a means for enabling a larger number of trips over a facility at a given travel speed. Capacity expansion can take various forms, including reduction in train headways, physical expansion of a highway segment, or optimization of traffic arrangements and signaling at a busy intersection[9]. In all of these cases, our objective is assessment of the net economic benefits obtained from the additional volume of trips traveled between an O-D pair, at a given time period, using the specific facility or mode.[10]

The price or cost of a trip paid for by users was defined in Chapter 4 as the generalized cost of travel, which is composed of the direct costs of the trip, including the price of gasoline, tolls, parking, or transit fare, and the monetized value of time spent traveling between O-D locations. Because the data available rarely permits individual measurement of these factors, COBA commonly replaces them with resource costs and categories of time value. Again, we need to emphasize that these are users' costs and *not* societal costs, which also include the value of externalities like pollution.

Since demand does not distribute uniformly during 24 hours, what is the proper time period for which changes in travel volumes and costs, used as inputs in the measurement of benefits from capacity expansion, are to be examined? As already noted, in most cases, the declared reason for capacity investment is relief of congestion at peak periods. Therefore, one approach might be to regard *peak-period* travel flow and costs only. However, off-peak users also stand to benefit from capacity expansion as they might face more favorable travel conditions due to, say, better road design. But even if the pertinent peak and off-peak O-D data were available, the measured benefits for each group might be biased if some trip makers switch from off-peak to peak period travel, following the capacity investment. While there are models that consider the time of departure as a function of travel costs (e.g., Small, 1982), by and large they are not dynamically integrated with the traffic assignment models used by planning agencies to estimate travel costs and volumes.[11]

Another possible approach to measuring benefits is to use a weighted average of travel volumes and costs between the peak and off-peak periods. This approach is also not problem-free. First, there is the issue of weights to be employed or the time length of the peak and the off-peak period. Second, save for very special cases, the demand and the supply functions are of the nonconstant elasticity type, meaning that use of a "weighted average" may result in incorrect estimates of the "before" and "after" benefit levels.

Still another approach would be to compute the net benefits of peak-time users, based on peak-period travel volume and time. We would subsequently apply a constant (e.g., the ratio of off-peak to peak hourly travel volumes) when computing the net economic change for the off-peak users. While this approach may be useful for some demand conditions (see below), it may inadequately reflect travel shifts from the off-peak to the peak period if caused by declining travel costs, induced by the capacity expansion. This is shown in Figure 8.1 as a segment of the demand curve: $V_2 - V_1$.

In what follows, travel demand is treated as the number of peak-period trips between an O-D pair over a specific facility for a given level of generalized travel costs. Furthermore, following capacity expansion, total travel demand over the relevant sections of the network must increase. Otherwise, the only effect would be trip diversion with zero gross benefits.[12]

4. SOURCES OF CHANGES IN DEMAND FOLLOWING TRANSPORTATION IMPROVEMENTS

Traffic congestion tends to maintain a self-limiting equilibrium. Expanding roadway capacity reduces congestion delays, allowing more peak-period trips—consisting of combinations of shifts in time, mode, route, and destination—and, over time, changes in land use. These travel shifts obviously provide consumers certain benefits or the shifts would not be made.

What is the magnitude of consumer benefits from these changes? Does the nature of the change matter? Stated differently, do the shifts in time, mode, route, or destination materializing in response to a marginal increase in capacity provide similar levels of marginal benefits? From society's perspective, are there large differences in the overall costs and benefits among these different types of change? For example, shifting time or route does not affect parking costs although shifting mode and destination does. The same can be said regarding pollution emissions, accident costs, downstream congestion, and land-use impacts. These issues are taken up next.

4.1 Short-, Medium-, and Long-Term Effects of Transportation Improvements

It is useful to begin our discussion on the various demand effects from transportation improvements by categorizing those effects relative to the time length required for their emergence.

  A. Short-Term Effects:
    1) Trip diversion between routes
    2) Temporal changes, mainly between peak and off-peak hours
  B. Medium-Term Effects:
    1) Change in modal split shares
    2) Change in O-D patterns, with total demand unchanged
  C. Long-Term Effects:
    1) Changes in total O-D demand
    2) Changes in motorization (car ownership) rates
    3) Land-use changes

The effects listed result from changes in public policy and exogenous variables. Policy changes can include changes in the capacity and layout of the network or the introduction of a new mode whereas exogenous changes include rise in income, car ownership, population, and economic activity over differing lengths of time. Since these two types of changes operate concurrently when analyzing the longitudinal demand changes from transportation improvements, it is indispensable that we control for the changes caused by external variables in order to correctly estimate benefits.

Quite often transportation planners assume fixed travel demand. At the O-D level, fixed demand implies that the margins of the O-D trip distribution matrix (the trip attraction and production vectors) are fixed for all i and j locations, determined at the previous phase of trip generation.[13] At the link or facility level, the same concept implies that the link's travel demand function is totally inelastic. With regard to the above underlying causes of changes in demand, observed temporal shifts can only result from exogenous factors since inelastic demand, by definition, is insensitive to policy-related changes in service level. In Section 6, below, we show that under the assumption of fixed demand, benefits are overestimated relative to the case of elastic demand.

A distinction is sometimes made between O-D demand and *realized demand*, where the latter is the demand actually accommodated by the in-place transportation system. Accordingly, comparisons of actual traffic volumes, recorded from the working network, with computed O-D demand can reveal some significant discrepancies. One element explaining this phenomenon is high travel costs especially on saturated networks; these effectively prohibit some trip makers from actually traveling. If so, link travel demand must be elastic and use of inelastic demand functions, which, as noted, is a common practice, is quite misleading. Allowing a queue for each route (or link)—with sufficiently high travel delay time—makes route demand non-fixed even though the O-D demand is taken as fixed.

4.2 A Formal Exposition of Changes in Travel Demand from Capacity Expansion

Consider a trip table (the O-D matrix), $T_{ij,l}^m$, which indicates the number of trips between zones i and $j (i,j = 1,\ldots,M)$, using link l on route $r (l \in r \in R)$, by mode $m (m = 1,\ldots,Q)$. The total number of trips is given by $T = \sum_{i,j} \sum_{l,m} T_{ij,l}^m$. This table reflects total travel between i and j, irrespective of time of day. Using this framework enables us to distinguish between several demand situations: First, T_{ij} is totally inelastic for any given ij pair; as a result, T is also fixed. Second, T is fixed but not T_{ij}; this means that trip patterns between origins and destinations can change while holding total travel constant. Third, both T and T_{ij} are variable for a given travel mode m. Fourth, T, T_{ij} and mode m are variable so that travel demand is elastic within and between modes. Fifth, reductions in travel costs induce demand that is *external* to the present O-D matrix.

With these definitions in mind, assume a capacity improvement that lowers travel costs on link l. What could result? First, reduced travel costs on this link can induce more travel by existing motorists. That is, $D_l = f(P_l)$, where P_l is travel costs exhibiting the property $(\partial D_l/\partial P_l) < 0$. How can that happen if T_{ij} is fixed for any ij pair? Recall that capacity expansion primarily aims at reducing peak-hour congestion and thus peak travel time. It follows that travel on link l, formerly undertaken at off-peak to avoid congestion, now switches to the peak periods.[14]

A second effect is traffic diversion from other links on alternative routes between the same ij pair. The underlying rationale is that the demand for travel on link l is a function of the travel costs on this as well as on alternative links, that is, $D_l = f(P_l, P_{l'})$, where $P_{l'}$ is travel cost on an alternative link, $l' (l \neq l')$. From a computational perspective, network equilibrium is defined as the condition where the marginal travel costs on all routes (or set of links) between i and j are equal. Therefore, when moving from a preexpansion to a postexpansion network equilibrium, lowered travel costs on link l will result in the diversion of trips from other links, given T_{ij}.

The above two effects assumed demand inelasticity with respect to interzonal travel costs for each ij pair and total O-D demand (T). Within these boundaries, $\Delta V = V_2 - V_1$ (shown in Figure 8.1) reflects the degree to which trips were actually switched between time periods and between links. However, if we allow for demand elasticity, which is certainly appropriate for the medium and long run, additional changes are likely to take place, the most conspicuous being the decision by existing motorists to intensify their use of the expanded facility. This could be done by increasing trip frequency per time unit.

An additional major effect of improved highway travel time is modal switching, mainly from public transit to automobiles. That is, $T_{ij}^m = f(P_{ij}^m, P_{ij,l}^{m'})$ with $(\partial T_{ij}^m / \partial P_{ij,l}^{m'}) < 0$, where T_{ij}^m represents the amount of travel between i and j on mode m (e.g., public transit) and $P_{ij,l}^{m'}$ the travel costs between i and j on mode m' ($m \neq m'$) on the expanded link l. Thus, if $P_{ij,l}^{m'}$ declines, so does the amount of travel on the alternative mode, T_{ij}^m, as trip makers on mode m switch to mode m'.

Two major sources of change in external demand are population growth and economic expansion. In large metropolitan areas, population growth can result in a 1%–2% annual increase in travel that, in turn, translates into a 5%–6% increase in peak-period traffic. Hence, significant amounts of additional travel can be expected even if no transportation improvement transpires. It has been estimated that by 2025, the US population will have grown by 26%, GDP will have doubled and total passenger-miles by all modes will have increased by 72% (US DOT, 2002a). A related source of external demand is general economic growth, as rising economic activity tends to generate more trips. For example, forecasts indicate that by 2020, intercity truck tonnage will have grown by 75% (US DOT, 2002a).

We next focus on the case where the volume of travel has increased following capacity expansion but observed travel time has remained at the preexpansion level. In Figure 8.2, the demand function is shown either as a total inelastic function D' or as an elastic function D_1. Let's assume that in the latter case, the supply function shifts from S_1 to S_2 in the wake of the capacity increase. If nothing else occurs, equilibrium will shift from E_1 to E_4, with the price of travel falling from P_1 to P_2 and volume increasing from V_1 to V_2. However, if the entire demand function moves from D_1 to D_2, as explained, trip volume will increase from V_1 to V_3 and equilibrium will shift from E_1 to E_3, keeping the price level at P_1.

Under these conditions, how should we measure the net change in benefits caused by the expanded capacity? The consumer surplus associated with previous users (V_1) has remained unchanged because travel prices have remained at P_1. Yet, the new users, ($V_3 - V_1$), who did not travel on this facility previously, now benefit from the ability to travel at price P_1. To measure the net gain, should we compare equilibrium $E_3 = \{P_1, V_3\}$ with the prechange equilibrium $E_1 = \{P_1, V_1\}$ or with the postchange equilibrium $E_4 = \{P_2, V_2\}$? The shift in the entire demand function ($D_1 \rightarrow D_2$) means that the net change in benefits should be measured as the area bounded by the demand curve, D_2, between the point where it intersects the price axis and point P_1, less the area bounded by the demand curve D_1, between the point where it intersects the price axis and P_1. Note that demand can shift to a new equilibrium point, where the price level is below P_1. But such a case is irrelevant to us here because our concern at the moment is to try and explain the constancy of travel prices before and after the capacity expansion. We stress once more that the changes shown in Figure 8.2 do not represent social equilibrium because the congestion externality remains unpriced.

Travel Costs

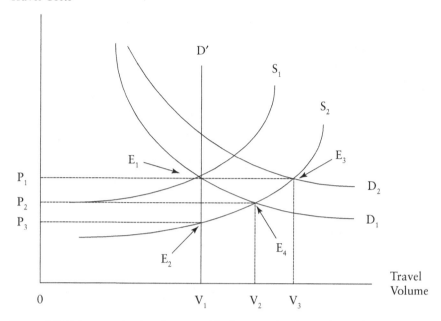

Figure 8.2 Volume and price changes with elastic and inelastic demand.

In real situations, we cannot observe demand functions; what we see is only the price of travel (P_1) in addition to the pre- and postinvestment travel volumes (V_1 and V_3). We thus face the question of how to measure the economic value of this investment given the observed information. This question is examined next.

5. MEASUREMENT OF BENEFITS FROM CAPACITY EXPANSION WITH INELASTIC AND ELASTIC DEMAND

5.1 Users' Benefits

The common approach to estimating net users' benefits from a transportation improvement is to compare travel conditions under the planned investment alternatives with those under the benchmark alternative (see Chapter 6, Section 2.1). These conditions include peak-hour travel times, travel speeds, and flows, delays at major intersections, and the peak period's time length. Other variables to be considered are users' direct monetary costs and sometimes parking costs, too. The net change in these variables, converted into monetary values, constitutes the project's annual users' benefits. Since these computations are done ex ante, with the actual demand still unknown, all that we can presently observe are the two equilibrium properties, P_1 and V_1 (see Figure 8.2).

These conditions nonetheless allow us to identify several possible cases for the estimation of net benefits from capacity change, first assuming inelastic (fixed) demand and then elastic demand.

Case 1: Fixed demand (D' in Figure 8.2). This case implies that for a given link l and mode m at time of travel t, T_{ij} is fixed for each ij pair. Following capacity expansion, the supply function shifts, $S_1 \rightarrow S_2$, with price falling from P_1 to P_3. The area $V_1(P_3 - P_1)$ thus represents the change in peak-period users' benefits. With demand fixed at V_1, estimation of the new travel cost (price) P_3 becomes simple when using a standard Volume-Capacity (V-C) function such as BPR. Denoting the ratio of off-peak to peak traffic volume by α, an estimate of the total economic gain for all users is given: $(1 + \alpha)[V_1(P_1 - P_3)]$. Because of its simplicity, this approach is commonly applied in the analysis of net benefits from capacity investments.

Case 2: Movement along an elastic demand function (D_1 in Figure 8.2). Following the supply increase $S_1 \rightarrow S_2$ and the equilibrium shift from $E_1 = \{P_1, V_1\}$ to $E_4 = \{P_2, V_2\}$, the area $P_1E_1E_4P_2$ indicates the change in benefits. Previous users (V_1) benefit from the reduction in cost ($P_1 - P_2$), with the area under the demand curve D_1 between $V_2 - V_1$ representing the change in utility for new users. If demand is approximated by a linear curve in the vicinity of P_1 and P_2, total benefits is approximated by the rule-of-half:

$$\frac{1}{2}(V_1 + V_2)(P_1 - P_2) \tag{2}$$

Case 3: A total shift in the elastic demand function (D_1 to D_2 in Figure 8.2). The underlying rationale is that the present equilibrium, E_1, was intolerable, thus requiring a capacity expansion investment, with S_1 shifting to S_2. As a result of induced demand (see Section 6, below), $D_1 \rightarrow D_2$ and the new equilibrium is $E_3 = \{P_1; V_3\}$. What is the change in benefits from this increase in supply? Following equation (1), the difference between the area under the demand function D_2 bounded by 0 and V_3, less the area under D_1 bounded by 0 and V_1, constitutes the change in benefits. That is:

$$\Delta NB = \int_0^{V_3} D_2(v)dv - \int_0^{V_1} D_1(v)dv \tag{3}$$

This analysis ignores possible changes in travel volumes and times on other links caused by the redistribution of traffic over time and space, following the capacity investment on link l. In a second-best world, where travel is carried out over congested facilities, the total sum of consumer and producer surplus over all links ($l \in L$) is the correct measure of total benefits from this investment (Kidokoro, 2004, 2006).[15]

5.2 Government's Nonresource Revenue Benefits

With elastic demand and supply functions, a move to a new equilibrium following a supply increase affects both consumer and producer surplus. This is shown in Figure 8.1 and estimated by means of equation 1. Yet, under Case 1, with fixed demand and a capacitated network, producer surplus—which reflects social gains from improved efficiency in service provision—is nullified by the new traffic and congestion.

However, for the other two cases, additional travel $(V_2 - V_1)$ implies additional government revenues in the form of taxes on travel expenses (e.g., gasoline tax).[16] Depending on the tax structure (e.g., fixed percentage sales tax), the additional tax revenue can be approximated by $(V_2 - V_1) \cdot C \cdot (1 + \tau)$, where C and τ denote users' expenses per trip and the tax rate, respectively.

In the case of public transit, revenues from additional travel are given by $(V_2 - V_1) \cdot (F + S)$, where F denotes transit fare and S subsidy. Of these, the amount $(V_2 - V_1) \cdot (F)$ equals transit users' expenses. If the amount of subsidy, $(V_2 - V_1) \cdot (S)$, can be shown to exactly equal additional taxes, and if the marginal utility of subsidy equals the marginal utility of taxed income, the subsidy amounts to a transfer from the public to the transit system and should not be counted as part of producer surplus. However, as argued in Chapter 6, when conducting COBA, subsidy revenues should be counted against the capital, operating, and maintenance costs associated with provision of the new service or new facility.

6. MEASUREMENT OF BENEFITS FROM CAPACITY IMPROVEMENT WITH INDUCED DEMAND

The actual measurement of benefits from a transportation investment that expands capacity needs to grapple with the phenomenon of induced demand. In the following sections we examine the measurement of benefits for various forms of induced demand.

6.1 Induced Demand

Once capacity has expanded and travel times fallen, traffic tends to increase, filling up the new capacity at the preexpansion travel times in the short and immediate run. This so-called "induced demand" effect has been examined extensively in the literature.[17] Three key questions arise with respect to induced demand: First, what are its potential sources? Second, what are the pertinent elasticities (i.e., the effect of a 10% increase in capacity on induced demand)? And third, how can we account for induced demand when measuring a transportation improvement's benefits? The last question is taken up in Section 6.2.

A shift in demand on a facility following capacity expansion represents additional traffic, which is measured as the change in peak-period traffic, the incremental average daily vehicle traffic, or additional Vehicle Miles Traveled (VMT). What are the possible sources of this additional traffic? As already noted, they may include traffic diversion from other time periods (e.g., from off-peak to peak), facilities (e.g., links), or modes. Additional traffic can also result from movement along the demand curve for trips, representing travelers who, at previous prices, refrained from traveling or traveled to other destinations. Furthermore, if economic development has taken place in the area of the new capacity investment, additional trips can be expected from either new economic activity or spatial rearrangement of regional economic activity.

Of all these trip types, which represent induced demand? If we consider only new or longer trips—net of general population and motorization growth—as genuine induced demand, trips diverted over time periods and routes should be excluded from the analysis. Yet, if it can be shown that economic growth is indeed one result of the capacity investment, trips engendered by this growth should be regarded as induced demand. In reality, however, it is impossible to distinguish between "real" induced demand traffic and all other additional trips following a capacity increase, especially if other changes—such as fluctuations in fuel prices—have taken place concurrently. Such a distinction might be possible if a general equilibrium analysis of *joint* land use and transportation characteristics were to be carried out (see Section 7). As a rule, then, shifts in demand from capacity enhancement are commonly lumped together either in terms of traffic volumes (as shown in Figure 8.2), or VMT, and represented by a shift in the entire demand curve.

Studies show that induced demand appears mainly in the form of greater VMT rather than additional trips. Since location decisions are sensitive to travel costs, reduced travel times encourage further dispersion (suburbanization) of existing residential, commercial, and employment activities, hence the increase in VMT. A corollary of this finding is the positive elasticity of VMT with respect to highway lane-miles, used as a measure of capacity. The magnitude of these elasticities depends, of course, on the specific database and model used.[18] For example, Marshal (2000), using cross-sectional aggregate data of congested roadways in 70 US metropolitan areas, reports elasticity of VMT with respect to per capita lane-miles of 0.85 for highways and 0.76 for major arterials. Noland (2001), applying cross-sectional and longitudinal aggregate analyses to data from the 50 US states, reports short-run elasticity of VMT with respect to lane-miles in the range of 0.3–0.6 and long-run elasticity of 0.7–1.0. Another finding is that capacity enhancement (increase in lane-miles) indeed precedes growth in regional VMT (Fulton et al., 2000). This result does not, per se, prove causality but does lend support to the basic induced demand hypothesis.

Alternatively, Mokhtarian et al. (2002), using pair-matched data on improved and unimproved highway segments in California, were unable to conclude that capacity expansions have led to discernible induced demand effects (they do suggest that their sample might have been too small to detect this effect). Cervero (2003), using California data on freeway expansion during the period 1980–1994, also concluded that part of the induced travel demand elasticity (a high-end value of 0.24) represented route diversion. More recently, a study by Hoover and Burt (2006) demonstrated that building highway infrastructure at a rate that matches the growth in the driving-age population does not significantly increase road usage by motorists. Other factors, mainly residential location, urban density, income, and use of congestion tolls have much larger impact on the effective amount of travel than does capacity expansion.

What really matters for our purposes here—the measurement of benefits from capacity expansion—is the fact that shortly after a project's completion, the traffic demand returns to the equilibrium associated with preexpansion travel prices. While a significant part of this additional travel comes from redistributed demand and only a smaller proportion represents real new travel, travel times before and after may not change. What, then, are the investment's benefits and how are we to measure them? Should we consider the additional traffic volume or perhaps the shortened length of the peak period as benefits? These questions are discussed next.

6.2 Measurement of Benefits with Induced Fixed Demand

As observed previously, the concept *fixed demand* is founded on two observations. First, total travel demand, represented by the margins of the O-D matrix is fixed relative to changes in travel costs. Second, in reality, our direct observations are limited to traffic volumes on links, volumes that match the network's capacity and are therefore fixed in congested networks.

Consider Figure 8.3, which shows the estimated equilibrium before and after supply changes. Here we consider a peak-hour capacitated network, where $(V/C) = 1$, so that demand, denoted by D_1, is treated as totally inelastic. This function intersects the supply function S_1 at equilibrium travel time (price) and volume, P_1 and V_1, respectively. In response to peak-hour congestion (given by travel price, P_1), supply (capacity) has been expanded to S_2, which lowers travel time to P_2. If D_1 remains unchanged, total benefits from the increased supply are given by the expression $(P_1 - P_2)V_1$. However, if the lower price, P_2, actually induces demand, the inelastic demand function shifts to D_2 and equilibrium is achieved at the preexpansion price level P_1 but with volume V_2. What, then, are the benefit gains from the capacity expansion?

Consider demand at two periods: the a.m. and the midday peaks; for simplicity, assume them to be independent relative to LOS.[19] Total benefits are, therefore, the sum of each period's benefits. Theoretically, there are two basic approaches to answering the above question. First, we can consider the alternative costs of not expanding capacity, that is, the "null" or "do-nothing" approach.[20] Second, we can compute the benefits of the new users only: $V_2 - V_1$.

Suppose that capacity has not been expanded. However, due to increases in population, car ownership rates, or VMT, demand for existing capacity

Travel Time

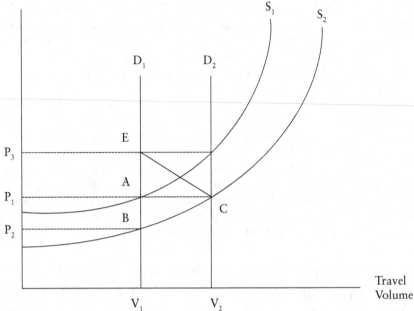

Figure 8.3 Measurement of benefits from shifts in supply and induced fixed demand.

(S_1) is expected to grow from D_1 to D_2. Because capacity is finite $(V/C \leq 1)$, we can reasonably expect longer queues on major facilities, which implies additional time spent in traffic or more time spent in lieu of travel to work. In Figure 8.3, this situation is equivalent to P_1 increasing to P_3, where D_2 intersects S_1.[21] The alternative users' costs of keeping capacity at the present level (the "do-nothing" alternative) is consequently defined by the area P_3EAP_1 or $(P_3 - P_1)V_1$. To avert these costs, capacity is expanded and the supply function S_1 moves to S_2. With demand at D_2, equilibrium is now at point C, where total benefits for present users (V_1) as well as new users, $(V_2 - V_1)$, is represented by the area P_3ECP_1, which is equivalent to $(P_3 - P_1)[V_1 + \frac{1}{2}(V_2 - V_1)] = (P_3 - P_1)\frac{1}{2}(V_1 + V_2)$.[22]

The same result would be obtained if an increase in supply from S_1 to S_2 was assumed, followed by the phenomenon of induced demand, which motivates a shift from D_1 to D_2. Either way, what this analysis actually shows is that trip makers who previously decided not to travel at present prices face opportunity costs of that decision in the form of forgone benefits from not traveling at all or not traveling at their desired time period or route or mode. In public transit, for example, if a train can currently accommodate 500 passengers per time unit while 600 potential passengers demand service, the additional wait time for the remaining 100 passengers is part of their total door-to-door travel time cost, irrespective of where they wait—at the train station or at home—to avoid peak-period congestion. Adding an additional rail car to shorten wait time (but not in-vehicle time) does confer benefits as it allows travel at desired times.

Turning to the second approach, previous users, V_1, do not benefit from the capacity increase because, as a result of induced demand, they now face the same travel time costs, P_1, confronted prior to the change. The new users, represented by $(V_2 - V_1)$, who previously chose not to travel at this price, now enjoy an economic gain, given by the area AEC.

Obviously, these two approaches to the assessment of benefits following capacity improvement differ substantially with respect to the magnitude of these benefits as well as their underlying rationale. The difference in the measured benefits is given by the area P_3EAP_1, which represents users' opportunity costs, resulting from the escalating congestion costs caused by ordinary increases in economic activity and population and thus the demand for travel. Because these costs are quite tangible—in the form of lost productivity or forgone leisure time, to name just two—the first approach is the preferred one. The willingness to pay (WTP) principle in effect implies that preventing a consumer from being worse off should count as an investment benefit, which is then added to the benefits enjoyed by new users. However, to the extent that the shift in demand can be attributed to induced-demand exclusively, the second approach is more appropriate in cases of capacity expansion. As welfare maximization requires that benefits be valued at the margin, time saved should be valued at peak-period or trip-to-work VOT in both cases. Again, it should be emphasized that S_1 and S_2 in Figure 8.3 represent private marginal costs and *not* marginal social costs.

When using the first approach, how can P_3 be estimated? At the start, remember that at the new equilibrium C, V_2 represents peak-hour travel volume at the preinvestment travel price P_1. With S_1 and S_2 as well as P_1, we compute the travel volume resulting from the intersection between S_2 and P_1, namely, V_2. This volume is then loaded onto the network under S_1 to produce P_3. The benefits can subsequently be estimated.

The approaches to measurement of benefits from capacity investments outlined here together raise two key questions for empirical evaluation. First, is it possible to assign values to the volume-capacity function beyond the effective range of $V/\overline{C} = 1$, where $\overline{C}$ is the capacity constraint? Second, how much does the assumption of fixed demand bias the results relative to elastic demand? The first question was examined in Chapter 7, where it was concluded that the relevant supply function should be the Marginal Cost function, which represents the queue that forms at the entrance to the facility, such as an artery road leading to an expressway. Thus, for a given $\overline{C}$, as the queue increases, the marginal costs of using this facility increase as well. The second question is examined next.

6.3 Comparing Benefits under Elastic and Inelastic Demand Schemes

In principle, demand is elastic with respect to LOS. In actual applications, the assignment algorithms used often intrinsically assume totally inelastic (fixed) demand. How do benefits obtained from a fixed demand analysis compare with those obtained under elastic demand?

Williams and Yamashita (1992) have shown that the estimated benefits under inelastic demand exceed those estimated under elastic demand. To illustrate this result, consider a linear demand function of the type $q = \alpha - \beta \cdot p$, where q represents quantity (trip volume), p is price per trip (in units of monetized travel time), and α and β are parameters. The demand elasticity with respect to price, η, is subsequently $\eta = \beta \cdot (p/q)$, which varies along the curve with changes in price and quantity. In reality, only p and q are observed. Assuming demand price elasticity, $\eta \approx -0.5$ (Goodwin, 1996), we can measure the change in benefits from a price change caused by a capacity improvement, ΔCS. For the linear demand function case, this change is:

$$\Delta CS = \frac{1}{\eta} f(p_1, q_1, p_2, q_2); \ \Delta CS > 0 \tag{4}$$

In (4), p_1, p_2 and q_1, q_2 denote prices and quantities before and after the change, respectively, with $f(\cdot)$ being a positive function. What, then, will be the change in the value of ΔCS as a function of price elasticity η? From expression (4), when demand price elasticity (in absolute value) declines (e.g., $\eta = |1|$ becomes $\eta = |.5|$), benefits from capacity improvements, in terms of the change in consumer surplus, increase. In particular, when using a fixed demand function[23] as opposed to an elastic demand function, benefits from capacity enhancement will overestimate the true benefits.

6.4 The Value of Traffic Flow Reliability

In Chapter 7 it was shown that improved traffic flow reliability—or reduction of the uncertainty of journey travel time variations—should be regarded as a potential benefit. What, then, is the effect of capacity improvement on traffic flow reliability? Most available studies did not directly address this question. Cohen and Southworth (1999) specified total delay from an incident as composed of half the average delay during the incident (due to queue formation) plus the delay incurred while the queue is dispersing, following termination of the incident.[24] Their model includes road capacity (in vehicles per hour at a given LOS). Assuming a Gamma distribution of incident duration,[25] based on data from other studies, they calculated the expected delays for highways of 2, 3, and 4 lanes with V/C ratios ranging from 0.1 to 1.0. As expected, when holding the V/C ratio constant, the expected delay (in hours per vehicle-mile) was higher for 2-lane than for 3-lane highways, which were still higher than the delay for 4-lane highways. Even for a V/C ratio of 1.0, both the mean and variance of the delay were smaller for 4-lane than for 3- and 2-lane highways. We can thus conclude that $\partial TD/\partial C < 0$, where TD denotes time delays. Similarly, for the same V/C ratio, the variance of the delay was also found to decrease with the number of lanes. In other words, while the variance of trip travel time increases with congestion, it decreases with greater capacity, that is, from more lanes in each direction. This analysis does not, however, account directly for trip scheduling, which is the mechanism motorists use to reduce the costs of traffic variability.

Given these results, it stands to reason that under conditions of induced demand as shown in Figure 8.3, greater reliability or lesser travel time variability can be expected when capacity increases. One possible explanation for this phenomenon is the capacity scale effect, implying that having more capacity (e.g., more lanes) enables better traffic maneuverability, thereby providing greater flexibility when overcoming nonrecurrent incidents. In public transit improved timekeeping enables passengers to better schedule their daily activities. Still, for COBA of any specific capacity investment, information on how trip makers' value improves reliability is needed. In general, policies aimed at improving highway incident removal or transit punctuality seem to have a significant effect on the costs of travel. In freight transportation, for example, shippers are willing to pay a premium for greater reliability, especially under just-in-time delivery schedules. When carrying out COBA of a project, then, improved reliability should be regarded as a benefit even though its actual dimensions may vary by trip or commodity type, commodity value, mode used, and regional spatial organization.

7. KEY PHASES IN THE TRANSPORTATION PLANNING PROCESS

To promote better understanding of the issues detailed in Section 6, this section returns to these issues within the context of overall transportation planning, a process used to assess benefits from planned transportation improvements.

7.1 The Transportation Planning Process

Figure 8.4 depicts the key phases in this process, known as the four-steps transportation planning process, which contains two major modules, labeled *land use* and *transportation* (for a review see McNally, 2000).[26] The figure also shows several loops between and within these modules.

From the perspective of this process, how can we explain observed shifts of entire demand curves—such as those shown in Figure 8.3—following a transportation capacity investment? The O-D matrix, T_{ij}, is obtained by allocating the trip production ($O_i = \sum_j T_{ij}$) and attraction ($D_j = \sum_i T_{ij}$) vectors to traffic zones using a trip distribution procedure. These vectors are

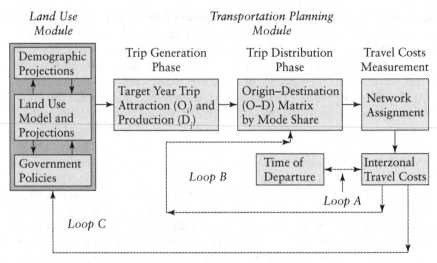

Figure 8.4 The transportation planning process.

typically estimated using regression or category analysis methods, which use the socioeconomic characteristics of travelers in a zone as independent variables. More sophisticated approaches consider demographic trends and planned land-use patterns to project longitudinal household growth rates, changes in residential and employment location, motorization rates, etcetera. If these trends and future spatial patterns are estimated correctly by means of an equilibrium procedure (see section 8.4), the derived O_i and D_j vectors contain all the pertinent information on future travel demand and thereby preclude the possibility of unaccounted for demand. In reality, of course, future demand cannot be estimated with certainty. Here, however, we focus on the reasons for those demand shifts arising from the very nature of the planning process itself rather than from any uncertainty of estimation.

Following the trip generation phase, the O-D matrix is estimated using a doubly constrained spatial interaction model (Ran and Boyce, 1996). Computation of T_{ij} relies mainly on gravity-type models, which estimate the linkages between the trip-ends predicted by the trip-generation model. For the subsequent modal split phase, discrete choice models are normally applied to compute the percentage of travelers using each mode. The results from these steps are O-D matrices for each travel mode T_{ij}^m, where m denotes a mode. As noted above, the principal attribute of the O-D matrix is that it is fixed with respect to trip-ends, travel costs, and actual times of the trip. The term *fixed demand* therefore reflects the idea that interzonal travel demand enters the assignment phase in fixed rather than variable (i.e., elastic) quantities.

Next, the T_{ij}^m matrix is loaded into the planned network, which includes the link(s) or facility(s) whose capacity has been expanded in order to compute interzonal travel times and costs by mode. Standard assignment schemes enter the entire volume of T_{ij}^m into the network even if $(V/C) > 1$. Conceptually, however, a network with finite capacity implies that at equilibrium, $(V/C) \leq 1$, and some demand may remain unserved at existing travel prices.[27]

In theory, travel times (prices) obtained at iteration n within an equilibrium framework are used at $(n + 1)$ to produce estimates of future activity patterns that, in turn, are employed to derive revised trip production and attraction vectors. This iterative scheme, represented by Loop C in Figure 8.4, continues until travel demand and supply reach equilibrium with respect to the network's finite capacity and potential demand for travel, aroused by reorganizing and developing land uses. If such an analysis were not conducted, some potential demand would remain unrecognized and thus unfulfilled in the four-step transportation planning process. This demand would nevertheless reappear in the form of more VMT—to be regarded as induced demand—once travel costs are lowered in the wake of capacity expansion. Moreover, normally in practical application, no feedback loop is established between the assignment (which produces the interzonal travel costs) and the trip distribution phase (Loop B) as well as between the assignment phase and the time of departure (Loop A), thereby further biasing the estimated peak-time travel costs.

To summarize, the overall effect on travel flow and cost of capacity expansion complexly depends on various demand and supply elasticities, the rate of change in exogenous variables such as annual population growth and network design parameters. The lack of a joint land-use–transportation model framework such as that illustrated in Figure 8.4 can explain induced demand once capacity has been increased. More importantly, failure to use the equilibrium loops shown in Figure 8.4 is likely to critically bias estimated travel costs and volumes following the capacity expansion and, as a result, the investment's benefits.

7.2 Typology of Traffic Assignment Models

During a typical application of the transportation planning model (Figure 8.4), the O-D matrix, once loaded onto a precoded network by means of a traffic assignment model, produces equilibrium travel time and volume on each link. These times are then aggregated to generate interzonal travel times. The process is repeated after the network has been modified to account for the change in capacity initiated by the new investment. The difference in aggregate travel time before and after the change is then used to compute the project's transportation benefits. Clearly, the assignment model plays a crucial role in determining travel time savings—and thus benefits—from the investment.

Five main types of traffic network equilibrium assignments can be identified: static, dynamic, micro-simulation, elastic demand, and activity based.

In the following, we survey the key factors, germane to the measurement of transportation improvement benefits, which differentiate between the methods.

1. The Static Traffic Assignment (STA) Model

This is the most prevalent approach currently used by planning agencies to measure network travel cost savings and traffic flows.[28] The principal short-comings associated with STA are first, its inability to capture temporal vehicular congestion and queuing phenomena. That is, in effect, the procedure allows total demand in existing facilities to exceed capacity (i.e., $(V/C) > 1$); second, the large portion of demand that remains unserved; third, its use of fixed or inelastic O-D demand. As a result, the measurement of benefits is quite unreliable and biased, with inflated travel time savings generated consequently.

Analytically, it is possible to have a static assignment with elastic demand. The equilibrium solution is obtained by solving a convex network optimization problem using methods such as the broadly used Frank–Wolfe algorithm. While this algorithm is swift, requiring relatively reasonable computational capabilities, solutions based on it suffer from inaccuracies relative to route choice and traffic distribution over routes. Multiple equilibrium solutions can, however, be obtained when using the model (Sheffi, 1985). Appendix A provides the formulation and empirical illustrations of STA with fixed and elastic demand.

Several approaches have been proposed to overcome the lack of time-dependent O-D data in STA. These include the use of real-time data for short-term predictions (Ashok and Ben-Akiva, 2000) and the generation of dynamic demand data from the use of fixed demand O-D matrices with a set of behavioral rules relative to time of departure (de Palma and Marchal, 2000).

2. The Dynamic Traffic Assignment (DTA) Model

Unlike the STA model, the DTA model computes a dynamic equilibrium, defined as an equilibrium that varies over time periods (e.g., peak and off-peak). DTA models are based on the principle of dynamic user equilibrium (DUE), in which the model allocates vehicles over the best paths on the network for each origin-destination pair so that vehicles leaving the same origin at roughly the same time experience approximately the same travel times. In contrast to the STA model, DTA models ensure consistency in route choice over large networks and, as a result, they provide equilibrium bench-marks for scenario evaluations.

DTA models, while accounting for the time of trip making, suffer from several empirical and theoretical failings. First, data on time of departure are, by and large, unavailable. Whereas 24-hour trip tables are readily obtainable, planning agencies do not collect time-dependent demand data on a regular basis. Second, the model assumes that trip makers can freely adjust their time of departure to changing travel conditions. This assumption ignores the fact that a good proportion of trip makers are constrained in their departures by various workplace and household arrangements. Trip chaining, for example, where time of departure is contingent on other activities such as dropping children off at school, largely inhibits flexible time-of-departure decision making. But even if appropriate data could be obtained, DTA models, while providing better estimates of interzonal travel time savings than do STA models, still cannot solve the induced demand problem, which, as explained above, represents a rather serious constraint on the estimation of benefits from a transportation improvement. Finally, equilibrium in DTA can only be achieved through iterative procedures where convergence cannot be guaranteed (for a review see Patriksson, 1994; Peeta and Ziliaskopoulos, 2004).

3. The Micro-Simulation Model

This model's objective is to reconstruct the movements of individual vehicles in the network. The model enables simulation of traffic's reactions to disturbances of the network relative to traffic incidence (e.g., a stalled vehicle) or a planned capacity reduction (e.g., road repair). Yet, for several reasons, conventional micro-simulation models have met with limited success when used for very large networks. First, simultaneous traffic simulation and path computation yield inconsistent route choices; second, complex models make calibration challenging as assignment results do not always exhibit those user equilibrium properties amenable to scenario comparisons (Chu et al., 2005); third, micro-simulations usually entail high computation costs due to the long run-times.

4. The Elastic Demand Model

As already noted the key problem with the fixed O-D demand matrix—relative to the measurement of benefits from transport improvements—is its insensitivity to Level of Service (LOS) parameters (see Dafermos and Nagurney, 1984a, 1984b). A plethora of studies have attempted to account for LOS parameters within the framework of fixed interzonal O-D demand. More recently, attempts have been made to develop such models for the purpose of assessing the impacts of changes in LOS from policy measures such as congestion tolls (Yang, 1997).

The basic objective of this research is to establish what we call the *demand-performance equilibrium level* between elastic demand and LOS. To this end, the demand function is expressed in terms of economic activity (e.g., location), travel LOS, and a vector of parameters that characterize the demand function (e.g., elasticity). The supply function, which describes the

LOS, is defined by a vector of those parameters that characterize link performance as well as policy instruments (e.g., capacity expansion). While it is conceivable that location is sensitive to LOS in the long term, for short-term analyses, the focus remains on adjustments in travel demand from policy changes, assuming activity level and location as given. We are unaware of any application of this method to large-scale networks to date, primarily due to the computational complexities and lack of relevant data on demand function parameters.

5. The Activity-Based Model (ABM)

These are, in essence, tour-based travel demand models aimed at providing detailed demand forecasts for use in planning applications. A tour is usually described by a purpose: work, work-based activities, schooling, etcetera. (Recker, 2001). The model provides inputs for destination choice models belonging to the traditional four-step transportation planning type. The approach has also been applied with a micro-simulation model to show the effects of tour characteristics on destination and mode choice (Rindt et al., 2003). But how well ABM models provide solutions to the fixed demand problem is still an open question.

8. APPROACHES TO ESTIMATING BENEFITS FROM TRANSPORTATION IMPROVEMENTS

In recognition of the fixed demand problem described above, attempts have been made to provide other modeling solutions by linking various phases of transportation planning by means of a unified optimization model or an iterative process aimed at converging into an equilibrium solution. The three loops in Figure 8.4 (identified by the dashed lines) indicate possible ways of linking interzonal travel costs—that is, network assignment phase output—with previous phases. Loop A was discussed above in the context of DTA models. Later, the following approaches are discussed: (a) successive runs of trip distribution and assignment models; (b) a combined trip distribution–network optimization analysis; (c) demographic and land-use sensitivity analysis; and (d) a joint land-use–transportation model. Prior to doing so we briefly discuss identification of the relevant population for the analysis of benefits.

8.1 Identifying the Relevant Population

When carrying out a COBA of investment alternatives, the question arises as to the population whose welfare changes we wish to measure. For example, with respect to alternative alignments of a rail project, each of which passes partially or totally through a different geographical area the question is: which is the relevant population? It can be argued that any project of significant size will affect the entire urban population because of the city-wide spread of travel time changes. In theory, this may indeed be true; but in reality, considering the magnitude and spatial extent of the existing network, even a large-scale project is likely to affect interzonal travel time only marginally. Hence, the majority of an area's residents may still be unaffected by the investment, which accentuates the need for identifying the relevant population.

A necessary first step when conducting such analyses is to demarcate the corridor containing the project and to delineate the affected population within its boundaries. For example, the first phase of the Second Avenue Subway (SAS) in New York City (discussed in Chapter 15), 286,000 employees (328,000 projected for 2030) and 11,900 low-income households, are currently found within a half-mile radius of its boarding areas. It can be safely surmised that the germane population for benefit assessment in this example would be that residing within the corridor.

8.2 Linking the Trip Distribution and Assignment Models

Several attempts have been made to link the trip distribution phase with the assignment phase of the four-step model for the purpose of deriving O-D matrices that reflect travel times in congested networks, the focus being on Loop B in Figure 8.4.

1. Estimation of an O-D Matrix from Congested Network Flows

In the four-step model, the O-D matrix is estimated from trip-generation vectors using average interzonal travel times. Chen and Florian (1996) have formulated a Demand Adjustment Problem (ADP) approach for estimating the O-D matrix, based on observed links flowing from a congested network. While the solution lacks dynamic properties and represents local optimum, by accounting for travel times in this type of network, the model provides more realistic estimates of O-D matrixes than do conventional approaches.

2. Recursive Looping of the Trip Distribution and Travel Assignment Phases

By successively feeding the interzonal cost matrix back into the trip distribution model, it is possible to better adjust the O-D matrix to changing network travel conditions. The key disadvantage of this approach lies in it not being an optimization model with proven convergence properties. It is therefore impossible to assess the accuracy of the results after several successive iterations. As to its advantages, the derived O-D matrix is based on flows from a congested network, which better reflect interzonal travel demand relative to the fixed-demand O-D matrix.

3. Combined Trip Distribution and Network Assignment

A further attempt to model Loop B is represented by the Combined Trip Distribution and Network Assignment equilibrium model, proposed by Williams (1976). The idea behind this approach is to derive a measure of transportation benefits that is based on the doubly constrained spatial interaction model given in (5):

$$T_{ij} = A_i B_j O_i D_j \exp(-\beta \cdot C_{ij})$$

$$\sum_j T_{ij} = O_i$$

$$\sum_j T_{uj} = D_j$$

$$(5)$$

As before, the subscripts i and j denote zones; O_i and D_j are vectors of trip production (origins) and attraction (destinations), respectively; C_{ij} is the interzonal travel cost matrix, with β the "impedance" parameter reflecting the sensitivity of travel demand to travel cost; A_i and B_j are the so-called "balancing factors." Using the superscripts "0" and "1" to denote the project's state "before" and "after" (or "with" and "without"), Williams (1976) proposed the following measure of change in total consumer surplus induced by the project:[29]

$$\Delta CS = -\frac{1}{\beta}[\sum_i O_i \cdot \ln(\frac{A_i^1}{A_i^0}) + \sum_j D_j \cdot \ln(\frac{B1_j}{B_j^0})]^{30} \qquad (6)$$

A key drawback of this formulation is that it assumes that the trip matrix (T_{ij}) and the trip generation vectors (O_{ij} and D_j) are invariant to travel cost changes (i.e., C_{ij} before and after the project). Martinez and Araya (2000) derived a variant of Williams's measure[31] that accounts for changes in these vectors following from a change in C_{ij}. It is given by (7):

$$\Delta CS = -\frac{1}{\beta}[\sum_i \frac{1}{2}(O_i^1 + O_i^0)]\ln(\frac{A_i^1}{A_i^0}) + \sum_j \frac{1}{2}(D_j^1 + D_j^0)\ln(\frac{B_j^1}{B_j^0}) + (T^1 - T^0)] \qquad (7)$$

where $T = \sum_i \sum_j T_{ij}$ and the constant 1/2 is related to the Rule-of-Half (RH). In this formulation, trip origins and destinations are assumed elastic with respect to travel costs.[32] The two summation terms in this expression describe changes in the accessibility of origin and destination zones. The third term in (7) describes the benefits resulting from improved trip aggregation.

In effect, changes in travel costs, which are reintroduced into the trip distribution model (Loop B, Figure 8.4), generate two distinct effects: a trip distribution effect and a trip generation effect, both expressed as zone-specific trips. These are captured in expression (8):

$$\Delta CS = -\frac{1}{\beta}[\frac{1}{2}\sum_i \sum_j (T_{ij}^1 + T_{ij}^0)\ln(\frac{A_i^1}{A_i^0} \cdot \frac{B_j^1}{B_j^0}) + (T^1 - T^0)] \qquad (8)$$

Using the Rule of Half (RH), Jara-Diaz and Farah (1988) have proposed the following measure for changes in Marshallian Consumer Surplus, ΔMCS:

$$\Delta MCS = \frac{1}{2}\sum_{i=1}^{n}\sum_{j}^{n}(T_{ij}^0 + T_{ij}^1)(C_{ij}^0 - C_{ij}^1) \qquad (9)$$

Expression (9) holds provided that several conditions are met, including the integrability of the demand function (Green's theorem[33]), the absence of second-order price effects on demand, that changes in prices are relatively small, and, most importantly, the existence of a Marshallian demand function. Another important result is that if the demand function is highly convex in the range affected by the price change, the RH method will produce erroneous results. Thus, despite its popularity, the RH can only approximate the true benefits obtained from improved infrastructure because those approximations are strictly bounded by intrinsic assumptions about the true demand function.

The advantage of these measures is that they provide direct, absolute values for the net gains flowing from a transportation improvement, thereby avoiding the need for separate computation of the "before" and "after" benefits. Moreover, they do not require detailed information on the underlying travel demand function. Regarding their disadvantages, they ignore the induced fixed demand issue. That is, these measures do not provide an answer to the case where $C_{ij}^0 = C_{ij}^1$, that is, "before" and "after" prices are the same (see point "C" in Figure 8.3). Most importantly, while these measures constitute an improvement over the conventional approach of the four-step transportation planning model, the key impediment remaining unresolved—the invariability of the total number of zonal trips with respect to travel costs. Hence, all that can be achieved by this linkage is a better distribution of existing trips.

8.3 Demographic and Land-Use Sensitivity Analyses

In the absence of available land-use models, planners often devise scenarios of future demographic and land-use configurations to facilitate exploration of potential benefit distributions. Common scenarios include a range of population growth rates, changes in employment size and composition, changes in activity location, changes in residential density, etcetera. Based on these changes, new trip generation vectors are derived and used to compute new O-D matrices. These, in turn, are fed as inputs into the assignment model to produce new interzonal travel time matrices. This procedure is carried out with and without capacity enhancing investments in order to estimate net benefits. By varying the assumptions on future demographic and spatial patterns, it is possible to obtain a range of travel time savings from the investment, meant to account for alternative future states of the area. The key difficulty with this approach is that it does not produce the equilibrium results that enable correct welfare comparisons of travel time savings before and after the investment. That is, because the variables in these scenarios are exogenous to the transportation system, the scenarios are insensitive to the travel time changes that in reality affect zonal distribution of activities.

8.4 Equilibrium Analysis: A Joint Land-Use–Transportation Model

A more complicated but much more accurate way to estimate travel time savings from a transportation improvement project is to estimate a joint land-use–transportation model. Future annual land-use projections are first calculated. These are then entered into trip generation functions to produce future-year zonal travel. Based on these, an O-D trip matrix is derived and subsequently used as input into a traffic assignment model that loads these trips onto a network with capacity expanded links. The resultant interzonal travel times are next fed back into the land-use model to produce revised land-use patterns (Loop C in Figure 8.4). The overall process repeats itself until a convergence rule is completed. In theory, at least, the process can converge into an optimal equilibrium solution if an agreed-upon social welfare objective function can be specified.[34]

If future land-use patterns and demographic trends are properly projected and if a dynamic traffic assignment model (or, for that matter, Loop A in Figure 8.4) is used to account for time of departure shifts, the phenomenon of induced demand will not appear because it has already been accounted for. Thus, a joint land-use and transportation framework should be the preferred method of analysis. However, such a comprehensive model requires major modeling and data collection efforts that are, by and large, beyond the scope of most planning agencies.

9. OTHER APPROACHES TO THE ESTIMATION OF BENEFITS FROM A TRANSPORTATION INVESTMENT

Accepting the fact that at best, transportation planning can be equated with a partial equilibrium analysis, are there other methods available to assess changes in the benefits generated by a capacity investment project? Two such major approaches are discuss below: random utility and aggregate demand function approximation.

9.1 Random Utility Measures of Benefits

Begin with the standard multinomial logit model, where the probability of choosing an alternative from a set of alternatives is given by:

$$P^{sk} = \frac{\exp(\beta^s V^{sk})}{\sum\limits_k \exp(\beta^s V^{sk})} \qquad (10)$$

In (10), s denotes a user class (identified among the overall relevant population of choice makers), k denotes a chosen alternative (e.g., mode) from choice set R, β is a parameter[35], and V^{sk} is a vector of the measurable attributes (strict utility) of k (de La Barra, 1989). Based on expression (10), Cochrane (1975) has shown that the average utility perceived by class s, AC^s, is given by

$$AC^s = \frac{1}{\beta^s} \ln[\sum\limits_k \exp(\beta^s V^{sk})] \qquad (11)$$

As shown by Williams (1977), expression (11) is equivalent to the traditional consumer surplus measure. Based on this expression, the following measures of the change in welfare from a transportation improvement is derived:

$$\Delta CS^s = \frac{1}{\beta^s} \ln(\sum\limits_{\forall k \in R} e^{V_{ik}^1}) - \frac{1}{\beta^s} \ln(\sum\limits_{\forall k \in R} e^{V_{ik}^0}) \qquad (12)$$

Or,

$$\Delta CS^s = \frac{-1}{\beta^s} \ln\left[\frac{\sum\limits_{\forall k \in R} e^{V_{ik}^1}}{\sum\limits_{\forall k \in R} e^{V_{ik}^0}}\right] \qquad (13)$$

In this notation, ΔCS^s is the change in consumer surplus for class s users, and k is an alternative selected by individual $i (i \in s)$ from the choice set R. The superscripts "0" and "1" denote "before" and "after" the change, respectively.[36]

Small and Rosen (1981) have shown that for multinomial logit specification such as (10)—in the absence of income effects—the expected change in consumer surplus is given by:

$$\Delta CS = -\frac{1}{\lambda} \ln(\sum\limits_{\forall k \in R} e^{V^k}) \qquad (14)$$

In (14), λ is defined as the marginal utility of income $(\partial V_i/\partial I)$.[37] The change in indirect utility is converted into some currency value (e.g., dollars) by means of the factor $1/\lambda$ (the inverse of the individual's marginal utility of income). Assuming a compensating variations-type demand function, (14) can be rewritten as:

$$\Delta CS = -\frac{1}{\lambda} \ln \left[(\sum_{\forall k \in R} e^{V^k}) \right]_{v_0}^{v_1} \tag{15}$$

In (15), v_0 and v_1 are the mean of the indirect utility for travel scenarios 0 and 1, respectively.[38] Expression (15) is a consistent measure of welfare, inherent to the logit model.

Several attempts have been made to apply these measures in the assessment of benefits from changes in transportation conditions. For example, Ortuzar and Gonzales (2002), when examining the effect of changes in travel conditions—for example, fare, travel time—on mode choice, used a discrete mode choice model of inter-island travel to derive measures similar to expression (15). Niemeier (1997) used a similar Small–Rosen measure to empirically calculate the monetary value of mode-destination accessibility for morning journeys to work. De Jong et al. (2007) used the log-sum welfare measure (the expected consumer surplus from an improvement) to calculate benefits from a reduction in generalized costs of travel. This measure is defined as the log of the sum of the choice utilities of sampled individuals, obtained from a random utility model (e.g., multinomial logit) and divided by the marginal utility of income.

9.2 Induced Demand: A Demand Function Approximation

Because a joint land-use–transportation analysis is hardly ever actually performed, how are we to account for induced demand when assessing benefits from capacity investments? Despite the limited information available on pre- and postinvestment equilibria, it is still possible to estimate the shift in demand (D_1 to D_2 in Figure 8.3) and, subsequently, the change in benefits. First, approximate the demand function with a linear function of the type $v = \alpha - \beta \cdot p$, where v is travel volume, p is travel price, and α and β are parameters. To estimate these values, make use of the observed volumes and prices, v_1 and p_1, and the reported demand price elasticity, η_p (e.g., about -0.5; Goodwin, 1996). Once this information is obtained, it is possible to compute the linear demand function as in (16):[39]

$$v = v_1(1 + \eta_p) - \eta_p (\frac{p_1}{v_1})p \tag{16}$$

Computation of the shift in the demand function from D_1 to D_2, as in Figure 8.3, and the subsequent change in welfare represents the next step. To that end, we make use of lane-mile travel elasticities with respect to capacity change η_{LM}, as reported in the literature.[40] Assuming, for example, $|\beta| = 0.3$ and $\eta_{LM} = 0.5$, calculate D_2 and then the change in benefits from the capacity expansion. In general, the change in net benefits from the investment, ΔNB, is given by:

$$\Delta NB = \frac{1}{2}|\beta|(v_1)^2((1+\eta_{LM})^2 - 1) \tag{17}$$

Using these figures the change in welfare is $0.188(v_1)^2$.

10. PLAUSIBILITY OF THE ESTIMATED BENEFITS

Once a project's travel time savings have been derived, the reasonableness and reliability of these results are to be considered in terms of the project's nature and the surrounding urban area. Remember, however, that biases intrinsic to the transportation model and the database can often produce estimates that, when compared with external indices, appear unreasonable. We therefore suggest that once benefit estimates are derived, a separate analysis be performed to ascertain their reasonableness. Here we outline several impediments to obtaining reliable estimates.

As explained earlier, future travel patterns are derived from land-use projections, mainly of population and employment. These forecasts often represent pretentious urban development plans that are unlikely to materialize. Moreover, transportation authorities, in their eagerness to implement a capital-intensive investment project, are often disposed to coercing modelers and planners to accept these urban forecasts as the sole bases for their transportation projections. The results therefore tend to be inflated benefit estimates and underestimated costs. At the very least, investment project analysts should be allowed to independently ascertain the reasonableness of those regional population and employment forecasts before incorporating them into their models. Various indices can be used to that end. For example, one can compare local employment and population forecasts with regional, provincial, state, or even national forecasts. Alternatively, regional population and employment growth rates can be employed as upper bounds on local growth rates.

Another issue is that travel forecasts obtained from a specific model frequently do not add up to the aggregate forecasts. To illustrate, when applying the four-step transportation-planning model, the aggregate travel flowing through all the network's links can deviate significantly from total trip forecasts measured either by traffic volume or by VMT. It is therefore necessary to adjust traffic assignment results to the aggregate forecasts in order to obtain reasonable benefit estimates relative to travel time and cost savings. Adjustments of this type, while important, may nonetheless increase the likelihood of multiplicative error being built into the final travel forecasts. That is, if each step of the planning model is subject to errors either because of necessary adjustments, poor data, or an inadequate algorithm, this error is likely to amplify once it serves as input for the next phase. Keeping track of possible errors in each step is a prerequisite for obtaining reliable results.

As argued above, the use of inelastic demand functions results in overestimation of benefits—relative to elastic demand functions—by a large margin. Yet, another source of biased estimation is the use of target-year travel volumes. Even if an elastic demand analysis is carried out, the use of estimated future annual volumes may lead to overestimation of an investment's benefits. To avoid such biased results, a growth model—rather than specification of future volumes—should be incorporated into the overall cost-benefit model to allow for expanding motorization rates as well as income and population, factors that increase benefits over time (see Chapter 6).

Another important inaccuracy in benefit estimation stems from the fact that predictions of future travel times and volumes are conditional on the stability of key demographic and land-use parameters over time and space. For example, residential density parameters may not uniformly change at all locations, thus changing the estimated number of trips emanating from specific zones. Modal split ratios may likewise change in response to rising income or population aging, which can critically affect actual travel patterns. Unless properly accounted for in terms of longitudinal and spatial constancy, the use of current parameters to predict future benefits may render their accuracy as rather tenuous.

In the face of all these constraints, how can we assess the reasonableness of the results obtained from benefit estimation? One approach would be to compare the compatibility between currently observed trip length distributions with those forecasted by trip distribution and assignment methods. A second approach involves determining how well predicted trip rates per capita and per vehicle compare with current rates. Unreasonable future rates may indicate an intrinsic error within the model. A third approach is to ascertain whether the distribution of travel demand by time of day predicted by the transportation model is, in fact, realistic. A fourth criterion is the degree of correspondence between forecasted levels of demand with current trip data collected at key locations on the network. A related approach is to conduct cordon traffic counts and compare them with the model's forecasts.

To illustrate, let VMT_1 denote the per capita VMT forecast by the four-step transportation model. Compare this result with computed per capita VMT, denoted by VMT_2, as a function of the annual population growth rate, X_1, the trip generation growth rate (in trips per person), X_2, and the rate of growth in average trip length (in miles), X_3. Thus, the computed change in annual VMT is:

$$VMT_2 = f(X_1 \cdot X_2 \cdot X_3) / K \tag{18}$$

where K denotes vehicles per capita. The deviations of VMT_1 from VMT_2 provide a good test for the reasonableness of the forecasted results.

Turning to public transit investments, a key measure of the reasonableness of the benefit assessments obtained is the comparison of modal split rates with and without the project. All too often, the predicted rate of transit use does not match forecasted highway travel. That is, if a significant number of trip makers do switch from car to transit, highway congestion levels will decline, thereby inducing a "switch back" from transit to highway until the two systems settle into equilibrium. The reasonableness of actual modal split changes therefore needs to be ascertained through a transit-car equilibrium analysis.

11. SUMMARY AND CONCLUSIONS

The main objective of this chapter was to examine key computational problems involved in the estimation of benefits from a transportation investment project. From an economic viewpoint, the concept *economic benefits from capacity investment* refers to the change in consumers' surplus that, in transportation, is measured in terms of changes in travel time savings and traffic volumes. In principle, assessment of total benefits from an investment should likewise include any change in producer surplus. Yet, for reasons explained in this chapter, this is not commonly done.

It should be understood, though, that measured benefits, even if computed correctly, are only second-best approximations at best. First, the estimation of benefits is carried out under second-best conditions (e.g., capacity investment in the absence of congestion pricing). Second, benefit estimates are, by and large, derived from a nonequilibrium procedure, such as that shown in Figure 8.4 (without Loop C). Inaccuracies from data and measurement methods consequently tend to get compounded, especially when benefit projections are made for very distant periods (e.g., 20–30 years hence).

In general, traffic congestion tends to maintain a self-limiting equilibrium. Expanding roadway capacity reduces congestion delays, allowing more peak-period trips that express shifts in time, mode, route, and destination. Travel shifts necessarily enhance consumers' utility or they would not be made. However, for the purpose of benefit computation, these shifts, collectively known as induced demand, pose a serious challenge because prior to making the investment, the only variables to be observed at this point are travel times and volumes. Unless properly accounted for, these shifts result in grossly biased estimates of the ensuing benefits. In addition, it has been argued here that several factors lie at the bottom of this problem, including the practice of using fixed-demand O-D matrices; the use of inappropriate traffic assignment procedures; and the lack of iterative feedback between transportation and land-use components.

These biases in the estimation of benefits can be summarized as follows. First, the welfare analysis is correct but the model used to estimate future travel times and volumes does not accurately reflect reality. For example, the model ignores dynamic adjustments of time, route, and mode choice. Second, the welfare analysis is incorrect, irrespective of whether the model reasonably represents reality. For instance, benefits may be defined as the product of the new estimated travel volume (after the capacity expansion) and the preexpansion travel time or cost (i.e., the area: $P_1(V_2 - V_1)$ in Figure 8.3). From a welfare perspective, this area represents total expenditures on travel related to additional traffic but *not* true benefits. Third, even if the welfare analysis and the estimation model are correctly defined, biases are likely to enter if longitudinal and spatial changes in key demographic, economic, and travel parameters are not taken into account. For example, activity density *and* composition are likely to vary over time at particular locations. If not properly considered by the model, the estimated travel results are again grossly biased.

Several approaches, embedded in the three loops shown in Figure 8.4, were suggested to overcome these difficulties. One key recommendation was to use a dynamic traffic assignment (DTA) model to allow for temporal shifts, primarily from off-peak to peak periods after completion of the capacity expansion (Loop A in Figure 8.4). Compared with the Static Assignment Model, use of DTA will greatly improve the accuracy and reliability of the benefit assessment.

A second key recommendation was to use a feedback loop between the trip distribution and the travel assignment phases of the transportation model (Loop B in Figure 8.4). By successively feeding the interzonal cost matrix (derived from either the STA or the DTA model) back into the trip distribution model in a partial equilibrium set-up, it becomes possible to better adjust the O-D matrix to changes in travel costs. This procedure produces estimated travel time savings that are more accurate than those derived under current practices by far. A related approach is to use a combined trip distribution and network assignment equilibrium procedure. Such an approach has generated several analytical expressions for assessing total benefits before and after the capacity change.

The third key recommendation was to use an equilibrium joint land-use–transportation model (represented by Loop C in Figure 8.4). Under this approach, land-use projections are employed to derive trip generation and distribution patterns that also encompass potential future travel demand. The interzonal travel costs based on this demand are then iteratively fed back into the land-use model until equilibrium is achieved. The key result of this procedure is the absence of induced demand because all potential sources of demand are already accounted for. If a DTA model is also used, induced demand from temporal shifts is considered as well.

In the absence of a land-use model, an alternative approach would be to employ future demographic and land-use patterns to derive trip production and attraction vectors. The resultant O-D matrices are then computed and fed into the assignment model as inputs. By varying the assumptions on these future activity patterns, it is possible to obtain a credible *range* of travel time savings from the transportation investment.

Studies have shown that gaps between travel demand projections and actual trends grow exponentially as a function of the time elapsed. Given current transportation planning practices that include use of nonequilibrium models to assess travel time savings, projections made for distant time horizons are liable to produce considerably erroneous results. It might therefore be useful to require shorter term evaluations—a period of 7–10 years only—when assessing a transportation project's economic benefits. The use of equilibrium models, especially joint land-use–transportation models, could allow more realistic assessments for longer periods of, say, 15–20 years. Beyond such horizons, all projections are subject to significant uncertainties.

APPENDIX A: EMPIRICAL EXAMPLES OF ASSIGNMENT MODEL WITH FIXED AND ELASTIC DEMAND

Formulation:

$$\min. z(v,d) = \sum_{a \in A} \int_0^{v_a} t_a(x)dx - \sum_{w \in W} \int_0^{d_w} D_w^{-1}(x)dx \qquad (A1)$$

Subject to:

$$\sum_{r \in R_w} f_r = d_w, \quad w \in W$$

$$\sum_{r \in R} f_r \delta_{ar} = v_a, \quad a \in A \qquad (A2)$$

$$f_r > 0, \quad r \in R$$

Where: $d_w = D_w(u), w \in W$
  In this formulation:
  a = a link belonging to the set of links A
  w = an O-D pair belonging to the set of all link pairs, $w \in W$
  R = a set of paths in the network
  R_w = a set of paths between an O-D pair, w, $w \in W$
  v_a = a flow on link a, $a \in A$
  $t_a(v)$ = travel time (costs) on link a as a function of the link's flow, which is assumed to be strictly monotonic
  d_w = demand of an O-D pair, w, which is assumed to be a function of equilibrium travel times between all O-D pairs
  $D_w(u)$ = Demand on O-D pair, w, $w \in W$, assumed to be strictly monotone
  u = vector of shortest path costs between all O-D pairs
  d = vector of all O-D demands
  D_w^{-1} = inverse of demand function ($u_w = D_w^{-1}(d)$)
  δ_{ar} = link-path indicator, $\delta_{ar} \begin{cases} 1 \text{ if path uses link } a \\ 0 \end{cases}$
  Based on this formulation, we next carry out some numerical exercises whose objectives are, first, to compute travel times and volumes for a simple two-road network under fixed and variable demand; second, to show the

impact of capacity expansion on consumers surplus; third, to carry out this analysis under conditions of user and system equilibrium.

Consider two locations linked by two roads, denoted as "1" and "2", respectively. The volume-capacity functions of these roads are given by:

$$t_1(v_1) = a_1 + b_1 \cdot (\frac{v_1}{c_1})^{\alpha_1} \quad a_1, b_1, \alpha_1 > 0 \tag{A3}$$

$$t_2(v_2) = a_2 + b_2 \cdot (\frac{v_2}{c_2})^{\alpha_2} \quad a_2, b_2, \alpha_2 > 0 \tag{A4}$$

Where t_1, v_1 and t_2, v_2 are travel time and volume on roads 1 and 2, respectively, c_1 and c_2 denote the capacity of roads 1 and 2, respectively; a, b, and α are parameters.

The demand function for travel between these locations is given by

$$V(t) = V_0 - \beta \cdot (t)^{\gamma} \quad \beta, \gamma > 0 \tag{A5}$$

Where V is demand in vehicles per hour, t is travel time, V_0 is demand for $t = 0$, and β and γ are parameters. Note that under conditions of user equilibrium, $t_1 = t_2 = t$.

Assume the following hypothetical data (in units of thousands of vehicles for traffic volume and road capacity) shown in Table 8.A1.

What are the traffic volumes and travel times on each road? To that end we solve the following "user equilibrium" optimization problem:

$$\text{min.} \quad y(v_1, v_2) = \int_0^{v_1} \left[a_1 + b_1 (\frac{x}{c_1})^{\alpha_1} \right] dx + \int_0^{v_2} \left[a_2 + b_2 (\frac{x}{c_2})^{\alpha_2} \right] dx$$

s.t.

$$v_1 > 0;$$
$$v_2 > 0$$ \tag{A6}
$$v_1 + v_2 = V(t)$$

Given the results of problem (A6), what is the consumer surplus (CS)? The computation of CS can be done in two alternative ways. First, by computing the area under the demand curve along the vertical (cost) axis between t and the intersection of the demand curve with the cost axis (for which $V = 0$), that is, $t = V(t)/\beta$. Thus,

$$CS = \int_t^{\frac{V(t)}{\beta}} (V_0 - \beta \cdot x^{\gamma}) \, dx \tag{A7}$$

Alternatively, CS can be obtained by computing the area under the inverse demand function, that is, $t(V) = \sqrt[\gamma]{(V_0 - V)/\beta}$, between 0 and $V(t)$, less the revenues (or user costs) $R = t \cdot V(t)$. Thus,

Table 8.A1 Initial Values of Parameters

Parameter	Value
c_1	2.5
c_2	3.5
a_1	2
a_2	4
b_1	3
b_2	2
V_0	10

$$CS = \left[\int_0^{V(t)} (\gamma \sqrt{\frac{V_0 - V}{\beta}}) \, dx - R \right] \qquad (A8)$$

Producer surplus is computed for road 1 by (A9)

$$PS = (t_1 \cdot v_1) - \int_0^{v_1} (a_1 + b_1 (\frac{x}{c_1})^{\alpha_1}) \, dx \qquad (A9)$$

The expression $(t_1 \cdot v_1)$ is total user expenditures in road 1. To compute producer surplus for road 2, insert road 2's parameters.

Total surplus, which is our measure of welfare benefits, (W), is: $W = CS + PS$. Changing the capacity of any of these roads allows us to compute the resulting change in consumer and producer surplus (the difference in CS and PS values before and after the change). In what follows we will examine a combination of four major cases: inelastic and elastic demand and linear and nonlinear link volume-capacity functions. For each of these cases we compute the impact of changing the capacity of road 1 by 20%, (i.e., from 2,500 vehicles/hour to 3,000 vehicles/hour) on traffic volume and travel time on each road, total travel demand (V), Total Travel Time (TOT), defined as: $t_i \cdot v_i$; $i = 1,2$, consumer surplus (CS), producer surplus (PS), and total welfare benefits (CS + PS).

Case 1

User equilibrium for linear volume-capacity functions and fixed demand ($V(t) = V_0$), as shown in Figure 8.A1. The numerical results are shown in Table 8.A2.

By comparing the two sets of results shown in Table 8.A2 it is evident that following the capacity expansion, traffic will, as expected, be diverted

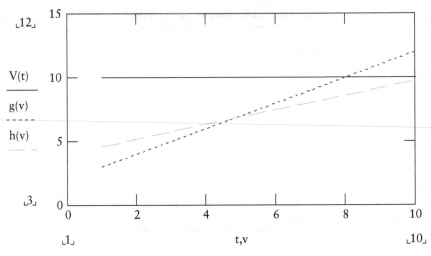

Figure 8.A1 Fixed demand with linear volume-capacity functions.

Table 8.A2 Results from Simulation (with Linear Volume-Capacity Functions and Fixed Demand; $\alpha_1 = \alpha_2 = 1$; $\beta = 0$ (i.e., $V(t) = V_0$))

Variable	Before Capacity Expansion	After Capacity Expansion
c_1	2.5	3.0
c_2	3.5	3.5
v_1	4.355	4.909
t_1	7.226	6.909
v_2	5.645	5.091
t_2	7.226	6.909
$V(v_1 + v_2)$	10	10
TOT1 $(t_1 \cdot v_1)$	31.467	33.917
TOT2 $(t_2 \cdot v_2)$	40.791	35.174
CS	0	0
PS_1	11.379	12.05
PS_2	9.105	7.405

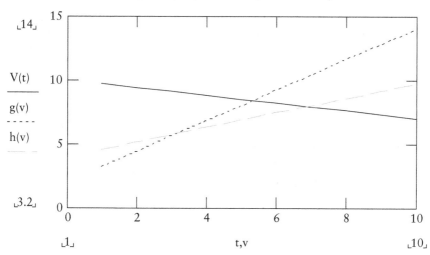

Figure 8.A2 Down-Sloping linear demand function with linear volume-capacity functions.

Table 8.A3 Results from Simulation ($\alpha_1 = \alpha_2 = 1$, $\beta = 0.3$, (i.e., $V(t) = V_0 - \beta \cdot t$))

Variable	Before Capacity Expansion	After Capacity Expansion
c_1	2.5	3.0
c_2	3.5	3.5
v_1	3.728	4.23
t_1	6.474	6.23
v_2	4.329	3.902
t_2	6.474	6.23
$V\,(v_1 + v_2)$	8.058	8.131
TOT1 $(t_1 \cdot v_1)$	24.137	26.348
TOT2 $(t_2 \cdot v_2)$	28.029	24.305
CS	108.214	110.193
PS_1	8.34	8.944
PS_2	5.356	4.349
$PS\,(PS_1 + PS_2)$	13.696	13.294
$W\,(CS + PS)$	121.909	123.486

to road 1 from road 2 while travel time on each road will decline. Because we have assumed inelastic demand, we neither compute the change in consumer surplus for this case nor the total change in welfare (W ($CS + PS$)).

Case 2

User equilibrium for linear volume-capacity functions and down-sloping elastic demand function ($V(t) = V_0 - \beta \cdot t$), as shown in Figure 8.A2. The numerical results are given in Table 8.A3.

Notice that in Table 8.A3 while total producer surplus ($PS = (PS_1 + PS_2)$) has declined after capacity was expanded total welfare ($W = (CS + PS)$) has increased, caused by the increase in consumer surplus.

9 Risk and Uncertainty in Transportation Project Evaluation

1. INTRODUCTION

All investments, private or public, are subject to risks, mainly in connection with the expected costs and benefits. The magnitude of these risks is a function of project type, size, complexity, management, and political environment. Transportation infrastructure investments are, invariably, no exception because they are quite complicated to design and implement as well as require huge sums of capital, significant portions of which are sunk costs. Moreover, the demand for transportation services varies considerably over time and space, making it difficult to predict. On the other hand, transportation investments are indivisible and, once committed to politically, legally, and financially, are largely irreversible. Hence, the risks associated with transportation investments include cost overruns, unmet schedules, lower than expected demand, significantly reduced levels of service, and, at times, financial insolvency. This reality notwithstanding, the common practice in transportation project evaluation is to forgo a comprehensive risk analysis, a decision that often leads to disastrous results.[1] In part as a warning, this chapter examines a range of transportation investment risks, their measurement and integration within the overall project evaluation process.

Beginning with Knight (1921) the economic literature uses the term *risk* when referring to the likelihood of a future state of nature when the probabilities of an occurrence are known or can be assessed. The term *uncertainty* is used for cases when these probabilities are unknown or unobtainable in an objective way.[2] In reality, however, there is a continuum of cases extending from a well-defined distribution of future states of nature to the polar case where the distribution of such states is totally unknown. For example, it is possible to quite accurately assess safety benefits from a highway investment by using past data on traffic accidents to derive the probability of an occurrence by accident type and facility-design characteristics. On the other hand, it is quite a challenge to produce the probability distribution for future travel demand for a new facility, especially when its life span exceeds 5–10 years.[3]

Because of the said continuum, the transportation literature often uses the terms risk and uncertainty interchangeably to indicate that transportation cost and benefit projections are to be treated with some measure of reservation. Because the major objective of project evaluation is to calculate an investment's welfare contribution, risk can be defined as the probability that a computed welfare contribution will, in fact, fall significantly short of expectations. The evaluator's objective therefore becomes the assessment of the risk incurred when making a given investment. Alternatively, risk could be defined as the opportunity cost forgone by investing in one rather than another project. Section 5 uses the latter definition as a means to assess a project's overall risk. For practical purposes, however, the former definition is used as the principle guiding this chapter.

Before delving into methods of risk analysis and measurement, we need to consider the theoretical argument first made by Arrow and Lind (1970) regarding the question of whether risk matters in public investment analysis. Arrow and Lind argued that when the government undertakes large-scale public works projects, risk could often be ignored because it is spread among a very large number of taxpayers and each individual's cost of risk bearing[4] is negligible.[5] Stated differently, while the nonexistence of some insurance markets may result in suboptimal overall risk distributions, the deviation from optimality is rather insignificant in such cases due to the very large number of individuals who are exposed to the risk.

How applicable is this reasoning to large-scale transportation projects? If we consider the likelihood that negative externalities, which imply disutility to individuals, will accrue disproportionately to an identifiable group of people, the Arrow–Lind argument may not hold. Given that transportation projects generate externality costs whose incidence is spatially concentrated, the argument that risk can be ignored in transportation investment is erroneous. For example, people residing along a highway construction project are likely to suffer extensive disutility from noise, pollution, and disruption of daily activity whereas those residing further away will not. A similar argument can be made if a transportation investment is financed by local taxes because local real estate owners assume the greatest risk of cost overruns de facto. In these and similar cases, we cannot argue that the risk of cost bearing is spread among the entire population and can thus be forgone in analyzing an investment.

Many public agencies, increasingly faced with limited budgets in recent years, have turned to the private sector for project funding, construction, and operation. These so-called Public–Private Partnerships (PPP or P3) require contracts that assign (albeit at times implicitly) the risk allocation among the parties. Such distributions invite the theoretical question of how risk should be allocated between the state and the private partners. Is there a fair risk-sharing formula? Section 9 examines this issue.

An important issue in transportation risk analysis is the attitude towards risk exhibited by public decision-makers. It has already been noted (in Chapter 5) that public officials often regard capital costs as benefits because these costs are translated into economic returns such as new jobs and real estate development. This attitude tends to be further exaggerated when funding for local projects comes from the state or the federal government. I therefore suggest that the level of risk aversion depends on the proportion of funding that is provided by sources external to the decision maker's jurisdiction. The higher this proportion, the higher is her propensity to accept risky projects. Section 6 provides a formal statement of this idea.

To summarize, this chapter is concerned with the following two key issues. First, how are we to define and measure a project's various risk components and, accordingly, its overall risk level? Second, how can we incorporate risk analysis into the project evaluation process? An important caveat is the differentiation to be made between the risk level of a single project and that of a set of technically interdependent projects because the concept of risk as presented here is most applicable to the evaluation of single, independent investment projects. However, when the analysis is at the level of strategic transportation planning (see Chapter 2) and refers to projects that might be technically dependent, the focus shifts to the plan's overall risk, which is *not* a linear combination of the risks of the individual projects. This chapter is mainly concerned with the risk level of a single project; yet, it rests with the analyst to make clear what type of risk is actually being examined when analyzing an entire investment plan.

The structure of this chapter is as follows. Section 2 discusses sources of risk and uncertainty in transportation investment projects. Section 3 examines methods of risk measurement in project appraisal. Section 4 examines probabilistic and simulation methods, while Section 5 explores curve fitting methods. A decision-tree analysis is presented in Section 6. Section 7 explores optimal investment timing rules under uncertainty. Issues pertaining to risk sharing in public–private partnerships are discussed in Section 8. Section 9 presents a private sector approach to the measurement of total project risk, which can be used as a benchmark for public project risk analysis. Section 10 discusses methods of incorporating risk into project evaluation and ways of mitigating risk in project implementation. A summary and conclusions are found in Section 11.

2. SOURCES OF RISK AND UNCERTAINTY IN TRANSPORTATION INVESTMENT PROJECTS

Transportation investments are subject to various types of risk, ranging from those related to construction to those related to patronage. But before these categories are examined in detail, we must confirm what we mean by risk and uncertainty.

2.1 Defining Risk in Public Investments

As explained previously, when making decisions, risk implies future events with known probabilities of occurrence whereas uncertainty implies unknown probabilities. Thus, the key distinction between the two concepts rests on knowledge or the degree to which information on future events is available (Frame, 2003).

The literature commonly defines risk as the "exposure to the possibility of economic or financial loss or gain, physical damage or injury, or delay, as a consequence of the uncertainty associated with pursuing a particular course of action" (Cooper and Chapman, 1987). Sturk et al. (1996) and Jaafari (2001) define risk as the exposure to loss/gain, or the probability of the occurrence of loss/gain multiplied by its respective magnitude. Hence, risk can be viewed as the product of the probability of an event occurring and the actual outcomes (consequences) of this event. That is:

$$\text{Risk} = \text{Probability} \times \text{Consequence} \tag{1}$$

However, in defining risk we need to distinguish between two concepts: the probability that an event (e.g., construction delay) will actually take place and the distribution of this event's consequences (e.g., the magnitude of cost overruns). Accordingly, Ayyub (2003), defines risk as:

$$RISK\left[\frac{Consequence}{Time}\right] =$$

$$LIKELIHOOD\left[\frac{Event}{Time}\right] \times IMPACT\left[\frac{Consequence}{Event}\right] \tag{2}$$

Expression (2) implies that the risk of a certain event is the probability of that event occurring times the probability of its size, which is conditional on this event occurring. This probability is then:

$$P(\theta) = P(e)P(\theta|e) \tag{3}$$

For example, the event "traffic accident" can have several outcomes (e.g., car damage, body injury, fatal injury). Thus, the risk of a fatal injury (θ) from an accident (denoted by $P(\theta)$) is the product of the probability that an accident will take place ($P(e)$) and the conditional probability of a fatality in the event of an "accident" taking place ($P(\theta|e)$). Sections 4 and 5 present methods for estimating the probability distribution of cost overruns of a transportation investment project.

2.2 A Typology of Project Risks

All categories of project risk share one factor in common: They are random variables with known probabilities. For estimation purposes, however, it is useful to identify specific risk items by type and magnitude as follows.

a. Underestimated Cost Forecasts (Cost Overruns): Data show that forecasts of capital costs, in particular of urban rail, have systematically underestimated the true costs of construction and service delivery (Pickrell, 1990). Flyvbjerg et al. (2003) provide data showing that of the 258 projects surveyed, cost overruns of 40% were quite common, with overruns of 80% not infrequent. This is, by far, the most serious type of risk because it may contribute to a project's insolvency and failure.

b. Overestimated Benefits: Projections of future transportation benefits from investments—number of passenger-trips, vehicle-trips, vehicle-miles traveled, and travel time saved—are notoriously inaccurate. Several *ex post* studies have substantiated this observation (e.g., Flyvbjerg et al., 2005; Pickrell, 1990; Kain, 1990). Factors common to benefits overestimation are:

1. Poor database quality: Often, the databases used for demand projections are poorly assembled, recorded and updated. Especially vulnerable are the networks data used to assess travel time savings. Land use and demographic forecasts, essential for the derivation of future travel demand, are commonly based on outdated data or, quite frequently, reflect unsubstantiated urban and regional aspirations rather than hard facts.
2. Disregard for contradictory or mutually exclusive trends in urban development and investment. When urban rail projects are planned, planners frequently choose to disregard other factors that may negate their ridership forecasts. An example is Buffalo Light Rail, where the project's rationale rested on ridership to the CBD area. Planners nevertheless failed to account for the concurrent large-scale shopping mall and highway developments in adjacent suburbs that diverted substantial traffic from Buffalo's downtown (Berechman and Paaswell, 1983).
3. Use of flawed methodologies for benefit forecasts. A most serious issue is the failure to use an equilibrium framework when computing future travel prices and volumes. Other factors similarly ignored are market imperfections, such as monopolistic behavior by public transit, rail, or airports, which can render forecasts incorrect (see Venabels and Gasiorek, 1996). Therefore, mere extrapolation of traffic based on, for example, expected population growth rates, is likely to result in grossly inaccurate forecasts.
4. Unwillingness to estimate the probability of a "worst case" scenario, defined as the case when unexpected technological, economic, political, and social changes—the conditions necessary for a project's viability— transpire. While it is not possible to foresee such events, it is nonetheless crucial to consider the probability of a worst case scenario in order to ascertain the boundaries of the project's economic feasibility as well as benefits. For example, if the project's break-even point is quite sensitive to small changes in regional unemployment, this may signal excessive vulnerability to contextual conditions. By and large, the project's susceptibility to changes in core variables is too often ignored.

5. Fixed future year projections. Demand projections are calculated for specific future years. When substantial delays in project completion become a reality, updates of the original demand projections are too often not performed.
6. Ridership projections carried out at the initial feasibility phase but never revised in the wake of detailed transportation and engineering planning.

c. Substandard Levels of Service: Effective levels of demand (e.g., number of users) are strongly influenced by the actual Level of Service (LOS) a project provides. LOS captures the time saved, reliability, ease of access and egress, crowding, and other amenities. Often, the risk of producing poor levels of service that in turn affect demand is left unaccounted for.

d. Technological Change: A technology adopted at the planning stage may turn out to be inappropriate once construction begins. In some cases the new technology represents improvements in equipment and methods. Such events are especially common during excavation and burrowing. The inadequacy of equipment and methods often force their replacement by newer, more effective but more expensive tools while work is in progress. Whatever the reason for the switch, it raises the risk of higher than projected capital and maintenance costs.

Adoption of inappropriate technology can also create risk. In transportation, construction of high-speed rail in dense metropolitan areas is not considered wise because a greater number of stations are required, as are long acceleration and deceleration distances, generally unavailable in cities. As a result, lower than expected speed levels are achieved. These render the enormous costs of this technology unviable in the face of the low expected benefits.

e. Financial Risks: Large-scale projects require the commitment of substantial funding over long periods of time. The consequent risk factors include:

1. Changes in interest rates, which increase debt service costs
2. Changes in exchange rates, which affect factor prices such as those for imported rolling stock or fuel
3. Drying up of funds due to the bankruptcy of a private partner or changes in the economic environment, such as reductions in the real estate tax revenues used to fund new public transit projects
4. Longitudinal decline in the farebox or toll revenues that support public transit and highway construction projects

f. Agency Risk: Project risks can also stem from the administrative structure and behavior of the public agencies that plan and manage infrastructure projects (Public Financial Management Inc., 1989):

1. Reauthorization risk: Need for annual legislative reauthorization of an agency's budget, a requirement that introduces political uncertainties into budget approval

2. Legislative appropriations risk, which may render long-term funding commitments uncertain

g. Failure to Meet Timetables: Flyvbjerg et al. (2004) have shown that cost overruns are highly correlated with the project's time horizon. Nonavailability of right-of-way, interest group objections, difficulties in securing the necessary funding, unforeseen engineering and construction difficulties can all delay project completion.

h. Risk Associated with Government Policies:

1. Unforeseeable changes in government transportation, land-use, and fiscal policies can threaten project initiation and even completion. Notable examples of such changes are new land-use policies that negate transit objectives by encouraging sprawl and highway use.
2. Macroeconomic realities such as economic down cycles often necessitate the government budget cuts that dry up funding and bring a project to a halt.
3. Failure of governments to live up to prior commitments, which represent the necessary preconditions for a project's construction. Examples are the failure to secure right of ways or to complete land clearance by a given date.

In practice, the above sources of risk manifest themselves as one of three major categories of project risk: cost overruns, insufficient demand, and financial insolvency. Of these, cost overruns especially have been shown to afflict a very large proportion of all transportation investments, particularly rail projects. Due to their frequency, we next discuss the causes of cost escalation and overruns in transportation projects.

2.3 Causes for Cost Overruns

Given the significance of cost overruns in transportation investments, it is useful to first consider the evidence available regarding this phenomenon. Table 9.1 contains data on this subject.

The Aalborg report that provided some of the data shown in Table 9.1 also noted that the rates of project cost overruns did not mitigate over the 70 years (1927–1997) covered by the study, with the phenomenon more prevalent in developing than in developed countries. What, then, are the major if not universal causes of these overruns?

1. Changing Nature of the Output

Transportation service attributes continuously change in response to technological improvements, changes in user preferences, and government regulations. A rail car manufactured today may be quite different from one built 10 years ago due to the use of different materials, electronic improvements,

Table 9.1 Cost Overruns from Various Studies

Study	Sample Size	Mean Cost Overrun	Range Lower Bound	Range Upper Bound
Auditor-General, Sweden[a]	15	86%	2%	182%
US DOT[b]	N/A	61%	−10%	106%
TRRL UK	13	—	−10%	500%
Aalborg University, Denmark[c]	258	28%	—	—

Source: Flyvbjerg et al., (2003).
Notes: [a]Study covering rail and road projects. [b]Rail projects only. [c]Including tunnel, bridge, road, and rail projects in 20 countries, completed between 1927 and 1998.

and improved safety features and passenger amenities. All of these imply increasing costs, which at the time when the project's economic feasibility study was done were not accounted for. Government plays a decisive role in determining costs by means of its revised regulatory legislation. For example, Canada recently announced an agreement made with automakers ensuring the reduction of emissions by 25% from the 1995 level by 2010.[6] At present, it is difficult to predict the implications of this agreement for car manufacturing costs. The point is that vehicles available today, including buses, trucks, and rail cars, deliver a different bundle of services than will those produced in the future, and at unknown costs. The same argument can be made for infrastructure facilities like highways, bridges, or rail terminals.

2. Noncompetitive Input Factors' Markets

For a range of reasons, the number of firms manufacturing specific types of the equipment used for the construction of fixed or rolling stock for rail has declined considerably over time. This has resulted in above-normal rents for manufacturers, which imply rising input factors' costs. Noncompetitive labor markets are another source of increases. For example, the US Federal Government mandates that only unionized labor will be employed in all federally funded transportation projects. Since changes in labor contracts cannot be anticipated, labor costs extending estimations going beyond current agreements are unreliable if made at the time of the project's analysis.

3. Cost of Land

The land prices used as inputs in the COBA conducted today may be poor predictors of future prices. Given land availability, landowners in the project's corridor are liable to charge monopolistic rents, a practice realized by keeping land off the market. While most countries allow land expropriation for the construction of public facilities, the various transaction costs associated with such acts, including litigation, assessment, clearing, and delays escalate the final costs.

4. Construction Costs

Construction is more susceptible to cost overruns when it entails difficult tasks such as burrowing or complex bridge building, with its unexpected engineering problems (e.g., water seepage) and management difficulties. This is especially the case in most mega-projects, light and heavy surface as well as subway rail.

5. Statutory and Right-of-Way Costs

In many cases, when detailed planning has not been completed prior to COBA, costs related to right-of-way acquisition can exceed initial estimates by a large margin, particularly when statutory constraints restrict land acquisition or use.

6. Legal Costs

The legal costs of infrastructure projects often entail many costs beyond that of contract preparation. Lawsuits brought by citizens and interest groups claiming damages due to construction disruptions, environmental nuisances, or safety are one major category of such unpredictable although historically anticipated costs. Similarly, opposition to the project may result in high direct and indirect legal costs brought on by the long delays that give rise to contract violations. These costs, although also difficult to predict, are quite common and substantial.[7]

7. Cost Estimates Made at Different Planning Phases

In general, we can distinguish between several stages of project planning, with correspondingly higher levels of capital cost estimates. The initial sketch planning or prefeasibility study phase is performed with initial capital costs estimates. A detailed plan is subsequently prepared together with revised costs estimates. In the third phase, a thorough engineering plan is completed with revised capital costs estimates that can widely exceed the previous ones. Once implementation begins, the actual capital costs turn out, by and large, to be well above the estimated engineering costs. Most commonly, the COBA that precedes the decision to implement does not take cost estimates beyond the second planning stage into account even though substantial revision of those estimates can be expected. Hence, the increasing likelihood of cost overruns.

2.4 Perception of Project Risk

While this and previous chapters focus on public investments whose funding and implementation normally requires collective decision making, still it is pertinent to ask about the perception of various risk types by participants in the investments decision process. Akintoye and MacLeod (1997) conducted a survey of UK contractors and managers for the purpose of obtaining some understanding of their relative perceptions of risk. The results are shown in Table 9.2.

As indicated by Table 9.2, managers are somewhat more sensitive to risk than are contractors. Shapira (1994) reports a similar finding. He argues that managers tend to place more emphasis on the value of outcomes than on probabilities of their occurrence as they are inclined to believe that risk is controllable. What these and similar studies imply is that contractors and managers depend on their intuition and subjective judgment to guide them when managing risk. Furthermore, while about half of the people filling these positions claim to be familiar with sensitivity analysis, very few use this technique in practice because both groups doubt the usefulness of quantitative risk analysis techniques in practice. These findings raise the issue of the appropriateness of these subjective estimations of risk and their impact on project cost overruns.

Table 9.2 Survey of Risk Perceptions

	Perception of Risk Premium	
Sources of Risk	*Contractor*	*Manager*
Environmental (e.g., weather)	Low	Moderate
Political, social, & economic (e.g., inflation)	Moderate	High
Contractual (e.g., distribution of responsibilities)	High	High
Financial	High	High
Construction (e.g., productivity, injury, safety)	Moderate	High
Market/industry (i.e., availability of skilled labor)	High	High
Company (i.e., corporate risk)	Moderate	Moderate
Developments in information technology	Low	Low
Project (design information)	High	High

3. METHODS OF RISK MEASUREMENT IN PROJECT APPRAISAL

The investment literature contains numerous risk analysis studies, the majority describing cases where the decision maker's preferences are identifiable and the investment variables are well defined and measurable. In transportation investments, especially mega-projects, this is not always the case; more general and imprecise methods of risk analysis have therefore been developed. These methods can be roughly divided into qualitative and quantitative categories.

Qualitative analysis attempts to assess probabilities and results using subjective judgment based on past experience or expert opinion. Ayyub (2003) argues that qualitative analysis may be sufficient for identifying a project's overall risk. Yet, Frame (2003) contends that qualitative risk analysis is often unclear and prone to varied interpretations by different people. Moreover, they are often not testable, which makes them difficult to assess. Still, many managers and public decision makers tend to rely on such methods, claiming that quantitative methods are also imprecise and too complicated to apply. The position taken here, as the motto of this part of the book states, is: "It is better to be approximately right than precisely wrong." In the ensuing sections we therefore examine several methods of quantitative risk analysis, including scenario analysis, profitability measures, probabilistic methods, and optimal investment rules.

3.1 Scenario Analysis

The key question explored by scenario analysis is how would the project's performance measured by, say, its NPV, respond to varying levels of demand and costs. One practical approach involves examining the project under worst- and best-case scenarios relative to key risk-prone variables such as future ridership (Boardman and Greenberg, 1996). Another makes it possible to examine the same project under "optimistic," "most likely," and "pessimistic" state-of-the-world values for each uncertain variable. Consider a hypothetical example of a new rail transit line relative to three variables: annual demand (passenger-trips), annual operating costs, and total capital costs (see Table 9.3). If the project is judged by its yield (NPV/PVC) and B/C ratio, our objective is to establish the range of risky results as well as to ascertain the variable to which the results are most sensitive.

Assuming a discount rate of 5%, a $5 fare per trip, a 5-year construction period, and a 30-year life span, we can calculate the project's B/C ratio for each of these states of nature. For example, for the "optimistic" scenario, the project's yield (NPV/ PV(C)) is 1.5, and its B/C ratio is 2.5 (see Chapter 6 for these calculations). Calculating the same optimistic passenger trips and operating costs but with "most likely" capital costs, the results are 0.25

Table 9.3 Hypothetical Scenario Analysis of a Rail Project

	Values of Uncertain Variables		
Annual Data	*Optimistic*	*Most Likely*	*Pessimistic*
Passenger-trips	10,000,000	5,000,000	2,500,000
Operating costs ($)	1,000,000	1,750,000	2,500,000
Capital costs ($)	250,000,000	500,000,000	750,000,000

and 1.25, respectively. In the case of "pessimistic" capital costs, this scenario implies a negative yield (–0.167) and a B/C ratio of 0.833, clearly an undesirable situation. With "most likely" demand but "optimistic" operating and capital costs, the yield is 0.224 and B/C is 1.224. For "pessimistic" demand but "optimistic" operating and capital costs, the results are –0.413 and 0.587, respectively. Repeating these calculations for all possibilities (45 cases) will show the range of risk (negative yield) attached to this project, and the variable to which the results are most sensitive. In reference to the above figures, we see that when demand drops below 4.15 million annual passenger-trips, even with "optimistic" scenarios for the other variables, the B/C ratio is less than 1, indicating that the project's results are most sensitive to the variable passenger-trips (see also Section 4.2).

A major component of scenario analysis is, therefore, sensitivity analysis, which is concerned with determining the impact of minor perturbations in key parameters on an investment's overall performance. These parameters include the project's discount rate and life span as well as major demand parameters like mode shares and demand price elasticity. Thus, if in response to a 1% increase in the discount rate the NPV declines significantly, the project should be regarded as highly risky. Note that the sensitivity of a project's performance with respect to a given parameter is, in general, nonlinear. That is, the effect on NPV of raising the discount rate from 5% to 6% is unlikely to be the same as raising it from 6% to 7%.

A related sensitivity concept is the *shadow price* of a constraint. In Chapter 6 we saw how a budget constraint can impact on the ranking of alternative projects. What might be the impact on this ranking if we relax this constraint? The answer to this question amounts to the computation of the shadow price of the budget constraint or, in mathematical programming terms, the change in the value of the objective function (maximum social welfare as measured by the project's NPV, for example) from a marginal change in the constraint.

In general, every resource whose supply is constrained at a level below the free market equilibrium quantity has a positive shadow price. A high shadow price indicates that the constraint is quite binding and that its costs, in terms of forgone social welfare, is also quite high. As our focus here is on capital investments, a shadow price analysis can help indicate to which among a set of projects we should allocate additional capital funding.

3.2 Use of Profitability Measures as Risk Indicators

Chapter 6 offered several measures of project profitability, some of which can be used as indicators of the project's risk level. In the following, we refer to the measures most salient for this purpose.

1. Payback Period

This measure was defined as the number of years necessary for the stream of benefits to recover the project's capital costs (equation 16, chapter 6). The longer the payback period, the higher is the project's risk level. The reason for this type of relationship is the likelihood that the key parameters, affecting a project's future streams of benefits and costs, remain unchanged, declines as a function of time. Consider the growth rate of future demand: It may attenuate over time, making present predictions of benefits inaccurate.

2. Minimum Benefits Necessary for the Investment to Break Even

The COBA model raises an important question: What are minimum benefits necessary for the project to break even? Analytically, NPV can be defined as:

$$NPV = \left[\sum_{t}^{T_C} \frac{(\frac{C}{T_C}) + r \cdot C}{(1+r)^t} \right] + \sum_{t=T_C}^{T+T_C} \frac{B_t \cdot \left\{ Q) \cdot \left[(1+g(t))^{t-T_C} \right] \right\} + (\delta R) - (MO) - (r \cdot C)}{(1+r)^t} \tag{4}$$

In (4), δ is the percent of fare box revenue that the project receives as external subsidy ($\delta \geq 0$), Q is ridership, with all other variables as defined in Chapter 6. In analytical terms, then, what is the minimum level of Q, denoted as Q_{min}, required for the project to break even (i.e., $NPV = 0$)?

If, under a given scenario, Q is relatively close to Q_{min}, the project can be judged as risky. We can likewise compute the minimum level of B_t (annual benefits) necessary for the project to break even. Benefits per user are comprised of the per-user amount of time saved and the value of time. If B_t's minimum is rather close to the scenario's level, it signals a risky project because any unforeseen decline in B_t will reduce the project's NPV to a level below the acceptable. In similar fashion, it is possible to compute the maximum level of capital costs for which the estimated benefits will yield a positive NPV and subsequently compare it with specific capital cost scenarios.

3. Project's NPV over Short Periods

NPV is defined as the difference between the discounted future streams of benefits and costs over the project's life span. However, the robustness of long-term predictions of benefits and costs decline rapidly over time, thus increasing the risk that the derived NPV values are incorrect. Hence, it is useful to perform the NPV analysis over periods shorter than the project's time horizon, say over 10–15 years. If the project's NPV < 0 for this period, it should be judged as risky.

4. PROBABILISTIC AND SIMULATION METHODS

If the probability distribution of key variables such as annual benefits can be established, we can employ a number of methods to decide whether the project should be undertaken.

4.1 Probabilistic Methods

Consider first the case where analysts can produce the probability distribution of the project's consequences. Following the notation in Chapter 6, let $P_{jt}(j = 1,\ldots,N)$ be the probability of realizing monetized benefits of size B_{jt} and subsidy of size R_{jt}, at time t. Hence, $\sum_{j=1}^{N} P_j \cdot (B_{jt} + R_{jt})$ is the expected value of total benefits at year t. In order to account for the dispersion of the underlying distribution of future benefit values, it is useful to normalize the expected value by dividing it by the standard deviation, σ, of this distribution. Thus, NPV becomes,

$$NPV = \left[-\sum_{t}^{T_I} \frac{C_t}{(1+r)^t} \right] + \sum_{t=T_{I+1}}^{T+T_I} \sum_{j=1}^{N} \frac{\left(\dfrac{P_{jt} \cdot (B_{jt} + R_{jit})}{\sigma} \right) - M_t - O_t}{(1+r)^t} \qquad (5)$$

If we also know the probability distribution of future costs, the same approach can be used to compute the standardized expected value of these costs at time period t. Boardman et al. (2001) provide a detailed analysis of the use of expected value methods in cases of uncertainty. Still, the critical question is how to obtain, *ex ante*, estimates for the demand and cost probabilities. This question is examined next.

4.2 Simulation Methods

A common approach to obtaining these probabilities is to consult a team of experts and use their subjective probabilities as proxies for the true probabilities (Pouliquen, 1970). Another approach is to assume a prior distribution, for example, a Poisson that, for fairly predictable events such as bus headways and arrivals, is quite adequate (Frame, 2003). A third possibility is to generate random values for the events' variables. The Monte Carlo method is the most well-used approach for this purpose.[8] A fourth approach would be to fit a curve to observed phenomena, such as cost overrun distributions.

To illustrate the second and third approaches, suppose that at each future period, travel time savings distribute uniformly between the "low" and "high" values. A normal distribution can be assumed around the "medium" level.[9] Using the Monte Carlo method we then execute repeated random drawings for each time savings value taken from the assumed distribution. The average of these draws constitutes a reasonable approximation of the expected value of traveler time savings. For each project alternative considered, plugging these numbers into the above NPV equation, (5), will produce the frequency distribution of NPV values from the random drawings. We can obtain this distribution's key statistics, including the average, variance, and other moments, if any.[10]

As shown in sectino 5.1, while commonly used in risk analysis, a Monte Carlo simulation may produce inferior results compared with those obtained from other methods. In particular, time-dependent events like project costs can better be approximated using curve-fitting methods (Regnier, 2005).

5. CURVE-FITTING METHODS

A particularly useful approach for obtaining probability distributions of key investment variables (e.g., costs) is the use of data on the past performance of a selected type of investment project (e.g., highways). This approach is next examined for the purpose of assessing the probability of a project having cost overruns of a given magnitude.

5.1 Assessing the Probability of Cost Overruns

Cost overrun is defined as the case where the project's actual or realized total costs at the time of its completion exceed the budget that was used as the basis for the project's appraisal. For estimation purpose, we define the Cost Overrun Ratio (COR) as the ratio of actual total costs to planned budget.[11] For example, if the planned budget is $1 billion and actual costs are $1.2 billion, COR = 1.2; if the actual cost is only $800 million for the same budget ($1 billion), then COR = 0.8 (no cost overruns). Some studies (e.g., Flyvbjerg et al., 2002; Jahren and Ashe, 1990) have used the percentage of cost increases to measure cost overruns. Under this definition, *COR* = 1.2 corresponds to a 20% cost overrun, whereas *COR* ≤ 1 implies a 0% cost overrun. When using observed data for COR calculations, the objective is to fit a probability distribution function that can best approximate the actual data distribution. The following analysis, based on Berechman and Chen (2008), tests four probability distribution models using goodness-of-fit statistics to obtain the distribution best approximating the observed COR distribution.

Analytically, for a given COR probability distribution model, we compare the estimated probability $P(COR) \geq a$, with the *observed* proportion of COR in the database, denoted by "r" for: $a = 1.0, 1.1, 1.2 \ldots, N$; where N is the maximum COR value (e.g., 2). The distribution model is said to underestimate or overestimate the true distribution of COR if:

$$\begin{cases} (P(COR) \geq a) \ < r \quad \text{underestimate} \\ (P(COR) \geq a) \ > r \quad \text{overestimate} \end{cases}$$

To illustrate, suppose a distribution model estimates the probability of COR to be greater than or equal to 1.3, $(P(COR) \geq 1.3) = 0.45$; however, based on the germane database, the observed probability of COR = 1.3, $R((COR) = 1.3) = 0.4$. This distribution model is then said to overestimate COR at values of 1.3 or above. On the other hand, if this distribution model estimates $(P(COR) \geq 1.5) = 0.2$ while the observed $r((COR) = 1.5) = 0.25$, the model is said to underestimate COR at values of 1.5 or below.

To simplify the analysis we use intervals rather than unique values for COR. The numerical example given below (Section 7) includes three intervals: $(COR) \leq 1.0$; $1.0 \leq (COR) \leq 1.2$; and $1.2 \leq (COR) \leq a_{max}$, where a_{max} is an arbitrary value (e.g., 2.0). The approach proposed for deriving COR probabilities contains the following steps:

1. Based on observations of actual cost overruns of investment projects, plot a COR histogram.
2. Based on this histogram, determine the distribution function that provides the best fit, using distribution-fitting statistics.
3. Estimate the relevant parameters (moments) of the selected distribution(s)

The database used by Berechman and Chen (2008) is comprised of a set of investment projects carried out on Vancouver Island (1993–2003), labeled here as the "Vancouver Island Highway Project (VIHP)." Of the total 163 independent projects, 127 were road and highway construction projects, and 36 were bridge and tunnel projects. It represents 174 kilometers of highway improvements and 146 kilometers of new construction. Because these investments were carried out in various parts of Vancouver Island and at different times, they are assumed to be independent relative to planning and costs. Of the 127 road and highway projects and 36 bridge and tunnel projects, 104 and 29, respectively, had cost overruns. Figure 9.1 shows a COR histogram of the entire VIHP projects. It is evident that a significant number of projects experienced some cost overruns (COR > 1). To verify

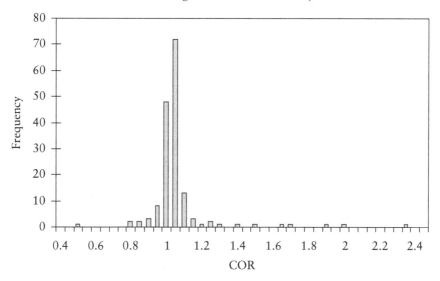

Figure 9.1 COR histogram of VIHP database.

how well this database represents the cost overruns phenomenon, we reviewed studies by Flyvbjerg et al. (2002, 2003) and Jahren et al. (1990). The COR histograms representing the respective databases exhibit a similar picture.[12]

The next question is: Which distribution function best represents the actual COR distribution for the VIHP database? To obtain an answer, four alternative distributions were fitted. These were: Normal, Generalized Gamma, Beta, and Cauchy. The parameters of these distributions included location, scale, and shape, as follows:[13]

a. Normal Distribution: $N(\mu,\sigma)$, where the mean μ is the *location* and the standard deviation σ is the *scale* parameter.

b. Generalized Gamma Distribution: $Gamma(\theta,\beta,\gamma)$, where θ is the *location* (threshold) parameter reflecting the minimum value of the distribution's variable, β is the *scale* parameter, and γ is the *shape* parameter.

c. Beta Distribution: $Beta(P,Q,A,B)$, where P and Q are *shape* parameters whereas A and B are *scale* parameters reflecting the minimum and maximum values, respectively, of the distribution's variable (e.g., COR).

d. Cauchy Distribution: $Cauchy(a,b)$, where a is the *location* parameter (indicating the median of the distribution's variable, namely, the location of the distribution's peak), and b is the *scale* parameter, playing a role similar for the standard deviation.

Table 9.4 Goodness-of-Fit Statistics (for all VIHP projects)

Fitting Statistics		Distribution			
		Normal	Gamma	Beta	Cauchy
Log-Likelihood (LL)		44.0746	72.8516	141.3540	**243.6415**
Kolmogorov–Smirnov Test	KS	0.3360	0.2964	0.3495	**0.1470**
	P-value	9.61e–017	3.34e–013	4.53e–018	**0.0015**
Chi-Square Test	χ^2	1.08e+005	6.93e+003	4.10e+003	**25.1132**
	P-value	0	0	0	**3.52e–006**

Notes: [a]KS Test Critical Value: 0.1073 ($\alpha = 10\%$); 0.1191 ($\alpha = 5\%$); 0.1429 ($\alpha = 1\%$); [b]Chi-Square Test Critical Value: 4.6052 ($\alpha = 10\%$); 5.9915 ($\alpha = 5\%$); 9.2103 ($\alpha = 1\%$); [c]The *p-value* is the probability of obtaining (by chance) a test statistic greater than the computed statistic. The null hypothesis is rejected if the p-value is smaller than or equal to the level of significance.

To ascertain which of these distributions best fits the observed VIHP database, three tests were conducted. First, the log-likelihood of each model was calculated, followed by the Kolmogorov–Smirnov (KS)[14] and Chi-Square (χ^2)[15] goodness-of-fit tests under the null hypothesis that a given distribution "correctly" represents the data distribution is rejected when the test statistics—either KS or χ^2—are below the critical value at a given level of significance. Table 9.4 shows the results of these tests.

Table 9.4 indicates that the Cauchy distribution best fits the database. First, under the Log-Likelihood (LL) test: LL(Cauchy) > LL(Beta) > LL(Gamma) > LL(Normal), implying that the Cauchy distribution fits the data better than the three other models do. Second, the values for the KS and χ^2 tests for the Cauchy distribution are the smallest when compared with those of the other three distributions; and, its p-value is significantly higher. We can therefore, concluded that the Cauchy distribution best fits the COR distribution of the VIHP database. This conclusion was confirmed by running the same tests on the Flyvbjerg et al. (2002) and Jahren et al. (1990) databases.

To yet further confirm this conclusion, Table 9.5 shows the observed and estimated probabilities for different risk levels, representing the COR range, under the four tested probability distributions as well as the probabilities generated by the Monte Carlo simulation.

As expected, the Cauchy probability estimates the best approximation to the observed COR probability values for all risk levels. The Cauchy distribution is apparently able to capture the high peak and fat tail characteristics of the VIHP COR data. We next examine the question of how to use risk probabilities in project appraisal and selection. To that end, we make use of the Cauchy probabilities in the context of a decision-tree analysis.

Table 9.5 COR Probabilities Estimated from the VIHP Database (Roads & Highways)

COR	Observed	Monte Carlo Simulation	Normal N (μ, σ) $\mu = 1.0355$ $\sigma = 0.1848$	Gamma Gamma (θ, β, γ) $\theta = 0.2693$ $\beta = 0.0329$ $\gamma = 23.2896$	Beta Beta (P, Q, A, B) $A = 0.4$ $B = 2.4$ $P = 5.9872$ $Q = 12.3864$	Cauchy Cauchy (a, b) $a = 1.0046$ $b = 0.0173$
COR ≤ 1	33.07%	42.33%	42.38%	43.73%	42.92%	41.73%
1 < COR ≤ 1.2	60.63%	42.33%	38.95%	41.30%	33.06%	55.46%
COR > 1.2	6.30%	15.34%	18.67%	14.97%	24.02%	2.81%

6. DECISION-TREE ANALYSIS

Decision Tree Analysis (DTA) is an investment decision-making tool in which the probabilities of cost overrun risk levels are established a priori. We assume that a decision maker has a gain or utility function that she wishes to optimize. An example would be the maximum NPV attainable by the investment.

6.1 Components of DTA

DTA contains three key elements:

1. *Decision alternatives.* A set of possible actions that aim at achieving a predefined objective, such as the maximization of NPV. Possible actions could be: implement the project as is, redesign, or discard. Let $A_i(i = 1,2,...,m)$ denote the decision alternatives.
2. *States of nature.* Defined as a set of future conditions on which the decision alternatives may have different effects. Let $S_j(j = 1,2,...,n)$ denote states of nature. For example, S_1 = low-level risk ($COR \leq 1.0$); S_2 = medium-level risk ($1.0 \leq COR \leq 1.2$); S_3 = high-level risk ($COR > 1.2$).
3. *Probability of incidence.* Let $P_j(j = 1,2,...,n)$ denote the probability of incidence of the respective states of nature S_j. Below we use the Cauchy probabilities as estimates for P_j.

Assume a project with present value of estimated benefits $PV(B)$, and present value of estimated costs of $PV(C)$. Given the risk of cost overruns, the Net Present Value (NPV) of this project is:

$$NPV = PV(B) - COR \times PV(C) \tag{6}$$

Since COR is a random variable, NPV is also a random variable. Each decision alternative A_i is associated with a different NPV. The dilemma revolves around how to select the "best" alternative. To that end, we propose three decision criteria: maximum gain (the gain function), maximum expected utility, and maximum utility (the utility function).

A. Maximum Expected NPV (Gain Function)

Using NPV as the gain function, the objective is to select the decision alternative A_i with the maximum expected NPV, denoted as: $\max E(NPV_i)$. Thus, $\max\limits_{i} E(NPV_i)$, where

$$E(NPV_i) = \sum_{j=1}^{n} \left[NPV_{ij} \times P_j \right], i = 1,2,...,m; j = 1,2,...,n \tag{7}$$

In (7), NPV_{ij} is the net present value of decision alternative A_i under state of nature S_j; P_j is the probability of state of nature (or COR of a certain level) S_j occurring.

B. Maximum Expected Utility

We assume that transportation decision makers are risk averse in that they attach a higher utility to a *potential loss* from a project (i.e., $COR > 1$) than to a potential gain, defined as ($COR \leq 1$).[16] Let $U(NPV_{ij})$ be a concave utility function associated with the net present value of decision alternative A_i under state of nature S_j. Expected utility from A_i, denoted by $EU(NPV_i)$, is then:

$$EU(NPV_i) = \sum_{j=1}^{n} \left[U(NPV_{ij}) \times P_j \right], \ i = 1, 2, \ldots m; \ j = 1, 2, \ldots, n \tag{8}$$

In (8), P_j is the probability of state of nature (COR level) S_j. The maximum expected utility measure is thus:

$$Decision = \underset{i}{Max}\, EU(NPV_i) \tag{9}$$

Note that when the utility function is provided, $EU(NPV) = U[E(NPV)]$. Let U^* be the utility level obtained with present (or preproject) resources, Y^*. Let Y' be the level of resources corresponding to $EU(NPV)$. The difference, $\Delta Y = Y^* - Y'$, is the risk premium a person is willing to pay in order to avoid the project's risk. This premium, known as the Cost of Risk Bearing (CRB), represents risk in terms of the cost that the project imposes on the investor. In utility terms, it equals $\Delta U = U^* - EU(NPV)$.

C. Maximum Utility Function

It stands to reason that in the presence of the risk of cost overruns, decision makers would be risk averse and respond differently to a project's *potential loss* (i.e., $COR > 1$) than to its potential gains. In utility terms, such behavior implies that negative outcomes (high COR) would receive relatively high weights while positive outcomes (low COR) would receive relatively low weights. The decision maker's objective would then be: Find the alternative with the maximum utility. That is, the decision criterion is: select $\max U(NPV_i)$, or select alternative A_i that maximizes the utility $U(NPV_i)$.

[i] The maximum gain function (7) requires that each NPV result be weighted by its specific probability value. The maximum utility function decision criterion, on the other hand, requires that all NPV values be weighted by a convex probability function to reflect the decision maker's risk-averse behavior. Following Yaari (1987), the utility associated with each decision alternative A_i is defined as in equation (10):

$$U(NPV_i) = \sum_{k=1}^{n} \left[NPV_i^{(k)} \times h^{(k)} \left(P_i^{(1)}, P_i^{(2)}, ..., P_i^{(n)} \right) \right]$$

$$= \sum_{k=1}^{n} \left[NPV_i^{(k)} \times \left(f(\sum_{l=k}^{n} P_i^{(l)}) - f(\sum_{l=k+1}^{n} P_i^{(l)}) \right) \right] (i = 1, 2, ..., m)$$

(10)

and $f(P) = \dfrac{(1 - e^P)}{(1 - e)}$.

In (10), the variable $NPV_i^{(k)}$ indicates ordering the NPV of decision alternative A_i under the state of nature S_j $(j = 1, 2, ..., n)$. Since under different states of nature a decision alternative is likely to have different NPVs, we order the random variable $NPV_i^{(k)}$, with k $(k = 1, 2, ..., n)$ the ordering index. That is, $NPV_i^{(1)} \le NPV_i^{(2)} \le \cdots \le NPV_i^{(k)} \le \cdots \le NPV_i^{(n)}$. The term $P_i^{(1)}$ is the probability of $NPV_i^{(l)}$ occurring, whereas l $(l = 1, 2, ..., n)$ is an order index equivalent to k in $NPV_i^{(k)}$.

The function $f(P)$ is a convex function in P. This transformation reflects the decision makers' risk-averse behavior in relation to the selected alternative (Yaari, 1987). That is, $h^{(k)}(P_i^{(1)}, P_i^{(2)}, ..., P_i^{(n)}) = \left(f(\sum_{l=k}^{n} P_i^{(l)}) - f(\sum_{l=k+1}^{n} P_i^{(l)}) \right)$ is the decision weight applied to the kth value of the random variable $NPV_i^{(k)}$. Note that this weight depends not only on the kth probability value $P_i^{(k)}$, but also on the entire probability vector $(P_i^{(1)}, P_i^{(2)}, ..., P_i^{(n)})$.

6.2 A Decision-Tree Model

States of Nature

We define three states of nature, corresponding to the three stated levels of cost overrun risk, S_j $(j = 1, ..., n; n = 3)$, and their associated probabilities: $P_i(P_i = P(S_i))$

S_1 = Low risk $(COR \le 1)$ with probability P_1; $P_1 = P(COR \le 1)$

S_2 = Medium risk $(1 < COR \le 1.2)$ with probability P_2; $P_2 = P(1 < COR \le 1.2)$

S_3 = High risk $(COR > 1.2)$ with probability P_3; $P_3 = P(COR > 1.2)$

Decision Alternatives

We assume A_i design alternatives, each reflecting a different level of benefits and costs, that is, A_i with $PV(B_i)$ and $PV(C_i)$, $(i = 1, 2, ..., m)$. This problem has m decision alternatives, A_i, and n states of nature, S_j $(j = 1, 2, ..., n)$, for the various COR levels.[17] Figure 9.2 shows a decision tree with m decision alternatives, each associated with three cost overrun risk events: Low,

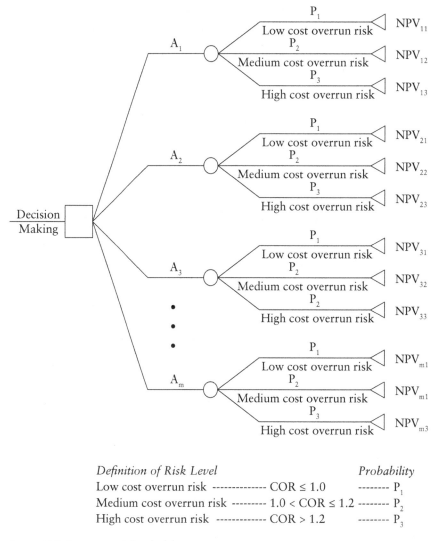

Definition of Risk Level		Probability
Low cost overrun risk ------------- COR ≤ 1.0		-------- P_1
Medium cost overrun risk -------- 1.0 < COR ≤ 1.2		-------- P_2
High cost overrun risk ------------ COR > 1.2		-------- P_3

Figure 9.2 Structure of the decision tree.

Medium, and High, with probabilities P_1, P_2, and P_3, respectively. Note that in this analysis we assume the probabilities P_i to be alternative-independent. It may be quite difficult to estimate P_i, which are dependent on A_i, primarily for lack of proper data. In any case, even if we could obtain $P_i(A_i)$, the structure of the analysis would be invariant although the final results would, of course, change.

The end nodes of the tree are labeled with NPV_{ij}, indicating the NPV for alternative A_i with risk level S_j. We then calculate the decision criteria for each alternative in the tree: expected NPV, expected utility, and maximum utility (equations 7–10). The last equation is further expanded for m alternatives with three states of nature. That is, for each decision alternative A_i ($i = 1,2,3...,m$), we order the NPV so that:

$NPV_i^{(1)} \leq NPV_i^{(2)} \leq NPV_i^{(3)}$. Thus,

$$U(NPV_i) = NPV_i^{(1)} \left(f(P_i^{(1)} + P_i^{(2)} + P_i^{(3)}) - f(P_i^{(2)} + P_i^{(3)}) \right) +$$
$$NPV_i^{(2)} \left(f(P_i^{(2)} + P_i^{(3)}) - f(P_i^{(3)}) \right) + NPV_i^{(3)} f(P_i^{(3)})$$

Next we present a numerical example.

6.3 A DTA Numerical Example

Table 9.6 shows data for a hypothetical highway investment with four design alternatives, denoted as $A_1,...,A_4$.

Each alternative has three risk events: S_1 = low COR ($COR \leq 1$); S_2 = medium COR ($1 < COR \leq 1.2$); and S_3 = high COR ($COR > 1.2$). Table 9.6 provides the NPV information for the four alternatives under the three risk levels (assuming a specific time horizon and discount rate).

To simplify the calculations we use the upper bound of each COR range. That is: COR = 1 for $COR \leq 1$; COR = 1.2 for $1 \leq COR \leq 1.2$; and COR = 1.5 for $COR \geq 1.2$. To select the best alternative we need to obtain the state of nature probabilities P_j ($j = 1,...,n$). To that end we will make use of the Cauchy function estimates shown in Table 9.5. The two decision criteria—Maximum Expected NPV and the Maximum Utility Function, equations (7) and (8), respectively—are computed as follows:

(A) Maximum Expected NPV

For each of the four alternatives the expected NPV is:

$$E(NPV_i) = \sum_{j=1}^{3} \left[(NPV_{ij} \times P_j) \right], (i = 1,...,4).[18]$$

Table 9.6 Hypothetical NP Value of Benefits and Costs for Four Design Alternatives

Design Alternative	A_1	A_2	A_3	A_4
PV(Benefits)	$2,000,000	$2,200,000	$2,500,000	$1,600,000
PV(Costs)	$1,200,000	$1,375,000	$1,650,000	$900,000

(B) Maximum Expected Utility

For this analysis we assume the following utility function:

$$U(NPV_{ij}) = 1 - e^{-\lambda(NPV_{ij})}, \; i = 1,2,...m; \; j = 1,2,...,n$$

This utility function belongs to a family of constant absolute risk-aversion functions. The parameter λ is the level of risk aversion; a large λ indicates a high level of risk aversion. For a given λ, $U(NPV_{ij})$ values are in the $\{0,1\}$ range.[19]

(C) Maximum Utility

From equation (10), the utility of NPV for the four alternatives and three states of nature is: $\sum_{k=1}^{3} \left[NPV_i^{(k)} \times \left(f(\sum_{l=k}^{n} P_i^{(l)}) - f(\sum_{l=k+1}^{3} P_i^{(l)}) \right) \right]$ $(i = 1,...,4)$.[20] Table 9.7 shows the results of these computations for each project alternative.

Based on these hypothetical data and assuming Cauchy risk probabilities as in Table 9.5, together with risk aversion $\lambda = 0.4$, the results from the DTA and the three decision criteria are shown in Table 9.7.

These results indicate that under the maximum expected NPV criterion A_2 is the preferred alternative. However, if we adopt the maximum expected utility and the maximum utility criteria, alternative A_1 is preferable. Under either criterion, alternatives A_3 and A_4 are inferior to the first two alternatives and should be discarded.

Table 9.7 Expected NPV and Utility NPV Results[a]

		NPV[c]			
Range of COR	*Probability*[b]	A_1	A_2	A_3	A_4
S_1: COR $\leq$ 1	41.73%	$800,000	$825,000	$850,000	$700,000
S_2: 1 $\leq$ COR $\leq$ 1.2	55.46%	$560,000	$550,000	$520,000	$520,000
S_3: COR $\geq$ 1.2	2.81%	$200,000	$137,500	$25,000	$250,000
Expected NPV: $E(NPV_i)$		$650,036	**$653,166**	$643,800	$587,527
Expected Utility: $(EU(NPV_i))$		**0.9113**	0.9069	0.8914	0.8950
Utility NPV: $U(NPV_i)$		**616,551**	614,798	597,758	562,413

Note: [a]The preferred alternative under each decision criterion appears in bold; [b]Cauchy probabilities (Table 9.5). [c]From equation (6).

7. OPTIMAL INVESTMENT TIMING RULES UNDER UNCERTAINTY

Several authors (e.g., Dixit and Pindyck, 1994; Pindyck, 1991) have investigated decision rules for new investments that, once committed to, are irreversible even though their future streams of benefits are subject to substantial uncertainty. Irreversibility can take several forms, such as long-lasting environmental damage (Pindyck, 2000). In transportation, irreversibility implies significant sunk costs because many such investments are indivisible, and once committed to, the invested resources have no alternative use. Consider the case of a bridge: Once built, has no alternative use; hence, the resources invested cannot be recovered. It might be argued that there are also "sunk benefits" (social-opportunity costs), such as time wasted due to present congestion conditions caused by insufficient capacity. Therefore, benefits can be gained by early investment. Under these conditions—irreversibility and demand uncertainty—what is the optimal timing of the investment?

The approach advocated is to delay implementation of the project by the period of time necessary for additional information about the "true" benefits to become available. The rationale behind this recommendation is that postponing implementation introduces the options of either not investing at all or adopting a better transportation once new information arrives, each of which may have greater value.

While this approach focuses on the benefits side, postponement can also affect the project's cost in two major but opposing ways. First, costs may also be subject to considerable uncertainty generated by factors such as incomplete engineering data, site conditions, or final design attributes. On the other hand, a major source of cost overruns is the time lag of implementation, which can result in escalating labor, material, and right-of-way costs. If the investment's purpose is maintaining a state of good repair of an existing facility, project deferral usually implies additional maintenance as well as rehabilitation costs.[21] Since these two cost impacts move in opposite directions, postponement can result in greater certainty regarding the true costs of the project but also in higher input costs (Crousillat and Martzoukos, 1991). Given that most studies of investment timing focus on benefits, which are prone to greater uncertainty than are costs.

Dixit and Pindyck (1994) have shown that an irreversible investment should be made if the value of its output (PV of benefits) is larger than the sum of its variable and discounted capital costs *so long as* the variance of future benefits (σ) is zero. However, if $\sigma > 0$, implying possible uncertainty over future benefits, opportunity costs may be incurred by delaying the investment given the possibility that benefits may increase in the future.

To illustrate, and following Pindyck (1991), consider a transportation project whose irreversible capital costs, denoted by C, expended in the current year ($t = 0$), are expected to generate annual benefits of B_1 over the project's lifetime of T years, beginning at $t = 1$. However, future ridership and therefore the project's benefits over subsequent years ($t = 2, 3, \ldots, T$) are subject to uncertainty. Over time, additional information may become available, thereby reducing uncertainty. With probability P, benefits can rise to B_2 ($B_2 > B_1$), but with probability $(1 - P)$, benefits can fall to B_3 ($B_3 < B_1$). The question is, then, under what conditions should the project be delayed to allow for more information to arrive. Under these conditions, the decision rule is: Delay the project if the difference between its *NPV* delayed by one year and its NPV of investing in the current year is positive. That is:

$$\Delta NPV = P \cdot \left[\frac{-C}{(1+r)^1} + \sum_{t=2}^{T+1} \frac{B_2}{(1+r)^t} \right] - \left[\frac{-C}{(1+r)^0} + \sum_{t=1}^{T} \frac{B_1}{(1+r)^t} \right] > 0 \tag{11}$$

How applicable are timing rules to transportation investment decision making? For well-defined, small-scale investments such as bus fleet expansion or the addition of new lanes to an existing highway, the use of timing rules can be quite beneficial. However, for large-scale projects, which often are exposed to weighty legal, contractual, political, economic, environmental, licensing, and funding uncertainties, the timing rules defined here may be of little value. The key problem with large-scale transportation infrastructure projects is not determination of the optimal year of investment. Rather, it is the ability to make a correct judgment on the overall welfare, equity, economic, and social implications of the project together with the numerous problems that hinder actual implementation. Under some circumstances, especially when the state is about to commit substantial capital funds but user level is quite uncertain, it is useful to examine the economic consequences of deferring the investment under the assumption that future demand might be higher.

8. RISK SHARING IN PRIVATE–PUBLIC PARTNERSHIP PROJECTS[22]

Frequently governments turn to private sector participation in the construction, operation, and funding of transportation infrastructure facilities and services. Known generically as Public–Private Partnerships (PPP or P3), these forms of cooperation can be defined as "arrangements whereby private parties participate in, or provide support for, the provision of (transportation) infrastructure or services" (Grimsey and Lewis, 2004).[23]

Traditionally, PPP assigned the private sector the role of design-bid-build only, while the public sector financed, maintained, and owned the infrastructure. New forms of PPP have extended the role of the private sector and accordingly we can distinguish several types of PPP, ranging along a continuum of public/private involvement in the provision of the infrastructure. These include construction, maintenance, and operation as well as financing and leasing of infrastructure facilities and services (e.g., public transit). These partnerships are now regarded as instruments for furthering transportation development, an objective that may otherwise not be realized due to shortfalls in the public sector budgets. It is also seen as a means to exploit private sector efficiencies in construction, financing, and project management that more than offset the additional costs entailed, especially private financing. This view notwithstanding, how real are these efficiency gains considering the transaction costs incurred?[24] Is PPP merely a transfer of public resources to private enterprise for an agreed-upon fee? In Chapter 10 we discuss the funding aspects of PPP arrangements. Here we focus on their risks and how to incorporate PPP risk into COBA.[25]

A PPP contract requires, among other things, an agreement on how the project's overall risk is to be shared between the parties. These risks include exceeding capital costs limits, failure to meet schedules for service delivery, difficulty in complying with environmental and other regulations, delays due to unforeseen site conditions, in addition to the risk that demand—and thus revenues—may be insufficient to cover capital, debt-service, maintenance, and operating costs. Of particular importance are various financial risks (e.g., unexpected changes in interest and exchange rates) for PPP projects with private sector funding. The PPP contract that defines the responsibilities of each side is also expected to stipulate the risk that each side will assume, along with the judicial contingencies for failure to comply with the contract's terms. The latter may require agreement regarding international dispute settlement as foreign corporations may bid for local projects.

Clearly, risk can be divided along a continuum between the public and the private sector, ranging from full to zero risk assumed by the private enterprise, where the balance constitutes the risk borne by the public sector. If the public sector bears nearly all of the risk of a particular project, the private sector's role is essentially that of a subcontractor or money-lender who faces a risk-free investment as the public sector is unlikely to become insolvent. For example, in the case of Highway 407, a 70-mile express toll road on the north side of metropolitan Toronto, Canada, private partners refused to assume the financial risks. As a result, the Province of Ontario financed the project's capital costs, thereby effectively assuming all financial risks, while the private partner became a fixed-price subcontractor who assumed only construction and operation risks.

It might be argued that once the risk level of a PPP investment has been properly assessed, we can safely disregard risk allocation between the parties because, for the economy as a whole, it would not matter.[26] However, this argument is true only if we can assume that the private and public sectors exhibit similar attitudes towards risk (e.g., same level of risk aversion) *and* if both parties are equally efficient in managing risk. Stated alternatively, the main reason why risk allocation matters is the asymmetry between the public and private sectors in dealing with and managing different forms of risk. Hence, we can categorically state that the specific allocation of risk is consequential and significantly impacts on the economic value of PPP investments.

In general, the private sector is better at putting together financial packages and managing financial and construction risks. The public sector, on the other hand, is more efficient in dealing with political and legal risks, land assembly and eminent domain risks, environmental damage risks, and demand related risks. Hence, *risk specialization* is the proper mechanism to be employed when allocating risks between public and private partners in an infrastructure project. The crucial point to remember is that the higher the share of risk the private partner assumes, especially of the demand risks, the higher the rate of return it requires to participate in the project. At the same time the likelihood that the project will default increases.[27]

The germane literature does not provide formulae for the allocation of risk between the parties. Actual risk-sharing schemes are often the result of ad hoc agreements and political negotiations. However, it is possible to suggest several approaches to the derivation of more balanced and efficient risk-sharing arrangements for PPP projects.

A. Risk Factor Control Approach

Under this approach, the state assumes control over those risk factors more-or-less immune to private investor control, implying that the state can deal with these factors much more effectively. State-controlled risk factors include:

1. Risk of extra costs from land expropriation, securing rights of way and transferring those rights, free of claims, to private partners
2. Risk of extra costs from preserving various cultural and religious sites (e.g., archeological sites, old cemeteries)
3. Risk of extra costs due to citizens' objections and lawsuits regarding land expropriations and environmental nuisances
4. Risk of demand shortages caused by changes in policy, such as the construction of competing projects (e.g., parallel roads), or by general economic decline
5. Political risks emanating from poor legislation and changes of government

Private enterprises, on the other hand, are normally more efficient in managing risks of the following types:

1. Borrowing and other financial risks, (e.g., changes in the inflation rate, interest rates, and foreign currency exchange rates)
2. Planning and design risks
3. Construction risks
4. Operation and maintenance risks
5. Technological change risks (e.g., new tunneling technology)

This approach, which uses "degree of control" as the key risk allocation criterion, seems to underlie many PPP contracts. Yet, it does not respond adequately to one key issue, namely, which side should assume the risk associated with the level of future demand and thus future revenues.[28] Should the private partner be totally shielded from demand fluctuations, or should it bear some of the risk induced by its own actions, including toll setting, level of service rendered, and maintenance quality?

B. Allocation of Risk Associated with Future Revenues

This approach calls for separating demand into its underlying market and nonmarket components and letting the private partner assume the market risks. For example, change in demand pursuant to changes in the toll regime (e.g., toll rates by vehicle type, time of day, or distance traveled) can be considered a market-related factor. In contrast, regulated transit fare or future highway layout patterns are nonmarket factors capable of affecting demand. Assigning the market-related risk to the private partner represents an efficient and reasonable risk-sharing scheme. In reality, however, this risk is all too often negotiated between the private and public partners on a case-by-case basis, with the state eventually bearing most of the risk. As a result, the shielding of the private sector from demand-related risks frequently leads to the adoption of projects generating inferior social benefits. It may also effectively hinder initiation of those future network improvements that affect demand.[29]

C. Risk Allocation-Based Contracts

With respect to PPP contracts, we can distinguish between "full cost" and "net cost" contracts as well as between "efficiency" and "performance" contracts. Under the "full cost" type of contract, potential private bidders tender for the lowest price (revenues) they demand for building the project or for providing the transportation service, irrespective of future demand (with the effective revenues going to the state). In the "net cost" type of contract, the private partner receives the full revenue from the project (e.g., tolls revenues) and bids for the payment that it will disburse to the state.

"Efficiency" type contracts require the private partner to compete over the costs of building the project or of providing the services but enable her to charge any price that she sees fit. "Performance" contracts, on the other hand, require private partners to deliver a certain level of output (with matching compensation for enhanced performance) while bidding for the requested revenue level.

Obviously, under each very different contract type, the risk to the private partner varies but, in all cases, it is an integral part of the contract. The bidding process has two key functions in this regard. Competition among bidders acts to reduce the project's overall costs, including the amount of risk borne by the public sector. Second, bidding is an effective mechanism for revealing how much risk private investors are willing to assume. This is valuable information needed by the public sector in its contract negotiations. On the other hand, bidding is a costly and time-consuming process; it therefore needs to be designed and carried out prudently.

Whatever the contract type, an important element affecting risk allocation is the contract's life span. Long-term contracts expose bidders to the risk of escalating input (fuel or labor) costs. Governments commonly attempt to cope with such events by introducing the degree of flexibility that allows them to adjust contract payments to specific cost or, perhaps, standard inflation indicators. As a result, private operators are inclined to reduce their demand for guaranteed fixed revenues because some proportion of their risk-exposure is covered. However, from the government's perspective, this approach implies taking on a higher share of the project's overall risk because such steps significantly shield the private party from considerable market risk.

In capital-intensive projects like underground rail, the state often guarantees currency exchange rates or major bank loans to the investor, which can cover 75%–80% of the total investment. A major predicament triggered by this step relates to bank policy: Banks are generally reluctant to lock in any funding before the potential investor actually wins the bid even though this condition may be a principal requirement for bidding. The state often provides a safety mechanism to overcome this impasse should it arise. All types of government guarantees need to be factored into the project appraisal in order to arrive at the correct assessment of its economic value.

The allocation of revenue risk can formally be presented as follows. Consider a Built Operate and Transfer (BOT) project in which user toll revenues are the investor's main source of income. Revenues, in turn, are the product of the toll level and actual demand. Let v denote the expected demand (e.g., the number of annual auto trips) and t the toll level. The risk allocation model indicates that if realized demand: $\alpha \cdot v$, $(0 < \alpha < 1)$, falls short of expected demand, the state will wholly or partly make up for the revenue difference. This difference is: $(t \cdot v - \alpha \cdot t \cdot v) \cdot \beta$, where β $(0 \le \beta \le 1)$ is the proportion of revenue shortfall that the state is willing to cover. Thus, the value of the state's guarantee of the revenue risk is: $t \cdot v(1 - \alpha) \cdot \beta$, where the value of β is negotiated between the state and the BOT investor. The larger the β, the greater is the risk that the state assumes. Note that the variable β can be defined as an increasing proportion of revenue shortfall rather than as a single number.

Beyond the above risks, the following list briefly describes some additional risks threatening PPP projects. These, too, must be accounted for when computing their true costs.

1. Loss of Control by the Public Sector

A PPP project, which involves significant capital outlays by the private sector, often increases the firm's involvement in decision making regarding how services are delivered and priced. This often leads to concerns about who actually controls service delivery. Objections to the long-term leasing of public infrastructure to the project's private partners often result from such apprehensions.[30]

2. Increased Costs and User Fees

The costs of overhead, administration, and depreciation of assets are usually not directly included in the fees that transportation users pay for highway and transit services. Yet, fees should be priced to reflect all the investor's relevant costs. If such pricing results in increased user fees, opposition to the project can result. This often compels the state to assume these costs.

3. Unacceptable Levels of Accountability

With PPP—as opposed to full public delivery—the lines of accountability are less clear to the public. This fuzziness may arouse criticism of the partnership and increased involvement of the public agency in ensuring compliance with public demands. Increased public control of the private investor may raise the private partner's effective costs and, in turn, his demand for greater compensation.

4. Unreliable Service Provision Caused by Unanticipated Events

Private firms are prone to labor disputes or other constraints external to the project's features that may prevent them from honoring their commitments. Such events expose the public sector, which is responsible for the continuous and smooth provision of services, to undue political and financial risks. This is a particularly acute issue because public transit services cannot be interrupted, irrespective of the source of the private partner's difficulties.

5. Inability to Benefit from Competition Due to the Limited Availability of Potential Private Partners

The public sector may be deprived of the benefits that competition brings if only a limited number of private enterprises have the necessary expertise or financial ability to enter into a partnership. The implications of this type of risk are costs higher than those incurred under competitive conditions or exclusively public provision of services.

6. Bias in the Selection Process

Public agencies have often been accused of bias in the selection of a bidder for a PPP project. Such complaints are heard most often when the lowest bid is, in itself, insufficient to win the contract as other conditions, such as experience, play a role in selecting a winner. This situation exposes the public sector to additional transaction costs from litigation, renegotiation, as well as direct costs from project postponement.

Three important conclusions can be drawn from this analysis of PPP risk. First, from a social-welfare perspective, there are ways to share risk between the public and private partners that are efficient as well as fair. Second, careful risk analysis of a PPP project must be conducted to ascertain the exact amount of risk borne by the public sector. Third, once this risk has been identified and measured, it must be incorporated into the COBA using one of the methods suggested in this chapter. The key message is that the more risk the government assumes, the more costly the project is to the public, a condition affecting the project's overall profitability. Finally, if the project is judged by a formal COBA as inferior (i.e., its benefit to cost ratio is less than one), the use of P3 is unlikely to make it worthy. Rather the project's deficiencies will soon emerge (e.g., cost overruns or insufficient demand) triggering renegotiation for a reduce risk exposure by the private partner, or for a larger share of state funding. Hence, a precondition for an efficient risk allocation scheme is that the project has passed a bona fide project evaluation test to ascertain its transportation-economic worthiness.

9. A PRIVATE SECTOR APPROACH TO THE MEASUREMENT OF PROJECT RISK

How should we measure a project's overall risk level? One approach would be to apply a private sector risk assessment model. The key argument behind such models is that the taxpayer can be viewed as a diversified private investor, and the public sector as a holder of a large portfolio of investments (Mayston, 1993). Yet, whereas private investors voluntarily pursue profit maximization objectives, taxpayers are forced to pay taxes even though their individual preferences regarding where those tax monies should be invested are not necessarily reflected in public infrastructure projects. It might further be argued that the government enjoys scale economies in the financial markets (e.g., it can borrow at rates below those obtained by private firms) or that it can better diversify risks than the private market is able to. However, such claims have to be balanced with the public sector's inefficiencies and lack of incentives for strict financial discipline (World Bank, 1994). Thus, use of private sector risk analysis may provide useful information about a particular project risk level because it reflects the opportunity costs of the invested capital.

In general, we distinguish between two major types of risks when deciding whether to invest in a particular project. These are risks are either *intrinsic* to the project or, alternatively, *external* to it (i.e., related to the economy at large). The first, which in the finance literature is known as *specific* or *nonsystematic* risk, stems from the type of project, its location, and specific market. For example, a port development project may face the risk of private shippers' reluctance to use this port due to more favorable conditions in rival ports, unforeseen costs from environmental or engineering issues, or construction delays due to local labor disputes. The second type of risk, which in financial jargon is called the *systematic risk*, arises from the systematic uncertainty about the future performance of the economy as a whole. Using the port example, a slump in international trade following on macroeconomic recession will affect the movement of goods even if the project was built as planned. During any investment analysis, it is necessary to use different approaches to deal with these two risks.

One possible way to deal with specific risk is to use a risk-adjusted discount factor, derivable from the Capital Asset Pricing Model (CAPM). Let r_f be the risk-free interest rate, r_M the market return (e.g., on the Dow Jones or S&P indexes), $E(r_M)$ the expected return from r_M and β, the "beta coefficient.[31] The risk-adjusted discount factor r_a is, then: $r_a = r_f + [E(r_M) - r_f] \cdot \beta$.

Turning to the measurement of a project's total risk, a private firm investing in a capital-intensive project will typically use 20%–30% of its equity, with the balance in long-term debt. Let s^E and s^D be the share of equity and debt in the total financing package, respectively, and let r^E and r^D be the real after-tax return on equity and on debt, respectively. Hence, the total return, r, is: $r = s^E \cdot r^E + s^D \cdot r^D$. Let r^F be the market risk-free interest rate (e.g., the rate paid by short-term government bonds). The difference between r and r^F represents the market's risk premium for this project. The higher the risk premium, the riskier is the project. Note that the rates r^E and r^D are based on the competitive financial market's assessment of the project's overall risk. Thus, even if the entire project is to be financed by the government, this risk cannot be eliminated; it is simply rolled over to taxpayers.

10. RISK ANALYSIS IN PROJECT EVALUATION AND CONTROL

10.1 Incorporating Risk Analysis into Project Evaluation

The methods and approaches to the measurement of risk previously introduced can be divided into two categories: those that aim at computing risk-adjusted benefit and cost variables, and those that provide estimates of the project's overall risk level. Expressions such as "expected value of benefits and costs" or "risk-adjusted discount rate" belong to the first category. Methods that assess the likelihood of cost overruns belong to the second. The decision-tree analysis described in Section 6 represents a method for selecting among different project alternatives under various risky states of nature. What other approaches can be used to incorporate risk analysis into the project evaluation process?

One such approach is to set an upper limit on the level of risk that a transportation investment project should assume. Thus, if the overall project's risk level (e.g., the likelihood of cost overruns) exceeds a certain threshold value, this project will, in theory, not be undertaken. A similar approach can be adopted for any specific risk factor, for example, overestimation of expected ridership. If the probability that future demand will fall short of a required level (e.g., the level necessary for $B/C \geq 1.2$) is greater than, say, 20%–30%, the project should not be initiated. A further approach is to adjust the rate of return of all the alternative projects considered to their respective risk levels and then rank the projects accordingly. This can be achieved through the computation of expected benefits and expected costs, factors that enter the rate of return equation (Chapter 6, equation 15).

Chapter 14 presents several approaches for selecting among investment alternatives, each characterized by several decision criteria including NPV, economic development, and environmental and community impacts. Each criterion is assigned a weight to reflect its importance in overall decision making. In a similar way, the compound risk index of each project can be added to the other criteria with a proper weight. Since decision makers are likely to be risk averse, especially when the project is funded from local resources, the weight they assign to the project's risk level invariably reflects their own levels of risk aversion.

10.2 Risk Control and Mitigation

Once a project's risks have been identified, quantified, and incorporated into COBA, it is necessary to develop strategies aimed at controlling them. The key objective is to lessen the likelihood of risky events as well as to reduce their impact (e.g., the amount of cost overrun), thereby increasing the likelihood of the project's success. Reduction of the variance of total cost distribution is an example of risk mitigation.

We can distinguish between several key strategies of risk mitigation: managerial control methods, contingency planning, contracting out, and insurance (Flyvbjerg et al., 2003, Chapter 7). Beginning in 2003, the US Federal Transit Administration (FTA) has required risk assessment as a condition for final design and approval of transit projects.[32] As important as this prerequisite is, it does not specify who should conduct the assessment and how, nor does it establish a probability threshold or range for project acceptance or rejection.

The identity of the body conducting the risk assessment of a large-scale project—that is, the sponsoring agency (e.g., the local MPO or transit authority), the funding authorities (at the state or federal level) or an independent agency—is crucial. While the sponsor might know most about the project, his risk assessment might also be biased because he has a vested interest in implementing the project. In addition, his assessment might reflect a level of expertise below that required for thoroughness. Clearly, an independent team, in consultation with the project's staff, is better equipped to provide an impartial risk analysis. This analysis should be a continuous process, conducted at various phases of the project. As risk is reassessed, further steps for risk mitigation can be introduced. The analysis should also be transparent to allow all the involved parties to provide input into the process.

Finally, since each step of the project's planning, evaluation, and implementation involves a certain measure of risk, a risk-management program needs to be developed, institutionalized, and effectively implemented throughout the project's construction period. There is a vast literature on the subject of risk management, although it is applicable primarily to private sector investments. Yet, there is no reason why such plans should not be adopted for the public sector as well (see for example Arrow, 1996).

11. SUMMARY AND CONCLUSIONS

Ample evidence indicates that large-scale transportation investments, mainly in rail, are inundated with cost overruns, grossly missed schedules, and unmet demand forecasts. The ability to reduce these risks through careful risk analysis, and the need to correctly assess the value of a project under risk, are the issues that motivated this chapter. The key questions asked were: What are the various risk factors that affect transportation investments, how can they be quantified and measured, and how are we to incorporate them into project assessment and selection?

The chapter examined a number of risk-assessment approaches. These included: scenario analysis, risk-adjusted profitability measures, probabilistic and simulation methods, curve fitting, decision-tree analysis, and rules for optimal timing of investments. In addition, the chapter examined the issue of risk sharing in public–private partnerships and methods used by the private sector to assess risk. Ways to incorporate risk assessment into the project evaluation process were also presented.

The key conclusion reached from this analysis is that no transportation investment project is free of risk, a condition that, in turn, affects its true transportation-economic value. Therefore, a formal risk analysis of each project should be an integral component of COBA and, it follows, a prerequisite for project decision making and selection.

Because risk implies that the investment's outputs and costs cannot be specified with certainty, it is necessary to establish a range of the calculated effects rather than provide specific point estimates. For example, following COBA of a given project, a prudent analyst would estimate a range for the

NPV results that reflect the risks associated with future streams of benefits and costs.

With respect to PPP-type projects, the underlying motivation of such analyses should be transportation-economic efficiency and construction effectiveness (e.g., complying with a strict construction schedule) and not simply removal of expenditures from the public sector's budget. To that end, a careful risk-sharing analysis is mandatory, using risk specialization and degree of control as the key sharing criteria.

Finally, why are project's risks so often ignored or inadequately evaluated during project assessment? When a significant proportion of the project's funding comes from sources external to the region where the project is to be implemented (i.e., federal funding), local decision makers tend to regard monetary costs as benefits (e.g., jobs creation), a perspective that makes them predisposed to accept riskier projects. A further explanation is embedded in the lack of good governance and transparency, features too often characterizing public decision making. A mandatory detailed risk assessment, such as the one required by the FTA, may therefore thwart acceptance of unworthy or wasteful projects. This is, indeed, one principal conclusion from this chapter.

10 Financing Transportation Investment Projects

1. INTRODUCTION

Experience shows that selection of a welfare-improving transportation investment, even if based on a proper evaluation, does not guarantee that the project will be built. Without secure funding, such a project remains merely an idea, unlikely to reach fruition. Political realities often render the evaluation process neither necessary nor sufficient for project implementation. Alternatively, the political ability to marshal and ensure funding can result in a project being completed even if it did not undergo orderly assessment. In cases like these, secure funding is often the raison d'être for undertaking the project even if the COBA has shown it to be unwarranted.[1]

When considering project funding, we distinguish between the *source of funding* and the *type of finance*.[2] Transportation projects are traditionally funded from a variety of sources: local agencies, city, regional, state, and federal governments as well as private investors. Each adopts a different financing method, whether taxation (earmarked or general), user charges, debt, or sale of public assets and equity. This distinction between source and type of funding underlies this chapter's main contention, namely, that the source of funding affects decision makers' propensities to select projects whereas the type of finance affects its true social-welfare value.

We should make it clear that this chapter is *not* about how transportation capital investments are or should be funded, nor is it about fiscal federalism as opposed to federal allocation of capital funds. The germane transportation literature is quite extensive. It reveals that a key concern among many national governments is the growing gap between transportation needs and funding availability. Numerous solutions have been proposed to ensure adequate and sustained funding, although political obstacles and public opposition often interfere with the viability of these measures (Smith and Gihring, 2004; TD Bank, 2004). Importantly, it has been observed that over time, a marked shift from federal and state funding to local funding has materialized (Goldman and Wachs, 2003; Wachs, 2003).

Our purpose here is to examine the related but neglected question of whether the source of funding affects transportation investment decision making and, if so, in what ways. We also turn to the issue of whether and how the form of a project's finance affects its welfare value, another topic not adequately addressed in the professional literature. What we do know is that normally, the "optimal" project is selected during the project evaluation stage while totally disregarding the form of finance, a practice implying that decision makers view project financing as a separate policy issue.

Against this background, we have chosen to focus on two main issues: the effect of funding source on project selection and the effect of financing on project value. We argue that: (a) Contrary to common practice, the funding source should not affect decision makers' attitude toward project selection, and (b) the financing method does affect a project's value; therefore, it should be integrated into the project's COBA.

The data and examples shown in this chapter reflect mainly US and Canadian experience, with some references to other countries. The reader should be aware, though, that parallel levels of government might reflect different political and institutional realities as we shift from country to country. For example, the federal governments of the US and Canada have different mandates and authority with respect to the planning and funding of public infrastructure.

This chapter is structured as follows. Section 2 surveys various sources of funding of transportation investment projects while Section 3 examines how the source of funding can affect project selection. Section 4 reviews the debate on the question of whether the method of finance should affect a project's social-welfare value. Section 5 examines various project financing methods. Section 6 investigates how these methods affect the investment's value. Section 7 considers the case of public–private partnerships in relation to a project's financial value. A summary and conclusions are presented in Section 8.

2. SOURCES OF TRANSPORTATION PROJECT FUNDING

2.1 Funding Needs versus Availability

A useful way to start the discussion is by considering the larger context of funding needs versus its availability. In general, transportation funding is meant to provide the resources for meeting four principal needs: routine maintenance, rehabilitation, replacement and modernization, and new infrastructure. Often, countries try to assess the gap between these present and future needs together with the levels of resources required. For example, a recent review found that the overall public infrastructure gap in Canada, including transportation, is in the range of $50–$125 billion (TD Bank, 2004). While this is a quite wide range, it nonetheless characterizes a worldwide phenomenon, namely, that transportation needs by far exceed funding availability.[3] This funding gap—alluding to the scarcity of public funds— partially explains the fierce political rivalry between communities for federal and state funding. Yet, it stands to reason that when resources are scarce and competition for those resources is acute, only the most efficient and effective projects should be selected. The irony is, however, that quality decisions are usually not made, with funding too often channeled to inferior projects (we return to this issue in Section 6). Table 10.1 shows the sources of funding against the types of finance employed for transportation capital investment projects in the US, information necessary to help frame this discussion.

To illustrate the trend described, consider the distribution of US state and local transportation revenue (1995 and 1999) by funding source and finance type, as shown in Table 10.2.

As evident from Table 10.2, about 50% of all revenues in the respective years came from state user fees whereas local and state taxes increased from 16.0% in 1995 to 24.5% in 1999. In addition, state borrowing increased from 6.2% of total revenue in 1995 to 9.3% in 1999. Another factor, not shown in Table 10.2, is gasoline taxes: As a source of revenue for highway projects (about 35% in 2001), these have been declining steadily, mainly due to improved fuel economy. The tax has also lost its popularity although rate revisions still require legislation.[4] The main point conveyed by Tables 10.1 and 10.2 is that in analyzing the impacts of funding on the value of a capital project, both the source of funding and the type of finance need to be considered in relation to each other, as we will demonstrate.

Table 10.1 Earmarked Transportation Funding: Source versus Type of Finance

Source of Funding	Type of Finance				
	Taxation	*Bond & Debt*	*User Charges*	*Equity*	*Other*
Local (city)	Property, impact fees, and other taxes	Municipal bonds	Tolls Parking Fees		Fees & assets sale
State	Income tax Payroll tax Fuel & tire tax	State bonds	Tolls Facility Entry fee		Fees & assets sale
Federal	Income tax Fuel tax	Treasury bonds	Security fees		
Public Agency		Agency bonds	Airport charges	Investment income	Transfer
Private Sector		Corporate bonds/ borrowing	Tolls	Private funds	Various

Table 10.2 Percent Distribution of US State and Local Transportation Revenues

Revenue Source and Type of Finance	1995 (%)	1999 (%)
State borrowing	6.2	9.3
Local taxes including sales taxes	6.5	8.0
State taxes	9.5	9.6
Local general funds	17.8	17.9
Local property taxes	7.6	7.2
State user fees	52.4	48.1
Total Revenue ($million)	$69,114	$88,872

Source: US Department of Transportation (2002).

2.2 Sources of Transportation Project Funding

Given the information found in Tables 10.1 and 10.2, does it matter whether the debt financing a project is issued by the city, the state, or the federal government? Put differently, why is the source of funding important for project selection? Based on the literature, this importance is rooted in political decision making. First, the greater the political distance between the level of funding (e.g., the federal government) and the level on which the project is carried out (e.g., local government), the greater is the uncertainty surrounding actual approval and delivery of the funds. More importantly, however, is the attitude towards risk exhibited by decision makers when funding comes from a higher political level. As argued in Chapter 4, when a project is funded from external sources, local politicians and decision makers treat the costs of the projects as benefits, mainly in terms of jobs, economic development, and political power. Hence, the costlier the project, the greater the perceived benefits. And so, the proclivity of local decision makers to accept a project regardless of its actual benefits and risks increases with the proportion of funding obtained from higher levels. The case of the Vancouver RAV line, where the majority of funding comes from federal and provincial governments in addition to the airport authority, is a case in a point (see Chapter 15). This observation also explains why US federal subsidies to local public transit inherently provide incentives for selecting capital-intensive projects irrespective of their efficiency or effectiveness (Jianling and Wachs, 2004). To illustrate this trend, Table 10.3 reports changes in the NY Metropolitan Transportation Authority (MTA) capital funding for the period 1981–2004 by sources of funding.

Table 10.3 shows that over time, the MTA has increased its reliance on "external" funding, mainly state support, at the expense of local (city)

Table 10.3 MTA Capital Funding Sources by Plan, 1982–2004[5]

Period	Federal (%)	State Dedicated Funds[a] (%)	City[b] (%)	Bonds & Debt[c] (%)	Local[d] (%)	Annual Average ($ million)
2000–2004	27	18 (0)	3	47	5	$3,784
1992–1999	33	12 (1)	9	26	20	$2,783
1981–1991	32	0 (15)	10	29	13	$2,675

Note: [a]The figures shown are dedicated state funds. The figures in brackets represent state service contracts and appropriations; [b]Bond and debt restructuring; [c]MTA bonds and debt restructuring; [d]MAC, PANYNJ/Nassau County, Lessor Equity/Asset Sales, Investment Income, Capital-Operating Transfer/PAYAG, Other (developer contributions, settlements, and miscellaneous revenue).
Source: Based on Seaman et al. (2004).

funding. "Dedicated funding" has become the state's main financing instrument for supporting transit investment since 1991. In addition, debt finance has increased substantially over time. Another example of the structure of funding sources is the Canadian system for support of urban transit shown in Figure 10.1.

Figure 10.1 indicates that in Canada, municipal (local) funding amounts to about 33% of total revenues and, as a result, the bulk of funding comes from other sources.

While these examples do not in themselves establish a clear trend in transportation funding, they support the previous conclusions—especially when considered together with other evidence (see Chapter 15)—that local authorities are increasingly relying on external financing, mainly state and federal (USA) subsidies, to fund large-scale capital projects. Furthermore, this observation explains the predisposition of local decision makers to select capital-intensive mega-projects for implementation. Section 3.2 analyzes this issue.

2.3 Funding Transit through Property Taxes

The quandary of how to cover the capital costs associated with constructing and maintaining public transit facilities nonetheless remains before us. A traditional proposal for resolving the issue involves raising real estate taxes to reflect the ensuing increased property values. This suggestion assumes that the property tax collected will effectively cover the immense costs of land acquisition and facility construction (Smith and Gihring, 2004). While this contribution to covering costs can be quite sizeable, this proposal raises several difficulties. First, property price increases are likely to transpire over time, continuing after the project has been built and accessibility has been improved. Yet, tax revenues need to be collected in order to fund planning

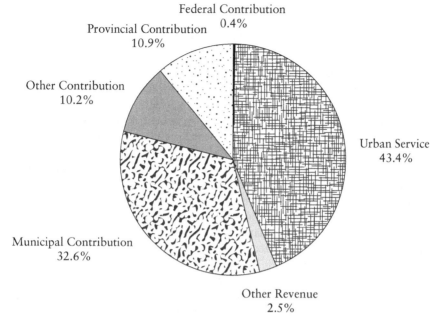

Figure 10.1 Funding for Canada's urban transit: total revenue by source (2003).

Note: "Other" includes revenues from charter, school bus, and other passenger services.

Source: Transport Canada Tabulation, adapted from Canadian Urban Transit Association (CUTA) data, (http://www.tc.gc.ca/pol/en/report/anre2004/7C_e.htm).

and construction costs, that is, prior to project implementation and the anticipated price rises. Second, the introduction of this tax is likely to affect social equity as landowners will, undoubtedly, transfer the tax to renters, whose demand for housing is rather inelastic. Third, the question of how to differentiate the increase in property value between improved accessibility and other factors (e.g., zoning effects and property-specific amenities) is a formidable empirical task. Despite these qualifications, the imposition of property taxes as a method to support transportation has been advocated by the academic community (e.g., Anas, 1983b) as well as urban decision makers.

3. SOURCES OF PROJECT FUNDING AND DECISION MAKING

3.1 The Effect of External Funding on Local Decision Making

We now return to a question posed earlier: Does the source of funding affect transportation project evaluation and selection? The salience of this question stems from the trends discussed regarding investment funding from sources outside the localities. Our hypothesis states that local authorities, as recipients of federal and state money, tend to regard external funding as "costless" and as political benefits. They are therefore predisposed to promoting infrastructure projects containing a large external funding component. Moreover, the larger this external component, the greater is their support for such projects as is the likelihood of their implementation, regardless of the social welfare to be gained—or not (Jianling and Wachs, 2004). A corollary to this premise is that, *ceteris paribus*, the same investment projects would not be as vigorously endorsed if funding were based mainly on local revenues, that is, taxation and user fees.

Another aspect of this dependence on external funding is the disregard for investment risk it encourages among local decision makers. The political reality captured in such behavior is simple: Infrastructure construction lasts for many years, often beyond the political life span of the elected officials who made the decisions; as today's incumbents are free of political liability for poor projects, this lack of accountability drives their inclination towards riskier projects.

Of course, from a societal perspective, such dispositions invite severe consequences. First—as always—there is no "free lunch": Money allocated to one project bears opportunity costs in the form of forgone returns from alternative investments. Second, this tendency promotes the implementation of inefficient projects, selected without any regard for their social rate of return. Third, once built, such projects often become "white elephants"— facilities draining local government budgets with their burdensome operational and maintenance costs. The Buffalo Light Rail case demonstrates this point (see Berechman and Paaswell, 1983).

3.2 External Funding and Local Decision Making

In this section we continue to examine the linkage between the level of external funding and project selection. We do so by translating our argument that local decision makers tend to equate capital investment costs with political benefits into formal terms.

Suppose that a certain investment project of size C (dollars) is funded from two sources: external and internal (to the region or city). Let α be the proportion of external funding and $(1 - \alpha)$ the proportion of internal funding (e.g., real estate tax revenues). Decision makers then derive the utility from the project as an increasing function of project size, as affected by the level of external funding. Let C be the decision variable. When faced with an external funding level of α, what is the optimal C to be selected?

Let γ represent the level of risk associated with external funding, such as the probability that funding will be terminated. Let δ denote the risk assigned to internal (local) funding, for example, how much decision makers will jeopardize their reelection should they raise local taxes. Both risk types are a function of α, but in opposite directions. Thus, whereas γ increases with α, δ declines with α. For simplicity, we assume that once approved, external funding is guaranteed, so that $\gamma = 0$; also, when $\alpha = 1 \rightarrow \delta = 0$.

What size of an investment, as a function of external funding, $C(\alpha)$, would a local decision maker prefer? We assume $C(\alpha)$ to be a monotonic increasing function of α, implying that larger proportions of external funding are associated with larger projects. Further assume that the decision makers' utility function from $C(\alpha)$ also increases monotonically with capital costs, and $C(1) = \overline{C}$, which is determined by the federal transportation budget.

If $(\alpha \cdot C)$ is funded externally, the amount $[(1 - \alpha) \cdot C]$ must be funded internally, a situation that implies risk to decision makers. The magnitude of this risk is also a function of population size, P, because local funding is collected by means of a per-unit tax. The following model represents this hypothesized scenario:

$$Max.\, U(C, \alpha) = U\left[C, \delta \cdot (\frac{1}{P}(1 - \alpha) \cdot C) \right]$$

(1)

$C,\ \alpha$

In (1), the utility gained by decision makers is an increasing function of capital expenditures *and* a decreasing function of the risk associated with the portion of the per-capita capital costs funded internally $((1 - \alpha)/P)$.[6] For illustrative purposes, let the utility function in (1) be written as:

$$U(C) = A\log(C) - \left[\frac{1}{P}(1 - \alpha)C \right]^{\delta},$$

where A is a scalar parameter, and δ $(\delta > 0)$ is the degree of disutility from internal (local) funding. Let C^* denote the level of investment that maximizes utility (equation 1). It follows then that as the proportion of external funding (α) increases, so does C^* $((\partial C^*/\partial \alpha) > 0)$ as well as the decision maker's utility $((\partial U(C^*)/\partial \alpha) > 0)$.[7] The key conclusions from this demonstration are that from the perspective of local decision makers, given population size, a larger proportion of external funding implies greater utility and thus higher proclivity for the selection of a larger capital investment project. It also confirms the assumed negative relationship between local funding and investment project size.[8]

Model (1) serves here primarily as a means to elucidate the relationship between local decision makers' attitudes towards the source of funding and the level of capital investment they support. It demonstrates that when faced with a set of alternative investments, local decision makers are more prone to approving costlier projects with increasing proportions of external funding.

4. FINANCING TRANSPORTATION INVESTMENTS: THE FUNDAMENTAL DEBATE

One school of thought considers a project's social-welfare contribution as a separate issue, distinct from its form of finance. According to this argument, the package used to finance a project should *not* affect either its value or its acceptability. This view further suggests that while the exact finance method may affect the distribution of benefits and costs among households, it bears no relevance for the project's social-welfare value.[9] It follows that in the case of Public–Private Partnerships (PPP), for example, the public sector should first determine the project's value using the social discount rate and only then turn it over to the private sector for financing and construction if that value is sufficiently high.

Although this approach may appeal to planners as it does away with cumbersome consideration of specific finance packages in the project's COBA, we reject it, based on its several theoretical and technical flaws. First, as argued in Chapter 6, the social discount rate reflects either the opportunity costs of societal resources or consumers' rate of time preference. If risk could be assumed away (the Arrow and Lind (1970) argument), both approaches would result in similar project welfare values because in equilibrium, the rate of time preference equals the net rate of return of expended resources. But, as shown in Chapter 9, risk cannot be assumed away. The correct approach is, then, to compute the marginal cost of public funds (MCF), which reflect the social costs of an additional dollar of tax revenue (see Section 6.2 below).

Second, exclusive reliance on the social discount rate for project selection implicitly assumes that social goals were clearly defined and are attainable, and that government investments are more efficient than private ones in noncompetitive markets. Again, the latter is not always the case, as attested to by the numerous failed transportation projects (Flyvbjerg et al., 2003). How should we regard a project that has passed the social discount rate test but proved itself a disappointment during or after construction?

Third, in general equilibrium settings, methods of finance affect the derived general welfare results of public (in this case transportation) investments (Proost et al., 2004). For instance, financing a project through an income tax will affect the propensity of workers to supply labor. Property and fuel taxes tend to affect consumption of nontransportation goods and services while corporate taxes affect investment decisions. If all transportation projects were financed using the same mix of taxes and other charges, and if the social-welfare discount rate had been correctly computed to measure the marginal cost of this mix, then the finance method would be inconsequential. Since this is clearly not so, especially in the case of mega-projects, the specific financial mix does appear to have a bearing on a project's social-welfare value.

Fourth, again as seen in Chapter 6, the selection of a project from a set of alternatives can vary according in the presence of budget constraints. Budgetary limitations, as we have shown (see Chapter 9), have motivated the growing trend toward financing and constructing transportation investments as PPP projects, in which the private sector invests substantial capital in return for what it considers an appropriate rate of return. Moreover, in PPP projects, risk is mainly borne by the public sector—a practice that influences actual project costs. Under these conditions, use of the social discount rate as the decisive criterion can lead to implementation of inferior projects.

A fifth theoretical argument has to do with the impact of funding on financial markets and consumers' rate of time preferences. Public capital investments are commonly funded through debt (mainly bond issues) that requires large interest payments (see the case of NYC's MTA, Table 10.3). Key results from this practice are, first, the potential crowding out of corporate bonds from capital markets, a phenomenon that affects the cost of capital to the private sector, hence, its level of investment in the economy.[10] Second, and most importantly for us here, interest payments on these bonds also impact on the social rate of time preference—and thus the social discount rate—as it requires the de facto transfer of resources from future to present generations. We are consequently forced to conclude that the funding method does have consequences for an investment project's true value.

Turning to technical arguments, one criterion often used to assess a project is its annual cash flow, which must conform to a predetermined budget (see Chapter 6). Since debt service payments are determined by the form of finance and directly affect annual cash flow, the financial package's makeup is crucial for project appraisal and selection.

A further technical argument relates to the correct computation of a project's benefits. Often unnoticed is the fact that some forms of financing represent implicit policy instruments because they influence the level of a facility's use. For example, the imposition of tolls to finance a highway project will necessarily affect demand and, it follows, the present value of its benefits. If we compare "tolls" versus "no tolls" scenarios, demand estimates would differ. Moreover, if the taxing of one mode subsidizes another, such taxation will necessarily affect demand for both. Obviously, the project's true value should be estimated only subsequent to determining its financing strategy.

Still another issue pertains to the debt limits (legal, institutional, or political) attached to the different sources of finance; when reached, these limits act like budgetary constraints, affecting the shadow price of the capital acquired. For example, a public agency may reach the legal limit of borrowing after floating a bond, a constraint affecting the price of any additional dollar the agency may need to borrow.

In conclusion, if planners wish to affect project selection, they should do so directly, through the weights they attach to specific impacts (e.g., encouraging public transit use) and *not* through a selection process that disregards the project's direct as well as indirect costs. Methods of financing should therefore not be considered independently of project design and evaluation; rather, they should be integral components of the assessment.

5. FINANCING TRANSPORTATION PROJECTS: MAIN TYPES

Taxation, debt, and user fees are, in general, the three main types of financing used in transportation capital project implementation: PPP projects add a private equity capital component to these types. Before examining each, it is worth recalling the fundamental debate on the merits of user charges versus taxation (or debt) as a form of finance. The increased use of taxation (sales, property, and income taxes) to fund transportation, coupled with the decline in user charges, has weakened the price-usage linkage, thereby encouraging more travel but also more maintenance activity and new construction. For example, truckers who do not pay for the wear and tear of the road system use highways more extensively than those who pay directly for their consumption of the same arteries. Clearly, an efficient users' pricing scheme reduces the amount of new investment together with its greater capital funding demands. Bearing this phenomenon in mind, tax revenues must be categorized as either direct (levied on income) or indirect (levied on consumption or transactions).

5.1 Indirect and Direct Taxation

To illustrate the use of *indirect taxes* for transportation purposes, consider the State of New York and the New York City MTA, which relies upon various revenue sources. Due to significant operating budget deficits projected for the coming years, the 2005–2006 New York State's budget added three new or enhanced indirect taxes targeted for support of the MTA:

- An additional 0.125% (1/8th of 1%) regional sales tax in those New York State counties served by the MTA, effective June 1, 2005. This source was expected to generate approximately $110 million in 2005, approximately $202 million in 2006, and approximately $230 million annually beginning in 2007.
- An increase in the MRT-1 tax (mortgage recording tax), effective June 1, 2005, from 25¢ per $100 of recorded mortgage to 30¢, expected to generate approximately $29 million in 2005 and approximately $50 million annually thereafter.
- Increases in specified motor vehicle fees, effective January 1, 2006. The MTA would receive 34 percent of the increase, expected to generate approximately $61 million annually.

We can predict that these indirect taxes will distort the allocation of resources primarily by increasing the gap between the prices received by suppliers and those paid by buyers (users). As was shown in chapter 5 (section 3.2), when faced with an average tax rate t levied on all goods and services, consumers will pay $\$(1 + t)$ for each \$1 of purchase, of which producers will receive \$1, with $\$t$ going to government coffers.

Turning now to *direct taxation*, suppose that the government wishes to invest an additional \$1 in transportation and decides to finance this investment through an income tax. To do this, it must raise taxes by *more* than \$1 because the increase in direct taxation implies a reduction in disposable income and hence a fall in indirect tax revenue. Direct taxation must in fact be increased by $\$(1 + t)$. Disposable income will then fall by $\$(1 + t)$. Given that the proportion $t/(1 + t)$ of all consumers' spending is direct government tax revenue, indirect tax revenue will fall by $\$t$.[12] The net effect on government tax revenue is therefore $\$(1 + t) - \$t = 1$. The implication of this example is that each extra \$1 collected by the government as direct taxes negatively impacts total tax revenues due to the decline in disposable household income.

This type of analysis obviously makes implicit simplifying assumptions, for example, that the marginal propensity to consume is constant. Still, it is pertinent to ask about the economic costs of a project financed in whole or in part from taxation, given the effect of indirect and direct taxes on consumption and disposable income. Using the market cost of capital for consumption (see Chapter 6 for details) does not fully answer this question because it does not account for deadweight losses from taxation although it does debit the social price of taxation from project costs.

5.2 Dedicated Tax Revenues as a Form of Finance

Table 10.3 provides indications of the growing use of dedicated funding as a source of funds for transportation projects. In general, dedicated or earmarked taxes[13] imply that specific sources of revenue are assigned to particular uses. In conjunction with vehicle taxes and fees, the US Highway Trust Fund, which earmarks federal fuel tax revenues for highways and transit, funded over 50% of highway expenditures in 2001 (see Figure 10.2).

What are the economic implications of using earmarked taxes as a source of funding? Efficiency in the allocation of tax revenue depends on the flexibility available to direct these funds to the highest-yielding public investments. Dedicated taxes hamper this efficiency by introducing inflexibility into resource allocation. Moreover, they hinder effective long-term budget control and public decision making. Earmarked taxes in effect carry the opportunity costs of forgone investments.

It might be argued, though, that the use of dedicated resources provides a minimum and uninterrupted level of funding, so important for the continuous planning, maintenance, and upgrading of the transportation network. Also, if earmarked taxes are levied on a transportation-related activity (e.g.,

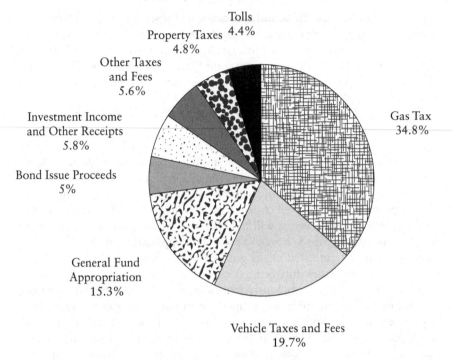

Figure 10.2 Revenue sources for highways in the US (2001).

Source: Wachs, (2003).

gasoline taxes), these funds come to approximate user charges, a fact that reduces the misallocation of tax revenue (Enoch et al., 2004). How, then, do earmarked taxes impact on a transportation project's costs? Section 6 discusses this issue.

5.3 The Debt Component of Capital Project Financing

As noted above, many cities and local transportation agencies use debt (borrowing and bonds) to wholly or partially cover the capital costs of their infrastructure projects. As an example, consider the 2006 debt structure of the New York Metropolitan Transportation Authority (MTA), shown in Table 10.4.

What, then, is the cost of this or a similar mix of debt to a capital investment project? A direct approach to estimating this cost would be the use of a weighted average of interest rates, where the weights represent the amount of debt associated with each type of debt. Such an approach makes it possible to compute the annual debt service payment on the project's outstanding debt.[14]

Table 10.4 MTA Debt Outstanding ($Millions), 2006

Type of Credit	Principal Issued Amount	Rating[a]	Current Amount Outstanding	Average Annual Debt Service	True Interest Costs (%)
MTA Transportation Revenue Bonds	$9,417.525	A2/A/A	$9,206.715	$602.9 thru 2032	4.90
TBTA General Revenue Bonds	$5,425.715	Aa2/AA–/AA	$4,579.860	$292.8 thru 2032	4.60
TBTA Subordinate Revenue Bonds	$2,474.990	Aa3/A+/AA–	$2,342.785	$147.0 thru 2034	5.29
MTA Dedicated Tax Fund Bonds	$3,740.975	AA–/A+	$3,278.415	$197.1 thru 2034	4.57
MTA State Service Contract Bonds	$2,395.205	AA–/A+	$2,310.930	$165.0 thru 2031	5.19
MTA Certificates of Participation (2 Broadway)	$807.330	Aaa/AAA/AAA	$430.965	$ 27.2 thru 2030	4.46
Grand Total: Bonds & Notes	$24,261.740		$22,149.670		

Note: [a]Bond rating relative to risk level is performed by specialized financial analysts such as Moody's and Standard & Poor's. AAA indicates highest quality.
Source: March 14, 2006, MTA (http://www.mta.info/mta/investor/pdf/mar06debt.pdf).

While financing debt with current taxes does not introduce a direct risk element (save for the risk of shortages per se) into the project, that is not the case of debt financing, which introduces the risk of debt service default. Bond ratings, as shown in Table 10.4, are good indicators of the risk level attached to this form of debt financing and should become part of the project's overall risk level (see Chapter 9).

6. TYPES OF FINANCE AND PROJECT VALUE

It was argued in Chapter 6 that if the rate r, used to discount the streams of benefits and costs from a project, reflects the correct shadow price of the project's capital, the derived net present value correctly measures its welfare contribution. But what if the marginal cost of the public funds, applied to a specific project, is in fact different than r due to the particular financial package of this project?

Consider a typical case of a new light rail line to be financed by federal grants (taxation), user charges (consumption), local government funding (mainly property taxes), debt, and private sector equity. Like all transportation projects, the project's benefits and costs are discounted by r, which is set by the federal government and based on general macroeconomic considerations (see Chapter 6). Now, the true costs of this financing package for the project may be much higher due to various deadweight losses (from taxation), the shadow price of the capital obtained from consumption (user charges), the risk-adjusted interest rate on bonds and the cost of private capital. To the economy, the opportunity cost of the resources used for this project is therefore higher than the discount rate r. Disregarding this discrepancy will bias the project's net present value. How should the specific form of finance be accounted for when computing the project's true cost of capital? How should it affect the project's value and what should be the annual debt service level?

6.1 The Corporate Finance Approach

In corporate finance theory, the well-known Modigliani–Miller theorem states that under conditions of symmetric information and no taxation, the form of finance (equity or debt) does not affect a firm's value. Stated otherwise, under these conditions, the firm's cost of capital—and thus its valuation—does not depend on the debt-to-equity ratio.[15] Can it therefore be concluded that the same result also applies to public investments so that, under similar conditions, the form by which a transportation project is financed is inconsequential to its valuation?

It should be remembered that the conditions underlying the Modigliani–Miller theorem rarely exist in real life. After all, firms and investors do face a variety of taxes, bankruptcy carries high costs, and information is vastly asymmetric. It is precisely because these assumptions do not hold that a firm's capital structure does matter. For example, in the US, the government grants tax deductions on interest paid, an allowance that contains an intrinsic bias towards debt financing.

In the case of public infrastructure investments, market efficiency assumptions pertaining to the source of funding *and* the type of finance cannot be supported. If anything, equity and borrowing decisions are highly political but also subject to legal in addition to institutional arrangements and regulation. Moreover, the equity funds used in public funding come from taxation, which in itself introduces market inefficiencies (reflected in deadweight losses). This means that the type of project finance does matter and should be assessed relative to its impact on the true costs of a public project and its value.

What, then, is the impact that the method of project financing is likely to impose on a project's benefit and its cost. We have already mentioned local property taxes, which affect local residents' disposable income and thus their demand for travel as well as their value of time. Property taxes can generate deadweight losses, too, thereby further affecting welfare.[16] Similar results occur from increases in local, state, or federal income tax when proceeds are earmarked for a project's financing. Alternatively, if user charges or congestion tolls are used to finance a project, they directly impact on demand for the facility and its benefits stream.

What remains to be reviewed in greater depth is the cost side of project funding. Alternative financial schemes have different impacts, whether through annual debt service charges or the discount rate. In general, the project finance method has three major effects on the present value of a project's costs. These are the project's true cost of capital and thus the discount rate, the annual debt service payment, and the project's risks, particularly the risks of cost overruns and financial insolvency.

If the project's true cost of capital, including debt service, exceeds the discount rate, the computed NPV will surpass its true value. One way to correct for this is to compute NPV as:

$$NPV = \left[-\sum_{t=1}^{T_C} \frac{C_t + kC}{(1+r)^t} \right] + \sum_{t=T_C+1}^{T+T_C} \frac{B_t + R_t - M_t - O_t - kC}{(1+r)^t} \tag{2}$$

where k is additional capital costs in excess of the discount rate, r. In the case of the MTA, for example, if $r = 3\%$ but interest charges are 5% (see Table 10.4), an additional $(k =)$ 2% should be added to the project's annual capital expenditures when calculating its NPV.

If a project is financed by several sources, such as debt, taxation, and user charges, the true cost of capital is computed as a weighted average cost of capital (WACC). The WACC takes into account the relative proportion of each component of the capital structure and then calculates the expected cost of new capital. To illustrate, assume a PPP type project, financed through equity and debt. Let:

r' = weighted average cost of capital (%)
y = required or expected rate of return on equity, or cost of equity (%)
b = required or expected rate of return on borrowings, or cost of debt (%)
x_c = corporate tax rate (%)
D = total debt and leases ($)
E = total equity and equity equivalents ($)
K = total capital invested in the project ($)

The weighted average cost of capital is then defined by:

$$r' = (\frac{E}{K}) \cdot y + (\frac{D}{K}) \cdot b(1 - x_c) \tag{3}$$

where $K = D + E$. This rate, r', should be used to discount future streams of benefits and costs. If the discount rate is externally set by the overseeing agency, the difference, $(r' - r)$, should be added to the capital cost as in (2).

To summarize, each form of financing affects a project's benefits and costs—and thus its net present value—in some way. If a project is evaluated and selected prior to the determination of a financing method, decision makers are likely to err in their choice.

6.2 Project Financing in a General Equilibrium Framework

To reiterate, transportation investments, particularly mega-projects, are generally funded through a financial package that contains a large tax revenue component. Although these revenues come from various sources (e.g., income tax, property tax, gasoline tax, and corporate tax) they have one common denominator, namely, their impact on other sectors of the economy, mainly on labor, consumption, and savings and investments. General equilibrium models of finance take these effects into account when deriving the net welfare effects of transportation investments (Proost et al., 2004).

A key element in these models is the marginal cost of the public funds raised by the specific tax (e.g., head tax, labor tax[17]). The concept marginal cost of public funds (MCPF or MCF) refers to the welfare cost incurred per additional dollar of tax revenue. The income tax levied on labor is such a tax.[18] Kleven and Kreiner (2003) have carried out extensive calculations of the MCF in OECD countries for the purpose of accounting for the tax's effect on hours worked and labor market participation.[19] Assuming standard labor supply elasticities, Table 10.5 reports estimates for Canada, the UK, and the US for a regressive tax (head tax), a proportional tax, and a progressive labor tax.

What these estimates show is that for the US, when including unemployment benefits, the welfare cost of raising tax revenues by $1 using a

Table 10.5 Estimates of Marginal Costs of Public Funds in Canada, the UK, and the US

	Proportional Tax	Regressive Tax (Head Tax)	Progressive Tax
Canada	1.30	1.01	1.83
UK	1.37	1.09	1.83
US	1.15	1.00	1.34

Source: Kleven and Kreiner (2003, Table II).

proportional tax is $1.15, which increases to $1.34 using a progressive tax. In other words, every $1 raised by progressive labor tax for investment in transportation carries an efficiency cost of $1.34.

A key implication of these estimates lies in the support it lends for our argument that the method of financing transportation investments has major impacts on a project's value and needs to be incorporated into its COBA. Thus, the social-welfare contribution of a project (measured by its NPV) is:

$$NPV = \sum_{t=0}^{\infty} \frac{B_t}{(1+r_n)^t} - MCF \cdot \sum_{t=0}^{\infty} \frac{\Delta C_t - \Delta R_t}{(1+r_g)^t} \tag{4}$$

In (4), B denotes consumers' benefits (measured by their consumption stream), ΔC is the direct capital investment and maintenance cost stream, ΔR denotes the stream of induced tax revenues, and r_n and r_g are the net and gross rates of return prevalent in the economy, respectively. That is, $r_n = r_g(1 - \tau_k)$, where τ_k is the tax rate on capital income. The MCF is defined as:

$$MCF = \left[\left. \sum_{t=0}^{\infty} \frac{w_t L_t}{(1+r_n)^t} \middle/ \frac{\partial \left[\sum_{t=0}^{\infty} \frac{R_t}{(1+r_g)^t} \right]}{\partial \tau_l} \right. \right] \tag{5}$$

In expression (5), w and L are the annual wage rate and labor supply, respectively; R is total annual tax revenue; and τ_l is the tax rate on income (income tax rate).

What expression (4) shows is that when a multiperiod investment project is financed through tax revenue, payments that affect labor supply and consumption, it is necessary to take these effects into account when carrying out project assessments. Crucially, it implies that when a project is funded through a specific finance package, the social discount rate is not the appropriate rate to be used for discounting future streams of benefits and costs. Instead, benefits should be discounted using consumers' after-tax discount rate, a net rate representing consumers' valuation of the transport services to be produced. Capital costs should be discounted using the government's gross return on capital, which represents the opportunity costs of government tax revenue in the economy. For COBA purposes, the market rate of return on private capital, which incorporates the market risk premium on private investments, is a good proxy for the economy's rate of return on capital investments. Thus, direct use of both market rates eliminates the difficulties encountered when using a single social discount rate that is only assumed to reflect consumers' rate of time preferences.[20] Expression (4) further indicates that the present value of net costs should be weighted by the MCF prior to its comparison with the present value of its benefits.

7. PUBLIC–PRIVATE PARTNERSHIPS

In Chapter 9 we examined in some detail the risk-sharing issues connected with Public–Private Partnership (PPP) investment projects, of which Private Financing Initiatives (PFI) is a common subtype. We noted that following a tendering process, the private firm or partner finances, constructs, operates, and maintains an infrastructure facility for a designated period of time. In return, the state compensates the PFI throughout the franchise period by means of an annual payment scheme or, alternatively, the tolls it collects. At the end of the franchise period, the private firm transfers the facility to the public's full possession, sometimes for a fixed sum. The bidding process, which includes a number of financial, technical, and service parameters, in many cases hinges on the requested annual payments.

The key motivations prompting state or local government to enter into a PFI contract are tight budgets, which preclude implementation of many worthy projects,[21] as well as the belief that a PPP setup can produce more efficient and better-managed projects. Yet, from the private sector's viewpoint, the main reason for participating in a PFI project is the generation of an "acceptable" rate of return on its investment. This rate must meet several conditions. First, it must reflect a steady and guaranteed stream of income. Second, it must reflect the market's yield on alternative investments. Third, it must contain a risk premium that is commensurable with this particular type of investment. Fourth, it must contain a financial spread that reflects an acceptable profit for the funding institution (e.g., a bank). Following the basic tenet of this book—that project assessment should be carried out from a social-welfare perspective—the relevant questions become: Should PFI financial arrangements affect the project's value and, if so, how?

As argued above, the value of a public project should also be a function of its financial profile. What, then, should the value of a PFI project be? The answer is a function of service demand and project costs. If the PFI contract contains clauses concerning future tolls, their level, and private partner responsibility, this information must be factored into the project's COBA to account for their impact on the future demand levels that determine the project's true welfare gains.

Turning to the project's costs, the private partner's accepted rate of return is a function of: (a) expected direct revenues from tolls; (b) the government's annual payment plus a fixed sum, if any, paid at the end of the contract; and (c) the government's share in the project's overall risk (see Chapter 9). Components (b) and (c) are those costs borne by the public that must enter directly into the project's COBA in addition to its capital, operating, and maintenance costs.

A related question is: What is the appropriate discount rate for a PPP contract: the social discount rate or the private sector rate? If government evaluates the PPP contract using its own costs of construction and maintenance, the social discount rate will be below the private sector rate (Grout, 2003). We obtain such a result because the social discount rate overlooks the additional costs incurred by the private partner's demanded rate of return and the government's disproportional share of project risk. Therefore, before committing to a PPP project, authorities need to consider the actual, sometimes implicit costs of the contract. A case in a point is the SR 91 toll road in Southern California. Apparently, the true costs of this project exceeded those implied by the use of the social discount rate.[22]

A recently proposed form of PPP is the *facility-lease* agreement. According to this arrangement, a private firm leases an existing transportation infrastructure facility, such as a bridge or a tollway, for a long-term period (e.g., 99 years). The major benefit derived by the private firm is a steady and quite reliable stream of income. For the public, its benefits are captured in delivery of an upfront, lump-sum payment that can then be used for further transportation or any other public investments in addition to relief from routine maintenance and repair costs, which are paid for by the private firm for the duration of the lease. For example, following a public tender, $1.83 billion were offered for lease of the Chicago Skyway Bridge.[23] Since bridges and similar facilities can be considered as enjoying a "monopolistic position" in the transportation network, income from tolls is guaranteed for the foreseeable future. While there is always the risk that the government will build another bridge, this is highly unlikely for various economic, political, geographic, engineering, and environmental reasons. In the Chicago Skyway case, the social benefits from the PPP arrangement were the lump-sum payment plus the opportunity costs associated with this sum (e.g., risk-free interest) *and* the operating and maintenance costs paid for by the private operator. The PPP costs were the forgone toll revenues over the lease's period.[24] Whether the public ends up paying higher tolls to the private operator than it would have paid to a public operator remains an open question.

8. SUMMARY AND CONCLUSIONS

This chapter has made a fundamental distinction between the "source of funding" of a transportation investment project and the "form of its finance." That is, a project can be funded from local, state, or federal sources, while taking advantage of debt, taxation, user charges, or private equity finance. The chapter's key tenets are that the source of funding affects the propensity of local decision makers to select and promote a project, while the form of finance affects its true welfare value. Together, project funding and finance have major impacts on the size and type of investment projects implemented, especially at the metropolitan or local level.

In general, funding availability for transportation infrastructure investments from all sources, at all levels of government, significantly falls short of needs for new construction, upkeep, and modernization of existing facilities. Moreover, as earmarked funding from the gasoline tax (a traditional major source of funding) has been in persistent decline, the competition for federal and state dollars has intensified, with a marked increase in the proportion of funding coming from nonlocal sources. What, then, is the impact of external funding (federal and state) on local decision makers' tendencies to select capital investment projects? Save for 100% external funding, part of the money for transportation investments must come from internal (local) sources such as taxation, a method usually arousing opposition among local residents and stakeholders. It was shown here that when faced with a given proportion of external funding, decision makers will select projects with the highest capital costs, adjusted by their attitude towards the risk associated with internally raised funds.

Turning to the issue of financing, the chapter argued that use the social rate of return to evaluate projects independently of a particular funding package is incorrect. Several reasons were mentioned to support this conclusion. Key among them was the contention that the purpose of project evaluation is to decide whether a specific project's implementation is worthwhile. Given that society must pay for all the resources it requires, the financial package must be considered as a factor determining project worthiness. Irremovable financing constraints—such as legal limits on public debt, which affect the marginal cost of debt funds (MCF)—should therefore be included in a project's COBA.

Several approaches were subsequently outlined for appropriately computing a project's value while taking into account available forms of finance. It was shown here that, in general equilibrium settings, benefit and cost streams should each be discounted separately, using a different discount rate, and that the PV of the capital costs stream should be adjusted to the MCF (see expression (4)).

Another issue reviewed was the growing use of PPPs as a means for acquiring investment funds that reach beyond a public authority's legal budgetary limits. This arrangement likewise raises the question of how to correctly assess the socioeconomic value of such projects. It was argued that PPP projects should be discounted at a rate reflecting the private-sector rate of return for the private capital contributed together with the government's share of the project's overall risk. Using any other discount rate can result in the adoption of socially inferior projects.

11 Transportation Improvements and Equity

1. INTRODUCTION

The transportation literature has long addressed issues of social equity (hereinafter simply equity) in the provision of transportation infrastructure mainly in relation to accessibility, travel costs, and mode choice. In some cases—most commonly in public transit—the investment's declared intent is to ensure greater equity or an improved equity distribution. In general, transportation improvements distribute nonuniformly over space, implying that they affect diverse populations disproportionately. Equity cannot, however, be regarded as a pure externality, equivalent, for example, to the environmental degradation following from a road investment that increases traffic volumes and thus emissions. For this reason, equity effects are discussed in this part and not in Part D, which focuses on the major externalities produced by transportation investment projects.

The literature on equity in the provision of transportation facilities and services can be broadly divided into four categories. The first follows the traditional Pareto Improvement approach and the Kaldor-Hicks compensation principle (see Chapter 3). Accordingly, equity effects of all types, so long as they emanate from a public investment, are accounted for if compensation can be made to the injured party, even in principle. This approach nonetheless suggests that income distribution effects can be disregarded because they tend to cancel one another out. While based on a sound economic rationale, the practical application of these principles is quite problematic, especially when dealing with location-based, indivisible investments. Furthermore, as Stough and Haynes (2002) point out, mega-projects are often built with excess capacity aimed at satisfying future needs. Such a pattern imposes inequitable intergenerational transfers, favoring the future rather than the present generation.

Another branch of the literature attempts to ground transportation equity in the overall concept of social justice and the modern welfare state's responsibility to provide spatial mobility to all members of society. Basic levels of transportation are thus regarded as merit goods, similar to health or education, which the state is obligated to provide (Hamburg et al., 1995; Hay and Trinder, 1991; Martens, 2005). From this perspective, the substance of spatial mobility reaches beyond personal mobility to encompass access to emergency services as well as key locations such as the CBD. Subsidization of the transit services may be an implicit condition for reaching the model's goals. This view of the role of the state notwithstanding, it still leaves open the question of how much mobility the state ought to supply.

A third branch of the literature has stimulated empirical studies attempting to assess the degree to which accessibility, a major indicator of transportation equity, is (un)evenly distributed among socioeconomic urban populations together with the implications of inaccessibility for social segregation and economic well-being. Examples include the Paaswell and Berechman (1977) and Wachs (1979) studies of the prevalence of urban carlessness and its effect on the welfare of the poor and the elderly, as well as the Rosenbloom and Altshuler (1977) investigation into the mobility needs of distinct socioeconomic groups and the degree to which existing transportation systems meet these needs. A related literature has examined the financial burden exacted by transportation expenditures on household income. The data show that the proportion of household income spent on transportation decreases with income (BLS, 2001). This regressivity increases when parking costs are added (Jia and Wachs, 1998).

The fourth category of literature examines equity outcomes from federal and state allocation of transportation funds to lower government authorities. For example, using US data, Seaman and de Cerreño (2003) have identified winners and losers at the regional and state levels, based on various allocation criteria.[1]

As previously mentioned, the declared objective of some transportation investment and improvement projects is to influence equity. Yet, even in such cases, the debate over the project's acceptance continues to revolve around the equity issue.[2] We thus need to distinguish between two key questions: How to identify the extent to which diverse populations will be affected by the planned project; and which investments should be implemented to improve the welfare of targeted populations. We would argue that whereas the first question relates to impact, the second is about reaching objectives. Hence, the first question belongs to the benefits-costs appraisal phase of project evaluation whereas the second fits the project selection phase (for an explanation see Chapter 2).

A point worth stressing is that in real-world situations, especially in well-developed urban areas, empirical measurement of equity effects is a difficult undertaking, with the necessary information largely unavailable or unobtainable. Another constraint to accurate assessment is the value of time, which differs substantially among socioeconomic groups, a fact that affects the total monetary value of the project. Finally, the spatial impact of a large-scale transportation investment is difficult to demarcate because accessibility spillovers are quite common to such investments (Berechman et al., 2006).

When considering environmental nuisances, transportation investments are often linked with what has been called, "environmental injustice," implying selective excessive exposure to pollution and other nuisances (see Alsnih and Stopher, 2003; Feitelson, 2002; Schweitzer and Valenzuela Jr., 2004). In Chapter 9 it was argued that in cases where identifiable groups bear a disproportionate share of a project's indirect costs, mainly in the form of environmental nuisances, their costs of risk bearing should be added to the project's costs. Environmental issues, including environmental injustice, are increasingly becoming a major concern to the public; they should therefore be incorporated among the criteria evaluated during the project selection phase. In section 4.2, we further elaborate on this point.

Accepting that equity impacts are inherent in transportation investments, this chapter is designed to meet three main objectives. The first is to review key equity concepts and empirical evidence regarding the relationship between transportation and equity. The second objective is to analyze the effect of transportation development on the welfare of low-income groups in the context of selected intervening factors. The final objective is to examine how a Cost Benefit Analysis (COBA) can take equity into account. Our discussion of these issues by no means represents an exhaustive analysis of the relationship between transportation and equity, which goes beyond the scope of this book. What it does do is make a preliminary determination regarding the role of equity, in conjunction with other factors, in the project evaluation process.

The design of this chapter is as follows. Based on the available literature, Section 2 examines the incidence and scope of three fundamental equity effects: poverty, mobility of the transportation-disadvantaged, and access to labor markets. Section 3 presents an empirical model for testing the effect of improved accessibility on the labor market participation of low-income households. Section 4 explores ways to incorporate equity effects into the project evaluation process. The concluding Section 5 presents a summary and key conclusions.

2. A TYPOLOGY OF MAJOR EQUITY EFFECTS

Equity analyses commonly differentiate between horizontal and vertical equity. The former, horizontal equity, is defined as the equal allocation of resources—or costs—across individuals and groups. The latter, vertical equity, is concerned with the differential treatment of different population segments, particularly the mobility-disadvantaged. Given the temporal and network character of transportation service delivery, it is difficult to ascertain horizontal equity. As vertical equity is easier to determine, the literature pays more attention to this phenomenon. Three such vertical impacts are discussed below: poverty, mobility of the transportation-disadvantaged, and labor market participation (see Section 3). We should repeat: The ensuing discussion's objective is limited to highlighting key issues and difficulties associated with the empirical measurement and incorporation of equity effects into transportation project evaluation. We suggest turning to other sources for a comprehensive analysis of these complex subjects (e.g., Banister, 1994; Rosenbloom and Altshuler, 1977; Litman, 2002b).

2.1 Poverty

It has long been observed that low income—perhaps the fundamental indicator of poverty—is associated with low spatial mobility, defined as the degree of access to desired destinations. In most contemporary metropolitan areas, spatial mobility is highly correlated with car ownership and availability. Thus, several studies have examined the relationships between car ownership and availability and income (Paaswell and Berechman, 1977; Rosenbloom and Altshuler, 1977). Before reporting results from these and similar studies, it is important to emphasize that the causal direction of the factors appearing in this relationship is not quite clear. That is, does low income imply low rates of car ownership or, alternatively, is low car ownership—and thus mobility-deficiency—a major contributor to poverty? Some studies of transportation and poverty appear to have overlooked this fundamental question.

Data on car ownership rates and availability among various income groups are seldom available. Yet, data on transportation expenditures as a proportion of total household expenditures are routinely collected, which explains the prevalence of this index in studies of transportation and poverty. Due to the availability of the data, it has often been argued that high transportation costs, mainly automobile costs, present a major barrier to the poor's access to economic opportunityies. Blumenberg (2003), however, has contended that the statistical evidence does not support this claim. Her analysis, which is based on household expenditure data from the US Bureau of Labor Statistics (BLS), shows that low-income households in fact spend a smaller percentage of their income on transportation than do other households. Thus, while average transportation expenditures as a percentage of total household expenditures reaches 17% among the lowest income group, this same variable reaches 18%–21% among higher income groups.[3]

The data further show that in 2001, households with annual income of less than $20,000 spent $3,200, on average, on transportation, of which only $405 was for public transportation. Because trade-offs exist between transportation and housing costs, a claim can be made that excessive automobile costs are directly responsible for reduced home ownership among low-income households. Again, Blumenberg's study concludes that these assertions are not supported by the data.

In a study of the transportation profile of residents of the South Bronx, one of New York City's poorest areas, it was found that a very low level of car ownership characterizes its residents (Berechman and Paaswell, 1997).

While not a complete substitute for auto use, the ubiquity of public transit in this area made mobility quite affordable. Hence, in the South Bronx at least, car ownership per se does not seem to have a significant impact on income and thus poverty (see Section 3 for a further analysis). Viewed from this perspective, the observations appear to support arguments in favor of more public transit investments at the expense of highway expansion.

"Transportation needs of the poor," a concept often appearing in the literature (e.g., Rosenbloom and Altshuler, 1977), is a related issue. Using the above definition of mobility—access to desired spatial opportunities— what is the necessary level of mobility required by low-income populations? Theoretically, this concept is elusive because the term "necessary level of mobility" implies the problematics of defining another person's needs. Providing an empirical response to this question is also intricate task due to the methodological prerequisite of objectively distinguishing "genuine needs" from "claimed needs." Even if this could be accomplished, "genuine needs" are unlikely to be either quantifiable or measurable. In addition, the mobility-disadvantaged poor constitute a heterogeneous group with a range of needs. For example, the mobility needs of single-mother households (found in high proportions in the South Bronx) are entirely different from those of the elderly poor.

Given these difficulties, one might ask why is it at all necessary to estimate the "genuine" transportation needs of different socioeconomic groups? The most direct answer is that these needs have become a charged political issue, governing many debates on a proposed investment's justification. No wonder that some studies (e.g., Rosenbloom and Altshuler, 1977) suggest methods for assessing the transportation needs of the poor and the mobility-disadvantaged. What remains unknown is how much various city and state agencies spend on providing transportation to these needy populations as well as what is the effective level of the service's utilization.

One final question pertains to the validity of the above definition of spatial mobility as the level of access to spatial destinations. Colonna and Fonzone (2004) provide OECD data showing road and vehicle spatial opportunities versus economic indicators, such as GDP per capita,[4] for four income groups: low income, lower-middle income, upper-middle income, and high income. As might be expected, the higher the income, the more available are the road and vehicle opportunities. This result supports the use of the level of access to spatial opportunities as an indicator of spatial poverty.

2.2 Mobility of the Transportation-Disadvantaged

The concept *transportation-disadvantaged* is often associated with socioeconomic characteristics such as income (e.g., low income), demographics (e.g., age), ethnicity (e.g., minorities), or physical constraints (e.g., mobility-impaired). A comprehensive study by the Transport Studies Group (2005) has shown that the mobility concerns of these different groups are rather similar, manifested primarily in restricted travel distances and thus in limited access to spatial opportunities and labor markets. Earlier research by Paaswell and Berechman (1977), Paaswell and Recker (1977), and Wachs (1977) likewise showed that the carless, the elderly, and the handicapped have similar mobility limitations and needs. As with poverty, some policy situations, especially those associated with the rationalization of specific transportation investments, may require quantification or at least ordinal measurement of these needs, particularly when faced with competing investment alternatives.

A different type of equity effect flowing from transportation investments is social exclusion. Studies have shown that limited accessibility, based on a lack of adequate transportation facilities and services, is a key factor in explaining urban social exclusion (Hine and Mitchell, 2003). Yet, on an objective level of exclusion, rural populations are highly accessibility-disadvantaged when compared with urban residents. When providing solutions to these situations we need to stress that transportation investments made to improve the accessibility of rural populations are, by and large, disproportionately more costly per capita than are similar urban investments. Thus, in designing policies aimed at reducing social exclusion, the question becomes how to allocate a limited budget among various disadvantaged groups, including urban and rural populations. There is no simple transportation-economic answer to this question, which in most real-world situations is "solved" through the political process.

2.3 Accessibility and Labor Market Entry

It has long been suggested that poor accessibility adversely affects the low-income household's capacity to participate in labor markets, a situation detrimental to its well-being. The Spatial Mismatch Hypothesis (SMH) states that inner-city minority residents suffer from high rates of unemployment due to their restricted accessibility to employment opportunities, which have spread to the suburbs. These minorities, with their low incomes and low rates of car ownership, are unable to relocate to the same suburbs because of the discrimination characterizing suburban housing markets. Under these conditions, improved accessibility, mainly through improved public transportation, can facilitate the labor market participation rates of inner-city minorities (Ihlanfeldt and Sjoquist, 1998; Kain, 1968; Ong, 2002).

In general, transportation developments generate efficiency gains, transfer effects, and activity relocation effects. Taken together, these effects may inconsistently impact the supply of labor (Banister and Edwards, 1995; Berechman, 1995; Forkenbrock and Foster, 1990). For instance, Cervero and Landis (1995), who studied the employment effects from the San Francisco Bay Area Rapid Transit (BART) system, found that most employment growth took place in corridors not served by BART and that BART's employment effect was confined primarily to the service sector (e.g., finance, insurance, and real estate). It was also found that employment densities near BART stations were higher than those observed at match-paired freeway interchanges (+12% for suburban and +28% for urban). These findings clearly indicate that the relationship between accessibility improvements and labor market participation is far from straightforward. The following section proposes a model that does link the two variables.

3. A MODEL OF IMPROVED ACCESSIBILITY AND LABOR MARKET PARTICIPATION

A study conducted by Berechman and Paaswell (2001) in New York's South Bronx examined the extent to which improved accessibility from a transportation investment affects access to labor markets by the area's poor residents,[5] who travel mostly by public transit (about 70% of all trips in 1990). In this study, access to labor markets was measured as the rate of labor market participation. The main hypothesis tested was that given demands for labor, reduced accessibility costs would, *ceteris paribus*, enhance the propensity of residents in the affected region to join the labor force.

Accessibility was regarded as an endogenous variable in this study because factors such as mode choice, time of departure, car ownership, and utilization are used by individuals to effectuate their travel times and costs. On the other hand, mode availability, bus and train headways, fares and road tolls are largely exogenous. Thus, in the analytical model, accessibility was regarded as an endogenous variable, with several exogenous travel variables introduced into the accessibility function.

In the model employed, the level of accessibility between residential and employment locations i and j, respectively, measured in units of weighted travel time and costs, denoted by T_{ij}, was specified as a function of the following five components[6]: c_{ij}^m, the monetary costs of travel by mode m, (m = car, transit, walk), weighted by the proportion of people using that mode between defined locations (w_{ij}^m),[7] where; t_{ij}^m, travel times by mode, also weighted; d_{ij}, time of departure; C_i^H, car ownership by household (at residential location i); Y_i^H, household income level. That is,

$$T_{ij} = f(w_{ij}^m c_{ij}^m, w_{ij}^m t_{ij}^m, d_{ij}, C_i^H, Y_i^H) \tag{1}$$

The specific accessibility function used in this study is given by (2):

$$T_{ij} = \eta_0 + \sum_m \eta_1^m (w_{ij}^m c_{ij}^m) + \sum_m \eta_2^m (w_{ij}^m t_{ij}^m) + \eta_3 d_{ij} + \eta_4 C_i^H + \eta_5 \ln Y_i^H + \varepsilon_1 \tag{2}$$

where ε_1 is the error term. While model (2) does not account for route or mode choices, it explicitly asserts that whatever transportation improvement is made (e.g., a new express bus), its accessibility impact is captured through changes in travel time and costs, accounted for time of departure, car availability, and income.[8]

Next, we specify the labor supply function, where $Q_{ij}^{k,s}$ denotes the number of employees in job type k (e.g., executive, technician, clerical), employed in industry type s (e.g., retail, manufacturing, construction), who reside in location i and work in location j, respectively.

$$Q_{ij}^{k,s} = \lambda_0 + \lambda_1^k \exp(-vT_{ij}) + \lambda_2 \ln Y_i^H + \lambda_{3,k} \ln W_j^{k,s}$$

$$+\lambda_4 E_i + \sum_{l=1}^{3} \lambda_{5,l} F_{l,i} + \lambda_6 SB + \varepsilon_2 \tag{3}$$

In (3) $Q_{ij}^{k,s}$ is assumed to be an inverse function of the accessibility level, T_{ij}. It is a direct function of income level Y_i^H; the actual wage rate paid in job type k in industry type s, $W_j^{k,s}$; the level of education, E_i, measured in school years; and the number of children in age groups l, $F_{l,i}$; ε_2 is error term. A dummy variable (SB) was used to indicate whether a person who lives in the South Bronx also works there (SB = 1) or not (SB = 0).

For the empirical analysis, the accessibility function's decay factor, v, was set to 1.0 (experiments with other values for v did not yield significantly different results). Three age groups ($F_{l,i}$; $l = 1, 2, 3$) were used: 0–5; 6–13; 14–18.

Equations (2) and (3) were estimated simultaneously using a 2SLS procedure. In the first stage, T_{ij}, the level of accessibility between residential location i and employment location j was estimated. In the second stage, $Q_{ij}^{k,s}$, the number of employees living in i and working in j, working in job type k in industry type s was estimated.

The database used for this analysis was taken from 1990 census data. The major data files contain data at the census block group level, not at the individual household level. The observations pertain to the employment, travel behavior, and socioeconomic attributes of South Bronx residents. Employment was categorized into 13 job types in 17 employment sectors. The study area contained approximately 56,000 census block-based origin-destination pairs, including persons living and working in the Bronx and people living in the Bronx but working elsewhere. This database does not account for part-time employees or for changes in the number of weekly work hours actually worked.

The results showed that changes in accessibility costs had a discernible effect on labor market participation in the area. However, with respect to job type, the effect of accessibility was *not* equivalent, either in terms of magnitude or significance. Depending on skill requirements, wage rates, household income, and age of children, participation in some job types such as Executive, Technician, Administrative, and Transport was more responsive to travel cost reductions than was participation in the other job types. The empirical estimates also showed that labor supply in some industry categories, including Retail and Wholesale and Personal Services, was largely impervious to changes in accessibility costs.

Another key result was the rather modest magnitude of the estimated net employment effect. However, in an economically distressed area like the

South Bronx, even a relatively small increase in employment can provide an important boost to its residents' welfare. This is especially so with respect to improvements in women's labor market participation. In areas like the South Bronx, where the proportion of all households headed by a woman is rather large, any reduction in female unemployment is of major policy interest.

Lastly, the results showed that individual and household attributes such as educational level and number of young children had a much more profound impact on labor market participation than did accessibility improvements per se. This conclusion should, however, remain qualified because the reported results were obtained from an urban region with a well-developed public transit system, a condition that tends to accentuate the effects of nontransportation factors on labor market participation. Other studies, conducted in regions characterized by different transportation structures, have shown that vehicle ownership can be an important factor in helping low-income people obtain and maintain employment (Sawicki and Moody, 2000). In one such study, Ong (2002) employed a logit model for estimating the probability of employment, with auto ownership and household attributes as explanatory variables. Using data from Los Angeles, where the supply of public transit is quite limited, the author concluded that auto ownership is associated with a 12% increase in the likelihood of being employed.

4. INTEGRATING EQUITY INTO PROJECT EVALUATION

As explained at the outset of our discussion, a main question dealt with in this chapter is: At which phase of project evaluation should equity effects and considerations be regarded, at the alternatives appraisal phase or at the project selection phase (see Chapter 2, Figure 2.2)? This section probes this question.

4.1 Incorporating Equity into Cost-Benefit Analysis (COBA)

As explained in Chapter 2, COBA constitutes the central component of the alternatives appraisal phase of the evaluation process. From a theoretical viewpoint, the main rationale for incorporating equity effects into a transportation investment's COBA is that equity changes can shift the marginal social *benefit* curve, the marginal social *cost* curve, or both. While the size of these shifts depend on the assumed income distribution, the measured benefits are nonetheless likely to differ in the two models (i.e., with or without equity effects). From a policy perspective, decision makers are responsive to equity changes in that they are partial to the distribution of a project's direct and indirect benefits and costs among regional constituents: hence, their motivations for embedding equity analysis in COBA. How can equity be accounted for in COBA and is the alternatives appraisal phase (where COBA is carried out) most suitable for these purposes?

Martens (2005) has argued that the appropriate way to incorporate equity effects into COBA is by replacing the Value of Time (VOT) saved—a key COBA parameter—with an alternative measure, what he calls "value of accessibility gains." It follows that Net Present Value (NPV) calculations should be based on the value of accessibility improvements to locations rather than mobility gains, such as VOT savings (see also Beimborn and Puentes, 2003). This argument implies that because the utility of improved accessibility exhibits conditions of diminishing returns, low-income persons with limited accessibility will benefit relatively more than will higher-income persons from the same accessibility improvement. Although a novel approach, its theoretical underpinnings and empirical implications have yet, to our knowledge, not been shown or tested, a lacuna perhaps explained by the prohibitive technical complexities attending the argument's operationalization.[9] In terms of public policy, land-use strategies (e.g., location of public services) and pricing policies (e.g., public subsidy or road pricing schemes) may be much more cost-effective means of improving accessibility for low-income groups.

How, then, can equity effects be introduced into COBA? If the distribution of a project's travel time and cost savings over the relevant socioeconomic groups, before and after the investment, can be established, representative statistics of this distribution (e.g., the mean and the variance) should be used to assess the VOT savings. Such an approach can help to identify the relative position of low income groups within the overall distribution of trip makers, which subsequently can be used as an input for project evaluation.

Another approach is to adjust VOT parameters to account for equity effects. Suppose an investment project affects two groups: high- and low-income earners. While the measured travel-time savings of each group might be the same, their respective VOT would differ due to variations in their marginal utility of income, which affects their VOT. Using the VOT of the high-income group will generate a much higher total monetary value for the project than would using the VOT of the low-income group. A weighted average of VOT might take these differences into account if the weights represented the relative proportion of each income group. Yet, if income distribution in a metropolitan area is highly skewed (generally the case), this approach might produce biased results. A better way for decision makers to favor low-income groups in the overall evaluation is to relegate this task to the project selection phase, where higher weights can be attached directly to those alternatives that benefit low-income groups (see Chapter 14 for a discussion of this approach).

A further complication arises if trip rates by trip type for each income group diverge widely. In that case, the actual trip-generation vectors and distribution matrices used to assess future trip volumes may adversely represent disadvantaged groups due to the higher-income groups' higher car ownership and trip rates. We would consequently face the prospect that investment projects to be implemented in high-income areas will outrank similar projects intended for low-income areas. Similar to the case of VOT, it is possible to appraise the project's alternatives using different trip rates. Again, though, we may face the problem of a skewed distribution, an additional argument for preferring the project selection phase to the alternatives appraisal phase when assessing equity effects.

Still another approach to adjusting the COBA is to apply different discount rates to the stream of benefits associated with different populations. It is technically possible to "artificially" enhance the value of the annual benefits streams of diverse income or mobility-disadvantaged groups in order to allow for their preferential treatment. Such a step's effectiveness declines, however, in the face of the complexities of obtaining "correct" discount rates or benefit values as well as aligning them with the underlying rationale of COBA: comparison of alternative costs of resources. For all these reasons, it seems preferable to treat a project's equity impacts on low-income or disadvantaged groups at the project selection phase exclusively.

4.2 Incorporating Equity into Project Selection

As explained, the incorporation of equity effects into COBA is quite problematic even if these effects were properly identified and measured. If we accept that judgment of an investment project's equity effects is, by its very nature, a value-laden activity, we suggest that the proper approach for doing so is the project selection phase (see Chapter 2, Figure 2.2). At that phase, community needs and values are reflected in the criteria and weights module used for a specific project's selection from among the full set of welfare-improving alternatives assessed.

Another advantage of including equity effects in the project selection phase is its transparency, a feature that is frequently quite salient in its impact on community acceptance of a proposed project. Incorporating equity into COBA for the purpose of estimating NPV necessarily makes equity effects indistinguishable from other welfare-changing effects (e.g., travel time reductions). In contrast, the objectives of transparency can best be realized at the project selection phase.

The issue remaining is exactly how to introduce equity effects into the project selection phase when measured, for example, as the percentage of low-income households whose accessibility will be improved. One approach is to assign a specific weight to these effects, a criterion that reflects the decision makers attitude toward equity. This weight will then be used together with the weights assigned to other effects (e.g., environmental) taken into account when selecting a project.

A second approach entails stipulating an equity criterion that the project must satisfy. For example, favoring greater mobility for low-income groups may result in selecting a project that contains a significant transit investment. Such a preference could result in selecting an investment having a lower NPV together with a considerable transit component at the expense of a road investment with a higher NPV but no transit component. Chapter 14 presents the respective analytics.

Lastly, in France, where NPV measures are the key criteria used in project evaluation and selection, equity issues are dealt with in several ways (Quinet, 2000). First, each new project is assumed to affect users, taxpayers, neighborhoods, and operators. These effects are then broken down by evaluating the net surplus for each kind of user. Second, the project's impacts are partitioned spatially. Consumer surplus is thus allocated according to the users' locations.

5. SUMMARY AND CONCLUSIONS

This chapter has focused on the equity results from a transportation investment project in addition to questions of how to incorporate equity effects and considerations into the project evaluation process. Three major equity effects were examined: poverty, labor market participation of low-income populations, and mobility of the transport-disadvantaged.

The analysis showed two major results. First, equity impacts are real in the sense that transportation investments can indeed disproportionately affect poor populations by encouraging labor market participation of low-income households and improving the welfare of mobility-disadvantaged groups like the elderly and the handicapped. Yet, transportation's impact on these effects, inherently difficult to measure, may be small relative to other population characteristics such as education and labor skills, a result that should be considered when proposing projects aimed a reducing unemployment among low-income groups.

The second major conclusion is that equity effects are best dealt with in the project selection phase of the project evaluation process. The rationale for this conclusion rests on the value-laden character of equity, which can best be handled when decision-making criteria are applied. Moreover, at the project selection phase, equity considerations become transparent, making them open to scrutiny. Conventional COBA is, by and large, unable to handle equity considerations as unique criteria because these effects become indistinguishable from the other factors when computing NPV results.

Given these conclusions, equity impact reports must become integral parts of project evaluations. These reports should define and measure the equity effects from each alternative considered relative to population incidence, spatial boundaries, and magnitude. If equity concerns are to be adequately considered, the transportation investment's overseeing authority must explicitly address the project's potential effects along this dimension.

12 Environmental and Safety Externalities

1. INTRODUCTION

The growing literature on transportation, the environment, and safety attests to the importance that transportation professionals and decision makers—as well as the public at large—ascribe to these issues. The reasons are quite obvious: The impact of environmental degradation, global warming, and air and water pollution on health, together with the human and economic costs of accidents, have all achieved prominence on the public agenda. Moreover, it is universally recognized that transportation is a major contributor to these maladies.

The economic literature treats these effects as negative externalities generated during the production and consumption of transportation outputs—individual travel and the transport of people and goods. They are regarded as externalities because producers and users do not take them into account when making transportation decisions, nor do they directly pay for the costs these phenomena impose. Instead, society at large bears these costs. To illustrate the magnitude of these effects, the external costs of transport in the European Union (EU) were estimated at about 8% of GDP in 1995 (INFRAS/IWW, 2000). Of all possible externalities, accidents, noise, air pollution, and climate change were the main contributors to these costs. Car use captured the largest share of externalities (58%), followed by heavy-duty vehicles (21%). Road transport as a whole accounted for 92% versus rail and water transport, which contributed to the remainder. The combined results of these externalities were increased health care expenditures in addition to economic losses in terms of labor absenteeism, material damage, and wasted and lost natural resources.

Against these realities, it is not surprising that transportation-related capital projects are almost invariably required by law to undergo a thorough Environmental Impact Study (EIS) aimed at assessing the environmental impacts of the proposed investment prior to their final approval. These studies, however, suffer from two major problems. First, by and large, they consider the *average costs* of these externalities and not their *marginal costs*, as economic theory requires. Since an externality's marginal costs tend to be above its average costs, an EIS often underestimates the externalities' true costs. Second, although an important prerequisite for project funding and implementation, an EIS is frequently treated as a surrogate for a formal, comprehensive project evaluation.[1] Externality costs are, in consequence, inappropriately accounted for in the overall evaluation process.

In light of the key objectives of this book—guidance in the proper evaluation and selection of a transportation investment project—this chapter raises three main questions. First, what type of external costs should be included in the evaluation of a proposed project? Second, how are marginal externality costs, which we claim are the costs relevant for policymaking, to be computed? Third, how are these costs to be incorporated into project evaluation? Should they enter the COBA directly, as a cost item or, alternatively, as a separate effect to be treated exogenously in the evaluation's choice module (see Chapter 2, Figure 2.2)?

A wealth of literature and data is available on transportation's impact on the environment and climate (see for example Davis, 2008; Stern, 2007; VTPI, 2002). While making note of these data, the chapter focuses on those formal externality cost functions relevant for project evaluation and policy design. The chapter will not, however, deal with transportation policies aimed at reducing environmental externalities (these center on reduced travel and improved fuel consumption; see for example Vincent and Callaghan-Jerram, 2006), nor will it contend with the extent to which trip makers pay for total transportation costs—including externalities—through taxes, charges, and tolls (see Delucchi, 2000; Delucchi and Hsu, 1998; Litman, 2003).

Section 2 examines two major types of transportation externalities—emissions and noise—and then reviews methods for calculating their costs. Traffic safety externalities, including accidents and security, are discussed in Section 3. Section 4 focuses on the distinction between average and marginal costs of transportation externalities and their use in evaluating a new investment. Section 5 discusses discounting and uncertainty in the computation of externality costs. Incorporation of environmental and accident externalities into project evaluation is discussed in Section 6. A summary and conclusions are presented in Section 7.

2. EMISSION AND NOISE EXTERNALITIES

Various studies have attributed a large number of externality effects to transportation, ranging from environmental to land-use to social externalities. Among the authors viewing land consumption and free parking as transportation-related externalities, some have estimated their values to be quite significant, especially in dense urban areas (Litman, 2003; Shoup, 2005). Others have added the value of public services such as police and emergency responses to these calculations (Delucchi and Hsu, 1998). In this author's view, the degree to which these effects are true externalities is questionable. One major reason for this conclusion is the competitiveness of the land and facilities markets, which implies that competitive pricing encourages efficiency in their use. In addition, the public pays for these costs, albeit indirectly, through taxation and other charges. Environmental effects, on the other hand, largely escape market mechanisms and should therefore be treated as pure externalities. The same argument applies to that portion of traffic accident costs not covered by insurance. In keeping with this argument, two particularly noxious and widespread transportation-induced environmental externalities are discussed next: emissions and noise.

Several attempts have been made to compute the costs of externalities as a percentage of GDP. For example, Quinet (1997), using European data, reports that noise costs range from 0.02% to 2% of GDP, whereas accident costs are in the range of 1.1% to 2.6% of GDP. Verhoef (1994) reports similar results. Delucchi and Hsu (1998), who used US data for the years 1990–1991, report total external costs ranging from 1.9% to 13.9% of GDP. These results are quite indicative of the magnitude of these transportation-related externalities although their ranges are sufficiently wide to make intercountry comparisons difficult.

2.1 Emission Externalities[2]

As the major consumer of petroleum,[3] the transportation sector is also the major source of air pollution. Transport emissions include greenhouse gasses (GHG), mainly carbon dioxide (CO_2) and, to a lesser extent, methane (CH4), carbon monoxide (CO), and sulfur dioxide (SO_2) and other pollutants like nitrous oxides (NO_X). Volatile organic compounds (VOC) and small particles (less than a micron in diameter, such as PM10 and PM2.5) represent additional pollutants, associated mainly with diesel engines. Recent data show that the transportation sector as a whole is responsible for 14%–20% of world and 33% of US GHG emissions.[4] Of this amount, 73% is generated by road vehicles of all type, 8% by maritime transport, 11% by aviation (5% domestic and 6% international), and the balance by other forms of transport.

Yet, the effect of these pollutants is not ubiquitous. As the data in Section 4 show, emissions are a function of road conditions, the area where travel takes place, travel speed, and engine type. For example, in a recent study it was estimated that road gradient contributes to emissions by a factor of 1 to 2.3 whereas altitude does so in the range of 1.1 to 1.6. Topographical and meteorological conditions, as contributors to pollutant concentration levels, were estimated to account for 2.5 to 6.3 of emissions, whereas population density contributed 0.9 (Imprint, 2007).

2.2 Noise Externalities

Noise, produced by the vibrations and sounds emitted by motor vehicles, including rail, is a significant source of externality costs. Noise pollution is of various types, including acceleration, tire-road contact, braking, horns, and vehicle alarms. Heavy vehicles in particular cause vibration and low-frequency noise.[5]

Because properties adjacent to streets and highways are directly affected by noise generated from passing traffic, changes in property values serve as natural indicators for the cost of noise externalities. Hedonic price models are the most common method used to estimate these costs. Some researchers have argued that hedonic estimates fail to consider numerous factors (including the costs of noise reduction devices installed by homeowners) and thus account for only a small fraction of the true costs of noise to society. Verhoef (1994), for example, claims that hedonic noise cost estimates represent only about 1/8th of their total cost.

These qualifications notwithstanding, typical estimates of noise costs indicate a 0.5% decline in property values for each unit change in Leq[6] above 50 dB(A). Other studies estimate *average* traffic noise costs to be about 18¢ per Vehicle-Miles Traveled (VMT); Vehicle-Ton Miles (VTM) or Passenger Miles (PM) can be used when appropriate.[7] The Noise Depreciation Sensitivity Index (NDSI), developed by Nelson (1982), defines the ratio of the percent reduction in housing value due to a unit change in the noise level. Nelson suggested 0.40% as the average NDSI ratio.

2.3 Calculating the Costs of Emission and Noise Externalities

Normally, computation of the costs of the environmental externalities induced by a new investment focuses on average cost per unit of transport. Yet, given the piecemeal nature of capital augmentation in the transportation sphere, we are obliged to compute the Short-Run Marginal Costs (SRMC) of those externalities instead. Computation of their Long-Run Marginal Costs (LRMC) requires that estimation be conducted at the point where transportation capital is at its optimal level, quite a formidable task given piecemeal policymaking and implementation.

Calculation of the SRMC is important for determination of an investment's efficiency, namely, its marginal benefits (e.g., added capacity) as compared with its marginal costs. This figure is also important for setting correct Pigouvian taxes, meant to internalize environmental and congestion externalities.[8] Average costs, on the other hand, are useful for determining fairness in the payment of external costs, such as deciding whether the trucking industry pays a fair share of the environmental costs it imposes.

The literature provides several methods for calculating the average and marginal costs of environmental externalities (see for example Delucchi and Hsu, 1998; Verhoef, 1994). These are: (a) Society's Willingness to Pay (WTP) to forgo or reduce the risk (probability of damage) from a given environmental effect; (b) Damages, which are the costs of repairing the harm caused by a specific transportation activity (e.g., noise from increased auto traffic in a given corridor); and (c) Avoidance Costs, which are the costs of taking steps to avoid a given environmental externality. Assuming cost efficiency, the last method is equivalent to computing the shadow price of a ruined environmental resource (e.g., clean air). Among these methods, the most common is the second, namely, direct computation of environmental damage. Following Eriksen (2000), average and marginal external costs are computed as follows:

$$\text{Externality costs} = \begin{bmatrix} \text{unit} \\ \text{cost} \end{bmatrix} \times \begin{bmatrix} \text{level of} \\ \text{damage} \end{bmatrix} \times \begin{bmatrix} \text{intensity per} \\ \text{unit transport} \end{bmatrix} \times \begin{bmatrix} \text{number of} \\ \text{units transport} \end{bmatrix} \quad (1)$$

In (1), unit cost represents the societal cost of the damage, such as deteriorated health or loss of life. The level of damage is measured in units that are a function of spatial incidence and the population affected, for example, the number of exposed households within a half-mile tract on both sides of a transportation corridor. Intensity per unit transport is the amount of emissions per vehicle-mile (e.g., CO_2 per truck-mile) or the change in noise level (e.g., dBA per 1,000 vehicles per mile) caused by a transportation mode. Units of transport are expressed in traffic volume (number of vehicles per hour), VMT, VTM, as well as PM.

To illustrate the use of this formula, consider the computation of the marginal cost of noise, $C(\Delta N)$, where ΔN is the expected change in total noise from the expected increase in traffic. The amount of noise externalities in an area of type j is a function of the nature of this area, A_j (e.g., $A_1 = 1$ for urban areas; $A_2 = 2$, for rural areas); the exposed population in j, P_j (e.g., number of residential units/sq mile); the expected level of traffic per mile, Q, and speed, S, after the project's completion; the expected change in noise level per 1,000 vehicles/mile, ΔL_i, defined for a noise interval i, (e.g., $\Delta L_{i=1}$ = $dBA50 - 60$, $\Delta L_{i=2} = dBA60 - 70$, $\Delta L_{i=3} = dBA70 - 80$; $\Delta L_{i+1} > \Delta L_i$); the average distance of residential units to the new or expanded transportation facility, r, (e.g., $r = .5$ mile); and a noise unit cost parameter, β, defined as the percent decline in property values from a unit increase in noise level (e.g., the 0.40% arrived at by Nelson (1982)).

Based on these, the total cost of noise can be computed as follows:

$$\Delta L_{i,j} = [(Q \cdot S)^\alpha / r) \cdot A_i], \ (j = 1, 2, 3, ...) \quad (2)$$

$$\Delta N_j = \sum_i (\Delta L_{i,j}), \ (j = 1, 2, 3, ...) \quad (3)$$

The parameter α, ($\alpha \geq 1$), is used to introduce a nonlinear change in the noise level resulting from changes in traffic levels and speeds. Note that in (2), traffic is in number of vehicles (Q), which can be transformed into VMT using average VMT per vehicle.

Let V_j^0 be current average housing values in the affected area j. Thus, a change in the total cost of noise, $C(\Delta N)$, is:

$$C(\Delta N) = \sum_j \beta \cdot V_j^0 \cdot P_j \cdot (\Delta N_j) \tag{4}$$

As indicated by (4), total noise costs will increase with the noise level in each affected area j; as shown by (2), noise level is a function of traffic flow and speed, which can be predicted, and average distance to its source. Note that in this exercise, unit cost parameter β is assumed fixed for any level of traffic. A more likely assumption is that β will vary upward with traffic, that is, the unit decline in housing values will increase as traffic increases.

3. TRAFFIC SAFETY

Traffic safety, as a term associated with land transportation, is commonly applied to the incidence as well as prevention of highway accidents or those caused by other modes, such as rail. Crimes committed against public transit users are often subsumed under the same heading. In recent years, the security of transportation facilities of all types has achieved an increasingly prominent place on the transportation safety agenda. What, then, are the marginal safety costs of a new investment and how should they be treated in the evaluation process?

3.1 Traffic Accident Costs

Studies have shown that the magnitude of transportation accident costs is staggering. In Europe, for example, the costs of highway accidents have been estimated to range from 1.1% to 2.6% of GDP (Quinet, 1997).[9] As the data reported in Section 4 show, the costs of traffic accidents can exceed the combined costs of emissions and climate change. In such a reality, there should be little doubt why improved traffic safety or its corollary, reduced incidence and severity of accidents, has become a major objective of all transportation infrastructure development.

Strictly speaking, only a portion of total accident costs can be regarded as genuine externality costs. That is, to the extent that insurance compensates for a certain proportion of accident costs (e.g., auto damage and some medical expenses), only a fraction of total accident costs represents pure externality costs. These costs relate to public services like police and fire, highway damage, medical care for uninsured motorists, and nontangibles like pain and suffering. Loss of earning capacity, when not compensated for by insurance, should likewise be added to these externality costs. At equilibrium, a decline in societal costs from traffic accidents (externality or social costs + internalized costs) reduces the premiums paid by motorists, or enhances the profits of insurance firms, or both. These results represent societal benefits, the relevant policy variables.

Traffic accidents clearly result from numerous factors: (a) human error or reckless behavior, (b) poorly designed, constructed, and maintained infrastructure, (c) faulty traffic control systems (e.g., malfunctioning traffic lights or wrong traffic signs), (d) mechanical failures, and (e) unforeseen events, sometime referred to as "acts of God" (examples include sudden deterioration in weather conditions).[10] A new investment directly affects primarily the second and third categories, which represent the quality of transportation facilities and the level of services provided.

While improved infrastructure generally reduces the overall accident level, its effect on accident occurrence and severity, and thus accident costs, does not uniquely correspond with those factors. That is, the cost of an accident is an increasing function of its severity (e.g., property damage only, light injury, fatality), and accident incidence is, *ceteris paribus*, an increasing function of travel speed that, beyond a flow threshold, declines with congestion. Analytically, accident costs as a function of travel flow, thus speed, can be described as a ∩-shaped function, implying that accident costs per mile first increase with flow but then decline, in response to reduced speed. Hence, if a new highway investment results in higher speeds, accident costs may also increase. A similar result might occur—at least in the short run—if, in response to a new public transit investment, highway traffic volumes were to subside but speed would increase as a result. This unexpected effect should be accounted for when analyzing the marginal accident costs of a proposed project.[11]

Still another safety effect from a new transportation investment is change in motorists' risk-taking behavior. Research has shown that in response to improved travel conditions, drivers and passengers tend to behave less cautiously, thereby increasing accident incidence and costs. In their study of the effect of seat belts on accidents, Cohen and Einav (2003) show that seat belt regulations have led to an overall decline in traffic fatalities. However, the magnitude of this effect is significantly smaller than that estimated due to motorists' compensatory behavior. Cohen and Einav therefore conclude that seat belt use has an indirect but adverse effect on fatalities by encouraging reckless driving. It appears reasonable to conjecture that other highway improvements, such as better lighting and wider shoulders, may have similar effects. In general, though, empirical estimation of accident costs requires that strict assumptions be made about motorists' attitudes towards risk and their willingness to pay for risk reduction (see for example Jansson, 1994).

A key variable in calculating the monetary costs of traffic fatalities is the economic value of human life. While the proportion of fatal out of total accidents is relatively small, their impact on global accident costs is very large due to the high value normally placed on the human lives lost. Market prices are available for other features of accidents, such as car damage and lost working days and thus income and productivity, but no market price exists for human life or, in other terms, fatal accidents. Leaving moral and social arguments aside, researchers have been unable to reach a consensus on this issue; in fact, the opposite is true. Some (e.g., Schelling, 1968) estimate the value of human life as the value individuals are willing to pay to reduce the probability of their death from a traffic accident, for example, by buying better protected but more expensive cars. Others, like Hauer (1994), claim that economically (and perhaps ethically) this approach is incorrect. Instead, Hauer advocates use of a least-cost opportunity measure as the appropriate policy mechanism for allocating resources to saving lives.

From a practical perspective, two main approaches can be applied to the actual monetization of injuries and fatalities (Miller, 1991). The first is the *human capital* approach, which measures the market costs of property damage, medical treatment, and loss of income due to injury and death. The second is the *comprehensive* approach, which incorporates nonmarket costs such as pain and suffering and reduced quality of life. The VTPI (2002) has calculated that under the first approach, the value of saving a human life equals $0.5–$1.0 million, with less for injuries. Under the second approach, the value of a life lost is in the range of US$2 to $7 million, with a "working value" of $3.3 million.[12] For illustrative purposes, consider the Israeli distribution of the costs of fatalities, injuries, and damage-type accidents. Setting the cost of a fatality (including pain and suffering) at 100% (NIS4.1 million in 2004 prices), the value of a severe injury is 12.2% and a light injury 4%. Externality costs, including property damage, public services utilized, and accident-related congestion, are estimated as 14.6% for fatalities, 1.4% for severe injuries, and about 1% for light injuries (Shidlovsky and Sarel, 2005). In comparison, a Norwegian study reports a higher proportion of externality costs from crashes (including fatalities), lying in the range of 37%–44% of total accident costs (Elvik, 1994). Others (e.g., Jansson, 1994; Miller 1991) estimate a similar range for the noninternalized costs of traffic accidents.

For the purpose of project evaluation, how should accident costs be assessed within the framework of an infrastructure investment's overall impact? Should the change in the incidence and severity of accidents be regarded as a change in traffic accident costs or, alternatively, as a safety benefit? The two might not be identical if: (a) individuals do not regard them as equivalent due to risk-taking behavior; (b) they are treated differently in COBA; and (c) they do not enter the project evaluation process at the same point. We return to this question in Section 6.

3.2 Security

Following the September 11 trauma, security has come to dominate much of the debate on transportation services provision. While only scant data are available on the societal costs of maintaining the requisite level of transportation system security, we can turn to the airline industry for some estimates.

These turn out to be quite significant. Agreement has nonetheless been reached regarding the need to include security when assessing the capital and operating costs of investments in mass transit, bridges and tunnels, air and marine terminals.

Security problems arise mainly from the perpetrators' intention to commit violent acts. Highway accidents can be mitigated through education, planning, engineering, and enforcement. In contrast, security issues largely defy such actions due to the openness of transportation facilities and their vulnerability to malicious acts. It appears that although society can tolerate a certain level of accidents, tolerance steeply dips with respect to terrorism.

Security being a public good,[13] paying for it remains the core question. If shippers were to voluntarily inspect their cargoes or passengers, thereby ensuring their "safe" status, security costs could be fully internalized. Alternatively, if the authorities conduct all security checks at key stages of the transportation system, security costs would constitute purely externalized costs. However, because security costs are quite prohibitive, it is unlikely that private providers and operators would be able to assume a sizeable proportion of the expenditures. Moreover, as a network-structured industry, transportation systems require hub facilities such as airports, intermodal freight terminals, and transit terminals, the majority of which are publicly owned. Hence, in paying for hub maintenance and operating costs, the public sector in effect pays for security.

In brief, the marginal security costs of a transportation investment include two main components: the costs of purchasing and installing security systems such as surveillance and monitoring devices, and the costs of carrying out ongoing security activities such as the inspection of goods and individuals. To the extent that these costs are levied on users in the form of airport tax or as part of an airline's ticket, for example, security costs should be treated as internalized externality costs. Yet, in most transportation contexts, the major portion of security costs is borne by the public and should, therefore, be considered noninternalized externality costs. For this reason, as argued in Section 6, transportation security costs should be addressed in COBA within the framework of the project's direct benefits and costs

4. AVERAGE AND MARGINAL EXTERNALITY COSTS

Economic theory suggests that pricing rules be determined according to the Marginal Cost (MC) rather than the Average Cost (AC) curve. For example, optimal externality pricing should be set at the point where the social marginal cost curve meets the demand curve for the externality-producing service (e.g., travel). Still, data on average externality costs are useful for many comparative purposes, such as unit pollution costs per modal-mile or modal-kilometer.

4.1 External *Average* Costs

Studies of the external costs of transportation commonly include computation of the External Average Costs (EAC). Table 12.1 reports European EAC by mode and externality type.

As shown in Table 12.1, accident costs represent the major proportion of total EAC for most transit modes. Emissions—causing air pollution and thus climate change—constitute the second largest externality, followed by noise. Notice that passenger rail is not a pollution-free mode, especially with reference to noise and climate change effects, although on the basis of per passenger-kilometer, it performs better than alternative modes do according to this criterion.

EAC results from a study conducted in Switzerland indicate that accident costs are the main externality costs for private cars, followed by environmental costs (pollution and noise). This holds true for both flat and mountainous terrains. For heavy-duty vehicles, the reverse is true; air and noise pollution are the key externality cost factors, followed by accidents (Imprint, 2007).

Table 12.2 provides simulation results for rail versus air and car emissions per passenger-mile, assuming eight 110-mph trains between Chicago and St. Louis daily.

It is evident from the data shown in Table 12.2 that automobiles are the worst polluters in terms of CO and NOX but less so with respect to VOC.[14]

Table 12.1 Externality Average Costs in 17 West European Countries

Mode	Externality effects (US$ per 100 users/km, or per 100 tons/km)				
	Accidents	*Noise*	*Air Pollution*	*Climate*	*Total*
Car	$4.03 (64.6%)	$0.55 (8.8%)	$0.85 (13.6%)	$0.81 (13.0%)	$6.23
Bus	1.22 (47.8%)	0.51 (20.0%)	0.49 (19.2%)	0.33 (12.9%)	2.55
Motorcycle	8.54 (53.8%)	7.32 (46.1%)	—	—	15.86
Light Truck	1.22 (16.3%)	2.22 (29.7%)	2.44 (32.7%)	1.59 (21.3%)	7.46
Heavy Truck	2.81 (46.6%)	1.33 (22.0%)	1.04 (17.2%)	0.85 (14.1%)	6.03
Passenger Train	0.23 (18.7%)	0.38 (30.9%)	0.26 (21.1%)	0.37 (30.0%)	1.23
Freight Train	0.11 (13.5%)	0.48 (59.2%)	0.09 (11.1%)	0.13 (16.0%)	0.81

Note: The figures in the parentheses indicate the percent distribution of cost by mode.
Source: Small and Kazimi (1995).

Table 12.2 Pollutants in Tons per Millions of Passenger Miles

Pollutant	Rail	Air	Car
VOC	0.084	1.582	0.703
CO	0.703	2.619	5.981
NOX	1.214	1.164	1.955

Source: Midwest High Speed Rail Association.
(http://www.midwesthsr.org/whyRail_cleaner.htm).

Although often neglected in daily discussion of the causes of pollution, speed is a salient factor contributing to traffic-generated emissions. A report by the Transportation Research Board (1995) notes that emissions per mile tend to first decline but then increase exponentially as a function of speed. For example, carbon monoxide emissions per mile are quite high at very low speeds (less than 10 mph); they then decline rapidly with increasing speed but rise sharply at speeds exceeding 55 mph. Hence, low speeds from grid-lock conditions, which characterize many urban commuting patterns, are major contributors to emissions and therefore to air pollution.

4.2 External *Marginal* Costs

As argued above, the relevant costs to be considered for policy purposes are Externality *Marginal* Costs (EMC) and *not* the Externality *Average* Costs (EAC). Thus, for purposes of project evaluation, we need to compute Full Marginal Costs (FMC) to obtain the total addition to *societal costs* resulting from the investment. These costs include the internalized marginal externality costs (costs borne by users) *and* the noninternalized (or externalized) marginal social costs associated with the investment. Examples of internalized and noninternalized costs are changes in auto operating and in air pollution costs, subsequent to the new investment. Thus,

FMC – Internalized Marginal Costs + EMC

As to computation of FMC, a key question relates to the output measure to be used. Depending on the mode studied, common output measures are passenger-kilometer (PKM) for transit; ton-kilometer (TKM) for freight; and vehicle-kilometer (VKM) for private cars. In order to introduce some consistency in understanding the outcomes, FMC is computed in monetary units per 1,000 PKM or TKM or VKM.

A second issue concerns the items to be included when computing FMC. Studies have employed a broad range of cost items, the main ones being congestion, traffic accidents, noise, air pollution, and infrastructure wear and tear costs. Others have included climate change, urban effects (e.g., activity relocation), nature and landscape deterioration (including view obstruction), and nontransportation energy use, thus pollution, by industries affected by transportation expansion (e.g., supplemental electricity production motivated by laying additional electric rail). Sometimes, these externalities are referred to as "up- and downstream effects."

In a report by Schreyer et al. (2004), the authors assemble detailed EMC estimates, excluding congestion, obtained from several European studies. Table 12.3 shows some of these results for road and rail transport by vehicle type, using two output measures: PKM or TKM and VKM.

The data in Table 12.3 highlight several key points regarding the estimation of a new project's EMC. First, they stress the role of location—urban versus nonurban—on the range of results. They further show that in the same area, externality effects vary considerably by type of mode and fuel (gasoline vs. diesel), which in turn highlights the importance of correctly estimating traffic mix. A third point is the importance of the output measure used, PKM or TKM versus VKM. For example, for heavy diesel trucks, the marginal costs of air pollution are estimated as €33.50 per 1,000 TKM, but €227.29 per 1,000 VKM. Table 12.3 further indicates the high proportion of accident costs in total EMC, particularly for private cars and motorcycles. For light and heavy trucks, on the other hand, the predominant EMC item is pollution—noise and air. Finally, despite its image as an "environmentally friendly mode," urban passenger rail creates considerable noise costs—€399.1 per 1,000 VKM—with air pollution costs of €696.0 per 1,000 VKM (diesel rail), and €814 per 1,000 VKM of climate change.[15]

A direct comparison of AC with MC results (Tables 12.1, 12.2, and 12.3) is somewhat problematic due to differences in databases, computation methods as well as output and monetary units. Within these limitations, the important observation is that for each cost category and for each mode, the externality's *marginal* costs are greater than the corresponding externality's *average* costs. As explained earlier, this result is of special importance when designing policy instruments like congestion tolls and other Pigouvian taxes.

In another type of comparison, Eriksen (2000), using Norwegian data, calculated EMC for different highway modes (cars, buses, motorcycles, and trucks of various sizes) by fuel type (gasoline and diesel) and area type (big cities, built-up, and rural). His results show that in big cities, the largest EMC item for passenger cars (gasoline) is congestion (over 57%), followed by emissions (17.7%) and accidents (15.0%). For passenger rail (presumably electric), wear and tear is the largest EMC item (56%), followed by accidents (39%) and noise (4.3%). For heavy diesel trucks (over 23 tons), emissions are the largest EMC item (49%), followed by congestion (24.3%), noise (13.4%), wear and tear (9.7%), and accidents (3.4%). These results agree with the data shown in Table 12.3. In particular, they indicate the relatively high proportion of accident costs in total EMC for car and motorcycle modes in urban areas as well as the high proportion of emissions for buses and trucks.

Levinson et al. (1996), and Levinson and Gillen (1998), estimated the short- and long-run marginal and average costs per VKM for nonurban travel in California. Given prevailing traffic volumes, their results show that accident costs amount to 43% of total EMC, followed by congestion and pollution (emissions and noise). Another key result from both studies is that long-run EMC are significantly above long-run EAC. They reported long-run EMC of $0.0816/VKM versus long-run EAC of $0.046/VKM, results that hold for each external cost category examined: congestion, noise, air pollution, as well as infrastructure (construction and maintenance).[16]

With respect to noise, Delucchi and Hsu (1998) calculated *marginal* noise costs per 1,000 VMT for five vehicle classes on six urban roadway types. Their model takes into account the impacts of traffic noise above a given threshold on residential and nonresidential property values. As expected, heavy trucks generated the highest noise costs on all roadway types: $30.80/1,000 VMT on urban freeways and $20.07/1,000VMT on principal arterials.

The US Federal Highway Administration has provided estimates for external marginal crash costs (the purest externality marginal cost category available for vehicles) by vehicle and area type.[17] For example, for autos on urban highways, EMC lies in the range of 0.78–4.03¢ per VMT. It rises to 1.76–39.68¢ per VMT for rural highways, reflecting the higher speeds and thus more serious injuries and fatalities associated with nonurban areas. For buses, the corresponding figures are 1.08–6.25¢ per VMT (urban) and 2.36–14.15¢ per VM (rural).[18]

Ozbay et al. (2001; 2007) have developed a methodology for computing FMC of highway travel. For each FMC category, a dedicated cost model was developed that includes car operating costs, congestion costs (internalized and noninternalized), accident costs (internalized and noninternalized), infrastructure costs, air and noise pollution costs. Three traffic models were subsequently used to assess the impact of additional traffic on these cost categories. The first was a static assignment model, based on the shortest path between each selected OD pair. The second determined several paths (including the shortest path) between a set of OD pairs and calculated the FMC as the weighted marginal costs of these paths. The third methodology estimated FMC from additional trip demand, using a micro-simulation traffic model.

The results shown in Table 12.4 are based on the first traffic model, applied to the Northern New Jersey Network for an average trip length of 9–15 miles and a VOT of $7.60/hour.[19]

It is evident from these results that for an additional 1% of highway travel by all vehicle types for an average trip distance of 9–15 miles, the major portion of FMC ($7.153) is internalized (borne by users). Of the noninternalized externalities, accident costs are over 50% of EMC whereas noise and air pollution, constitute about 45%. Infrastructure costs comprise little over 3% of FMC.[20]

Table 12.3 External Marginal Costs by Mode (€ per 1,000 PKM or TKM and VKM)

	Road					Rail	
	Car	Bus	Motorcycle	Light Truck	Heavy Truck	Passenger	Freight
Accidents (range)	10–90	1–7	36–629	10–110	0.7–11.8	0.09–1.6	0.06–1.08
UK (high)							
Urban	35.2				4.0		
Interurban	40.7				4.7		
Swiss (€/1,000 VKM)[a]							
Urban	0.042	0.774	0.309	0.053	0.107	0.73	1.08
Interurban	0.016	0.208	0.055	0.021	0.053	0.09	0.06
Noise (range)	0.07–13.	0.05–4.6	0.25–33	2.4–307.0	0.25–32	0.09–1.6	0.06–1.08
MC (Average)							
Urban	13.1	4.61	32.9	307.0	31.98	0.73	1.08
Interurban	0.07	0.05	0.25	2.37	0.25	0.09	0.06
(€/1,000 VKM)							
Urban	18.42	92.1	36.84	92.1	169.47	399.1	574.64
Interurban	0.14	0.71	0.28	0.71	1.31	32.61	34.35
Emission (range)[b]	5.7–44.9	12–18	3.2	15–100	33.5	5.1	7.4
Urban							
Gasoline	5.72		3.21[d]				
Diesel	44.86	17.74[d]		15.14[d]	33.50[d]	5.1[d]	7.4[d]

Interurban							
Gasoline	5.80						
Diesel	18.32						
(€/1,000 VKM)							
Urban							
Gasoline	9.54		3.59[d]				
Diesel	74.74	310.7[d]		11.36[d]		696.0[d]	
Interurban							
Gasoline	9.54						
Diesel	30.12				227.29[d]		2,437.0[d]
Climate (range)[d]							
€/1,000 PKM[e]	1.7–27	0.7–9.5	1.7–11.7	8.2–57.4	1.8–12.8	0.3–7.1	0.4–5.3
€/1,000 VKM[e]	2.9–45	23.6–165.0	1.9–13.1	6.1–42.6	12.4–86.5	116–814[f]	237–1,658[f]
Nature & Landscape (range)	0–2.1	0–1.3	1.97	10.9	0.8	0.7–1.2	0.1
Urban Effects (range)[g]	1.1–9.6	0.1–2.2	0.7–7.1	3.0–32.3	0.9–7.1	0	0
Up- and downstream (range)[h]	2.0–4.1	2.6–6.0	1.3–2.7	13.0–23.4	3.6–7.4	0.9–8.3	0.2–1.7

Notes: [a]Medium traffic flow (1,000 VKM); [b]Health Costs; [c]All roads; [d]Representing minimum (€20) and maximum (€140) shadow prices per ton of CO_2; [e]Urban and interurban travel; [f]Diesel train; [g]Separation and space availability; [h]Effects from production and transport of energy for transportation purposes as related to VKM driven.
Source: Based on Schreyer et al. (2004).

Table 12.4 FMC by Categories for Average Trip Distance of 9–15 miles[a] (in $US)

Private (Internalized) Costs		Infrastructure Costs	Noninternalized Externality Costs			
Operating	Congestion	Accidents	Maintenance	Congestion Externality	Accident Externality	Air Pollution	Noise
1.389	3.786	0.664	0.062	0.635	0.345	0.114	0.158

Source: Ozbay et al. (2001).
Note: [a] 9–15 miles is the average trip length in this region.

To illustrate the use of the FMC estimates appearing in Table 12.4, consider the total societal costs from the increase in truck traffic at the Port of New York/New Jersey resulting from growth in international trade (Berechman, 2007). Between 2005 and 2006, container volume in ton equivalent units (TEU) rose from 4.78M to 5.09M, representing a 1-year increase of 6.4%.[21] Primarily due to limited rail capacity, over 80% of all cargo that arrives at the port is hauled by truck, with the balance transported primarily by waterway. For the purposes of this analysis, assume that the main destination of truck traffic is the Camden-Philadelphia market and distribution center, located about 80 miles from the port. This truck traffic runs along a well-defined corridor (the New Jersey Turnpike), which is congested throughout most of the day. The results show a total FMC of $884.16M per year assuming VOT of $7.60/hour and $1,620.96M for VOT of $32.3/hour.[22] These results, which provide a reasonable estimate of the overall impact of additional truck traffic from port-related trade expansion, should be included in the COBA of the port's infrastructure development.

What are the key conclusions to be reached from this discussion of transportation EMC and FMC? First, unsurprisingly, congestion is a major FMC item for urban transportation. However, users internalize a significant proportion of these costs (through the value of the time they spend in traffic) so that noninternalized congestion costs constitute a relatively small fraction of EMC. Second, accident costs, which also comprise a significant element in FMC, like congestion costs are internalized by users for the most part (through the insurance premiums that they pay). Emissions and noise therefore make up the bulk of noninternalized EMC.

5. DISCOUNTING AND UNCERTAINTY IN THE EVALUATION OF ENVIRONMENTAL EXTERNALITIES

5.1 The Discount Rate for Environmental Externalities

In order to assess the economic value of the environmental externalities produced by a transportation investment, the future stream of environmental effects (e.g., changes in CO_2 levels) requires discounting. Following Arrow (2007), the appropriate discount rate (r) to be applied is a function of three factors: the pure social rate of time preference (δ),[23] the expected rate of growth in average consumption (g), and the elasticity of the social weight attached to consumption (η). The last factor accounts for the diminishing social value of marginal consumption as consumption increases. Thus,

$$r = \delta + g\eta \tag{5}$$

What values should be used for these factors? Regarding δ, the US Office of Management and Budget (OMB, 1992) estimates δ to be between 1.5% and 3%.[24] Arrow (2007), on the other hand, following the Stern

Committee's report (Stern, 2007), accepts a zero value for δ. As to η, Arrow (2007) estimates this parameter to lie between 2 and 3 whereas the Stern committee sets it as equal to 1. Finally, Arrow has estimated the growth rate of consumption (g) to be 1.3% per year.

Using ranges of values for these factors ($\delta = 0 - 2$; $\eta = 1 - 2$; $g = 1.3$) results in a discount rate of 1.3% to 4.6%. This is a low rate when compared with the rates regularly used to discount transportation investments (see Chapter 6). It undoubtedly reflects the impact of environmental externalities on the economy.[25]

Weitzman (1994) has derived a sliding scale for the discount rate of environmental projects following a survey among economists. He recommends that in the short term (1 to 5 years), projects be discounted by 4%, in the medium term (6 to 25 years) by 3%, in the long term (26 to 75 years) by 2%, and in the very long term (76 to 200 years) by 1%. It warrants repeating that the underlying rationale of computing this sliding scale is to encourage selection of long-term environmental projects that, given the distribution of their benefits many years into the future, would otherwise generate negative NPV results.

5.2 Uncertainty of the Physical Quantity of Environmental Effects

The general formula for computation of externality costs described above (Section 2.3, expression (1)) contains two components characterized by considerable uncertainty: the "level of damage," a function of the number of people to be exposed to a pollutant; and "units of transport," measured in traffic volume, ton-miles or passenger-miles. Importantly, population and travel forecasts are subject to significant uncertainty, a feature that can diminish the validity of externality cost computations. In a study of travel demand and emissions for the Sacramento, California, area, Rodier and Johnston (2002) highlighted the impact of plausible errors in population and employment projections on the likelihood that the region's transportation development program will meet required pollution levels (mainly NOX) in a target year. In recognition of the uncertainty level of the states variables, their key conclusion was that Metropolitan Planning Organizations (MPOs), which are responsible for population and employment projections, should carry out sensitivity analyses in order to ascertain the probability that transportation plans will conform to emission constraints in a given time frame.

Uncertainty also exists with respect to the unit cost of pollution given that the severity and extent of damage to diverse population sectors cannot be fully known a priori. Assuming risk-aversion behavior, any uncertain damage should be treated as equivalent to a loss greater than the expected loss (Arrow, 2007). The fundamental policy implication of this observation is that estimated environmental costs represent the lower bound for the true costs, which in all probability are quite a bit higher.

6. INCORPORATING ENVIRONMENTAL AND ACCIDENT EXTERNALITIES INTO PROJECT EVALUATION

Environmental effects stemming from transportation development are, for the most part, pure externality costs. Motorists, transit users, or freight shippers seldom pay directly for the social costs associated with the noxious emissions and climate change effects engendered by their travel activities. In contrast, a significant proportion (about two-thirds to three-quarters) of all traffic accident costs is internalized, primarily through accident insurance.[26] Security costs are also significantly internalized through user charges, higher shipping prices, or public spending. Therefore, consistent with the approach taken in this book, we maintain that environmental costs should be dealt with by the project selection module whereas accident- and security-related costs should be part of the COBA assessment of a project's direct benefits and costs.

Translation of these conclusions into a COBA formulation (see Chapter 6, equation (4)) implies that when computing a project's NPV, annual benefits, B_t, should be the sum of direct travel time and cost savings *plus* the change in accident and security costs flowing from the investment. The latter change can be positive or negative, implying a decrease or increase in costs, respectively. Moreover, changes in accident and security costs should be discounted using the project's discount rate r but just so long as we can assume that r is the correct social discount rate (see the discussion in Chapter 6).

Chapter 14 discusses methods of incorporating various effects (referred to as "goals") into the project selection module. As noninternalized externalities, a project's environmental effects, properly computed, should be assigned weights that reflect their relative importance from the project analysts' or decision makers' viewpoints. Along with other goals and weights, the objective is to provide a complete scheme of all weighted goals, normalized to a common benchmark (e.g., 100), for each investment alternative. The "best alternative," defined as the option obtaining the highest score, should subsequently be selected. The difficult question is how to derive the appropriate weights for the various effects. Chapter 14 deals with this question. Here it will suffice to say that once the weights are defined and assigned to each goal, a sensitivity analysis should be conducted in which the weights are incrementally changed in order to ascertain the robustness of the final investment choice.

7. SUMMARY AND CONCLUSIONS

Ample evidence has been accumulated on transportation's impact on environmental deterioration and climate change. Similarly, the relationships between traffic flow and accidents are well documented, with voluminous data available on accident incidence and severity by mode type, flow conditions, and facility design. A casual review of the current transportation literature confirms the salience of these issues in the debate on transportation development and new infrastructure investments.

Three fundamental issues were dealt with in this chapter: (a) Identification of the main transportation-produced environmental and accident externalities and their measurement; (b) Computation of the marginal externality costs from a new project; and (c) Incorporation of these costs into the project evaluation process.

With respect to the first issue, it was argued that while transportation produces a myriad of environmental effects, the key ones are noxious greenhouse gases and noise. Traffic accidents constitute another major transportation externality. But whereas emissions are noninternalized externalities, a significant proportion of accident externalities are internalized through insurance and safety measures; the same applies to transportation-related security costs.

By and large, data on the costs of transportation externalities pertain to average costs, expressed in terms of vehicle-miles, ton-miles, or passenger-miles. However, for the purpose of new investment assessment, we need to compute total (or full) marginal costs, defined as internalized marginal externality costs plus noninternalized marginal externality costs. The available data indicate that marginal externality costs greatly exceed average externality costs, an observation that holds true for most externalities. Several alternative methodologies were proposed here for the computation of full marginal costs, including congestion and infrastructure costs (Section 4, above). Using network assignment methods, Ozbay et al. (2001, 2007) have shown that in dense networks (in their case, northern New Jersey), congestion was the main marginal externality cost, whether internalized, or noninternalized, followed by accidents.

The importance of transportation externalities for the economy can be expressed in two primary ways from the perspective of project assessment. First, the rate used for discounting environmental externalities should be set significantly below the rate used for discounting direct transportation benefits (e.g., travel time savings). Second, noninternalized environmental externality costs should be incorporated into the project selection phase of the overall evaluation process. Following computation of their NPV, these externalities are assigned weights reflecting their importance in the eyes of the project's decision makers (see Chapter 14). Alternatively, accident, safety, and security costs, most of which are internalized, should be introduced directly into the COBA when computing the NPV of the project's direct benefits and costs.

13 Transportation Investments and Economic Development

1. INTRODUCTION

Transportation infrastructure can be defined as a set of interconnected structural elements that provide the framework for supporting an entire system.[1] These elements are variously called "civil infrastructure," "municipal infrastructure," or "public works." Irrespectively, they collectively provide the underpinnings for the system's services, route, time of day, and mode, at all geographical levels.

An accepted maxim among transportation decision makers and planners is that transportation infrastructure development engenders economic growth at the local, regional, and national level. Empirical support for this view comes mainly from historical records, exemplified by the following *New York Tribune* editorial on the construction of the Central Pacific (CP) and Union Pacific (UP) railroads in mid 19th century America:

> The tribune calculated that, whereas the government was accustomed to paying as much as 40 to 50¢ per ton per mile to haul supplies to the troops in frontier outposts, the UP had reduced that rate to less than 10¢ per ton per mile. That meant that, though the cost of government supplies in 1867 was $699,698, it would have cost $2,625,536 had the supplies been transported by wagons. The government had saved nearly $2 million in one year alone, and that in a year when the track had only reached the Nebraska-Wyoming border. Meanwhile, the value of its public lands alongside or near the railroad had gone up far more than what the government would have received for *all* its lands had there been no railroad.

The report further reflected the optimism felt by the vast majority: "We shall look for a great stream of travel over the Pacific Railroad next year" the paper declared, "and its completion will give a wonderful impetus to mining, settlement and industry throughout the New Territories, as well as on the Pacific coast."[2]

Can we conclude on the basis of this and many similar accounts that investments in transportation infrastructure always yield comparable or even greater economic growth benefits? Although often challenged by academic authors, many writers seem to have accepted this view as a fundamental tenet and then proceeded to estimate economic growth benefits on the basis of extrapolated historical trends (see the survey by Lakshmanan and Anderson, 2002).

A common corollary to this view is that economic growth effects from a transportation investment should be counted among the project's overall benefits. From a normative economic perspective, this approach is correct because economic growth can have momentous social welfare impacts. This conclusion, however, should be qualified on three grounds. First, one must clearly show *ex ante* that economic growth effects will indeed accrue as a result of a particular investment. Second, many economic development benefits are, in effect, capitalized primary transportation benefits. Their inclusion among an investment's benefits amounts to double-counting of benefits. Third, even if growth benefits can be shown, transportation investments should be chosen, first and foremost, on the basis of their transportation benefits; externalities such as economic growth should constitute secondary considerations. We return to this argument in Chapter 14.

Large-scale transportation investment projects have been rationalized time and again on the grounds of nontransportation factors believed to be crucial for the project's political viability and funding eligibility. Historical records show that many transportation investments were justified primarily on the basis of declared political gains[3] or asserted yet unproven economic effects even though they would never have been accepted on transportation grounds alone (Berechman and Paaswell, 2005). The current chapter therefore examines the overall issue of transportation investment and economic development within the context of project evaluation against this background of often unsubstantiated claims.

There is a rich literature in economic history on the long-term relationships holding between transportation development and economic growth (for a review see Banister and Berechman, 2000). The impact of road construction on trade in the Roman Empire, the effect of improved sailing technology on European trade with Asia and the Americas during the Mercantile Era, and the decisive role of canal and railroad development in the American economy during the early and mid 19th century are notable examples. While these factors' underlying causes and scope of influence are still subject to debate,[4] we focus on the measurable economic effects emanating from transportation capital stock accumulation and individual transportation investments. It should be emphasized that measurable growth effects are obtained *ex post* whereas *ex ante* development effects are needed for project evaluation. Thus, whereas historical examples can provide a general understanding of macro- and micro-level relationships between transportation development and the economy, they can hardly be used as guidelines when assessing a specific investment in contemporary metropolitan areas.

The positive relationship between transportation development and economic growth is so entrenched in the public's mind that many regard transportation investments as, first and foremost, a fundamental means to ensure economic growth.[5] Some governments (e.g., China and India) are currently undertaking massive transportation projects of all types (e.g., roads and airports), trusting that the new infrastructure will eventually attract private-sector investments and induce economic growth. Yet, this strategy, which might be called the "build it and they will follow" approach, may prove to be rather ineffective unless supported by complementary policies, mainly regarding job creation, income augmentation, and land use.[6]

Given this reality, we must first answer three cardinal questions. First, what evidence do we have for the emergence of economic growth effects and how are we to define and measure them without double-counting benefits? Second, how are we to account for changes in development-promoting locations following a new transportation investment? Third, how can we incorporate economic development benefits into the overall evaluation process, especially if the project cannot be justified on the basis of its primary transportation benefits?

Relationships between transportation investment and economic growth are typically analyzed at one of two levels. At the macro level, the objective is to estimate the economic returns to a region or nation from the accumulation of transportation capital stock. At the micro level, the focus is on the project's economic development effects, mainly on the local economy. This chapter reviews evidence from the macro literature but retains its focus on the micro impacts of a single investment project and the inclusion of those impacts within the project evaluation process.

The rest of the chapter is organized as follows. Section 2 reviews the links between transportation investment and economic development at the macro level with the aim of shedding light on the relationships holding between changes in transportation capital stock and regional economic development. Section 3 examines the theoretical underpinnings of micro-level analyses, with a focus on the relationships between specific transportation investments and local economic development. Next, Section 4 proposes an approach for measuring the economic development benefits flowing from an investment. Section 5 presents a model for the measurement of employment effects. Section 6 examines the issue of improved factor productivity, including freight and logistics costs, as well as regional competitiveness. Section 7 explores the measurement of real estate development from transportation investments and the problematics of its use in project evaluation. Section 8 discusses the effect of transportation development on land use and urban form, while Section 9 examines the measurement of economic development benefits within the framework of partial versus general equilibrium analysis. Section 10 discusses how these externality effects should be incorporated into project evaluation. A summary and conclusions follow in Section 11.

2. TRANSPORTATION INFRASTRUCTURE DEVELOPMENT AND ECONOMIC GROWTH: A MACRO-LEVEL ANALYSIS

Macro-level models are meant to estimate the rate of return from transportation infrastructure capital stock accumulation. To that end, the most common approach is to estimate a production function-type model with regional, state, or national aggregate output as the explained variable and labor, private capital, and public transportation capital as the explanatory variables. Public capital in this context is defined as the fixed stock—such as roads, streets, and transit terminals—necessary to provide transportation.

When we turn to modeling, a distinction is made between "capital stock" and "capital flow" models. In the former model, the level of output is regressed against the capital stock level. In the latter, annual changes in output are regressed against annual changes in capital stock. The general structure of the stock model is shown in (1).

$$Q_{c,t} = A_{c,t} f(L_{c,t}, K_{c,t}) g(H_{c,t}) \tag{1}$$

In (1), A represents the Hicks-neutral level of technology, L and K are labor and private capital, respectively, and H is public capital stock (e.g., the regional highway network). The subscripts c and t represent region (e.g., state or county) and year, respectively. For the model to have a clear economic interpretation it must meet the conditions of positive marginal productivity of public capital ($g'(H_{c,t}) > 0$) in addition to positive marginal productivity of labor and private capital ($f_L > 0$; $f_K > 0$), but with diminishing returns ($f_{LL} < 0$; $f_{KK} < 0$). If markets can be assumed to be reasonably competitive and labor and private capital are mobile across regions, input prices equal their respective marginal revenue product, that is,

$$w_{c,t} = p \cdot A_{c,t} f_L(L_{c,t}, K_{c,t}) g(H_{c,t}) \tag{2}$$

$$r_{c,t} = p \cdot A_{c,t} f_K(L_{c,t}, K_{c,t}) g(H_{c,t}) \tag{3}$$

In (2) and (3), the variables w and r represent the price of labor (e.g., hourly wage rate) and private capital stock (e.g., interest rate), respectively, with p the price of output. Given this general formulation, we next explore some of the underlying analytical and empirical issues involved with estimating (1) – (3) and then report key findings from the germane literature.

In order to estimate a capital flow model, annual net additions to total capital stock must be computed. One approach common to doing so is to apply the perpetual inventory accounting method. In their study of the economic growth effect of highway capital accumulation, Ozbay et al. (2007) used the formula $K_t = (1 - \delta)K_{t-1} + I_t$, where K_t is the year-end capital stock in year t; δ is the geometric rate of depreciation (%), and I_t is real investment in year t.

2.1 Transportation Investments and Economic Growth: The Causality Question

A key question in the analysis of relationships between transportation investment and economic development is causality. Does transportation capital stock accumulation stimulate economic growth (measured by, say, per capita GDP), or does economic growth induce further demand for transportation infrastructure in addition to the resources necessary for investment? This question is quite consequential. If causality operates in reverse and economic growth drives transportation development, what are we to make of the results of the numerous empirical studies that have implicitly assumed the opposite?

The econometric literature has long addressed the causality issue with the standard Granger test of causality, applied to two related time series (Granger, 1969).[7] Because observations on transportation development and economic growth have spatial and longitudinal dimensions (see equations (1)–(3), above), other tests, such as the Holtz-Eakin (Holtz-Eakin et al., 1988) panel data test are often used. Appendix A describes the Granger causality test for panel data.

Specifically, when do we know whether a transportation investment has stimulated economic growth? Even if we can establish such causality, what is the nature of the respective relationship? Is it subject to diminishing returns? How does it vary at different spatial levels (e.g., national, state, county)? And what rate of return can be obtained from transportation infrastructure capital investments? These questions are dealt with in subsequent sections. Below we briefly comment on the relationship between transportation and economic development on the macroeconomic level.

Lahiri and Yao (2004) have developed a monthly aggregate transportation index that measures US transportation sector economic output. The index includes freight movements (trucking, rail, air, water, and pipelines) and passenger transport (transit and aviation). The importance of this index arises from the fact that it is closely synchronized with other indices (industrial production, sales, employment, and personal income) and can therefore predict periods of economic slowdown and recovery. The explanation given for its serial correspondence is that transportation is a key factor in the building up of inventories directed at industrial production, and so heralds the direction of economic cycles. Yet, macro data can often be misleading with respect to the significance of transportation capital stock expansion. In the 1980s and early 1990s, the Japanese government made huge investments in transportation infrastructure; the Japanese economy nonetheless remained stagnant (GDP actually contracted in 1998). In New York City, the economy has boomed since the mid 1990s even though no significant expansion of transportation capital stock had been initiated in the interim.

Even if we accept the contention that transportation development does engender economic growth, we still need to explain what is meant by "transportation development." The accumulation of capital stock does not, in itself, say much about the actual level of service rendered by that stock. Transportation infrastructure can be underutilized, or badly managed; it can also underperform for technical and administrative reasons. It is, after all, the actual level of service that matters, *not* the level of capital investment. Unfortunately, macro-level models are unable to provide level-of-service indicators; by and large, they use reported capital stock as their key explanatory variable (see Table 13.1 for a selection of such studies). Given that, a related question refers to actual model estimation: How can transportation capital stock be transformed into monetary values? The use of historical, current, or replacement values criteria is likely to yield different results.

These qualms notwithstanding, as the studies surveyed in this chapter show, the general view held by economists and planners is that transportation investments promote regional economic growth, although just how remains far from being clear. Much of that uncertainty surrounds the question of whether transportation generates regional growth or, alternatively, reinforces that growth, with growth in fact stimulated by nontransportation factors such as increased interregional and international trade. The latter scenario implies that if a region grows rapidly, inadequate transportation investments will inhibit or delay this growth at some point. A lack of transportation facilities obviously constrains the mobility of factors such as labor and capital. Econometric measurement of the transportation-economic growth relationship may therefore show a positive association but without revealing the explicit direction of influence (for a discussion see Berechman, 2001; for an empirical analysis see Berechman and Paaswell, 2005).

2.2 Review of Macro-Level Studies

Numerous empirical studies have been carried out for the purpose of elaborating the said relationship between transportation capital investments and economic development. The analytical tool predominantly used for analyses conducted at the aggregate or macro level is the production function, in which aggregate output is explained by labor, private, and public (transportation) capital.[8] A sampling of macro-level studies using this instrument is shown in Table 13.1.

The estimated output elasticities shown in Table 13.1 clearly vary widely, from a very high 0.39–0.56 (Aschauer, 1989) to a very low 0.04 (Garcia-Mila and McGuire, 1992; Waters, 2004). Also indicated is that output elasticities obtained from a higher-level spatial database (i.e., national) tend to be greater than those obtained from lower-level spatial database (i.e., state or province and county). We investigate this issue next.

Table 13.1 Survey of Output Elasticity Results from Various Macro-Level Studies

Study	Country	Level of Analysis	Data	Functional Form	Infrastructure	Output Elasticity
Mera (1973)	Japan	Regional	Pooled	C-D[a]	Transportation, communication	0.35 (Manufacturing) 0.40 (Service sector)
Eberts (1986)	U.S.	State	Time series	C-D, Translog	Public capital[b]	0.03
Costa et al. (1987)	U.S.	State	Cross-section	C-D, Translog	Public capital	0.20
Aschauer (1989)	U.S.	National	Time series	C-D	Public capital	0.39–0.56
Munnell and Cook (1990)	U.S.	National	Time series	C-D, Translog	Public capital	0.33[c]
Munnell (1990)	U.S.	State	Pooled	C-D, Translog	Highway capital[d]	0.06
Munnell (1990)	U.S.	State	Pooled	C-D, Translog	Public capital	0.15
Duffy-Deno & Eberts (1991)	U.S.	Metropolitan Area	Pooled	C-D, Translog	Public capital	0.08
Moomaw & Williams (1991)	U.S.	State	Pooled	Translog	Highway capital	0.25
Lynde & Richmond (1992)	U.S.	National	Time series	Translog	Public capital	0.20
Garcia-Mila & McGuire (1992)	U.S.	State	Pooled	C-D	Highway capital[e]	0.04
Ozbay et al. (2003)	U.S.	County	Pooled	Multiple Regression	Highway investment	0.09
Ozbay et al. (2006)	U.S.	County	Time series	C-D, Translog	Highway capital	0.21
Waters (2004)	Canada	Province	Time series	C-D, Translog	Highway capital	0.08

Notes: [a]C-D: Cobb-Douglas; [b]*Government Finances*, US Bureau of the Census Publications, defines capital outlays as direct expenditure for the construction of buildings, roads and other improvements, including additions, replacements, and major alterations to fixed works and structures, whether contracted privately or built directly by the government; [c]Labor productivity elasticity; [d]Includes sewage, water and others; [e]Includes education.

2.3 Time Lags and Spatial Spillover

To investigate the effect of time lags and spatial levels of analysis, Berechman et al. (2006) applied the following model to state, county, and municipal databases. Use of a log-form model simplified estimation of the parameters and their economic interpretation.

$$\log(Q_{c,t}) = \beta_0 + \beta_1 U_{c,t} + \beta_2 \log(L_{c,t}) + \beta_3 \log(K_{c,t}) + \beta_4 \log(H_{c,t}) + \varepsilon_{c,t} \qquad (4)$$

where: Q is gross state, county, or municipal product; U is the unemployment rate at a higher geographical scale (e.g., state level for a county-level analysis); L is employment (number of jobs); K is end-of-year nonresidential private capital stock; H is end-of-year highway capital stock; c is the index of the geographical level (state, county, municipal); t is the year index; β_i (i = 0,...,4) are parameters to be estimated, and ε is the error term.

1. Time Lags

In order to investigate possible lags between the time of the transportation investment and the time of its impact on output, the following model is estimated:

$$\log(Q_{c,t}) = \beta_0 + \beta_1 U_{c,t} + \beta_2 \log(L_{c,t}) + \beta_3 \log(K_{c,t}) + \beta_4 \log(H_{c,t-n}) + \varepsilon_{c,t} \qquad (5)$$

where: $n = 1,2,...,5$ years.

2. Spatial Spillovers

Next is a spillover model that takes into account the effects of a highway investment on areas proximate to the investment's location.

$$\log(Q_{c,t}) = \beta_0 + \beta_1 U_{c,t} + \beta_2 \log(L_{c,t}) + \\ \beta_3 \log(K_{c,t}) + \beta_4 \log(H_{c,t}) + \beta_5 \log(NH_{c,t}) + \varepsilon_{c,t} \qquad (6)$$

In (6), NH represents neighboring state, county, or municipality. Statistically, we test for *spatial autocorrelation*, which may occur when the error term associated with one locality depends on conditions at other localities.[9] From (6) we compute the elasticity: $\eta_{Q,NH} = (\partial Q/\partial NH)/(NH/Q)$, which is the parameter β_5. We conclude positive spillover effects if β_5 is significant and positive.

3. Output Elasticity

Given (4), output elasticity with respect to highway capital, β_4, is:

$$\beta_4 = \frac{\Delta Q}{Q} \bigg/ \frac{\Delta H}{H} \qquad (7)$$

By rearranging and substituting the values obtained for Q and H (for given years), the marginal output of highway capital, $\Delta Q / \Delta H$ becomes:

$$\frac{\Delta Q}{\Delta H} = \beta_4 * \frac{Q}{H} \tag{8}$$

Expression (8) measures the percent change in Q (gross state, county, or municipal product) in response to a 1% change in highway capital (H).

The database used in the Berechman et al. (2006) study is composed of state, county, and municipal data collected for the New Jersey/New York Metropolitan Area for the years 1990–2000. All monetary values are in millions of dollars (in 2000 prices). At the state level, the database contains 48 observations (for the 48 states) for each of the sampled years. At the county level, 18 observations per year were included, one annually for the 18 counties located in the New York/New Jersey Metropolitan Area; at the municipality level, parallel observations were obtained for each of the 389 municipalities found in this region.

The parameters estimated from the basic model (4), which were highly significant, clearly showed that the estimated impact of highway capital weakens as the geographic area under study becomes smaller. We return to this issue shortly. Turning to the lag model (5), the most sensible and statistically significant results were obtained for one-year lags. However, the results also showed that inclusion of a lag variable slightly reduced the magnitude of the highway capital impacts on output for all three levels of analysis. These results can be explained by the fact that at all three geographical levels, gross product has increased over time, in turn enabling allocation of more resources to highway projects and thereby shortening their time lag effect. It may also imply that the highway capital stock accumulated over time is a function of the previous level of highway investment, which is largely independent of time lags. As with the basic model, the impact of highway capital diminishes as the geographic level of analysis decreases.

The third set of results was obtained from spillover estimation (6). For a spillover effect to exist, investment in a given location, c, should reduce output in the selected location (β_4 is negative) while investment in a neighboring location should increase it (β_5 is positive). The results indicated that there are no significant spillover effects at the state and county level (the β_4 values are positive) but that they do prevail at the municipal level. These findings may result from the fact that most of the economic activity defined in the output variable Q is contained within the state and county levels almost exclusively. In addition, the transportation effect is measured at the regional highway network level so that the effects of local changes are likely to be manifested network-wide. The negative coefficient observed for the public capital variable (H) at the municipal level likewise indicates that spillover effects dominate at this spatial level of analysis.

Table 13.2 Output Elasticity of Highway Capital (year 2000)

Level	Direct Elasticity (β_4)	Output Elasticity
State	0.047	0.37
County	0.045	0.34
Municipal	−0.002	−0.01

To illustrate computation of the marginal output of highway capital (8), consider the county-level data. In 2000, total gross county product, Q, in the study area was valued at $633,692 million and total county highway capital at $85,235 million. From model (1), the coefficient for highway capital at the county level is found to be 0.045. Substituting these values into (8) yields marginal productivity of highway capital of 0.34.[10] This figure implies that a $1 increase in highway capital leads to a long-term accumulated increase in gross county product (GCP) of 0.34. The direct elasticity is 0.045, which implies an increase of $4.5 in GCP in response to a $100 capital investment. Table 13.2 summarizes the output elasticity results for the state, county, and municipal levels for the year 2000.

Figure 13.1 shows the percent change in gross state output as a function of highway capital accumulation.

Another way of interpreting the output elasticity results is by comparing them with the rate of return computed for the capital investments made at each of the three geographic levels. For example, for the year 2000, the rate of return of county-level highway capital is shown to be 7.55% (0.34 divided by 0.045). For the entire period (1990–2000), the average rate of return at the county level reached 5.09%. Figure 13.2 shows these results for the three spatial levels of analysis.

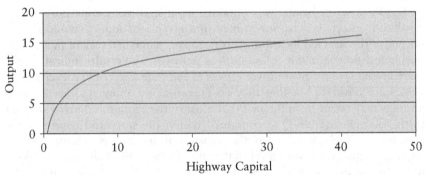

Figure 13.1 Percent change in gross state output as a function of highway capital accumulation.

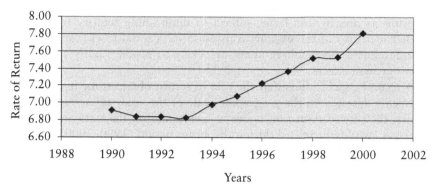

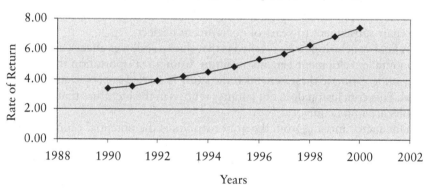

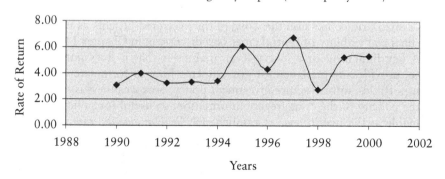

Figure 13.2 Rate of return on highway capital on the state, county and municipality level (1990–2000).

Several conclusions can be drawn from the above analysis. First, as illustrated by Figure 13.1, economic growth benefits from transportation capital investments are, by and large, subject to diminishing returns. In general, further increases of the existing transportation capital stock, especially in well-developed metropolitan areas, are likely to produce fairly small economic growth effects.[11]

A second conclusion is that the rate of return obtained for highway investments depends on the geographic scale of the analysis. As Figure 13.2 shows, the rate of return on highway investment on the state and county level has steadily increased during the entire period (1990–2000) whereas yields have exhibited a volatile pattern at the municipal level.

Regarding the rate of return on new infrastructure investments, activities such as construction, maintenance, and upgrading should be distinguished from one another. A 1988 US Congressional Budget Office report indicated that the real rate of return on new highway construction was 15%, on maintenance 35%, but only 5% on road upgrading (Gramlich, 1994). The high yield of maintenance investments probably indicates the dire conditions of present transportation capital stock and the crucial need to improve its state of repair subsequent to years of government neglect.

A final conclusion to be reached is that due to spillover effects, analysis of economic development benefits resulting from a transportation investment may underestimate these benefits if the study is carried out solely at the local level. This conclusion does not counter reports in the literature that spillover results are quite equivocal.[12]

One factor missing from the above studies is the potential economic impact of the method of project financing. For example, if state or local taxation is used to pay for the investment, economic growth might be reduced because consumption and production are highly responsive to taxation. A related issue is the spatial distribution of the project's benefits and costs. That is, in many cases, residents of a central city pay for transportation improvements, primarily through property taxes, while suburbanites, who are largely exempt from the same taxes, enjoy a significant proportion of the ensuing benefits. A common argument states that this "equity" phenomenon has a significant impact on the value of the measured benefits as well as on the financial viability of central cities (see discussion in Chapter 11).

A key limitation of a macro-level analysis is that it does not, by and large, provide any guidance for governments how to formulate a specific transportation infrastructure investment policy. This weakness is a product of the paucity of the disaggregate information, so useful for policymaking, available at the macro level (Gramlich, 1994). The *average* rate of return from a longitudinal increase in highway and transit capital stock, which a macro-level analysis elicits, may not accurately predict the economic benefits of a particular investment project. A related problem is that most studies assume that irrespective of location, the total monetary value of an investment has the same impact on the total value of public capital stock, hence on economic development. In fact, a new interchange in a populated area is more likely to encourage substantial commercial and retail development in adjacent locations than an identical interchange located in a sparsely populated area. These issues are taken up next.

3. MICRO-LEVEL ANALYSIS: THEORETICAL FOUNDATIONS

Broadly speaking, transportation investments generate two categories of benefit: direct travel benefits, such as travel time and cost savings, and indirect or secondary benefits, such as economic growth.[13] In this chapter, the first category is referred to as *primary transportation benefits* and the second as *externality benefits* to indicate that they are byproducts of primary transportation benefits and not merely their capitalized values (for an exact definition, see Section 3.1).

The literature cites a large number of growth-related externalities as emerging from transportation development (see, for example, Banister and Berechman, 2000; Lakshmanan and Chatterjee, 2005). An enlarged list might include the greater competition that weakens local monopolies, expansion of the labor markets from which local firms draw workers, enhanced productivity, increased government revenues from heightened economic activity, land development, intensified scale and agglomeration economies, increased clustering and regional specialization (which in turn raises productivity), new production chains, and improved logistics. Taken together, these impacts improve aggregate efficiency and lower costs. While these effects are often mentioned in the planning literature as indicators of the economic growth produced by transportation investments, the critical question—how to identify and measure them *ex ante* within the context of a proposed project—remains largely unanswered. Moreover, as repeatedly mentioned in this book, many of these effects are essentially consequences of the project's capitalized primary benefits—travel time and costs savings—and so, even if correctly measured, should not be included in a Cost Benefit Analysis (COBA) to avoid double-counting of benefits.

3.1 Economic Development Benefits: Analysis of Externalities

Chapter 3 examined the measurement of benefits from changes in transportation supply given the presence of externalities that cause the market prices of consumption and production activities to deviate from their true social costs. In cases where transportation improvements reduce these discrepancies, genuine economic development benefits do follow. To illustrate this process, consider the case where a firm enjoys a monopoly within a geographic region, which allows it to earn monopolistic rents as well as restrict output. A transportation project that lowers intra- and interregional transportation costs will buttress the ability of other firms inside and outside this region to compete, thereby reducing cost markups and expanding total output. These impacts, once translated into enhanced activity, improve social welfare and therefore constitute the project's economic development benefits. However, within the framework of transportation investment, these seemingly positive externalities should often be viewed as market capitalization effects, flowing from improved accessibility. Including them as part of the investment's direct benefits can lead to the double-counting of benefits (Mohring, 1993).

We next focus on three types of production externalities, each of which is amenable to transportation cost reductions: (a) scale economies, (b) forward and backward industrial linkages, and (c) agglomeration economies, implying increasing productivity with city size. These externalities are the key components of the so-called "new economic geography," aimed at explaining regional diversity and trade even in the absence of regional comparative advantages (Fujita et al., 1999; Krugman, 1995).

In the present context, scale economies imply that economic advantages can be gained from large-scale production units. To reduce production costs per unit and expand output, firms may decide to concentrate their production in fewer but larger spatial units. Such measures are adopted when inter- and intra-regional competition intensifies in response to falling transportation costs, circumstances that can force firms to economize by operating at a larger scale.

The concept *industrial linkages* refer to interfirm trade of intermediate goods and services, which frequently represent a sizeable proportion of firm activities. When faced with high transport costs, firms may choose to locate near their final product markets. When transportation costs decrease, these and other firms can move closer to their intermediate suppliers for the purpose of enjoying reduced upstream (buying from suppliers) and downstream (supplying other firms) costs. The end result is intensified regional industrial clustering, a key indicator of an agglomeration economy.

Externalities are normally associated with market imperfections. But only when the regional economy is quite imperfect will interfirm pecuniary externalities evolve. Put differently, when regional transportation costs are high, *ceteris paribus*, spatially dispersed production can be expected. When transportation costs fall, increased agglomeration will enable firms to benefit from such pecuniary externalities (Venables and Gasiorek, 1999). In addition, those falling transportation costs brought about by transportation investments are likely to induce increasing city size and productivity that, when combined with distortionary taxes, may result in yet larger economic gains (Venables, 2007).

Two major conclusions can be drawn from this discussion of the economic development pursuant to transportation investment. First, economic development impacts, especially if markets are imperfect, are best captured when measured at the regional level. At lower geographical levels (e.g., municipalities), the strong spillover effects that may appear are likely to distort the measurement of benefits (see above, Section 2.3).

The second conclusion drawn is that it is necessary to ascertain the degree to which the lowering of transportation costs will indeed motivate changes in the production, consumption, and location patterns of households and firms as well as in the organization of markets (for a detailed discussion see Banister and Berechman, 2000, Chapter 7).

The previous discussion did not address an important issue, namely, the impact of initial conditions on economic development effects. On the one hand, in well-developed metropolitan areas, the diminishing returns associated with additional or supplemental transportation investments can render insignificant the travel and accessibility effects of even large-scale projects. As a result, the potential impact of reduced travel costs on firm production and location decisions may be quite minor, as may the expected level of economic development benefits. On the other hand, in highly developed areas where further intensification has been hindered by an inadequate supply of transportation, transportation investments can signal large potential benefits. Alternatively, areas with little or no development are less likely to possess the necessary latent demand; hence the importance of recognizing initial transportation and economic conditions in a given area when predicting new transportation project's economic growth effects.

The approach to the identification and measurement of economic development benefits outlined above warrants several important caveats. First, it cannot explain the *dynamics* of these effects, particularly the time required before the local economy can actually enjoy these benefits. Some changes may come about almost instantaneously as expectations for enhanced accessibility precede the actual construction of a new facility; others can take years to materialize if local conditions are not sufficiently ripe.[14]

Second, this approach assumes that transportation is a significant factor in the formation of production and consumption patterns. In fact, for a large range of firms, transportation plays an inconsequential role in production and location decisions (Economic Development Research Group, 2005). For example, back office operations and local services are fairly immune to changes in accessibility. Moreover, in contemporary metropolitan areas, only a small proportion of all households in fact change their consumption and location patterns in response to transportation improvements in the short- to medium-run (e.g., 3–5 years). Housing prices, relocation costs, local taxes, public amenities, and household attributes are more consequential in their impact on relocation decisions (Chatman, 2009; Giuliano, 2004).

Third, the decisive role of regional policies in the realization of economic development benefits cannot be overemphasized. Even when positive externalities ensue from a major transportation investment, no economic development benefits will transpire if various land-use and other policies are not now nor soon to be in place. For example, if zoning regulations preclude high-density activity patterns, location-based economic agglomeration benefits would not materialize. Moreover, at the very moment that a transportation project is being implemented explicitly to boost economic activity in one specific area, other projects capable of negating these effects are often being constructed in another area. To illustrate, construction of a highway leading to suburban retail centers negates the accessibility benefits emerging from a rail project being built to revive a declining CBD area. From a regional perspective, the net effect of these incompatible investments will be limited to redistributing accessibility (Berechman and Paaswell, 1983).

3.2 Short- versus Long-Term Economic Development Benefits

Studies of transportation investments commonly distinguish between short- and long-run economic development effects. The former is associated with the so-called "investment multiplier effect" whereas the latter is with "regional economic growth effects." The concept of a multiplier effect refers to the value of economic activity accounted for by money spent on construction and purchases from local firms and the amount subsequently spent on local input factors (e.g., labor) or on final products (e.g., food), capital movements that generate additional revenues for additional local firms and residents.

How significant are these multiplier-induced economic gains when measuring a project's overall benefits? Many empirical studies indicate that these gains are quite high, to the point where they constitute a sizeable portion of the project's total benefits gained. To illustrate, a recent study of the Trans-Hudson Express Tunnel project (NJ Transit, 2006)[15] estimated that over the 10-year construction period, the multiplier effect gained from the $5 billion investment would include $2.7 billion of personal income, 4,000 jobs per year, and gross regional product of $4.5 billion (in 2004 prices).

Local decision makers often regard these sizeable gains as direct economic development benefits. But are they genuine benefits? Based on the previous discussion, the answer is generally *no*: If local markets are reasonably efficient and unemployment is fairly low, these gains constitute various forms of economic *transfers* rather than economic benefits. If the transportation investment in a metropolitan area is financed by taxation, at least some of the multiplier effects are pure transfers from taxpayers to local residents. Moreover, the economic gains enjoyed by local businesses from increased purchases by residents of one metropolitan area represent shifts in spending from other areas; so, these gains should be offset by a decline in business elsewhere. In addition, if demand for local goods increases from the infused investment funds, prices will go up, with the increases in producer surplus offset, in part, by declining consumer surplus.[16]

It is only when the rate of nonutilization of labor and other resources is rather high that the multiplier effect—which, among other things, results in decreased unemployment—can be regarded as a true economic development benefit. But even then, this is a short-term effect, lasting the length of the construction period. In brief, if input factors were fully employed, the public investment effect would be to increase factor prices (e.g., wage rates) and divert resources (e.g., mobile construction labor and heavy equipment) from other investments, or both. These impacts should be accounted for, in turn, against the increase in economic activity from the investment multiplier.

Two methods are frequently used to compute the multiplier effect: the "Economic Base" and the "Input-Output" (I/O) models (for a review see Batty, 1976).[17] Economic base models relate changes in the amount of goods and service sold within the region to the amount of goods and services sold outside it. Input-output models are essentially accounting tables whose aim it is to establish linkages between economic sectors by using fixed coefficients to indicate the unit contribution of one sector to the output level of another. Two types of linkages are possible: technological and trade. The former indicates the amount of inputs from one industry used to produce a dollar of output by other industries. The trade linkage indicates how much a given industry purchases from other firms in the relevant region. Once these linkages are established, the I/O model estimates the induced impact from the investment, sector by sector and for the region as a whole.[18] Electronic I/O model packages, calibrated for specific geographical regions like counties or states, are commercially available.[19]

A key difference between the multiplier effect and economic development is that the magnitude of the former is mainly a function of the investment's monetary size, whereas the magnitude of the latter is a function of the investment's primary (in this case) transportation effects and its ability to induce positive externalities in various markets. Thus, the multiplier effect is quite independent of the specific nature of the investment—highway, transit, or nontransportation—given that the crucial variable is the investment's financial size. In contrast, in the case of economic development benefits, there is a positive correlation between the time and cost savings obtained from a transportation investment and the investment's expected economic development benefits. Moreover, whereas the multiplier effect will end once the project has been completed, the economic growth effect will continue thanks to the structural changes instigated in the impacted markets.

Estimation of economic development benefits requires establishing a baseline for the conduct of measurement. Because economic benefits often materialize over long periods of time, setting that baseline year is highly consequential. Yet, the longer the period over which measurements are made, the more difficult it is to separate the impact of a specific transportation investment from all other land use, economic, demographic, and other transportation developments taking place in the interim. This complexity makes it necessary to use a general equilibrium model when estimating the economic development benefits resulting from an investment in transportation (see Section 9).

4. MEASUREMENT OF ECONOMIC GROWTH BENEFITS FROM TRANSPORTATION INVESTMENTS

A fundamental assumption underlying the analysis of economic growth benefits from transportation investments is that these benefits flow from the investment's primary effects in various markets. Thus, the measurement of economic development benefits, by type and magnitude, requires that we first identify the markets amenable to changes in their transportation systems. This requires identification of the regional and urban economic growth trends unrelated to the transportation project so that the net economic growth effects can be determined. In addition, modeling the relationships between the primary transportation effects and the various economic development effects within a general equilibrium framework is also necessary. Yet, the use of such a model framework is quite problematic within the realities of urban and transportation planning, a constraint calling for an approach more limited in scope. Such an approach is depicted in Figure 13.3.[20]

As Figure 13.3 shows, this methodology's first phase involves delineation of the area likely to be affected by the project's transportation results. One way of doing so is to use a network equilibrium model to determine which network segments will most likely be affected by the project. A second possible approach establishes the isoquant contours of accessibility (in terms of, say, travel times and spatial opportunities), then systematically determines which economic markets operate within these contours. These contours can, however, underestimate the true social-welfare changes elicited by the investment because the economic development effects are likely to spill over to other geographical areas. But, because decision makers are quite sensitive to the economic and employment situation in their own constituencies, which they associate with voter satisfaction and electoral support, they tend to disapprove of projects that confer benefits outside their districts.[21]

Application of the approach entails understanding that definition of the area of potential economic impacts is, in itself, insufficient for assessing the spread of future economic developments. Regional growth capacity limitations, unfavorable to further development, can effectively limit the relevance of these definitions. Precise identification of locational constraints, including the amount of built space, zoning regulations, and so forth, therefore represents a prerequisite for the approach's effective application.

Another understanding influencing the model's use is that urban areas continually experience periods of economic development, whether stimulated by natural population increase, general economic growth, or other public as well as private nontransportation investments. Care must thus be exercised in identifying regional growth trends unrelated to transportation development. Hence, in Figure 13.3 this module is labeled "unrelated growth trends."

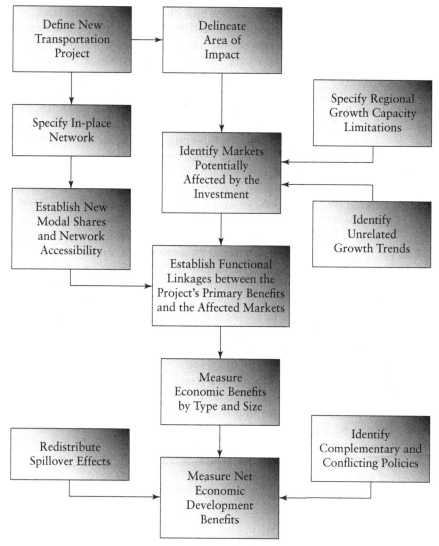

Figure 13.3 A framework for assessing a transportation project's economic development impacts.

Another key component in this framework is consideration of the project's impacts at the network level. Failure to measure outcomes at this level can introduce severe biases into the analysis. For example, adding a new subway line may not generate the travel time savings expected by the project's planners at the network level due to network externalities, trip diversion, latent demand, and off-peak to peak demand shifts. Thus the module, in Figure 13.3, labeled "new modal shares and network accessibility."

We should also not forget that accessibility changes tend to produce non-uniform markets effects. Whereas some economic sectors are quite susceptible to transportation modifications, others may be totally unresponsive. For some firms, transportation inputs are largely inconsequential so that even a large-scale transportation investment geared at improved accessibility may not result in within-industry (Marshallian) agglomeration. On the other hand, reduced travel costs are likely to increase participation rates in some labor markets and multiply or deepen cross-industry linkages. For these reasons, it is important to understand the potential of each market within the investment's impact area to respond to transportation improvements.

The evaluation of the relationships between the transportation primary impacts and economic development consequences, by type and size, is further affected by spatial policies and spillovers. Such state- or regional-level policies may contradict one another, as projects designed to encourage economic development in one area may simultaneously negate other policies aimed at encouraging development in another area. As a result, an investment's predicted economic development benefits may not fully transpire unless they are accompanied by measures that offset actions initiated elsewhere. One cogent example is attempted resolution of urban sprawl by passenger rail investments. To counterbalance sprawl with its unwarranted social and environmental effects, land-use policies must be enacted to ensure realization of the investment's full benefits.[22]

In closing this section, we return to a basic notion influencing our analysis so far. If we accept the assumption that economic growth can be triggered by transportation investments, it also holds that the level of growth is functionally related to the level of improved accessibility. Thus, once markets with potential for transportation-related growth have been identified, the next phase in the analysis depicted in Figure 13.3 is to specify the functional relationships between the two effects. Section 5 presents such a model.

5. EMPLOYMENT EFFECTS

When estimating changes in employment consequent to a transportation investment, the key empirical questions pertain to how transportation's primary benefits are to be associated with labor market decisions and how we are to account for the effects of intervening factors on these decisions. Berechman and Paaswell (2001) studied these questions in the context of a major transportation investment project in the South Bronx, a low-income, high-unemployment area in New York City.[23] The approach developed in their study first defined a labor market participation decision rule, which included travel costs. Based on this rule, a model was defined to empirically estimate the relevant elasticity parameters.

The labor market participation decision rule was based on Cogan's (1980) concepts *reservation hours* and *notional hours* of work. The former is defined as the minimum number of hours a person is willing to work; the latter is the number of hours a person would choose to work if she was required to spend at least a (positive) number of hours in the labor market. The Berechman and Paaswell study followed a similar approach by formulating reservation and notional work hour functions in addition to reservation and notional wage rate functions. Each function was augmented by an accessibility component estimated by a separate accessibility function. The study hypothesized that labor market participation decisions were based on three main variables: (a) potential employees' notional work hours relative to their reservation work hours; (b) their reservation wage rate relative to the offered wage rate; and (c) the costs of travel to work should they decide to participate in the labor market.[24]

The empirical model applied was composed of accessibility and employment functions, which were presented in chapter 11 (section 3)

A 2SLS procedure was used to estimate the model's parameters.[25] In addition, several statistical tests were conducted to account for the contemporaneous correlation in the error terms across equations, endogeneity and heteroscedasticity (Greene 2000).

The database used in this study includes observations obtained from 18 counties in Northern New Jersey and Southern New York for the year 2000. The observations included data on travel time by mode, time of departure, car ownership, and car occupancy by households, the number of people employed by job type,[26] the wage rate by industry sector,[27] household income and number of children per family by age group.

Three key results emerged from the empirical estimation of this model. First, controlling for skills, offered wage rate, household income, and children in the specified age groups, labor market participation in most job types were responsive to travel cost reductions. Yet, in some job types (e.g., retail and wholesale), this result did not hold. Thus, when assessing the policy impacts on employment of a project's accessibility improvements, we should recall that not all job types can be treated similarly.

The second major result was that the net employment effect from the investment was fairly small. Based on the estimated parameters, the model predicted a 10% transportation accessibility improvement would generate a 0.54% increase in new employment, which translates into a mere 4.57 new jobs for each 1,000 employees.

Lastly, the results showed that nontransportation variables significantly impact on labor market participation rates. Thus, for all job types included in this study's database, a higher wage rate was associated with a greater tendency to enter the labor market. Level of education had a similar positive effect on employment. For all job types, some formal college education positively contributed to employment seeking. As might be expected, the costs associated with child-care represented a major market entry barrier. For a given job type, having more children in a given age group was associated with higher market entry costs, thus a reduced market entry rate.

6. IMPROVED FACTOR PRODUCTIVITY AND REGIONAL COMPETITIVENESS

A claim commonly made in the literature is that transportation infrastructure investments improve firm productivity and thus regional competitiveness. These benefits may accrue to the firms themselves in the form of increased profits, or be passed along to consumers in lower prices, or a combination of the two. Such benefit are thought, in turn, to stimulate regional economic development by expanding the amount and range of goods and services produced and, consequently, regional income. As with employment, the two principal difficulties in assessing productivity gains from a transportation investment are, first, how to link improved accessibility with productivity gains while controlling for various intervening factors such as regulation, price rigidities, and institutional arrangements; and second, how to avoid double counting of benefits.

Time and costs saved from a transportation investment are usually regarded as the primary sources of enhanced labor productivity. Yet, as we have seen in Chapters 7 and 8, behavioral factors may render these savings inconsequential. Consider, for example, the case where individuals trade off travel time saved for leisure activities, or swap off-peak time of departure with peak time departures. And even if saved time is used for work purposes, it might still be difficult to empirically assess the productivity gains from an additional few minutes of time worked, especially if extra compensation is precluded.

6.1 Freight Productivity

Freight transportation productivity gains are often cited as a major benefit from the improvements achieved through investments in transportation infrastructure. These gains arise mainly from increased truck productivity, logistical cost savings, and consolidation of facilities. Collectively, these benefits can be equated with enhanced regional competitiveness. The argument goes as follows. High levels of traffic congestion tend to disproportionately affect truck movement, especially at key facilities such as bridges, tunnels, air and marine terminals, and intersections near to the CBD. Because truck hauling comprises, by and large, the largest share of regional freight transportation, the end result of stalled trucks is higher costs of doing business, expressed in the price of output, which reduces the region's ability to compete domestically and internationally. Reduced congestion improves truck productivity by enabling more runs per day, thus lowering the unit cost of output and enhancing regional competitiveness.

These arguments raise several economic and political hurdles. First, because congestion tolls, especially on truck movements, are politically difficult to impose, supporters of the regional competitiveness argument generally advocate further investments in local infrastructure instead. However, the use of local taxation to finance infrastructure projects is also unpopular and may, in any case, reduce the local economy's competitiveness. This situation makes external funding mandatory, which explains the common claim that without state and federal support for investment in additional traffic capacity, regions and cities are bound to lose their economic advantages.

Another problem arises from the use of value of time saved as a measure of improved truck productivity. There is no single value of freight that can be used in empirical analyses given that freight is typically multidimensional relative to value, durability, volume (containerized vs. bulk) and other product characteristics. The common approach, which entails use of an average value of truck drivers' time (see Chapter 4), does not account for the large variability in the value of the commodities hauled; it may therefore produce an erroneous estimate of truck productivity.

Finally, there is the logistics chain that affects truck productivity well beyond time savings because the relationship between the producer, shipper, carrier, and end-user can change in consequence. Thus, the benefits from significant truck time savings in highway travel may partially or wholly be negated by reduced productivity elsewhere in the chain, for example, by longer wait time at ports.

6.2 Logistics Cost Savings

A logistics (or supply) chain is a coordinated system for moving goods from suppliers to customers. Key components of a logistics chain include the supply of raw material, production or manufacturing, distribution, warehousing and (retail) sale channels to final consumers. Within each of this chain's components, freight transport is a key activity whose costs affect overall logistics costs.

What empirical evidence do we have about the impact of improved transportation on a firm's logistics costs? In a comprehensive review, Lakshmanan and Anderson (2002) examined the literature on this subject. The evidence they cite is relatively sparse and even conflicting. Another study, by Hickling et al. (1995), which used in-depth interviews with managers of a small sample of firms, concluded that a 1% reduction in average freight travel time would lead to a 0.548% reduction in logistics costs. However, it is doubtful whether these savings are the direct result of reduced transportation costs. For example, reduction of inventory carrying costs comprises another significant component of logistics cost savings; yet, these savings result mainly from more efficient supply chain systems and innovations in just-in-time delivery methods rather than the movement of inventory by truck.

In the study conducted by Shirley and Winston (2001), the authors attempted to derive an empirical linkage between provision of road infrastructure and inventory levels. Using the US Census Bureau's Longitudinal Research Database, they concluded that marginal inventory reductions for each dollar of infrastructure expenditure have been declining over time.

Hence, we can expect improved road conditions to have a minimal impact on unit inventory costs.

Another argument (McCann, 1998) proposed is that improved road conditions, which reduce freight transportation costs, enable shipment of larger batches that, as a result, lowers unit costs and thus total logistics costs. Yet, large shipments may also raise the carrying costs of inventory, which are an increasing function of shipment size due to factors such as storage, interest, and insurance. Furthermore, not all decisions regarding shipment size reflect firm inventory considerations. Lakshmanan and Anderson (2002) report on a survey of British producers of food and drink indicating that the key factor leading firms to utilize more transportation services was customer demand to receive shipments in a more timely fashion to enable them to reduce their own inventories (McKinnon and Woodburn, 1996).

In sum, considerations of a range of logistics issues have not unequivocally indicated that the lowering of freight transportation costs per se will significantly impact total supply chain costs. The empirical evidence is too meager to derive firm conclusions. Other factors, such as inventory costs, may have a more decisive impact on these costs.

6.3 Facility Consolidation

Another purported benefit of transportation infrastructure improvements is facility consolidation, in which firms concentrate production in fewer locations in order to take advantage of scale economies and production efficiencies. Hickling et al. (1995) produced the following results to show the effect of improved transportation costs on facility consolidation and thus on cost savings. (Table 13.3)

Before using these or similar results to estimate benefits from a transportation improvement, two caveats are in order. First, when activity concentrates

Table 13.3 Facility Consolidation Cost Savings: Medical and Surgical Products

	Before Consolidation	After Consolidation	Cost Savings (%)
Distribution Facilities	16	6	
Costs ($ Millions)			
Transportation	22	18	18.2
Warehousing	9	7	22.2
Inventory Carrying	11	9	18.2
Total Logistics Costs	42	34	19.0

Source: Hickling et al. (1995).

in fewer locations, their benefits often come at the expense of other locations, which may experience a concurrent decline in their economic activity (Forkenbrock and Foster, 1990). Second, concentration may also come at the expense of market competition as significant scale economies can result in fewer competing firms, capable of earning monopolistic rents. In combination, these effects can negate the social welfare gains associated with economic growth; they therefore require special attention when computing the investment's economic growth benefits.

McKinnon and Woodburn's 1996 survey of British firms showed how limited is the evidence indicating that declining transportation costs are a major factor behind consolidation of facilities and declines in average inventories. Perhaps these phenomena reflect long-run trends driven by technological advances and improved inventory management together with market trends towards firm takeovers and agglomeration.

All in all, what is needed is more empirical research into the interrelationship between transportation investments, the cost and quality of freight transportation services, as well as firm decision making. Only after sufficient findings have been culled will we be able to arrive at appropriate conclusions about their impact on business decisions regarding the respective variables.

6.4 Enhanced Regional Competitiveness

As discussed in Section 6.1, the empirical literature on the relationship between congestion and regional competitiveness has provided evidence collected mainly from studies on the impact of congestion on truck movements, equated with the costs of doing business in an area. In a study conducted by the Economic Development Research Group (2005) in Portland, Oregon (US), it was shown that congestion has substantially increased the costs incurred by Portland's businesses in recent years. The study estimated that if major capacity investments had been implemented, shipping cost savings would have accrued mainly to the region's trucking, warehousing, manufacturing, and trade sectors.[28] But what about the impact on regional competitiveness from upgraded specialized facilities such as air and marine ports? Evidence suggests that the scale of operations and productivity of such facilities, which link local with national and international markets, can have momentous impacts on regional and national economies. Thanks to the high volume of passengers using airports, many have become hubs for a myriad of industries. Commercial, industrial, information technology, retail, and service center activities have turned these hubs into de facto "airport cities" (Kasarda, 2000). By housing economic activities not necessarily related to the aviation sector, "airport cities" have become multimodal, multifunctional enterprises capable of stimulating regional economic development.[29]

Marine ports, which serve as major gateways for freight, seem to have a much stronger impact on the long-run growth of the national than the local economy. Marine shipping costs significantly affect the cost of manufactured exports produced nationwide. For many countries, exports are vital for the foreign currency earned and then used to buy imported growth-promoting capital goods. Low shipping costs are therefore closely linked with national economic growth. Because trucks do the bulk of port-related freight hauling,[30] reduced highway congestion is liable to reduce overall shipping costs.

The above factors notwithstanding, the difficulty in modeling the effect of improved infrastructure on regional competitiveness is largely due to regional dependence on global markets,[31] which are rarely integral to regional development models. Even if we could employ a well-constructed regional model, changes in regional competitiveness from, say, improved port facilities remain subject to the conditions (e.g., labor rules, tariffs and customs, and the demand for final goods) reigning in national and international markets. Highway improvements meant to benefit truck transport may only partially affect total shipping costs. These benefits are likely to be distributed nationwide—due to their varied sources—rather than within the local economy.

7. THE EFFECT OF TRANSPORTATION ON REAL ESTATE VALUES

Many studies have shown that transportation investments positively affect real estate values and new construction—important types of economic development benefits (see Huang, 1995, for a literature review). Moreover, the increased real estate values and floor space, commercial and residential, are thought to be transformed into higher property and other local tax revenues, which are then added to the list of the investment's overall benefits. This section examines the underpinnings of this effect and some key pitfalls involved with its estimation.

7.1 Assessment of Transportation's Impact on Real Estate Values

As we have noted in other parts of this book, numerous empirical studies have been carried out on the impact of transportation improvements on real estate values (see for example Anas, 1995; Cervero and Duncan, 2002; Hess and Almeida, 2007). But why would a transportation investment increase property values? The rationale underlying this argument is that the reduced travel times, subsequent to transportation development, affect the relative accessibility to a location, thereby enhancing consumer surplus. Improved accessibility is further capitalized in producer surpluses for residential and commercial real estate, which are then reflected in the value of land and structures (Anas, 1995; Mohring, 1961). Such results emerge with urban general equilibrium models that account for changes in consumer and producer surpluses in housing and transportation markets. The tax revenue generated from the expected increase in property values is also viewed as an important development benefit. Sometimes called "gained tax," it is measured as the difference between the annual assessed increase in land value and the revenue derived from the general property tax of properties adjacent to the new transportation facility (Gihring, 2001; Higginson, 1999).[32]

When assessing transportation investments, the key empirical question is how to assess, *ex ante*, the changes in real estate values from a planned transportation investment. Two approaches are explored here. The first uses results from *ex post* studies to derive coefficients that, within reason, are used for the analysis of a new planned investment.

The model most commonly employed to estimate changes in real estate values belonging to the first approach is the "hedonic price regression model." In this model, assessed property values constitute the dependent variable with proximity to the transportation facility, property characteristics, and locational and neighborhood amenities the independent variables. Parameter estimates of the model are interpreted as shadow prices and provide information on how the market values accessibility.[33] A common result from hedonic price studies is that the values of properties located in areas with commuter rail stations are higher by about 10% than those of properties located in areas without rail stations (Armstrong and Rodriguez, 2006).

The second approach calls for the assessment of the amount of new commercial and residential floor space added in the wake of a transportation investment. It subsequently uses fixed coefficients to convert floor space into employment and income. Present or projected tax rates are then used to derive expected tax revenues. Because the magnitudes of these coefficients are crucial, low, medium, and high values are often used. Figure 13.4 depicts these relationships.

At the foundation of this approach is the idea that a transportation investment raises the value of the existing properties adjacent to the new transportation facility, which spurs new residential and commercial development, thus new jobs and income. It also enhances sales of urban goods and services (e.g., tourism) or business captured from other regions. As a result of all these, the city realizes a significant increase in property, income, and sales tax revenues. This stream of future increases in tax revenues, properly discounted, is regarded as a major economic development benefit associated with transportation investments.

7.2 Some Caveats about Using Increased Property Values as Economic Development Benefits

A key result obtained from the empirical studies mentioned is the nonuniform spatial distributional of changes in property values. That is, the values of residential properties in very close proximity to transportation facilities (e.g., new railway station) are typically quite lower than those of properties located at some distance away, mainly due to noise and other environmental externalities. While peaking at short distances, the relationship between

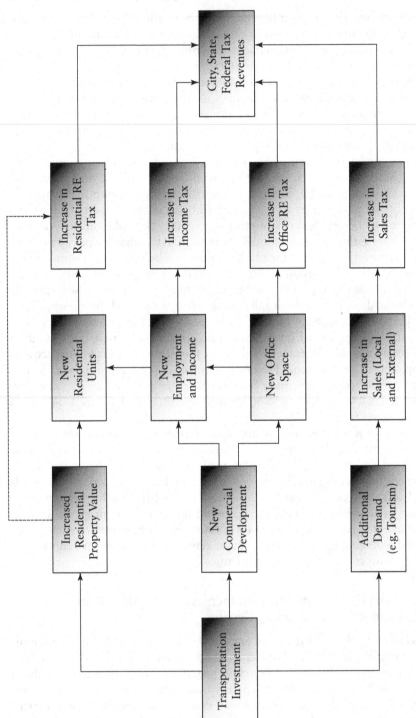

Figure 13.4 Real estate development and tax revenues flowing from transportation investments.

property values and distance tends to attenuate, reflecting the increasing costs of access time to more distant properties, perhaps requiring use of other modes (e.g., automobiles) to reach the main transportation facility. The value of commercial properties is also likely to peak near the transportation facility and then taper off with distance.[34]

Although these results are widespread, their use to assess changes in property values may be misleading. That is, under general equilibrium conditions, the value of some properties in the region may actually decline compared with the preproject values due to the intra-regional redistribution of real estate demand. Moreover, in anticipation of increases in value following a transportation investment, real estate supply (e.g., the number of building permits) also grows. The net effect is expected to be a rather small overall change in property values. Under partial equilibrium conditions, however, the measured market prices of properties are likely to overestimate the net capitalized value of the transportation benefits. Market imperfections may, of course, add to the complexities of using changes in property values as a measure of economic development. Consider, for example, a case where zoning regulations prohibit increases in density near the transportation facility.

Another empirical finding derived from a General Equilibrium Land Use and Transportation (GELUT) model is that identical improvements across modes do not yield similar impacts on property values and rents. Anas (1995) found that unlike the case for subways, across-the-board travel time improvements in bus, auto, and commuter rail reduce central area housing rents, whereas auto-targeted improvements yield higher total benefits and increases in commercial rents.[35]

Many studies have highlighted the importance of local conditions on the effect of transportation improvements on property values. Thus, the impact of a new rail line on property values in cities like Buffalo, New York, where the economy has been declining over the last several decades, is much smaller than in places where the economy is expanding (Hess and Almeida, 2007). Hence, the use of results obtained from one city cannot be straightforwardly applied to investment projects carried out in other cities.

A different problem relates to the use of property values in the assessment of equity. That is, subsequent to the increase in property values following investments in transportation, renters, residents, and business owners alike have to pay higher rents, part of which will be taxed. If not accompanied by comparable increases in renters' income or business owners' profits, this transfer of income from renters to property owners and then to the tax authorities may conclude in some being priced out of their particular markets, which has become a familiar event in cities throughout the world. For the purpose of project assessment then, how can we account for the reduced utility of renters relative to the enhanced utility of landowners in the framework of a transportation investment?

As shown in Figure 13.4, estimation of property value changes provides one basis for increasing city tax revenue forecasts. If the city taxes away part or all of the increase in a property's value, the deadweight loss from taxation must also be factored into the COBA. This further raises the question of what should be done with the additional tax revenues. Should the city use them to fund transportation capital costs, as some recommend (Regional Planning Association, 2004), or should it compensate low-income renters for the increase in their rents, or perhaps use the money to retire old debt? Each of these potential uses impacts differently on the transportation project's assessment.

Despite these qualifications, consultants and decision makers routinely attach great importance to changes in property values resulting from transportation investments. Their key argument is that the project's accessibility benefits, which are capitalized in the land and housing markets, reflect residents' willingness to pay a premium for the respective locations. These prices then provide good estimates of the transportation investment's primary benefits. However, in consideration of the implications of the current discussion, care must be exercised with respect to how changes in property values are measured and how they are included in the project's COBA.

8. TRANSPORTATION DEVELOPMENTS AND URBAN FORM

A fundamental principle of urban economics is that reduced travel costs affect activity location decisions and, it follows, urban form. Changes in location affect, in turn, the level of economic activity in the impacted area, which can thus be treated as an economic development benefit from the transportation investment responsible. This section therefore deals with three key questions: (a) How are we to model and measure the linkage between transportation changes and land-use changes? (b) What are the welfare effects from "more efficient" urban form? (c) How to incorporate these effects into the project evaluation process?

Chapter 8 examined the incompatibility of various phases of transportation planning with changes in travel demand. In particular, it examined the incongruity between trip generation rates and interzonal travel costs as well as the failure of assignment procedures to account for induced travel demand, factors directly affecting transportation benefit estimation. To resolve these and related issues, a linked land-use–transportation model was suggested (see Chapter 8, Figure 8.4). Analytically, such a model would associate the reduced travel costs, following transportation capacity expansion, with land-use projections, for the purpose of explaining potential changes in activity location and intensity.

Turning next to the question of the welfare implications it has been suggested that improved transportation increases the efficiency of land-use patterns. This result has direct welfare implications (i.e., changes in consumer and producer surpluses) that influence the investment's overall social welfare effect. The key issue in this regard turns on what it is meant by an "efficient land-use pattern." In general, transportation infrastructure development, whether road or rail, leads to a more dispersed urban structure and urban sprawl, which some view as highly inefficient (e.g., Cederbaum et al., 1996). Others (e.g., Gordon and Richardson, 1997) view urban sprawl, where jobs follow people, favorably because it helps maintain relatively constant work-trip times and distances. Still others (e.g., Banister, 1997) take a middle ground while refraining from characterizing urban forms as "favorable" or "unfavorable," focusing instead on urban land-use issues (e.g., specialization, concentration, mixed use) in relation to reduced trip length.

For transportation investments to have a significant effect on land-use patterns, transport must be an important factor in the location decisions made by households and firms. The literature is not unanimous on this question. Some researchers argue that over time, transportation has come to play a decreasing role in these decisions (e.g., Giuliano, 1996). Others suggest the opposite, claiming that localized land-use patterns are highly correlated with transportation costs and trip length (e.g., Cervero and Landis, 1995). In general, relationships between land use and transportation are complex, with the impacts of new infrastructure projects on the respective decisions, especially in highly developed urban areas, neither fully apparent nor readily identifiable. Nevertheless, the consensus leans towards the view that in the long term, urban land-use patterns are responsive to major changes in the transportation system's structure.

Accepting the view that transportation developments have at least some discernible impacts on land-use decisions, the mechanism most suitable for modeling and measuring these relationships is embodied in the set of Integrated Land Use and Transportation (ILUT) models.[36] Unlike macro-level models, ILUT models do not attempt to statistically estimate cross-sectional, longitudinal, or panel data relationships between transportation capital stock and output (see Section 2). Rather, ILUT models first analytically define the interactions maintained between transportation and location decisions in reference to residential, commercial, industrial, and other land uses. They subsequently simulate changes in location decisions, and thus urban form, from changes in the transportation system.[37]

Suppose that a chosen land use pattern can be predicted from a specific type of transportation project. One still needs to determine whether this pattern confers positive or negative welfare benefits. In their study of the impact of transportation investments on land use, Forkenbrock et al. (2001) developed a methodological framework that, the authors claim, enables identification of the type of transportation project required to `encourage certain types of land-use patterns. Yet, they qualify this assertion by stating that a consensus must first be reached on the type of urban forms considered "preferable." Can such a consensus actually be achieved in large metropolitan areas? Considering the presence of so many interest groups and stakeholders as well as the multifaceted socioeconomic composition of contemporary cities, the answer most probably will be negative.

Whether the results of a transportation investment are judged favorable or not with respect to urban form, the third key question before us refers to how we are to incorporate welfare effects from activity relocation into the project evaluation process. To the extent that the transportation model used for assessing an investment's transportation consequences is sensitive to land-use changes (as in Chapter 8, Figure 8.4), the results obtained already account for the revised land used. However, if the resulting land use pattern also confers externalities (negative or positive), these should be treated separately. For example, if a new large-scale rail project is likely to encourage further suburbanization and thus increase environmental externalities, these effects should be considered in the project selection phase of the evaluation process. We return to this issue in Section 10, below.

9. A GENERAL EQUILIBRIUM ANALYSIS OF ECONOMIC DEVELOPMENT BENEFITS

Most transportation infrastructure investments, implemented as they are in well-developed urban areas, have marginal impacts on total regional accessibility and localized economic development. For this kind of project, prudent use of benefit cost analysis will produce reasonable results. However, for other project types, including large-scale or mega-projects, interregional, national, or international in scope, COBA may underestimate the economic development benefits accrued to the economy as a whole. Furthermore, as an *ex ante* decision method, COBA must use predictions of future travel demand to account for future changes in all relevant sectors and in trade flows. Hence, to be meaningful, assessment of benefits from investments of these types require a general equilibrium (GE) approach, aimed at explaining production, consumption, and prices in the economy as a whole.[38] In contrast, partial equilibrium (PE) models, which characterize most of the empirical studies reviewed in this chapter, focus on specific segments of the economy (spatially or sectorally defined), while taking the rest of the economy as given. In addition, PE models tend to treat the demand for output as totally elastic while ignoring the down-sloping nature of true demand curves.

GE models are also used to study social welfare benefits when the economy cannot be assumed to be perfectly competitive, mainly due to the presence of scale and agglomeration economies, monopolistic competition, and distortionary taxation.[39] For instance, it has been observed that enhanced trade between well-developed neighboring countries like the US and Canada or Western Europe results mainly from economies of scale than from comparative advantages and regional specialization.[40]

How suitable is COBA for assessing economic development benefits in markets characterized by monopolistic supply of transportation services, mainly public transit? As with the case of any other externality, imperfect competition typically results in underestimation of the welfare gains from a transportation investment (see Chapter 3). Reduced transportation costs, however, tend to weaken monopolistic power and thus monopolistic rents; these in turn scatter throughout the economy in the form of greater output and improved productivity. Venables and Gasiorek (1999) studied these effects using a computable general equilibrium (CGE) model. Their simulation results indicate that the total welfare gains from a reduction in transportation costs—when using a CGE model—are greater than those revealed by COBA, depending on the elasticity of demand for transportation services, the degree of monopolistic market power, agglomeration economies, and interindustry linkages.

The above conclusion regarding the use of GE models applies especially to investments in facilities used for interregional and international trade, such as large maritime terminals, inland and coastal waterways, airports, or border crossings. Trade theory views decreased transportation costs as a major incentive for higher trade volumes, similar to the effects of reduced trade tariffs, removal of trade barriers, and introduction of pro-trade policies, where gains accrue mainly at the state or national level.[41] A GE analysis is particularly applicable when our interest lies in assessing the economic growth benefits of investments at these spatial levels.

Finally, decision makers commonly view highway and rail development as key factors for stimulating interregional and international trade. Some reservations to these conclusions have been raised in the literature. For instance, Lakshmanan et al., (2001) report that only 10.4% of US freight movements, which generally utilize domestic road and rail infrastructure, actually support international trade. Moreover, trade gains from further transportation investments abate over time as a function of diminishing marginal accessibility, greater regional integration and more ubiquitous access to markets.

10. INCORPORATING ECONOMIC DEVELOPMENT BENEFITS INTO PROJECT EVALUATION

The inclusion of economic development benefits into transportation project evaluation raises two conceptual questions. First, at what stage of the evaluation process should these effects be examined, at the COBA assessment phase or at the project selection phase? Second, what weight should be given to economic development effects relative to primary transportation benefits?

When attempting to answer these questions, a case study of transportation investment alternatives in New York City (Berechman and Paaswell, 2005) was considered. The anticipated transportation benefits from the projects analyzed in that study were computed using traditional measures of savings in access and egress time, wait time, in-vehicle travel time, and reduced exposure to overcrowding. These savings were computed for each corridor in which the project was planned as well as for other parts of the network. Cost savings from reduced auto use were also computed.

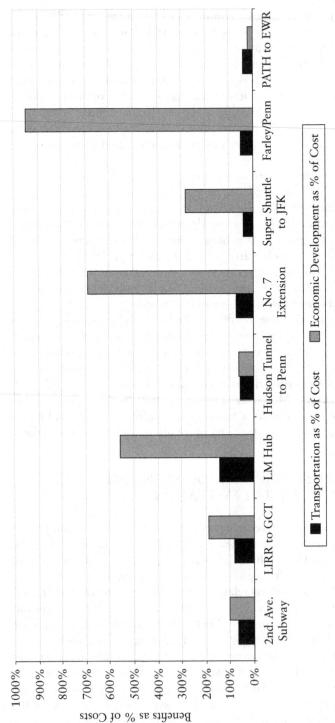

Figure 13.5 Transportation and economic development benefits as percent of capital costs by project.[a]

Notes: [a]Present Values of benefits and costs.

Legend: 2nd Ave. (Second Avenue Subway); LIRR to GCT (LIRR Connection to Grand Central–East Side Access); LM Hub (Fulton Transit Center and Permanent PATH Station); Hudson Tunnel to Penn (Access to the Region's Core: NJ Hudson Tunnel); No. 7 Subway Extension; Super Shuttle to JFK (LIRR and/or JFK Access to Lower Manhattan); Farley/Penn (Penn Station and Farley Post Office); PATH to EWR (PATH Extension to Newark Airport).

The economic development benefits for these projects were computed using the approach depicted by Figure 13.4. Benefits included job growth, new commercial and residential developments, and additional tax revenues. Figure 13.5 shows the Present Value (PV) of the primary transportation benefits and of the economic development benefits for each project as a percent of the PV of the project's capital costs.

The picture emerging indicates that the value of the economic development benefits, expressed as a percentage of a project's total PV of its capital costs, by far exceed those of the primary transportation benefits. In fact, in only two cases, (the Hudson Tunnel and the PATH to EWR or Newark Airport), do the transportation benefits appear in the same range as their economic development benefits. Thus, the positive assessment of these projects is almost entirely dependent on their economic development contributions.

Several questions are raised by these results. Is it rational to select transportation investment projects principally on such a basis? Should a transportation investment indicating expected transportation benefits significantly lower than its capital costs be denied regardless of the magnitude of the non-transportation benefits to be generated? Is it correct to directly sum the transportation and economic development benefits for the purpose of producing total benefits, a step that effectively assigns equal weights to each benefit category? If not, what weight should be assigned to each and at what phase of the overall evaluation process should this weighting take place? The questions are important because the assessment and selection of transportation projects on the basis of their economic development effects may result in approving transportation investments with insignificant transportation impacts.

Referring to the project evaluation process explained in Chapter 2, economic development benefits ought to be incorporated into the evaluation process at the project selection phase. When this occurs, a project's evaluation team should assign weights to each category of benefit so as to reflect their importance within the broader scope of transportation policymaking (see Chapter 14 on the issue of weights). If we agree that transportation investments should be accepted, first and foremost, on the basis of their primary transportation benefits, then these benefits should receive the larger weight. For example, in the cited study of NYC transportation projects, the primary transportation benefits were assigned 50% and the economic development benefits 30% (the balance was assigned to other benefit types).

11. SUMMARY AND CONCLUSIONS

This chapter focused on the identification and measurement of economic growth effects from transportation infrastructure investments. The discussion followed three main lines of inquiry: First, a macro-level analysis, where transportation capital stock was used to explain aggregate state, regional, or local economic growth; second, a micro-level analysis where improvements in local accessibility were used to explain local market performance such as labor market participation rates; third, an urban form analysis, where changes in travel costs pursuant to a transportation investment were linked with activity location and intensity. In all of these analyses, the key issues revolved around how to estimate the respective effects and how to incorporate them into the project evaluation process.

Our analysis indicates that economic development benefits, if correctly modeled and measured, should be considered at the project selection phase. This holds even when, as we have seen, direct transportation benefits are small relative to the estimated economic development benefits. Therefore, combining the two types of benefits to produce total benefits can result in rationalizing projects choice on the grounds of their economic growth benefits irrespective of their scanty transportation benefits.

The chapter has also advocated the use of a general equilibrium regional land-use–transportation model (GELUT) to correctly assess activity patterns and travel cost savings from transportation investments. Such a model is also necessary in order to avoid the double-counting of benefits, a persistent faulty outcome arising from the use of a partial equilibrium model.

The unavailability of operational GELUT models and the complexities associated with their calibration and application makes GELUT use rare within the context of current urban planning realities. This does not deny the availability of alternatives for obtaining reasonable assessments of a transportation project's economic development implications. First, the target population for welfare improvement is to be precisely defined. Second, the markets most likely to favorably respond to changes in accessibility (mainly labor and land markets) are to be identified. The competitiveness of these markets must also be measured in order to ascertain whether the proposed accessibility improvement will indeed increase welfare. Third, regional competitiveness in the context of national and international markets is to be assessed.

Perhaps the most crucial question demanding a response is how to identify and measure an investment's anticipated economic development effects *ex ante*. Because observed economic development benefits often represent capitalized travel time and cost savings, their correct measurement requires that we avoid the double-counting of benefits. Only positive externalities, such as agglomeration economies, or the reduction of negative ones, should be treated as a transportation project's genuine long-term economic development benefits.

APPENDIX A: THE GRANGER CAUSALITY TEST FOR PANEL DATA

Following Jiwattanakulpaisarn et al. (2006), for a panel database we can write expression (1) in Section 2 as:

$$\Delta Q_{c,t} = \alpha_0 + \sum_m^M \beta_m \Delta Q_{c,t-m} + \sum_m^M \gamma_m \Delta H_{c,t-m} + \rho_c + \varepsilon_{c,t} \tag{A1}$$

In (A1), the terms $\Delta Q_{c,t}$ and $\Delta H_{c,t}$ are growth in regional output and in regional stock of highway capital, respectively. The number of time lags is denoted by M; $\varepsilon_{c,t}$ denotes error terms. The term ρ_c represents unobserved shocks common to all regions but varying across time.[42]

The Granger test amounts to testing the hypothesis that expansion of the highway capital stock stimulates changes in regional output. Statistically, it amounts to rejecting the joint hypothesis that $\gamma_m = 0, m = 1,\dots,M$. If this null hypothesis is rejected, then highways can be said to cause regional output expansion.

Similarly, we can specify the expression:

$$\Delta H_{c,t} = \delta_0 + \sum_m^M \mu_m \Delta H_{c,t-m} + \sum_m^M \upsilon_m \Delta Q_{c,t-m} + \eta_c + \sigma_{c,t} \tag{A2}$$

In (A2), η_c represents unobserved shocks and $\sigma_{c,t}$ denotes error terms. The Granger causality test holds if we can reject the null hypothesis that all of the coefficients of the lagged output variable (υ_m) are significantly different from zero.

14 Alternative Methods of Project Selection

1. INTRODUCTION

Assuming the precise definition of project objectives and appraisal of all the proposed investment alternatives relative to all their transportation and nontransportation impacts, the next step in the evaluation process demands selection of the optimal or preferred project alternative (see Figure 2.2, Chapter 2). If one alternative appears superior to all others relative to all the criteria, no selection process is necessary. This rarely being the case, the question becomes that of choosing a procedure to determine the *optimal* alternative. The current chapter focuses on this issue by examining various methods that can assist decision makers in identifying the optimal project alternative.

In previous chapters, the theoretical underpinnings of COBA methods were discussed, as were their major deficiencies as tools for project evaluation and selection. One key problem raised was decision making in the face of conflicting views and interests.[1] In response, various methodologies have been proposed to facilitate selection of an optimal project under such conditions. To be sure, no one method can ensure the reaching of a full consensus among stakeholders; and no formal methodology is capable of directly producing reconciliation, a task usually delegated to the political system in democratic societies. Here, however, the focus is on methods capable of eliciting the trade-offs between objectives (e.g., transportation efficiency, improved equity, and reduced environmental externalities) in ways that enable decision makers to make rational and systematic choices regarding the preferred project. From another but related perspective, use of well-founded and systematic project selection methods predicate transparency, an attribute often lacking in real-world transportation investment decisions.[2]

Assuming multiple objectives, we can distinguish between two broad types of project selection approaches: hierarchical and complementary. The *hierarchical* approach maintains that a transportation project must, first and foremost, meet transportation-economic criteria such as a minimum benefit-to-cost ratio, with benefits being direct impacts of transportation activities. These impacts include, for example, reduced network travel time and costs, favorable modal shares (e.g., greater transit and fewer highway trips), or reduced peak demand. If a project passes this test, it must next meet other criteria, for example, sufficient economic development impacts. Section 6 proposes such a method.

The second approach regards all effects as *complementary* and entails the use of methods that enable simultaneous examination of all key effects, with the transportation-economic assessment of the project—carried out by COBA—just one such effect. Both approaches, however, require the use of weighted scoring of the various effects in order to determine the optimal alternative. In terms of the specific methodologies, we can distinguish between multicriteria and decision-support methods. This chapter examines these approaches and assesses their usefulness for project selection.

A momentous issue in public decision making is the identity of the institution charged with making the final choice of a project. Is it a committee appointed by the governor, or by the mayor, or by the ministry in charge, or perhaps a local planning organization or an independent committee of experts? Obviously, the identity and structure of the decision-making body critically impacts on the way choices are made. A related issue concerns the mechanism used to arrive at its final decision. The literature on public decision making discusses these issues in conjunction with others, such as concurrence-seeking, coalition formation, individual reputation, information sharing, and private views regarding the project's uncertainties (see for example Visser and Swank, 2007). It is beyond the scope of this chapter to delve into all these issues; yet, we stress, in real-world situations, such matters are often essential for understanding why a specific transportation project was selected (see Chapter 15 for case studies).

It should also be understood that the evaluation and selection methods, used in public investment decision making, cannot be divorced from each country's respective history and values. Thus, US legislation passed in the 1930s, requiring a COBA-like framework for the evaluation of public works, set the direction for subsequent development of federal and then local assessment of transportation projects. A country like the US, which has adopted the right to life, liberty, and pursuit of happiness among its key values, might decide on a different set of public investments than would a country that sets its priorities as peace, order, and good government.

The design of this chapter is as follows. Section 2 examines in some detail a prototypical multicriteria evaluation method. Other multicriteria decision methods are examined in Section 3, followed in Section 4 by a review of decision-support methods. Section 5 comments on the prevalence of multicriteria analysis methods. Section 6 proposes an alternative project selection procedure. A summary and conclusions are presented in Section 7.

2. MULTICRITERIA DECISION ANALYSIS: SCORING METHODS

Transportation investment policies are commonly expected to satisfy a large number of objectives in addition to their direct transportation goals. The US 1990 Intermodal Surface Transportation Efficiency Act (ISTEA), for example, cites economic growth, safety, accessibility, environmental, connectivity, intermodality, land use and urban form, efficiency, and the preservation of existing transportation systems as its objectives. Multiple criteria analysis (MCA) methods have been developed in order to allow each decision-making environment to engender its own set of criteria, measure and score them, and then generate a system of relative weights specific to the given context.

Prior to discussing MCA, an explanation of the rationale for using scoring techniques in project evaluation is due. It can be argued that the NPV (or some variant) of a project provides all the relevant information necessary for correctly assessing each investment option's overall contribution to social welfare. Furthermore, we might say that this rationale also holds in the presence of external benefits and costs. That is, the NPV of externalities should be added to the NPV of direct benefits to obtain the total NPV of a transportation project. Yet, such an approach raises several salient conceptual concerns.

The first concern springs from the fact that in metropolitan areas in the industrialized world, the transportation network is highly developed; hence, any transportation investment, even if sizeable, will make only a marginal improvement to overall accessibility in the area. Therefore, the actually measured direct transportation benefits are unlikely, by themselves, to generate a positive NPV sufficient to justify the project. In such a case, if we combine direct transportation with non-transportation benefits, the latter will effectively determine the project's overall value. But should we be willing to prefer a transportation investment primarily on the basis of its nontransportation benefits? Cases like these may coax decision makers to stress the project's direct transportation impacts by attaching a weight to these that is higher than the weight given to the indirect benefits. Under such conditions, it is undesirable to simply add up the direct and indirect benefits, a step that will subsequently call for application of a scoring and weighting method.

Another problem with the use of NPV as the selection criterion is that the project's direct transportation and other benefits (e.g., economic development) may not accrue to the same populations. Whereas the former will accrue largely to users of the transportation system, often within a confined corridor, the latter will accrue to region-wide nonusers as well, such as landowners and developers. With respect to this issue as well, decision makers might want to attach scores and differential weights to each type of benefit, thereby affecting the overall ranking of the projects.

A third issue is that alternative impact criteria may not be defined with the same metric. As the examples below show, some are defined in percentages (e.g., the investment's rate of return), some in monetary units (e.g., NPV), and some in time units (e.g., years of construction). Hence, methods are required that provide common scales that facilitate comparisons.

In sum, COBA, as explicated in previous chapters, is unsuitable for handling projects with multiple objectives, especially if some cannot be readily monetized. But even if these impacts were monetized, COBA further requires that all effects be expressed as a single measure of the investment's net welfare contribution. As a result of these constraints, trade-offs between impacts can neither be shown to nor considered by decision makers.

2.1 Weighting and Scoring: The Goal Achievement MCA Method

All MCA methods are comprised of essentially two main phases. Phase *one* requires that each different transportation and nontransportation impact category be systematically scored using any of various measurement scales (e.g., cardinal, ordinal, interval or ratio). Phase *two* entails the assignment of a weight to each category that reflects its relative importance for decision making. The investment alternatives are then ranked on the basis of their normalized weighted total score. One early and still used MCA scoring-weighting method is the Goal Achievement Matrix (GAM), also known as Simple Additive Weighting (SAW). While other methods have since been devised (see Section 3), GAM serves as the prototypical MCA method.

Pioneered by Hill (1968), the GAM method aims at providing a common denominator for all investment alternatives considered so that they can be ranked systematically and unambiguously. It places all criteria used for the evaluation and all project alternatives into matrix form; matrix entries are the normalized scores assigned to each alternative for each criterion. All criteria not being equally important, a vector of weights is also specified. Its purpose is to reflect the relative importance of each criterion (see section 2.4). The product of the score matrix and the vector of weights produces a weighted score matrix. Summing across each project yields a vector of ranked projects.

Technically, the method consists of a score matrix (Q) containing the raw score values assigned to each criterion for each alternative. The matrix is then transformed into a normalized score matrix (S) whose elements represent values ordered relative to a common denominator (e.g., the highest basic score). This matrix is subsequently multiplied by the vector of weights (W) to produce the weighted normalized score matrix (T). The vector of weighted scores for each alternative (V) is then derived from T. The alternative with the highest score is then selected. Appendix A presents the analytical structure of the GAM method.

2.2 Generating Weights

The critical factor in the application of any MCA method is the weights used. That is, if the final ranking of the alternatives is invariant according to the weights, then the use of MCA for project selection is superfluous. Alternatively, if the ranking is sensitive to the weights chosen, then it is necessary to determine the appropriateness of these weights.

In general, we can distinguish between four approaches to weight generation.[3]

1. *Expert Panel:* Weights can be generated by pooling the opinions of experts or of well-informed individuals relative to the nature of each criterion. Sampling techniques can elicit weights based on the distribution of responses. For example, Lootsma (1992) reports a survey among professionals who were asked to respond to a list of policy goals and their respective assessment criteria. The respondents indicated their views of the two variables by means of pair-wise comparisons on a qualitative scale. Answers were then scored on a numerical scale (e.g., in the range of +10 to –10). The weights were subsequently obtained by transforming these scores into a logarithmic scale.

2. *Simulation:* Over the uniform distribution {0,1}, a set of random numbers, one for each criterion, is generated. The weights are then computed by normalizing the set's values (e.g., by dividing each simulated value by the total sum) so that the sum of the weights equals unity. This essentially random generation process is used when no prior information on decision-maker preferences is available. The underlying rationale for using this approach is that it prevents the assignment of arbitrary (e.g., equal) weights. For more, see Janic and Reggiani (2002).

3. *Optimization:* Under this approach, the decision process is formulated as an optimization problem, with the objective function defined as the variance of the overall scores of each alternative under study (Jessop, 1999). The variables, whose values must be determined, are the decision weights; constraints on these variables are derived from explicit preference statements made by decision-makers. These are expressed in terms of trade-offs between pairs of criteria-weights (an example of such an optimization model is found in Sayers et al., (2003). Interactive procedures have been proposed when information on decision makers' preferences—and thus trade-offs—is unavailable (Nijkamp and Rietveld, 1979). These procedures are directed at obtaining decision makers' attitudes toward each criterion's acceptance range, information that is obtained through an iterative and systematic exchange between the decision maker and the policy analyst (see Cho, 1999, for an empirical application).

4. *Ex Post Analysis:* The weights are regarded as the decision criteria's shadow prices, reflecting their relative importance. Similar to the case of missing markets and absent prices, it is still possible to estimate the implicit weights (prices) used in previous comparable situations (i.e., projects of the same type). An interesting example is a study by

Nellthorp and Mackie (2000), who used a hedonic regression model to elicit the implicit weights used in already-constructed trunk road projects in the UK (their sample included 68 projects).

What is common to all of these methods is their explicit attempt to eliminate subjectivity in the generation of decision weights and thereby make the overall evaluation-selection process consistent and transparent. It is precisely for this reason that these methods are not universally accepted; that is, they constrain the ability of political decision makers to implement projects that suit their agendas.

2.4 An Example of the GAM Method

Consider the following application of the GAM method for project-ranking purposes (Berechman and Paaswell, 2005).[4]

Step 1: Specify the set of criteria and set the weights as in Table 14.1. In this case, the weights were generated through brainstorming by a panel of experts.

Step 2: The scores for each of the six criteria and their subcriteria are enumerated. To illustrate, Table 14.2 shows the second criterion, "other transportation benefits," for three investment projects.

Step 3: Normalize the score. One approach is to take the "best" score of each criterion and define it as 100.[6] That is, divide each row by the value of the best score and then multiply the result by 100. Note that for some

Table 14.1 Criteria and Weights (W)

Criterion	Weight
1. COBA Transportation	0.40
2. Other Transportation Benefits (e.g., transit ridership)	0.10
3. Economic Development	0.25
4. Project Construction Period	0.05
5. Environment	0.15
6. Community	0.05
Total	1.00

Note: If for some reason the values of one or more of the alternatives' criteria cannot be assessed, its weight is proportionally distributed among the other criteria.[5]

Table 14.2 Other Transportation Benefits Score (Q)

Criterion	Method	Variable	Units	Project A	Project B	Project C
2. Other Transportation Benefits						
2.1 Network time saved	Network analysis	Time	Minutes	15	20	10
2.2 Ridership	Network analysis	Volume	Passenger-trips	100,000	60,000	120,000
2.3 Modal Split	Assignment	Share of transit	Percent	15	20	40
2.4 Modal peak hour congestion relief	Network analysis (wait time)	Delays	Minutes	5	8	3

criteria, the best score is the lowest value, for example, as in the case of delays (a 3-minute delay is better than a 5-minute delay). In that case, the lowest score becomes the numerator, that is, every other score is divided into that value and the result is multiplied by 100.[7] The normalized scores for "other transportation benefits" are given in Table 14.3.

Table 14.3 "Other Transportation Benefits" Criterion—Normalized Score (S)

Criterion	Method	Variable	Units	Project A	Project B	Project C
1. Other Transport Benefits						
2.1 Network time saved	Network analysis	Time	Minutes	75	100	50
2.2 Ridership	Network analysis	Volume	Trips	83.3	50	100
2.3 Modal Split	Assignment	Share of transit	Percent	37.5	50	100
2.4 Modal peak hour congestion relief	Network analysis (wait time)	Delays	Minutes	60	37.5	100
Total				255	237.5	350
Normalized				72.9	67.9	100

Table 14.4 Total Normalized Scores

Criterion	Project A	Project B	Project C
1. COBA Transportation	100	48	40
2. Economic Development	100	94.4	83.3
3. Other Transportation	72.9	67.9	100
4. Project Construction Period	74.1	81.5	100
5. Environment	100	66.7	66.7
6. Community	68.2	81.8	100

To illustrate the calculations in Table 14.3, consider the criterion "modal peak hour congestion relief." measured as minutes of delay. As shown in Table 14.2, the best (in this case least) delay is 3 minutes. Thus, the normalized score is computed by dividing the 3-minute (least) delay by each project-specific value and then multiplying by 100 (60 = [(3/5) × 100]; 37.5 = [(3/8) × 100]; 100 = [(3/3) × 100]).

Step 4: Repeat Step 3 for each of the six criteria in Table 14.1. The six vectors of the total normalized score are given in Table 14.4.

Step 5: Multiply the normalized score matrix by the weights vector (in Table 14.1) to produce the weighted normalized score matrix, as shown in Table 14.5.

Step 6: From Table 14.5, the weighted (normalized) score vector of projects, V, is: $V = \{94.4, 61.6, 66.8\}$.

Table 14.5 The Weighted Normalized Score Matrix (T)

Criterion	Weight	Project A	Project B	Project C
1. COBA Transportation	0.40	40	19.2	16
2. Economic Development	0.25	25	16.1	20.85
3. Other Transportation Benefits	0.10	7.29	8.15	10
4. Project Construction Period	0.05	3.7	4.075	5
5. Environment	0.15	15	10.0	10.0
6. Community	0.05	3.41	4.09	5
Total	1.00	94.4	61.6	66.8

Step 7: The project with the highest score, denoted by V^*, is $V^* = max_j (V_j)$. According to Table 14.5, this is project A.

Similar procedures can be found in the literature (e.g., Janic and Reggiani, 2002) and in the operational specifications provided by various planning agencies.[8]

3. OTHER MCA METHODS

As pointed out, the scoring-weighting method underlies, to one or another degree, all other multicriteria evaluation techniques, including those proposed in the literature as alternatives to GAM. Three such methods—hierarchy, regime, and critical threshold value analyses—are very succinctly examined below.[9] We should bear in mind that the literature on decision-making methods in business and management is rather well developed, analytically quite sophisticated, and extensively applied.[10] In contrast, the lack of relevant data, the presence of many stakeholders, the frequent inability to agree on common objectives, and, most importantly, the usually charged political atmosphere in which public decisions are made, make the more sophisticated MCA techniques rather superfluous in the area of public decision making.

3.1 Hierarchy Analysis

Conceptually, the weight assigned to each criterion indicates the salience attached to that criterion by the decision maker. An alternative way of expressing the relative importance of a set of criteria is to arrange them in hierarchical order. To that end, the hierarchy method, also called the Saaty method (Saaty, 1980), is widely used to rank alternative proposals.

In general, the approach entails three main phases (Janic and Reggiani, 2002). First, decision makers are asked to what degree one criterion is of more or less importance when compared to another, which results in a hierarchical ordering of all the criteria. The objective is to decompose the set of criteria into two subsets: main criteria and secondary criteria. The second phase involves an ordinal pair-wise comparison of all the criteria, resulting in pair-wise matrices where each element in the matrix shows the (integer) score given to each criterion in each project. The third step demands synthesis of priorities, carried out by computing the overall score for each alternative in a way similar to that applied in the GAM model.

3.2 Regime Analysis

Regime Analysis is a discrete, multiattribute method of project evaluation (Winston, 1994; Zanakis et al., 1998). It can deal with binary, ordinal, categorical, and cardinal data in addition to mixed data. As with the other decision-making methods, its main inputs are an impact score matrix and a set of weights. Regime methods use concordance analysis to rank a set of alternatives by means of their pair-wise comparisons with chosen criteria. The analysis ranks projects based on a concordance index, found by taking the sum of the weights assigned to the criteria for which project i is better than project k and then subtracting the sum of the weights of those criteria for which k is better than i. Alternative i is considered more attractive than alternative k if the result associated with i is positive. Additional performance indicators can further be introduced to help arrive at a more unambiguous ranking of the alternative projects.

3.3 Critical Threshold Value Analysis

The purpose of this method is to help decision makers assess the degree to which competing alternatives meet predefined standards. This task is achieved by comparing the impacts of the various alternatives against a set of reference values, called Critical Threshold Values (CTV). The overall process is completed in four steps: First, identification of a set of measurable indicators; second, assessment of each project's impact on those indicators; third, establishment of a set of normative references; fourth, evaluation of the alternatives. An impact matrix serves as the model's input. It contains the values that the indicators assume for each alternative considered. The matrix itself is separated into indicator classes; for example, environmental, social, and economic. For each indicator, a CTV is defined. Decision making proceeds by inspecting each individual alternative against the CTV and then comparing the various choice options. The indicators can be measured quantitatively, qualitatively, or with a mixed approach.

3.4 How Useful Are These Methods?

In their study of airport expansion plans for the Maastricht area in the Netherlands, Vreeker et al. (2001) used an evaluation framework that blended three approaches: regime analysis, critical threshold value analysis (entitled the Flag Model[11]), and hierarchical analysis (the Saaty method). The criteria for analyzing potential impacts were grouped into three main categories—economic, social, and environmental—and applied to four different scenarios defining the airport's possible future functions (business as usual, the main regional airport, etc.). While this study does not compare the relative usefulness of each analytic approach, it concludes that taken together, multicriteria methods provide decision makers with more useful tools for dealing with investment decisions that require choosing between inherently conflicting objectives (e.g., economic development vs. environmental sustainability).

Janic and Reggiani (2002) have used three similar MCA methods to evaluate potential locations for new European airports.[12] They employed three different scenarios for generating weights: equal weights, simulation, and entropy. After applying the three MCA methods to the scenarios, the authors concluded that these methods produced essentially the same results in terms of selecting the "best" out of seven sites for a new European hub airport (Table 6 in their study). On the other hand, if a single decision criterion was used, the actual choice of an airport became objective-specific. That is, a different solution emerged for a cost-minimization as compared with, say, profit-maximization objective.

The main conclusion reached from these and similar studies is that the choice of an alternative depends significantly more on the way the weights were generated than on the specific MCA method used. This conclusion invites a second one: the need to conduct a sensitivity analysis on the weights used to ascertain the robustness of the final ranking relative to marginal changes in the weights (see Section 4.3). This conclusion notwithstanding, the use of a MCA model in the overall project evaluation process is essential for making coherent, systematic, and transparent investment choices.

4. DECISION-SUPPORT TOOLS

In addition to the reviewed scoring-weighting methods, the literature proposes what can be thought of as support tools, useful when making infrastructure investment choices. However, some scoring and weighting may continue to be necessary because the objectives associated with each support tool tend to conflict.

4.1 Performance Measures

Following Fielding (1987), performance measures have been adopted, mainly in public transit, as a means to assess and monitor current performance as well as determine which capital investments will yield the highest return. Table 14.6, taken from Stuart (1997), shows the most common performance indicators used in public transit.

Given these measures, the choice among investment alternatives is made on the basis of which alternative is judged as capable of providing the highest level of performance. Obviously, this approach does not reduce the likelihood that one alternative will be superior to others in one or several measures but inferior in other measures. In such cases, weighting may become necessary.

4.2 Ordinal Methods

Sometimes, assignment of a cardinal score to an effect (e.g., improved quality of life or expansion of transit options) poses difficulties; in such cases, ordinal methods are called for. Ordinal choice methods rank projects on the

Table 14.6 Public Transit Performance Measures

Category of Performance Measures	Performance Indicators
1. Cost efficiency	Cost per mile
	Cost per hour
	Cost per vehicle
	Ridership per expense
2. Cost effectiveness	Cost per passenger trip
	Revenue per passenger trip
	Ridership per expense
3. Service utilization/Effectiveness	Passenger trips per mile
	Passenger trips per hour
	Passenger trips per capita
4. Vehicle utilization/Efficiency	Miles per vehicle
5. Quality of service	Average speed
	Vehicle miles between road calls
	Vehicle miles between accidents
6. Labor productivity	Passenger trips per employee
	Vehicle miles per employee
7. Coverage	Vehicle miles per capita
	Vehicle miles per service

basis of selected criteria without assigning quantitative values to them. It is *ordinal* in the sense that one can say that impact A is "better" than B, but without quantifying the amount by which A exceeds B. All ordinal methods require the assignment of objectives (criteria) to the chosen evaluation classes. Comparison of the ordinal rankings indicates the most desirable alternative (Holmes 1972; Nijkamp and Van Delft, 1977).

Ordinal measurement may not actually be critical even if multiple items are added together. It has long been shown that adding up multiple ordinal measures approximates creation of *interval scales* (see the classic works of Thurstone, 1928, and Likert, 1932).[13] When individual items are properly scaled, the various ordinal levels come to represent differences in the measured attribute, making the addition of multiple ordinal measures conducive to producing increasing levels of variation, what come very close to representing an interval scale. This methodology is commonly accepted among survey researchers (Meyers et al., 2005). Still, a key objection to the use of ordinal methods remains the difficulty in generating a final ranking of project alternatives.

4.3 The Appraisal Summary Table

Another useful approach to project prioritization is a two-step procedure resulting in the construction of an Appraisal Summary Table (AST), which is then used to provide detailed summary information on key aspects of each project. This information is subsequently subjected to an MCA procedure in order to systematically prioritize the alternative projects under resource availability constraints.

First introduced in 1988 by the British New Approach to Appraisal (NATA),[14] the AST summarizes major project impacts according to five fundamental criteria, in our case, environmental impact, road safety, economic value, modal accessibility, and regional integration (Vickerman, 2000). Some of these are further divided into sub-criteria in order to capture a wider variety of impacts. For example, environmental impacts are categorized into noise, air quality, landscape, biodiversity, and water quality, whereas economic value is shown as the product of time savings, operating costs, capital costs, and regeneration (economic development). Accessibility can include access to public transport, degree of community separation, and pedestrian accessibility.

Should an element integral to these criteria be difficult or impossible to quantify, its value is qualitatively indicated on an ordinal scale (e.g., small, medium, large, or neutral). The AST data represent the net effect of the project on each of the chosen criteria relative to a no-build option, or a benchmark value. The table itself represents a summary statement of the project's quantitative or monetary value. If these cannot be assessed, a descriptive ranking on a point scale can be provided (Price, 1999). To be sure, the AST approach is not meant to provide an automated ranking and selection procedure. Rather, as stated in its title, it summarizes the outcome of each criterion or subcriterion.

The NATA and AST schemes have been criticized on several grounds. NATA in particular provides no guidelines for weighting the five selected criteria, relying instead on the decision maker's assignment of the proper weights, what may be an unrealistic expectation in numerous circumstances. Further, it overlooks double-counting issues. For example, economic regeneration, as shown in Chapter 13, which can represent a capitalized impact of improved accessibility, appears in the AST along with the project's direct travel time and cost savings. Yet, in order to model and estimate economic development effects, it is analytically necessary to use travel costs and time savings as inputs. Nor does NATA deal with important issues such as risk and uncertainty although the value of time, used in all calculations, is based on a constant marginal unit value regardless of time saved or passenger income level.[15]

4.4 Testing the Final Ranking's Robustness

The next step is conduct of a sensitivity analysis in order to determine the results' robustness with respect to changes in weights. As an illustration of how such a test is conducted, we repeat the example of the GAM method (Section 2.4) but with only four criteria, as shown in Table 14.7.

Because of their importance the transportation and the economic development benefits criteria were tested twice. First, each received an equal weight.[16] Subsequently, the weights were changed to 30% and 70%, respectively. The test results are shown in Table 14.8.

Among equally weighted projects, D, A, and H rank as the top ones. When the weights are set at 30% for transportation benefits and 70% for economic development, the previous ranking remains stable, indicating that the rankings are quite robust with respect to these key criteria.

5. PREVALENCE OF MCA METHODS

Despite their seeming analytical sophistication and effectiveness as evaluation and selection tools, MCA methods have not gained universal acceptance by all of the countries using formal project assessment schemes. A survey shows that most countries use the B/C ratio rather than MCA as their key decision tool (Banister and Berechman, 2000, Table 7.3).[17] Moreover,

Table 14.7 Criteria and Weights[a]

Criterion	Weight
1. COBA Transportation	0.50
1. Calculated benefits per ride	
2. NPV transportation benefits	
3. Minimum benefits per ride	
4. Calculated benefits as percent of minimum benefits	
5. Rate of return of investments	
2. Other Transportation	0.125
1. Network time saved	
3. Project Construction Period	0.065
1. Years	(0.063)
4. Economic Development	0.310
1. PV economic development	(0.313)
2. PV of economic development per annual ride	
3. Economic development ratio	
Total	1.00

Note: [a]Initial exact weights are in parentheses.

Table 14.8 Summary of Scores with Different Weights[a]

Criteria	Projects							
	A	C	D	E	F	G	H	I
Transportation benefits (50%)	45.553	32.073	32.032	28.224	34.534	27.972	30.658	34.288
Economic development (50%)	31.536	17.743	50.00	4.877	19.179	18.778	37.138	1.322
Total weighted normalized score	77.089	49.78	82.032	33.101	53.713	46.75	67.797	35.61
Transportation benefits (30%)	27.332	19.222	19.219	16.934	20.72	16.783	18.395	20.573
Economic development (70%)	44.15	24.84	70.00	6.828	26.851	26.289	51.994	1.851
Total weighted normalized score	71.482	44.062	89.219	23.762	47.571	43.073	70.389	22.424

Source: Berechman and Paaswell (2005).
Notes: [a]For brevity, other criteria are not shown.

even if an MCA method is used, transportation criteria (mainly, travel time and costs savings) do not always play a primary role in project selection. In Spain, for instance, environmental, distributive, economic development, and transportation impacts are the four leading criteria, with the first three accounting for 80% of the total weight (López Suárez and Monzón de Cáceres, 2006). When ranking railroad projects in Taiwan, the key criteria employed were: (a) the project's status with respect to immediate construction; (b) the ratio of additional investment to total costs; (c) the availability of funding from the national government; (c) environmental impacts; (d) population relocation; and (e) travel time savings (Su et al., 2002).

Often, disputes over the implementation of transportation projects center on anticipated nontransportation impacts. That is, the focus of the debate is on the balance between cultural, social, natural resource preservation, and commercial interests rather than transportation quality.[18,19] In the context of MCA, this common phenomenon has several implications. First, as implied, transportation projects are not always viewed as investments whose main goal it is to confer transportation services to the public. Second, the real issue is frequently how to define objectives acceptable to all stakeholders and thus applicable to effective evaluation. A related factor is the need to derive a set of agreed-upon weights for MCA use. In brief, the generation of transportation benefits by a transportation investment is all too often neither a necessary nor a sufficient condition for project selection. Time and again, social and political realities dictate the agenda and take over the project selection process.

Project evaluation and selection practices in France provide an interesting example of the present disfavor in which MCA finds itself. In the 1980s and 1990s, original practices were phased out to the benefit of MCA but then brought back as the main evaluation tools (Quinet, 2000). That is, as a result of what were perceived to be wasteful capital-intensive projects, MCA caught the brunt of public criticism. Particularly attacked were groundlessly high weights assigned to subjective items, the lack of harmonization between the modes evaluated, and the discrepancies in time value assignments. As a result, it was recommended that calculation of impacts be based in the future exclusively on economic theory and methods, especially NPV and IRR. In addition, the duration and residual value of infrastructure in addition to first year rate of return was included as ranking criterion in the new approach (see Chapter 6 for definitions of these measures). Environmental effects, including noise and air pollution impacts and, more recently, global air quality, have also been monetized and incorporated into the economic analysis. This emphasis on a return to COBA does not mean, however, that equity issues remain outside the French selection process. Similarly, the project's potential to increase population density in the center city, a policy favoring public transit use, is also taken into account. On the other hand, under the French approach, economic development effects, particularly employment, are not considered in the analysis because they are viewed primarily as redistribution effects—gains in one region are treated as losses in another.

COBA in France currently encompasses the following core phases:

- Specification of the project's general goals
- Analysis of the needs to be met
- Technical descriptions of key variables such as traffic, VOT, travel time and cost savings, and capital costs
- Economic assessments of project alternatives from the perspective of users, operators (e.g., bus companies), and the community as a whole, using primarily NPV-type criteria

As this schematization indicates, NPV-type measures, rather than MCA, serve as the key appraisal and selection criteria.

In 2002, Germany proposed a revised evaluation methodology for the Federal Transport Infrastructure Plan (BMVBW, 2002). The methodology contains three main modules: transportation COBA, environmental risk assessment (ERA), and spatial impact assessment (SIA). A key objective of this scheme is to avoid double-counting of benefits, a common phenomenon that mars the validity of many evaluation procedures. In addition, it does not assign weights to the various impacts. As a result, the German methodology leaves the door quite open to the selection of projects geared to political outcomes.

Finally, the UK evaluation and selection procedure (NATA) lacks explicit guidance as to how the MCA should be used to identify the preferred project, as was previously pointed out (Section 4.3). That is, NATA specifies neither the weights to assign to various impacts nor how should they be engendered. As a result, the project selection phase—a critical part of NATA—remains rather subjective and open to criticism with respect to transparency and consistency (Sayers et al., 2003).

6. A PROPOSED PROJECT SELECTION SCHEME

It should be clear from the discussion in this chapter that the development and use of MCA methods is predicated on the recognition that the selection of one among a set of transportation investment alternatives should not be based on the net contribution of the direct transportation effects alone. Impacts such as environmental quality, equity, economic development, and land use must be addressed as well. Notwithstanding this determination, use of the MCA methodology raises some difficult concerns that, as the French, German, and British experience show, can devaluate its effectiveness as a project selection tool. The way weights are generated and assigned to each effect can transform project selection into a rather subjective process, subject to the preferences of stakeholders or political decision makers in isolation of other criteria, especially the true transportation impacts.

There seems to be no easy solution to this predicament as state and local policymakers are reluctant to forgo their power over transportation investment even when large-scale capital projects are financed through federal grants. One possible remedy to this state of affairs might be a mandatory project evaluation protocol explicitly stipulating that funds allotted to transportation are to be used only for projects that make significant net transportation contributions. To illustrate this principle, consider the hierarchical three-phase selection scheme as shown in Figure 14.1.

Given the set of investment alternatives, the first phase is a standard COBA to determine which of the alternative projects considered can meet a required net transportation contribution threshold. For example, a selection prerequisite might be that, say, 80% or more of the project's total benefits would be direct "transportation benefits." "Transportation benefits" is of course a broad heading, covering a myriad of transportation impacts ranging from highway congestion abatement to improved regional freight

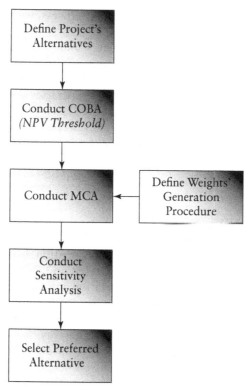

Figure 14.1 Proposed project selection scheme.

movement. Whatever the project's transportation objectives might be, such a clause would ensure that it will provide a minimum of transportation benefits and thus avoid the choice of inferior transportation investments. A subset of project alternatives that are worthy of implementation from a transportation perspective would result.

The second phase of this proposed selection scheme involves application of a MCA procedure that, like those described herein, is introduced to identify the "best" or the "preferred" project alternative. The key input in this phase is the set of weights generated by one of the procedures described in Section 2.3. We should recall, however, that even if a relatively low weight is assigned to a direct transportation effect, the project's total impacts will still be comprised mainly of transportation benefits thanks to the demands made in Phase One.

The third phase entails a sensitivity analysis conducted for the purpose of ascertaining the robustness of the results. In cases where the selection is shown to be rather sensitive to marginal changes in the assigned weights, the MCA procedure would be revisited.

In terms of the overall project evaluation process (Figure 2.2, Chapter 2), this proposed selection scheme should be incorporated into that part of the module labeled "project selection." That is, the figure's "choice" block would be composed of the above three-phase process, with the weights entered as inputs to the MCA phase (Step 2).

It is doubtful whether local stakeholders and decision makers would readily accept this or similar project selection schemes because they curtail the probability of implementing projects producing political booty. Furthermore, federal authorities in representative democracies are not immune to political pressure as exerted by representatives elected to state, provincial, or municipal government. At the minimum, however, we can hope that just having such a state or federal protocol will force stakeholders to introduce some rationality into their arguments and reveal the subjective weights they attach to each criterion.

7. SUMMARY AND CONCLUSIONS

Project selection is crucial to overall project evaluation. Its overt objective is to rank all alternative projects to be considered and, as a result, determine which is to be preferred. Since transportation infrastructure investments typically generate multiple transportation, equity, economic, land-use, and environmental impacts, the project selection process must account for as many as possible in a systematic and measurable way.

Multiple criteria analysis methods were developed for this very reason, as a means of bringing the consequences of investments into the project selection debate. All MCA methods therefore require the scoring of a full range of effects, the assignment of weights to reflect their relative importance and the use of a search method to identify the best alternative. To illustrate this process, a detailed description of the Goal Achievement Model appears in the appendix to this chapter.

While the scoring of the various effects is based, by and large, on quasi-objective measures such as travel time and cost savings, the weights assigned to each effect are not. They essentially reveal the subjective views of stakeholders and decision makers, which often reflect self-interest and political expediency. It is this subjective aspect of MCA that makes its application tenuous and open to criticism. Evidence from numerous transportation projects too often indicate that transportation investments are selected more on the basis of their alleged nontransportation effects, like economic development, than on their transportation impacts, whether modest or great. No wonder that MCA has been rejected as the key methodology for project selection in some countries (e.g., France) or supplemented with other measures (e.g., the UK).

To circumvent this and similar problems, given the basic tenet of this book that transportation investment projects should be selected, first and foremost, on the basis of their assessed transportation benefits, this chapter proposed a three-phase project selection scheme. At the core of this scheme is the idea that a transportation project should first pass a transportation benefits threshold test. That is, it must generate a predetermined level of significant and direct transportation benefits to qualify for implementation. Subsequent to meeting that threshold, it can be subjected to a formal MCA where the weights applied result from the use of an identifiable weight-generation procedure. The last phase of this scheme, sensitivity analysis, then ascertains the robustness of the final ranking with respect to changes in the weights.

Whatever procedure for project selection is adopted, this chapter's key message is that it must be rational, systematic, comprehensive, and, most importantly, transparent. All too often the lack of transparency, whether in reference to the criteria, the weights, or the selection process itself, results in totally erroneous transportation investment decisions. Since public resources are rather scarce, wasteful investments result in the weakening of the overall transportation system.

APPENDIX A: ANALYTICAL PRESENTATION OF THE GOAL ACHIEVEMENT MATRIX METHOD

1. The Score Matrix: Q. Let q_{ij}^k be an element in an $M \times N \times K$ matrix, Q, whose rows i, $(i = 1, \ldots, M)$ are criteria, each subdivided into k $(k = 1, \ldots, K)$ items, with columns j $(j = 1, \ldots, N)$ representing alternatives. Because each criterion is defined and therefore scored in different units, we need to normalize the scores. This can be done in various ways, provided that after normalization, all scores are comparable and linear-additive.

2. *The Normalized Matrix:* S. Let r_{ij}^k be an element in a $M \times N \times K$ matrix of normalized scores. Let $s_{ij} = \sum_k^K r_{ij}^k$ be an element in an $M \times N$ matrix, S, of total normalized scores for each of the main criteria for each alternative.

3. *The Weights Matrix:* W. Let w_i be an $M \times 1$ vector of weights, showing which M criteria are considered crucial and what weight (w_i) is assigned to each ($\sum_{i=1}^M w_i = 1.0$). Let w_{ij} be an element in an $M \times M$ matrix, W, defined as: $w_{ij} = [w_i]^T \times [I]$, where $[w_i]^T$ is the transposed w_i vector and thus is a $(1 \times M)(M \times M)$ product) and $[I]$ is the identity matrix.[20]

4. *The Weighted Normalized Score Matrix:* T. Let t_{ij} be an element in an $M \times N$ matrix, T, whose ij element is defined as:

$$t_{ij} = [w_{ij}] \times [s_{ij}] \tag{A1}$$

or

$$T = W \times S \tag{A2}$$

5. *The Weighted (Normalized) Score Vector of Projects:* V_j. It is defined as:

$$V_j = \sum_{i=1}^M t_{ij} \tag{A3}$$

6. *The Highest Scoring Project:* V^*. The highest score, V^*, is defined as:

$$V^* = \max_j (V_j) \tag{A4}$$

15 Why Are Inferior Transportation Investment Projects Selected?

1. INTRODUCTION

This book has examined a significant number of methods and techniques to be used in project assessment and selection. As Chapter 6 (Appendix C) has shown, many countries employ these and similar analytical tools for transportation project evaluation. Yet, all too often, projects that rank very low or even fail COBA tests are nonetheless implemented. A legitimate question to be asked in such circumstances is why decision makers implement projects that had been judged unworthy or inferior in the evaluation process that they themselves may have initiated? We define "inferior projects" as those that do not pass common benefit-cost analysis tests or obtain very low scores on comparative scoring tests (see Chapter 14). When applying a financial criterion, inferior projects are those whose alternatives can be clearly shown to yield higher rates of return. This chapter is therefore devoted to responding to the issue of inferior project selection as well as the policy implications of such tendencies for actual project assessment and selection.

Because a significant number of public investments in major infrastructure projects require the input of a highly diverse group of public authorities, special interest groups, political stakeholders, and technical experts, decision making—by definition—becomes a very complex process. To simplify the analysis, we cluster these diverse actors into two groups, "technical analysts" and "administrative/political decision makers," in the ensuing discussion. From the perspective of rational planning, members of the first group utilize their technical expertise to carry out systematic analyses of the transportation, engineering, economic, social, and environmental features of a set of alternative projects. They subsequently communicate their findings, together with conclusions as to which investment option yields the highest welfare contribution, to members of the second group. Based on this information, the latter group is mandated to reach decisions regarding the project to implement. If we content ourselves with this model we will reach an incomplete if not erroneous understanding of how decisions are in fact made. That is, members of the second group have access to additional information pertaining to project funding feasibility, constraints, and trade-offs stipulated by law, in addition to a propensity to "read" the electorate.

The core question should therefore be rephrased as to why do decision makers frequently *reject* the findings and recommendations of the technical experts, only to select inferior projects? Berechman and Paaswell (2005), for example, using accepted methodologies to evaluate a set of transportation investment projects in New York, ranked these projects according to a number of transportation, economic, and environmental criteria.[1] Decision makers nevertheless selected projects ranked inferior according to this analysis. To paraphrase the issue, what can we say is the role or weight, if any, of technical assessment in project evaluation and selection? Are the methods and techniques examined in this book merely used to support predetermined choices?

This chapter is consequently structured as follows. Section 2 proposes some hypotheses to explain why inferior projects are selected. Section 3 presents three large-scale rail investment projects currently under construction as "data" to be explained by Section 4, which compares these investments according to several key dimensions and then draws conclusions regarding the factors most responsible for the projects' implementation. A summary and conclusions are found in Section 5.

2. SOME HYPOTHESES REGARDING THE SELECTION OF INFERIOR PROJECTS

Why are inferior projects selected? One hypothesis states that the investment's objectives as well as its metrics are poorly defined and subject to political disagreement. Whereas transportation planners and analysts would point to transportation benefits, like improved accessibility, as the investment's main objectives, political decision makers would identify nontransportation benefits such as job creation and real estate development as its main goals. A second hypothesis is that different actors apply different selection criteria when making choices. A third hypothesis is that political considerations, such as the ability to secure funding or to form a coalition for the project's approval, or to satisfy some constituents and political supporters, are the driving decision-making motives. A fourth hypothesis is that the allotment of federal funding—a significant source of capital for local and state projects, especially mega-projects—is only loosely conditioned on evidence showing genuine transportation and economic development benefits. Finally, the lack of required transparency and accountability in public decision making eases implementation of unworthy projects. The task before us is, therefore, to identify the key factors that determine which project will be selected for implementation in practice.

To gain some insight into the process, we conducted a comparative analysis of three mega-projects currently under construction. Our objective was to understand why these projects were selected even though they could not be justified as the best transportation investment alternatives using a formal COBA. The projects were compared along several dimensions: investment objectives, project type and alternatives, system details, computed benefits and costs, COBA process, funding, and decision making. Obviously, this was not meant to be a comprehensive investigation into the issue, one that would require a large sample of projects. Instead, we use the results of this comparison to shed some light on the factors that best explain the selection of inferior projects.

3. THREE CASE STUDIES

The case studies examined below were selected for several reasons. First, they are mega-projects, which by their very nature are difficult to assess and implement; second, they are rail projects, notorious for cost overruns and overestimation of benefits; third, they are currently being implemented in three different countries, thereby facilitating a more global view of the issues examined.

3.1 Tel Aviv Light Rail

Background

In 1973, the Israeli government decided to promote mass transit in the Tel Aviv metropolitan area. At that time, the government allocated an initial sum for the purpose of examining the project's main engineering and transportation-economic features. Since then, a growing debate has been conducted among transportation professionals, the Ministries of Transportation and the Treasury, as well as the Tel Aviv Municipality, most vociferously during the 1990s, over the project's rationale and the kind of system to be built. The Municipality favored an underground subway that would be faster and more convenient while others, primarily the Ministry of Finance, argued that such a project was too expensive and that an above-ground light rail network was preferable. To promote the project as a policy objective, a Metropolitan Mass Transit Authority (NTA) was established by the government, with actual planning begun in 1997. Out of several alternative configurations, the one shown in Figure 15.1 was selected. In 2000, the first LRT (the Red Line) was submitted to national planning authorities for approval. The project's completion date was set at 2010 although 2013 currently appears to be more realistic.

Transportation Design and Planning

The overall system, as planned, consists of several Light Rail Transit (LRT) lines (indicated in Figure 15.1 as the Red, Green, and Purple Lines; the

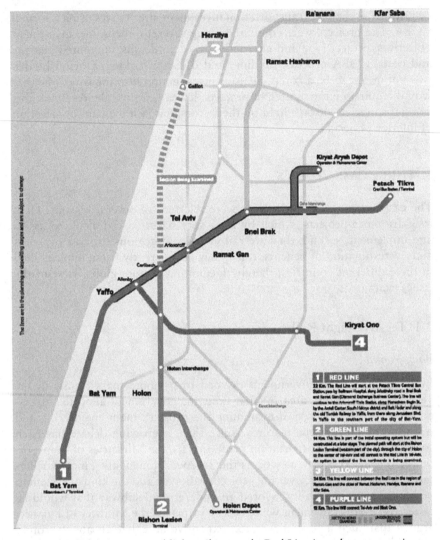

Figure 15.1 Tel Aviv proposed light rail network; Red Line is under construction.

Source: NTA—Metropolitan Mass Transit Authority, http://www.nta.co.il/site/en/
neta.asp?pi=41.

Yellow and Orange Lines are currently under discussion), and several Bus
Rapid Transit (BRT) lines. The project currently under construction is the
Red Line, whose length is 22 kilometers, with approximately 10 kilometers
underground. Twenty-two stations are planned for the route's above- and
underground segments. Expected total travel time from one end of the line
to the other is 43 minutes. Planned service frequency at peak periods is one
train every 3 minutes at ground level and every 1.5 minutes underground.

The project's planning included the traditional four stages. Traffic assignment was carried out with a static assignment model, using several iterations between the assignment, the modal split, and the trip distribution models. Other features of the model included market segmentation by ownership and car availability, five trip categories (home-work, home-school, home-shopping, home-other, nonhome), five time periods, direct and related parking costs (e.g., costs of parking search); and several combinations of main mode with other modes (e.g., bus with LRT). The database included then-current 1995 and 1996 population and travel census surveys augmented by two cordon and stated preference (SP) surveys.

Demand Projections

Initial ridership projections indicated 430,000 passenger-trips per day (in 2020) on the Red Line and 300,000 per day on the Green Line. These projections were soon criticized for being inflated and based on unrealistic assumptions. For example, planners assumed total parking unavailability in the Red Line corridor (thus excessive parking search time and costs); they applied peak modal split ratios to other hours of the day; and they made very generous population and employment projections in areas within or adjacent to the light rail corridor.

Cost Projections

Initially, the project's costs were estimated in the range of IS6–7 billion (Israeli shekels, about $1.75b–$2b in 2008 prices). Since then, these estimates have been revised several times; by 2008, they were estimated at $NIS^2 11$ billion ($2.75b–$3.15b depending on the exchange rate), a cost escalation of 57%–87% at the time of writing (these figures are not final). For lack of transparency, we were unable to determine what these sums actually cover. However, it is clear that they disregard the costs of traffic delays, fuel, loss of productivity, and loss of income by businesses in the region, estimated at NIS1 billion annually for the planned 6 years of construction.

Economic Viability

Because no detailed COBA report was ever published (based on the argument of commercial confidentiality), it is difficult to ascertain whether the project is economically viable. Indirect calculations raise doubts about its economic feasibility. Assume, for example, 300 days of operation annually and 430,000 passengers per day, each making 2 trips daily. Under the current public transit fare regime, these estimates imply total annual farebox revenue of NIS 258 million. If total annual debt service plus maintenance and operating costs constitute 20% of capital costs (about NIS2.2b), farebox revenue will cover only about 12% of the project's annual costs.

Funding

This is a public funding initiative (PFI) project. The duration of the contract, including the 6 years of construction, is 32 years. The government has agreed to pay the concessionaire (the MTS Group) the sum of NIS 8.6 billion (paid in NIS and in Euros), or about 80% of total capital costs. The rest is being funded by the MTS group.

Decision Making

The project's main stakeholders are the Ministries of Transportation and Finance in addition to the Municipalities of Tel Aviv-Yafo and adjacent towns. The mandate of the overseeing agency (NTA) includes conduct of the transportation-economic analysis of the project, engineering and urban planning, managing the tendering process for selection of a private sector concessionaire, and construction oversight. Save for the Ministry of Finance, all other stakeholders have vested interests in completion of the Red Line. As a result of their relentless pressure, once the Ministry of Finance approved the Red Line as a PFI project, it became a certainty. In addition, the present project has encountered virtually no authentic professional or political challenges, especially with respect to the NTA's costs and demand projections. This lack of open debate facilitated the project's acceptance by the public and the media.

3.2 New York City's Second Avenue Subway (SAS)

Background

Three north-south transit lines served Manhattan's East Side in the 1920s. To make way for residential and commercial development, the Second Avenue elevated rail line (the "El") was torn down in 1940; 15 years later (1956), the Third Avenue "El" was also torn down, which left only the underground Lexington subway line to accommodate the city's entire East Side. From the perspective of routes, it appears that the rationale for constructing the SAS was established in the 1920s, long before the "El" lines were demolished. In the 1970s, three tunnel sections were constructed but eventually abandoned due to the city's financial crisis. The current rationale for renewing the project rests on hopes of lessening overcrowding and delays on the Lexington Line as well as improving travel times for East Side residents. Politically, the SAS was linked to the East Side Access (ESA) project, which connects Long Island with Grand Central Terminal. Stated differently, if benefits were to be dispersed to the ESA's clientele (mainly Long Island's Nassau county residents), Manhattan's East Side residents must also benefit. New York's Metropolitan Transportation Authority (MTA) was put in charge of transportation-economic planning and construction.

Transportation Design and Planning

The entire line will stretch from Harlem (125th Street) to New York's financial district (Hanover Square). It is to be built in four phases. The present phase stretches from 96th Street to 63rd Street, with four stations; the other three phases are still to be scheduled.[3] The section of the project currently under construction is shown in Figure 15.2 as the Red Line. It is expected to open in 2014.

Demand Projections

About 591,000 daily passenger-trips were projected for the entire SAS project, with 200,000 daily passenger-trips projected for Phase 1. These projections were obtained from regional population and employment forecasts but not corroborated with other methods, network analysis, and local surveys, to name two.

Costs Projections

Initial estimates for the entire line were US$12.5 billion, not including debt service, operating, and maintenance costs, with US$4 billion allocated to the first phase. Thus far, the MTA has been forced to add an additional sum of US$54 million to its budget to acquire real estate and cover construction, with an additional US$17 million for tunnel drilling.

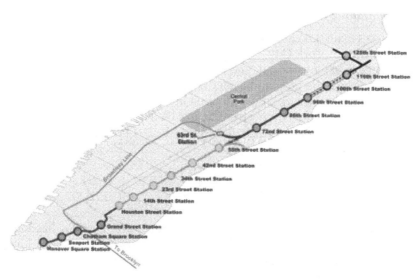

Figure 15.2 The NY Second Avenue Line.

Source: Metropolitan Transit Authority (http://www.mta.info/capconstr/sas/).

Economic Viability

Save for the analysis reported by Berechman and Paaswell (2005), neither the entire project nor its first phase have been subjected to a complete COBA. An environmental impact analysis was carried out in 2001. In 2003, a supplemental draft environmental impact statement (SDEIS) for the full length of the SAS was prepared, followed by public hearings and preparation of a final environmental impact statement (FEIS). Engineering planning (EP) of the project was subsequently carried out. In effect, the SDEIS, FEIS, and EP were treated as substitutes for a comprehensive COBA. It has been estimated that the SAS investment would produce the equivalent of 70,000 full-time direct and indirect jobs in addition to time savings, reliability improvements, and overcrowding relief valued at US$1.26 billion annually (Regional Planning Association, 2003).[4] Two other attempts to quantify the SAS's potential economic development benefits in terms of additional square feet of office space and residential unit development, tax revenues, and jobs stimulated were able to predict a respective $320 million and $100 million annually in terms of the present value of tax revenues.[5]

Funding

Federal government funding is to provide US$1.3 billion (over 7 years), which is one-third of the cost of the SAS's first phase ($4b). Additional funding is expected to come from the sale of bonds by the MTA.

Decision Making

The project's main stakeholders were the governor of New York State (NYS), the mayor of New York City (NYC), senators representing the State of New York, the Federal Government, and the MTA. Given that all of these stakeholders supported the project, together with a number of civic groups, once federal funding was secured, the SAS faced little opposition. Presently, however, the combination of cost overruns and MTA inability to raise funds may affect construction and, as a result, its meeting the 2014 completion deadline.

3.3 The Vancouver-Canada Line (RAV Line)

Background

The Vancouver International Airport-City of Vancouver corridor has long been recognized as requiring a rapid mass transit system. The Canada Line (previously known as the Richmond-Airport-Vancouver or RAV Line) was considered to be the means by which to link, by rail, Vancouver's Central Business District (CBD) with its international airport and thus reduce traffic congestion. RAV Project Management Ltd. (RAVCO), a public agency, was created specifically to oversee the project's design, procurement, construction and implementation. Despite its extensive promotion, the project ranked lower than other corridor projects in the region based on planning criteria set by RAVCO (2003) itself. A regional congestion study showed that by 2021, the region would be facing severe congestion conditions (levels E and F). While this impact would be felt region-wide, most of the congested roads would not be near or within the Canada Line corridor.[6] In terms of daily car trips, it was estimated that the Canada Line would remove 18,000 cars from the corridor's roads, representing just 6% of the corridor's daily car trips. The project is shown in Figure 15.3 as the Red Line.

Transportation Design and Planning

This project entails construction of an automated light metro system. The line's length is approximately 19 kilometers, with some sections at grade, others underground, and one elevated section. The number of planned stations is 16. The Canada Line project will augment Vancouver's existing transit system, which includes two automatic light rail lines (Skytrain), a commuter railroad, and an extensive bus network.

Demand Projections

It has been estimated that by 2010, approximately 100,000 daily riders will use the system. Travel time savings along the entire line was estimated to be 27–34 minutes, based on current travel times by a bus traveling along the proposed route.

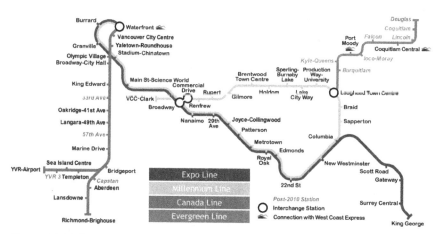

Figure 15.3 The Vancouver-Canada (RAV) Line.

Source: RAVCO (2003), (www.canadaline.ca/aboutoverview.asp).

Costs Projections

In 2001, the project's cost estimates had reached CAN$1.24 billion. By 2005, that estimate had grown to CAN$1.72 billion, with the bidding price at CAN$1.889 billion (in 2003 dollars), representing an increase of over 50% above the initial estimates.

Economic Viability

Save for some preliminary studies, no comprehensive COBA was carried out to estimate this project's net economic contribution (Siemiatycki, 2006).

Funding

The 2005 budget (CAN$1.72b) is to be covered as follows: CAN$450 million by the federal government, CAN$300 million by TransLink (the regional transit oversight authority), CAN$300 million by the Vancouver Airport Authority, CAN$365 million by the Province of British Columbia, and CAN$200–$250 million by the private sector. The private concessionaire will design, build, operate, and maintain the system for 30–35 years, after which it will hand the system to the Province of British Columbia at a set price to be paid by TransLink. It is also estimated that project will generate about $105 million of new revenues in parking and airport fees (RAVCO, 2003).

Decision Making

The main stakeholders in the Canada Line project are the federal and provincial governments, TransLink, the Vancouver International Airport Authority, the City of Vancouver and adjacent municipalities. Since about 80% of the funding comes from sources other than Province of British Columbia coffers, the project presented the province with strong incentives to aggressively lobbying for it. While it took 3 votes by TransLink directors to finally approve it, the project has faced little serious professional or political opposition.[7]

4. COMPARISON OF THE THREE SYSTEMS

In order to help draw some lessons from these three case studies, Table 15.1 compares them along several key dimensions.

4.1 Key Lessons

From the information exhibited in Table 15.1 it seems that history plays a significant role in determining how a project first appears on the public and political agenda. By "history" we mean the prior events that planted the idea of the project in the mind of the public and political decision makers. Each of the three cases has a long history that laid the groundwork for stakeholders' recognition of the project's "indispensability." Once the idea of such mega-projects became entrenched, it created a policy vision that framed a specific project as more feasible than its alternatives. When strategic choices came to be made, these visions ruled (Bradford, 2000). Supporting our causal account is the work of Lovallo and Kahneman (2003), who have argued that once a plan becomes anchored in their minds, executives and decision makers tend to conduct the kind of analysis that affirms their beliefs. They then go on to advocate these subconscious decisions by exaggerating their benefits and discounting their costs.

A second common factor that may explain why a particular project is aggressively promoted is the role of the institution—a public agency or private organization—assigned to analyze, plan, and then market the project. As the funding and operation of these bodies are linked to the project's planning and execution, a strong incentive is created in favor of lobbying for and promoting the project's selection and eventual completion. Lenient accountability standards and a lack of transparency facilitate the exercise of these forces. And so, as indicated in Table 15.1, the agency in charge of realizing the project in all three cases was the same agency in charge of conducting the transportation-economic evaluation as well as assessing its investment alternatives.

A third common factor is the substantial reliance of the three projects on external funding, whether federal or private. Tel Aviv light rail and the Canada Line would not have been approved for implementation unless they were structured as PPP or PFI-type projects. These realities have created strong pressures to implementing the projects irrespective of their transportation-economic value. As noted in Chapter 9, the greater the funding coming from outside the jurisdiction where the project is destined to be built, the greater the propensity of local political decision makers to assume more risk and select more-expensive projects. In addition, the potential for private sector funding creates strong incentives for local and federal governments to support the project, irrespective of its true contribution. One side effect of such arrangements is the loss of transparency. By their very nature, PPP projects require a large degree of confidentiality to protect the commercial interests of potential bidders. As a result, critical information—such as projected patronage, actual costs, risk-sharing arrangements, and the project's overall economic worth—remain hidden from public scrutiny.

The three projects examined above are rail mega-projects that, as noted by Altshuler and Luberoff (2003), resonate well with many powerful interest groups despite their poor performance. These groups include construction firms, consulting firms, labor unions, environmentalists, and social policy advocates. Not to build is a decision that would therefore incur the sizeable political penalties that reinforce the project's acceptance by decision makers.

Table 15.1 Comparison of Three Mega-Projects

Indicator/Project	Tel Aviv Light Rail	New York Second Avenue Subway	Vancouver Canada (RAV) Line
Objectives			
Declared objectives	Highway congestion relief; Environmental improvements	Subway congestion relief; Economic development; Air quality	Highway congestion relief; Economic development; Access to airport; Air quality
Quantitative planning objectives	No	No	No
Project and Alternatives			
Role of history in project selection	Significant	Significant	Significant (tentative)
Investment alternatives	LRT, BRT	Bus lanes	Unknown
Related transportation investments	Suburban rail	Suburban rail	Highways and bridges
System Details			
Type	Under/above-ground light rail	Subway	Under/above-ground light rail
Length & O-D	22 km; suburbs-CBD	4.8 km	20 km; CBD-airport-suburb
Stations	32	4	16
Time horizon	32 years (including 6 for construction)	35 Years	30 Years
Computation of Benefits			
Ridership forecasts/time savings	430,000/day passengers; highly unlikely	Phase 1: 200,000/day; highly unlikely	100,000/day (in 2010); 17–27 min./trip unlikely
Peak-period highway congestion	Limited effect	No effect	Limited effect
Effect on modal share	Assessed as significant	No effect	Assessed as significant
Economic development estimates	Not analyzed	Assumed to be very large	31,000 new jobs projected; $4.9b wages

Table 15.1 (Continued)

Indicator/Project	Tel Aviv Light Rail	New York Second Avenue Subway	Vancouver Canada (RAV) Line
Equity (benefits to population)	Mainly users living in corridor	Subway users on parallel lines	CBD employees and airport travelers
Environmental Externalities	Unknown	Computed as significant	Assumed high

Computation of Direct Costs			
Capital costs	Initial estimate: NIS 5–7b ; Presently NIS 10b	Entire project $12.5b; First phase: $4–$5b	CAN$1.24b (2001) CAN$1.889b bid
Maintenance costs	Not calculated for COBA	Not calculated for COBA	$28m–$36m/year (2010)
Risk of cost overruns in COBA	Not accounted for	Not accounted for	Not accounted for
Risk allocation (PPP)	Concessionaire receives 85% of costs	Unknown	Unknown

Formal COBA			
Benefit/cost ratio (transportation benefits only)	B/C < 1 ($r = 5\%$)	B/C < 1 ($r = 5\%$)	B/C ≈ 1 ($r = 5\%$); B/C ≈ 1 ($r = 7\%$)

Funding			
Source of funding	State, private sector	Federal, state, MTA	Federal, province, airport, private
PPP	PFI	No	BMOT

Decision Making			
Main stakeholders	Tel Aviv and adjacent municipalities, Ministries of Transportation and Finance	NYS, NYC, federal government, MTA	Province of BC; Airport (YVR); Vancouver; adjacent municipalities; federal government
Overseeing agency	NTA	MTA	RAVCO
Key decision makers	Ministries of Transportation & Finance	NYC Mayor, NYS Governor, US DOT	TransLink, Province's Premier, Federal Ministry of Finance
Role of private sector	Significant	Partial	Significant

A direct result of this decision-making environment is the dissemination of misinformation by project's proponents, including the organization designated to plan and implement it (Flyvbjerg, 2003; Siemiatycki, 2006; Wachs, 1989). Such misinformation is transmitted in intentionally underestimated costs and overestimated benefits along with undervalued environmental impacts and inflated urban/regional economic development benefits. A biased analysis of the project's benefits and costs follows directly from these conditions.

5. SUMMARY AND CONCLUSIONS

This chapter has attempted to respond to the question of why unworthy transportation investment projects are implemented while better alternative investments, having higher returns, are not. Edwards and Mackett (1996) as well as Pickrell (1992) have suggested that when it comes to rail projects, cities are quite irrational in their investment decision making. Lane (2008) has found that such decisions can be explained by the wish of decision makers to sustain a vibrant image of their city along with promises of potential economic development benefits.

In order to gain some insight into this issue, we delved into the key factors that tend to explain the selection of transportation investment projects. To that end, the chapter compared three rail mega-projects currently under construction in three different countries. The analysis showed that four factors can best explain this rather persistent phenomenon. First, each project has a long history that helped to embed the idea of such projects in the minds of the public and decision makers; second, we find the ability to secure funding, mainly from the central government, often prior to any comprehensive cost-benefit assessment of the project; and third, establishment of an agency or private organization to be responsible for the analysis, planning, *as well as* implementation of the project. The fourth factor is the lack of transparency and accountability, which is manifested in all three cases by the failure to published detailed COBA reports showing how these projects' benefits and costs were estimated and to whom they accrue. A union of these factors can practically guarantee a project's selection. While history is not controlled by sitting decision makers, attempts to secure funding, set up an agency, and divulge critical information to public scrutiny are, to a considerable degree, within their domain of responsibility. We are forced to conclude that the hypotheses cited in Section 2, especially the last three, have been confirmed by this analysis.

Based on the preceding analysis, we offer the following suggestions, all of which can potentially improve transportation investment decision making.

1. Different agencies should be put in charge of analyzing the transportation-economic rationales of proposed projects and carrying out any

detailed planning and construction. Alternatively, each project should be required to undergo a comprehensive COBA prior to the final selection stage. The analysis would then be reviewed by an independent panel of experts.

2. Mandatory transparency and openness to public scrutiny are to be integrated into the project selected process. Political factors and the relative weights given to the criteria applied by a COBA would also be subject to these requirements.

3. Every project COBA must include a risk analysis, including PPP or PFI type projects.

4. Legislation should be passed stipulating that funding will be conditional on the completion of a comprehensive COBA of each project and its alternatives.

Shareholders in private businesses demand that critical capital investments be made with the help of sophisticated yet transparent analytical techniques. Shareholders in major infrastructure investments—the general public—likewise deserve transparent decision tools. In closing, we can only say that all contemplated as well as implemented projects should convey to citizens that "these were dollars well spent!"

Notes

NOTES TO CHAPTER 1

1. Under the heading "Light rail, with an emphasis on light," *The New York Times* ran a story on the River Line light rail system running between Camden and Trenton, New Jersey, a 34-mile line along the Delaware river, which so far has cost the state over $1 billion to build, with annual costs of $65 million. It delivers fewer than 6,000 one-way trips per day so that each trip costs the taxpayers about $30 for operating and debt service costs. (More recently, New Jersey Transit reported 7,600 daily passenger-trips). The article quotes Prof. James Dunn of Rutgers University, who sensibly observed that for the political decision makers who built this and similar systems, transportation needs are beside the point; jobs, contracts, and influence are the project's true benefits (*The New York Times*, Metro Section, March 13, 2004).

NOTES TO CHAPTER 2

1. An excellent discussion of the political aspects of transportation project evaluation can be found in Altshuler and Luberoff (2003).
2. The massive drop in the demand for transit and auto travel following the tragic events of September 11, 2001, in New York City is a case in a point. This drop in demand (which has since picked up) partially reflects the loss of jobs and capacity. In general, though, the relationship between ridership and security concerns is far from clear.
3. See, for example, AASHTO (2003).
4. The model is based on the notion that economic outcomes and voting behavior are correlated (Downs, 1957). The model then predicts that if the distribution of voters by their skills were such that the distribution's Mean is greater than the Median, the result would be overprovision of public goods.
5. For a comprehensive discussion of transportation planning and project design see for example Ortuzar and Willumsen (2001).
6. For a detailed discussion of how transportation projects actually penetrate the public agenda see Altshuler and Lubeboff (2003, Chapters 7, 8).
7. "The West Side's Yours, Ground Zero Mine," the *New York Times*, (March 27, 2004).
8. In early 2002, following the September 11 tragedy, New York State's governor established a new public body, the Lower Manhattan Development Corporation (LMDC), to oversee the rebuilding of infrastructure and development in Lower Manhattan. The governor controls the LMDC's board. While the

rebuilding of damaged infrastructure remained the responsibility of the specific operating agencies (reopening of MTA transit stations and rebuilding the PANYNJ PATH station), the integration of these facilities and design approaches to new infrastructure was assigned to the LMDC. The corporation received unique planning and building powers that were usually kept within the purview of previously existing agencies and authorities.

9. Changing signaling to allow higher speeds in one section of a rail route makes no sense unless similar investments are made elsewhere along the network (Nash and Preston, 1993).

10. Often in large metropolitan areas there are several planning organizations overseeing land use and transportation systems, each with its own objectives and agenda. The TIP then represents the resolution of these agencies' collective negotiations.

11. Some claim that the Governor of New York's support for the direct rail project to JFK airport is just a red herring. The real reason for his support is the attempt to keep major brokerage firms presently located in Manhattan's downtown from moving to mid-town (Berechman and Paaswell, 2005).

12. The Buffalo Light Rail project, whose stated objective was to revitalize the declining downtown area, is a case in a point (see Berechman and Paaswell, 1983)

13. Here we ignore the recent literature on the role of travel for travel's sake. For a good analysis of this literature see Mokhtarian and Salomon (2001).

NOTES TO CHAPTER 3

1. This chapter assumes the reader's familiarity with microeconomics as well as welfare concepts and principles. For a basic introduction see Friedman (1985); for a more advanced analysis see Varian (1992).

2. One noted case is the attitude towards the financing of public goods, that is, consumers' willingness to contribute towards paying the costs of a public good. This willingness is significantly influenced by notions of fairness relative to a person's conception of his fair share of costs. Stated differently, an individual's notion of other people's contributions becomes the reference point for his/her decision making.

3. It should also be pointed out that interpersonal utility comparisons are routinely performed at all levels, including the political level, when conducting socioeconomic public policy analyses (see Friedman, 1985, Chapter 5).

4. Equity issues are discussed in Chapter 9.

5. In competitive markets, prices provide correct signals relative to the benefits and costs of the respective goods and services. Section 5 discusses benefits assessment when markets are noncompetitive.

6. Further references to the welfare underpinnings of COBA can be found in Vickrey (1960), Small (1999), and Boardman et al. (2001).

7. A strong Pareto optimum allocation is defined as the case in which no other feasible allocation is strictly preferred by at least one person and not opposed by all others. A weak Pareto optimum is defined when an allocation is strictly preferred by *all* individual, i.e., all must gain from it.

8. See Kaldor (1939), Hicks (1940), and Scitovsky (1941) for early discussions of the social welfare function. Arrow (1963) provides axiomatic treatment of the subject. An additional treatment is by Harberger (1978).

9. In the literature, the term "externalities in transportation" is often used to describe two distinct sets of effects, environmental externalities (e.g., air pollu-

tion), and secondary effects (e.g., job creation). Chapters 12 and 13 deal with these effects in turn.

10. Small (1999) argues that since transportation projects may also generate negative impacts such as environmental nuisances, the willingness to pay principle can be applied to indicate the amount of money consumers are willing to pay to avoid such harmful effects. The problem is that, by and large, these effects have no markets so that an individual's ability to correctly assess their value is rather questionable.

11. The Slutsky effect (or equation) refers to the change in demand from a one-unit change in price, which is the sum of two distinct effects—the substitution effect and the income effect—induced by a price change.

12. Historically, Dupuit was probably the first to use consumer surplus, also called the Marshallian consumer surplus (Quinet, 1998), as a measure of welfare in the context of public works projects (Dupuit, 1844). Krutilla (2005) reviews the Kaldor–Hicks distributional accounting method of wefare effects from a policy change.

13. Travel price, which reflects the total generalized costs of travel, includes monetary expenses (car usage and tolls, if any), travel time costs (including in-vehicle, wait, and transfer time), and other travel amenities (e.g., ease of access and egress).

14. This is a marginal cost function for the supply of additional units of road space. In transportation network analysis, S_1 represents the volume-capacity function, which shows travel time (cost) as a function of travel volume. See Chapter 7.

15. That is, $S = MC = \sum_i mc_i$, where mc_i is the marginal cost curve of firm i.

16. In the case where $MC = AC$, the supply curve S is horizontal and producer surplus is zero since revenues exactly equal production costs, including capital costs.

17. Since travel costs are a function of travel volumes *and* capacity, a true first-best solution requires that equilibrium is set where capacity is optimized. This, however, rarely happens, especially in urban transportation, where restrictions such as land availability and zoning preclude the attainment of optimal network capacity.

18. The term *Pigouvian taxes* is named after Arthur C. Pigou (1877–1959), a British economist, best known for his work in welfare economics. In his book *The Economics of Welfare*, Pigou further developed Alfred Marshall's concept of externality costs imposed or benefits conferred on others, ignored by the person taking an action. He argued that the existence of externalities was sufficient to justify government intervention. His reason: Someone's creation of a negative externality, e.g., congestion, implies that he is engaging in an excessive level of the activity that generated the externality. Someone creating a positive externality, say, by educating himself and making himself a better citizen, would not invest enough in education because he would not perceive education's value to himself as being equivalent to education's value to society. To discourage activities that cause negative externalities, Pigou advocated a tax on the activity. To encourage activities that created positive externalities, he advocated a subsidy. These are now called Pigouvian taxes and subsidies.

19. At times, the term "third-best" solution is used to indicate that as a result of several institutional, physical, and financial constraints, not even second-best type solutions are attainable.

20. For an analysis that takes these effects into account within the framework of aviation networks, see Blum (1998) as well as Adler and Berechman (2001).

21. It has been noted that if markets were sufficiently competitive, benefits adhering to one group would be fully offset by costs adhering to another (Small, 1999a). Put differently, in competitive markets, pecuniary externalities amount to transfers between economic entities. Yet, in the context of urban transportation, markets are rarely competitive; hence, pecuniary externalities are unlikely to be pure transfers.

22. The social marginal benefit is low because buses are, on average, only partially full per trip. Also, we assume that transit impact on highway congestion is negligible.

23. Total costs are: $TC(V) = S(V) \cdot V$, where $S(V) = AC(V)$ is the average cost function and V is volume.
$$MC(V) = \frac{\partial TC(V)}{\partial V}.$$

24. A related welfare-reducing effect arises from the fact that under this regulation scheme, the producer requires a public subsidy to sustain operations. Such a subsidy will have to be financed by increased taxation, which introduces further distortions in the form of deadweight losses from taxation. On the other hand, these negative effects have to be balanced against equity impacts on transit users (see Chapter 11).

25. In comparing this expression with previous ones (expression (16)), the areas over which the integration is carried out must be noted.

26. Note that as a result of the decline in volume, travel speed might increase, thereby making travel time shorter, implying lower travel costs p''. However, since we focus on the case of flat toll in the absence of congestion, total users' costs, including the toll, are greater than they were at the initial equilibrium price p^*. That is, $p' = (p'' + \rho) > p^*$.

NOTES TO CHAPTER 4

1. It should be noticed that for transit, costs are *not* a direct function of passenger-trips but, rather, of vehicle-hours or vehicle-kilometers traveled. On the implications of this costing method, see Berechman and Giuliano (1985) and Berechman (1993).

2. For literature on the positive utility of travel see Redmond and Mokhtarian (2001).

3. From the stated preference survey conducted in California by Hickling Lewis Brod Inc. (1997), the distribution of travel time is rather skewed to the right. Whereas about 19% of the respondents commute 5 miles or less, 5% commute more than 50 miles one way to work or school. National travel diary surveys, such as the NHTS, have produced simliar results.

4. In the longer run, relocation is an effective way to reduce travel time.

5. This result appears to contradict conventional microeconomic modeling of time allocations (see Appendix A), which precludes the possibility of TT having a positive coefficient. One possible explanation is that TT serves as a proxy for omitted variables related to trip benefits. Allowing TT to have a positive coefficient (for some segment of the population) is one way of capturing the effect of those omitted variables. However, a positive coefficient would then make the value inappropriate for use when estimating travel time savings.

6. For example, the New Jersey Department of Labor reports the average hourly wage rate in 2000 as $19/hour, resulting in VOT=$7.6 (40% of the *overall* average hourly wage rate in NJ) and VOT = $32.3/hour (75% of the average wage rate in *managerial* jobs in NJ) (http://lwd.state.nj.us/lpaapp/Occupation Explorer.html).

7. Other potential benefits may arise from the reduction of negative externalities such as auto emissions, or the enhancement of positive externalities such as improved land-use efficiency (Litman, 2007). In Chapters 12 and 13 we examine these effects.

8. The use of passenger-miles can be quite misleading because transit passengers' benefits are mostly a function of time and costs, not of miles traveled. Also, major transit systems, like the NYC subway, use a fare method that is independent of distance traveled.

9. Recently (November 18, 2005), the US Congress awarded Amtrak, the railroad that services the Boston-Washington Northeast corridor, a $1.31 billion subsidy. The bill, however, sought to limit Amtrak's ability to discount tickets and reduce the off-peak pricing that the railroad had been using (*The New York Times*, November 26, 2005).

10. The concept was originally developed in the context of environmental analysis, mainly the availability of open space. See Weisbrod (1964) and Johansson (1987).

11. Expected surplus is computed on the basis of the distribution of surplus outcomes with known probability of occurrence (see Chapter 9).

12. Boardman et al. (2001) raise the question of what is the sign of OV. They show that if transit is regarded as a normal good, for risk-averse individuals the sign of OV might be negative if future income is uncertain.

13. See also Chu and Polzin (1998) for estimates of option benefits.

14. Notice that we do not assume here that the hourly wage rate (w) depends on the amount of time spent at work (t_w) as some studies do (see for example Ramjerdi 1993). Similarly, we do not assume that the wage rate is location-dependent, i.e., $w(d)$; (see Gunn, 1991). Adding such assumptions would not alter the main conclusions reached here in any fundamental way.

15. The choice of 24 hours implies that other variables in the system, such as earned and unearned income, should be proportionate to this time period.

16. This characterization of the model is fundamentally different from Becker's (1965) household activity production model because we explicitly distinguish between time as a commodity (which enters the utility function) and time as a resource, which is subject to a resource constraint (see DeSerpa, 1971).

17. By definition, a unit of time of 24 hours is always binding so that strictly speaking, $\mu > 0$.

NOTES TO CHAPTER 5

1. Costs can also be differentiated by discipline, e.g., geotechnical, civil, and structural, architectural, mechanical, ventilation, and fire protection, electric and electronics, plumbing, traffic and safety (including employee safety).

2. The British Transport Guidance Analysis (TAG) recommends the use of a special software program called "QUADRO" to calculate delays caused by construction works on highways and to assess the costs of traffic disruption caused by major trunk road construction (TAG, April 2004a, http://www.web tag.org.uk/webdocuments/3_Expert/9_Major_Scheme_Appraisal_in_LTPs/3.9.2.htm#5_2).

3. $\sum_{t=1}^{20} \dfrac{50,000,000}{(1+0.07)^t} = \$529,700,000$

4. An example is a prefeasibility Study of a Fixed Rail Link between Labrador and Newfoundland, Canada (http://www.gov.nf.ca/publicat/fixedlink/pdf/AppendixF.pdf).

5. Alternatively, for each $1 of final sale price, sellers of labor will receive $1/(1 + t)$, while the government's share will be $t/(1 + t)$. For example, at 25% average income tax rate, for each $1 of labor sold, employees will receive $0.80 (1/(1 + 0.25))$ while the difference, $0.20 (0.25/(1 + 0.25))$, is government revenue.

6. For a comprehensive discussion see Boardman et al., (2001).

7. Data from the Light Rail Capital Cost study indicates that from 1981 to 1995, the average light rail vehicle cost just over $1.1 million. However, since 1996, the cost of the same vehicle swelled to over $2.8 million per car, a 160% increase. Furthermore, the US Federal Transportation Administration (FTA) database indicates that from 1999 to 2001, average light rail vehicle cost has escalated by 141%, an increase that far exceeded the general inflation rate of approximately 7% annually (Booz, 2004).

8. If demand and supply curves can be assumed to be linear in the relevant range, the correct opportunity cost of the input factor is the budget allocation $P_2(Q_2 - Q_1)$ less the net gain in producers' surplus, i.e., $1/2(P_2 - P_1)(Q_2 - Q_1)$.

9. Severance damage typically includes changes in setback of improvements, conformance to zoning, parking-to-building ratios, and neighborhood standards for parking, setback, and/or green space. Additional issues are environmental degradation from the transportation facility's impacts, including noise, pollution, and traffic. In areas where real estate prices are quite high, the amount of severance damage has often become more of a matter of legal issue than an economic fact.

10. The early tunneling of New York's Second Avenue Subway is just such an investment (see Chapter 15).

11. Consider New Jersey Transit. This authority provides commuter rail services in New Jersey by using rail tracks owned by Amtrak, which provides rail services in the US Northeast corridor. New Jersey Transit formerly paid Amtrak according to a formula negotiated by the US Congress in the 1980s. The latest transportation budget, passed in November 2005, nullified this formula. It stipulated that charges are now to be based on the "train mile usage of each commuter rail authority" (*The New York Times*, November 26, 2005).

NOTES TO CHAPTER 6

1. The act's actual wording is: ". . . the Federal Government should improve or participate in the improvement of navigable waters or their tributaries, including watersheds thereof, for flood control purposes if the benefits to whomsoever they may accrue are in excess of the estimated costs" (Arnold, 1988).

2. Related terminology includes "with and without" and "before and after" the project. The former indicates that the COBA of a new system is being carried out with a proper account of the in-place system or conditions whereas the latter indicates that the COBA is being done without such adjustments.

3. To illustrate, consider the Major Commercial Transportation System (MCTS) for the Greater Vancouver Region. The planners considered travel scenarios representing road traffic conditions with and without MCTS investments for the year 2021. The results indicate that without the MCTS improvements, the monetary cost of additional travel time delays (net of changes in travel distance) will grow to $414 million/year, including $280 million for truck delays and $134 million for business-related car travel delays. The planners also addressed the social value of travel time delays for personal travel, arriving at a total cost of $806 million annually (MCTS, 2003).

4. In continuous form: $NPV = -PV(C) + \int_{t=1}^{T} e^{-rt}(\Delta CS_t + \Delta PS_t)dt$.

5. For example, for $100 invested over 2 years at 5%, total capital expenditures, including debt service will equal: $(((100/2) + 100 \cdot 0.05)/(1 + 0.05)) + (((100/2) + 50 \cdot 0.05)/(1 + 0.05)^2) = \$100$

6. It can be argued that highway investments also receive state and federal subsidies, which should, therefore, be included in these projects' producer surplus. To the extent that these are direct and identifiable subsidies that benefit only local users, this would be the correct approach. As pointed out by Mishan (1971, Chapter 10), these kinds of considerations reflect political and institutional constraints.

7. In the US, bus and rail farebox revenues typically amount to 30% of total operating costs. In NY and Chicago, the largest public transit properties, the recovery rate is much higher, about 45% for rail and buses in Chicago, and about 50–60% for rail and buses in New York.

8. Known as the "Fisher Effect," $(1 + r) = (1 + r')/1 + f)$, where r is the real and r' is nominal interest rate. Hence, $r = (r' - f)/(1 + f)$.

9. The costs of building the Richmond-Airport-Vancouver (RAV or Canada) rapid transit line were estimated in 2006 at $2.05 billion, up from $1.9 billion calculated in 2003 in nominal prices. The difference reflects adjustments for inflation using the CPI. "It's exactly the same money, so the public agencies are not on the hook for any more money than they approved" said the chief executive officer of the Canada Line Rapid Transit Inc., the agency in charge of building the project (*The Vancouver Sun* March 4, 2006). This explanation, however, overlooks the possibility that the CPI may fall short of the construction industry's price index. Similarly, if funding commitments were made in nominal terms, their real value may have eroded over time.

10. It is also possible to introduce growth by defining NPV as: $NPV = [PV(B(t)) - PV(C(t))] \cdot e^{-(r-\alpha)t}$, $r > \alpha$. Yet, as is, equation (10) enables exact specification of the growth model.

11. To illustrate, in British Columbia, Canada, maintenance costs per lane-kilometer grew between 2000 and 2005 by an average of about 2% per annum (Source: http://www.bcbudget.gov.bc.ca/annual_reports/2005_2006/trans/Report_on_Performance.htm).

12. At a 5% discount rate, a $1 million dollar investment is worth about $613,900 at year 10, $231,400 at year 30, yet only $87,200 at year 50.

13. The reader is referred to Lind (1982) and to Boardman et al. (2001) for extensive coverage of the subject.

14. As a matter of fact, agencies quite often forgo discounting altogether (Coleman and Smetters, 1999).

15. For elaborate discussions see Baumol (1970), Stokey and Zeckhauser (1978), and The World Bank (1996).

16. An example would be a government ceiling on guaranteed savings funds, or regulations restricting the amount of interest that banks can pay on selected types of saving accounts.

17. For consumption, the appropriate rate would be the interest that consumers pay when borrowing for consumption purposes (e.g., rates charged by credit card firms).

18. The variable $\bar{r}$ essentially represents the shadow price of marginal output.

19. See Sandmo and Dreze (1971) for a discussion of these factors.

20. The Office of Management and Budget (OMB) estimates a 1.5% to 3% intergenerational discount rate.

21. For purposes of comparison, the coupon rate for a 10-year Treasury Inflation-Protected Security (TIPS), due January 15, 2018, currently (April 2008) stands at 1.625%.

22. For example, consider a 2-year investment whose initial capital outlay is 120, with $B_1 = 80$, and $B_2 = 60$; $NPV(i) = -120 + (80/(1 + i)^1)) + (60/(1 + i)^2) = 0$. This parabolic function has two solutions: $i_1 = 0.115$; $i_2 = -1.448$, which implies that any discount rate in the range $\{0,-1.448\}$ will yield a positive NPV.

23. This problem would not have risen if the annual net benefits changed their sign (positive to negative) only once. Most financial programs that compute IRR values report just one solution, which represents a weighted average of IRR values. In contrast, mathematical programs that solve for IRR will generate a vector of solutions.

24. If the project is financed by a loan, the annual debt payment is:

$$P_t = \left[C - (\frac{C}{T_C})(t - 1) \right] \cdot \rho + \frac{C}{T_C}$$

, where T_C is the investment period.

25. The European Channel Tunnel and the Buffalo Light Rail System are cases in point. See Banister and Berechman (2000) for a discussion.

26. The US Federal Highway Administration currently uses two major life-cycle cost models: (a) The Highway Economic Requirements System (HERS); and (b) the Highway Development and Management Tool (HDM-4). The first is used to compare improvements to highway segments, including resurfacing, reconstruction, widening, etc. The second, developed by the World Bank, estimates highway user benefits, infrastructure costs and externalities (e.g., accidents, energy, and emissions) for alternative investment strategies. (See: http://www.fhwa.dot.gov/planning/toolbox/costbenefit_forecasting.htm)

27. This approach is equivalent to finding the market-clearing price (the cost of funds), which equilibrates the given amount (supply) of funds with the projects' capital requirements (demand for capital).

28. Analytically, the problem is: Find i^* so that $\sum_j^{K \in J} PVC(i^*)_j = B$, where K is a subset of the set of all projects, J, and subject to $[PVB(i^*)_k - PVC(i^*)_k] > 0$, $\forall k \in K$, and B is the budget constraint.

29. This procedure raises questions about the uniqueness of the solution (i.e., several subsets meet these conditions), and project (in)divisibility.

NOTES TO CHAPTER 7

1. *Highway Capacity Manual*, (1965). Note that the *Manual* uses volume rather than flow, which is the more commonly used variable in traffic engineering. Volume is defined as observed flow divided by Peak Hour Flow (PHF) to account for variations in hourly flow.

2. Downs (2004) mentions a host of policy devices, in addition to capacity expansion, to contain congestion. Key instruments are peak-hour tolls, improved public transit, intelligent transportation systems, parking programs, and land-use restraints.

3. These estimates, although rough approximations, represent a composite of many past and ongoing congestion research studies.

4. These changes are mainly due to improved vehicle performance, which allows vehicles to better squeeze together on freeways. The empirical functions used presently for applications also consider signalized intersections, where improved signal synchronization is major cause for the increase in maximum flow.

5. Examples are the BPR or the Akcelik's function (Akcelik, 1996). An alternative function is that of Davidson (Akcelik, 1991), where the denominator is

(C-V) for $V < C$. But this function is not widely used; it also creates some computational problems in the Frank–Wolfe assignment algorithm, which is used for calculating the network equilibrium, since the Davidson function will not increase monotonically.

6. In practice, volume-capacity functions are often calibrated in a way that produces estimated volumes, which can match observed volumes obtained from traffic counts. These functions are indeed empirical and cannot be used to describe the phenomena discussed above.

7. The Texas Transportation Institute has developed a congestion index, used to calculate congestion levels for major US cities over time. See http://www. publicpurpose.com/hwy-tti20011986.pdf.

8. The growing use of Intelligent Transportation Systems (ITS) devices and methods is aimed to a large extent at reducing travel time uncertainty. Motorists' willingness to pay for information that allows them to better plan their trips is an indicator of the economic value of certainty.

9. It has been reported that when the Standard Deviation (SD) of travel time is included in a travel demand model that contains scheduling coefficients, the SD's coefficient is insignificant, presumably because it is already embedded in the scheduling variables (Small et al., 1999).

10. In their model, Noland et al. (1998) combined a supply-side model of congestion delay with a discrete choice demand model that predicts trip scheduling for morning commute trips.

11. Here, length of the queue is represented by the number of vehicles.

NOTES TO CHAPTER 8

1. Elsewhere in this book (mainly in Chapters 2 and 15) we argue that other objectives—such as political gains and acquisition of federal funding and economic development exclusive of improved travel conditions—all too often motivate transportation investment decisions. Nevertheless, in adherence to the normative approach of this book, direct travel benefits are seen as the principal rationale for undertaking transportation investments.

2. We do not distinguish here between constructing a new facility, adding capacity to an existing one, or bringing a facility to a state of good repair. In terms of traffic flow, the end result—an increase in network carrying capacity—is the same.

3. Unlike the common economic analysis presented in Chapter 3, the typical supply function used in transportation analysis does *not*, by and large, represent marginal social cost functions. Instead, it represents the marginal private costs of trip makers who, for the lack of congestion tolls, pay only their own costs. Williams et al. (2001) concluded that, in general, benefits measured under a regime of free highway use (no tolls) will significantly exceed benefits measured under a road pricing regime

4. Vehicles are usually defined in terms of Passenger Car Equivalent Units (PCU) to allow for vehicles of various sizes.

5. For a detailed analysis of these definitions and applications see Ran and Boyce (1996, Chapters II and VI).

6. This function is defined as: $t = t_0[1 + \alpha(v/\bar{c})^\beta]$, where t_0 is free-flow travel time, α and β are parameters, usually with $\alpha = 0.15$ and $\beta = 4$. Many other functional forms are available, including empirical ones such as: $(v/c) = \alpha + \beta \cdot s + \gamma \cdot s^2 + \varepsilon$, where s denotes speed and ε the error term (Keeler and Small, 1977). See also Section 5.

7. This analysis demonstrates the rule-of-half discussed in Chapter 3.

8. We can also regard as trips the movements of *individuals* between O-D pairs, such as in public transit. Given the capacity of transit vehicles (e.g., buses) and the level of service offered (e.g., the number of passengers allowed per bus), we can convert individuals' transit trips into vehicular transit trips per time unit.

9. It is important to note that from a traffic-engineering viewpoint, changes in capacity involve changes in the LOS regime. Thus, even if we assume a linear increase in volume resulting from capacity expansion of, say, 25% more lane-miles and 25% more volume, it may not be under the same Level of Service (LOS) and travel flow conditions. That is, suppose that the LOS "before" the change was level "F", while the "after" LOS it is "E", thereby keeping the same volumes per lane. Still, these different LOS regimes imply different flow stability, speed conditions, probability of breakdown, etc., which in turn affect travel times. While we fully recognize these engineering characteristics of travel flow, given the practical difficulties associated with the measurement of travel demand changes, volume, and costs, these issues are not considered here or in what follows.

10. The use of travel demand management or traffic control methods to better utilize existing capacity is not cost-free and requires resources, for example, enforcement and maintenance costs. From this, the need to examine the net economic gains from such capacity improvement schemes follows.

11. Note that the time of departure and the time of actual trip making on the congested facility, while related, are not the same. One can depart home at 7 a.m. and get into congestion at 7:10 (see Chapter 7, Table 7.1). Thus, information on the former decision variable may not wholly correlate with the latter.

12. Known as the Pigou–Knight–Downs (PKD) Paradox it states that with two untolled modes, perfectly substitutable in demand (e.g., road and rail), if total demand for travel remains fixed, expansion of the road will generate zero gross benefits as long as some travelers use the rail after the expansion (see Arnott and Yan, 2000).

13. For a review of the four-phase transportation-planning model see for example McNally (2000).

14. Figure 8.1 is not defined for any specific time period. However, if V_1 and V_2 are hourly rates, the argument holds.

15. This measure is also equivalent to the change in the sum of consumer and producer surplus on route l plus the change in deadweight losses on all other links.

16. Revenues by firms providing transportation goods and services (e.g., parking or gasoline) are assumed to be offset by the costs of producing these goods and services. If corporate net profits are taxed, this additional tax income should be accounted for as part of government's tax revenue.

17. For recent studies see for example Cervero (2003); Cervero and Hansen (2002); DeCorla-Souza, and Cohen (1999); Goodwin (1996); Hansen (1998); Lee, Klein, and Camus (1999); and Mokhtarian et al. (2002).

18. For a review see Mokhtarian et al. (2002, Table 1).

19. Of course there might be nonzero cross-elasticities between the two periods so that a change in LOS at the a.m. peak will affect demand at midday. However, if a time of departure function were added to the (dynamic) assignment model, the end result would be two distinct demand periods, as in Figure 8.3.

20. As noted in Chapter 7, this is a short-term perspective, since in the long-run location patterns will adjust to changes in LOS. For more on this issue, see Section 7 in this chapter.

21. For present users, this situation is equivalent to the supply curve S_1 shifting upward to intersect the demand curve D_1 at point E.

22. The practice of using the area $V_1 V_2 AC$ as a measure of benefits from capacity expansion is totally incorrect as this area actually represents total costs of travel for $(V_2 - V_1)$ users.

23. When demand becomes totally inelastic, (i.e., $\eta \to 0$), ΔCS increases. When demand is fixed, (i.e., $\eta = 0$), ΔCS is undefined.

24. They show that total delay varies with the square of incident duration. If the duration of the incident is reduced by x percent, total delay is reduced by $(1 - x^2)$.

25. $Gamma(\theta, \beta, \gamma)$; where θ is the *location* (threshold) parameter, which reflects the minimum value of the distribution's variable, β is the *scale* parameter, and γ is the *shape* parameter. See Chapter 9.

26. Carroll and Bevis (1957) have presented an early version of this process. In general, this process has been subjected to intense criticism for being arbitrary, unreliable, and for the errors in modeling and estimation amplified through the successive phases. Still, it remains the most-used transportation planning process employed by planning agencies.

27. In other words, total travel volume, obtained from aggregation of all traffic over all network links, would be less than or equal to the total volume of travel obtained from aggregation of the original O-D matrix over all zones. That is: $\sum_{i,j} \sum_{l,m} T^m_{ij,l} \leq \sum_{i,j} T_{ij}$. The difference reflects unserved demand, which equals total demand less realized demand, the latter being demand served at present travel costs.

28. Despite its known shortcomings the most common STA software is the EMM2. It uses standard Volume-Capacity functions such as the BPR.

29. Williams's (1976) derivation of expression (5) is based on an entropy maximization model that, strictly speaking, is not rooted in microeconomic principles. However, it has been shown that expression (7) has a close relationship with measures of users' benefits as derived from random utility theory (see Anas, 1983a).

30. Note that in (5), β is fixed for all users, thus requiring the assumption of no income effect in the model. Williams (1976) proposed transit market segmentation by homogeneous income groups, which resulted in β being segment-specific.

31. They characterize this measure as a long-run measure of benefits.

32. Notice that if total trips do not vary with travel costs, i.e., $\sum_i O^1_i = \sum_i O^0_i = \sum_j D^1_j = \sum_j D^0_j = T$, then expression (7) is equivalent to Williams's measure as in expression (6).

33. That is: $(\partial X_i)/(\partial P_i) = (\partial X_j)/(\partial P_j) \ \forall i \neq j$ where X and P represent quantities and prices, respectively.

34. For an examination of the analytical properties of this approach, including equilibrium conditions, see Berechman (1976); Berechman and Small (1988); Wilson, (1998).

35. β^s is the parameter of the exponential function used to approximate the joint cumulative distribution of the utilities of group s (Cochrane, 1975). de La Bara (1989, Chapter 4) further shows the relationship between the value of β^s and the probability of selecting an alternative.

36. A different specification of the multinomial logit model can produce accessibility measures that are expressed in different units (Ben-Akiva and Lerman, 1985).

37. Small and Rosen make the point that for good (alternative) k, belonging to a discrete choice set, $\lambda_k = -(1/x_k) \cdot (\partial V_k/\partial c_k)$ where x_k is the quantity of the choice (e.g., number of trips per time unit) and c_k is the price of good k.

38. Expression (15) can be interpreted as the expected *compensating variation* (the amount of income a consumer must receive to leave his utility unaffected

by the price change), or as the *equivalent variations* (the amount of income a consumer would be willing to forgo to avoid the price change).

39. $\eta_p = \dfrac{\beta}{p_1/v_1}$, or $\beta = \eta_P \dfrac{p_1}{v_1}$.

40. Cervero and Hansen (2002) estimated a 2SLS model with instrumental variables. They reported lane-mile elasticity of 0.559, i.e., a 10% increase in lane-mile will result in 5.59% increase in traffic volume. Noland and Cowart (2000) have used a nationwide metropolitan-level database to estimate a time-series cross-sectional model. Their results indicate that a 10% increase in lane-mile will result in an 8% to 10% increase in volume.

NOTES TO CHAPTER 9

1. The Montréal-Mirabel International Airport in Canada is a case in a point. It was completed in 1975 and meant to replace the existing Montréal-Pierre Elliott Trudeau (Durval) International Airport. However, due to insufficient demand caused by Mirabel's distance from Montreal and the lack of transport links, it was unpopular with airlines and passengers alike. It presently serves mainly as a cargo airport.

2. Here we do not follow the Bayesian approach, which uses subjective probabilities to replace objective ones when the latter are not known. The main reason is that transportation investments are public sector decisions, which require coalition formation, and collective decisions with conflicting interests. To use Bayesian methods we would need first to elicit individuals' preferences and then aggregate over prior subjective probabilities—two formidable analytical and empirical tasks.

3. Several major studies have noted large inaccuracies in reported ridership and traffic forecasts and costs (Flyvbjerg et al., 2003; Pickrell, 1990; Skamris and Flyvbjerg, 1997). Others (e.g., Wachs, 1989) maintain that this reality cannot be explained solely or even partly by forecasting uncertainty alone. Deliberate falsification of the data by the responsible authority in order to get the project started cannot be ruled out.

4. The risk to which individuals are exposed from an investment can be measured in utility terms. We can thus compute the risk premium that individuals would need to bear in order to maintain the same utility level effective prior to the project. This premium is known as the Cost of Risk Bearing (CRB).

5. Arrow and Lind have shown that when the number of individuals is sufficiently large, the *expected value* of net benefits closely approximates the correct measure of net benefits, defined as the willingness to pay for an asset delivering uncertain returns.

6. Reported in the *Toronto Star*, March 24, 2005.

7. As an example, consider Seattle's (State of Washington) monorail project. In 2002, voters approved a 22-kilometer system (up from the existing 1.6 kilometers), with an original cost estimate of about $2.5 billion. However, opposition grew after this cost estimate more than quadrupled to $11.4 billion. In November 8, 2005, the voters scrapped the project entirely by rejecting a 17-kilometer, $4.9 billion alternative that monorail proponents had offered.

8. Named for Monte Carlo, Monaco, where the state's primary income comes from casinos where games of chance—e.g., roulette wheels, dice, and slot machines—exhibit random behavior.

9. If travel time savings can be estimated as a function of, say, number of users and length of peak period, this function's parameters would be used for the normal distribution.

10. For further details see Raiffa and Schlaifer (1968).

11. Cost overruns are defined as a ratio here to avoid problems associated with projects of different size as well as negative values (budget exceeds actual costs).

12. Both studies used the percentage of cost increases (actual costs minus estimated costs) to represent cost overruns. In Flyvbjerg et al. (2002, 2003) the average percentage cost overrun was 28%, for the 258 transportation infrastructure projects. In the Jahren et al. (1990) study of 1,576 naval construction projects, average cost overrun was about 10%.

13. For further information see: http://www.itl.nist.gov/div898/handbook/eda/section3/.

14. The KS $F_n(x)$ function is defined as a step function that takes a step of height [$1/n$] at each ordered observation. For any value of x, $F_n(x)$ is the proportion of observations less than or equal to x, while $F(x)$ is the probability of an observation (from the proposed distribution) being less than or equal to x.

15. It is defined as the sum of the square of the difference between the observed and expected value divided by the square of the expected value.

16. Kahneman and Tversky (1979) raised the question of whether risk is about attitudes towards monetary results from an event or actually about the probabilities of this event occurring. Thus, the expected utility model can be replaced by a *prospect function* of the form: $W = v(P) \cdot U_1 + v(1 - P) \cdot U_2$, where the weighting function v describes the attitude towards the probability of an event (e.g., changes in wealth) occurring. Notice that this approach assumes that $v(P) \leq P$. Subsequent development (Schmeidler, 1989) of the model has suggested that the prospect function should be expressed as: $Z = v(P) \cdot U_1 + [1 - v(P)] \cdot U_2$. This formulation implies that the weights of the outcome should sum to one, and that gains and losses be treated differently. Importantly, risky outcomes may be underevaluated relative to sure outcomes ($v(0) = 0; v(1) = 1$).

17. We disregard the decision alternative "no build," defined as a project with one or more decision criteria that produce zero or negative results.

18. For example, $E(NPV_1) = \sum_{j=1}^{3} \left[(NPV_{1j} \times P_j \right] = 800,000 \times 0.4173 + 560,000 \times 0.5546 + 200,000 \times 0.0281 = 650,036$

19. When $NPV \rightarrow 0$, $U(NPV_{ij}) \rightarrow 0$; when $NPV \rightarrow \infty$, $U(NPV_{ij}) \rightarrow 1$.

20. For example, for alternative A_1, $(NPV_1^{(1)} = 200,000) \leq (NPV_1^{(2)} = 560,000 \leq (NPV_1^{(3)} = 800,000) \rightarrow (P_1^{(1)} = 0.0281); (P_1^{(2)} = 0.5546); (P_1^{(3)} = 0.4173)$ thus, $U(NPV_1) = (200,000) (f(0.0281 + 0.5546 + 0.4173) - f(0.5546 + 0.4173)) + (560,000) (f(0.5546 + 0.4173) - f(0.4173)) + (800,000) f(0 4173) - 616,551.$

21. In a study of the cost consequences of deferred investments, Paaswell et al. (2004) computed the cost escalations from the postponement of several tunnel, bridge, as well as highway maintenance and rehabilitation projects in New York City. As expected, they found considerable cost escalation due to capital cost increases, additional maintenance costs and increases in the scope of the projects due to further deterioration. In addition, they computed the losses in benefits from postponement of these projects, which were quite significant. As these projects involved existing facilities, issues of uncertainty were not considered.

22. This section draws on Berechman (2006).

23. Internationally, during the period 1985–2005, 390 PPP road projects were funded and a similar number planned, totaling $390 billion. During the same period, 133 PPP rail projects were funded and a similar number planned, for

a total of $270 billion. These figures notwithstanding, in most countries only a small proportion of total infrastructure has been developed through PPP to date (OECD, 2008, http://www.internationaltransportforum.org).

24. These transaction costs, which include bidding, contract negotiation, and monitoring, can amount to 10–15% of the total costs of the project (see discussion in Vining and Boardman, 2008).

25. Resources on PPP are: http://www.ncppp.org; http://www.fhwa.dot.gov/ppp http://www.nossaman.com/information/articles/articles.asp#Infrastructure.

26. One might also argue that if government is risk neutral, it would be more efficient to shift most of the risk there. Yet, the contractual relationships between the public and private sectors act to compel the government to live up to its specific commitments, thereby negating risk neutrality behavior. In addition, if by "government" we also mean entities such as local transportation authorities and municipalities, it is not at all clear that the "government" is indeed risk neutral.

27. One illustrious example of failure to risk-specialize is the European Channel Tunnel (Eurotunnel), which resulted in a colossal financial failure of about 80% cost overruns and suspension of debt service payments. In this case, the project's political risk was left to the private investors to manage rather than to the specialist, namely, the state. On July 11, 2006, The Eurotunnel Company filed for bankruptcy protection, caused by its creditors' refusal to accept a financial restructuring plan. Its total outstanding debt was then about €4.65 billion. The Company has been struggling for about 20 years to reduce interest payments on its debt while failing to meet traffic projections. Standard & Poor has cut its rating on Eurotunnel secured bank loans from BBB to C, which is one step above default (Bloomberg, AFP and Reuters, July 14, 2006).

28. An example of this model is the European Bank for Reconstruction and Development financial scheme for road development in Eastern Europe, especially the M1-M15, a BOT toll motorway in Hungary. Noncommercial risks were assigned to the government while the lenders assumed responsibility for financial risks such as interest and currency exchange rates. Still, in this case as well, actual traffic levels were far below the initial projections, resulting in reduced revenues and the project's technical bankruptcy. One major reason for the failure is the nature of travel demand, which is quite elastic with respect to toll level. So, increased tolls resulted in revenue losses.

29. A case in a point is the widely publicized SR 91 private toll road in Orange County, California. The overseeing agency, Caltrans, has signed a contract in which they agreed not to build any new (free) road capacity parallel to or competing with the privately financed toll road, excluding road improvements necessary to ensure safety. When Caltrans announced that they would widen some lanes on a nearby road for safety purposes, the toll road operators filed a suit against Caltrans for breach of contract, which settled out of court, agreeing not to widen the road. Formally, the case was not about risk sharing because the term "risk sharing" was not used. The essence of the case was translated into a guaranteed income suit.

30. One example is the opposition to attempts by New Jersey's governor (Jon Corzine) to sell the state's toll roads to private investors (see Belson, 2008).

31. It reflects the correlation between the firm's returns and market returns.

32. An example of how the FTA risk-assessment requirement has resulted in improved project management and risk control is the South Corridor Light Rail project (nicknamed the Lynx) in North Carolina, scheduled for completion by fall 2007. It is a 9.6-mile rail line, with 15 stations and 7 park-and-rides, which runs from uptown Charlotte to Pineville, North Carolina. Initial cost estimates were $398.7 million, which have escalated to $427 million

(April 2006). This relatively small cost escalation (about 7%) was achieved in large part by the risk-mitigation plans adopted in the wake of three risk assessment studies. These studies assessed the likelihood that the project could be completed at or below budget.

33. $E(D_1) = qD_u + (1 - q)D_d = 0.4 \times 10 + 0.6 \times 5 = 7$; $NB_1 = E(D_1)p_1 = 7 \times 2 = 14$.

34. If $r < \alpha$, the optimal strategy is always to postpone the project (Dixit and Pindyck, 1994, p. 144).

NOTES TO CHAPTER 10

1. *The New York Times* reported an initiative made by a US Senator from the State of Mississippi to legislatively earmark construction of a new rail line, costing $700 million, which would reposition a newly built $250 million Gulf Coast rail line. This case followed the $250 million budget appropriation for a bridge proposed for the Alaska outback (and named "son of the bridge to nowhere"), initiated by Alaska's US State Senator (*The New York Times*, April 23, 2006). At the time of writing, the bridge plan had been shelved although the money has nonetheless been transferred to the state for use for whatever transportation purposes it saw fit.

2. In this chapter we use the terms *type*, *form*, and *method* of finance interchangeably.

3. For the US funding gap see USDOT (2002).

4. A US Congressional Research Service report indicates that US Highway Trust Fund revenues fell from $21.2 billion in 1999 to $20.9 billion in 2002 (in 2001 prices) despite the increase in VMT. With this easily collected type of money no longer so available, other sources must be located to replace these revenues.

5. The MTA is North America's largest transportation network, serving 14.6 million people across a 5,000-square-mile region. MTA subways, trains, buses, tunnels, and bridges carried an average of 7.6 million passengers per weekday in 2004. The system includes 8,259 rail and subway cars, 4,895 buses, 734 rail stations, 7 bridges, 2 tunnels, and 2,058 miles of track.

6. Note that the above formulation accounts for the actual amount of external funding and not just for its proportion. That is, it is possible that when α increases, the dollar amount of local funding may also increase. For example, 50% external funding of a $500 million project implies $250 million of internal funding whereas 60% external funding of a $700 million project implies $280 million of internal funding. Thus, the term $(1 - \alpha) \cdot C$ is the actual size of external funding.

7.
$$C^* = \sqrt[\delta]{\frac{A}{\delta \frac{1}{P}(1-\alpha)}}.$$

Introducing C^* into the utility function we get:

$$U(C^*) = A \log\left(\sqrt[\delta]{\frac{A}{\delta \frac{1}{P}(1-\alpha)}}\right) - \left[\frac{1}{P}(1-\alpha)^{\delta-1}\frac{A}{\delta}\right].$$

8. A simple regression analysis on data from NY and NJ (1992–2004) shows negative and significant relationships between the proportion of local funding and the size of projects. The higher the percentage of local funding, the smaller was the investment project.

9. Essentially the argument says that the use of a social discount rate that reflects society's preferred rate for allocating resources between present and future generations is sufficient to produce the project's true welfare value.

10. Often interest payments on government bonds are tax deductible, which act to intensify the crowding-out effect.

11.
$$\$(1+t)\cdot\left(\frac{t}{(1+t)}\right)=t.$$

12. In the UK, earmarking is called "hypothecation," derived from the Latin *hypothecare* or *hypotheca*, which means "deposit," or from the Greek *hupothēkē* or *hupotithenai*, which means "to deposit as a pledge."

13. In railroad operations, the weighted average cost of capital is the cost of borrowing and the cost of equity. Revenues from railroad commerce, on the other hand, come mainly from medium-term contracts (typically about 80%) having an average 5-year life span. About 25%–30% of these revenues are locked in by older contracts. If these older contracts are below market price and prices are expected to rise, there is more pricing power to be realized by the railroads.

14. The basic Modigliani–Miller theorem asserts that, in the absence of taxes, bankruptcy costs and asymmetric information, assuming an efficient market, the value of a firm is unaffected by how that firm is financed. That is, it does not matter if the firm's capital is financed either by issuing stock or by selling debt; nor does the firm's dividend policy matter. The theorem is made up of two propositions, which can be extended to a situation *with* taxes (Modigliani and Miller, 1958).

15. In general deadweight losses from taxation can be quite substantial. Feldstein (1999) has estimated that in the US in 1994, for every $1 income tax collected, $0.30 is wasted in the form of deadweight loss ($181 billion which is over 30% of total personal income tax revenue collected).

16. The marginal cost of funds obtained from a head tax is likely to be about one. On the other hand, an increase in labor tax tends to increase the marginal cost of public funds by more than one, although this conclusion ignores the ensuing effect of transportation investments on total tax revenues.

17. Here we disregard possible second-order effects of a labor tax on the congestion of existing capacity.

18. They also accounted for unemployment compensation, social security contributions, participation effects, and the average indirect tax level as a proportional labor tax.

19. On the underlying rationale and problems of using a single social rate of discount see Baumol (1968) and Lind (1982).

20. The Texas Department of Transportation (TxDOT) has developed a form of PPP called Comprehensive Development Agreements (CDAs) to obtain badly needed private funding to supplement decreasing transportation revenues (mainly state and federal fuel taxes). The added funds are necessary to achieve an acceptable level of mobility by 2030, as well as shrink an $83 billion funding gap (http://www.txdot.state.tx.us/txdotnews/trans_challenges.pdf).

21. The SR 91 consists of a 10-mile-long toll lane along the median of a highly congested highway (30-miles long), built and operated by a consortium under a 35-year franchise. The toll lanes opened in late 1995 and used time-of-day tolls as its source of revenues. The project was quite successful in that it was able to cover the private partner's operating and debt service costs (but not a subordinated loan covering less than 10% of the project's costs) in less than 3 years while reducing travel time significantly. Yet, from the public interest viewpoint, it was not perceived as a success because it inhibited attempts by a different government authority (Caltrans) to upgrade the highway network and maintain it in a state of good repair and safety. As a result, in 2003 the project was turned over to Orange County Transportation Authority (OCTA) for $207.5 million, which now collects the toll revenues.

This example highlights the conflict between private and public sector views of a project's value.

22. In October 2004, after an international competition, a private consortium (Skyway Concession Company) was awarded a 99-year contract to operate and maintain the Chicago Skyway, a 7.8-mile toll road ($2 toll) that is the only toll facility in the state not operated by the Illinois Toll Highway Authority. The consortium has paid $1.83 billion to the City of Chicago upon closing the agreement (January 2005). In return, SCC has the right to all toll and concession revenue.

23. Foote (2006) makes the point that despite the seeming attractiveness of this investment to both parties, there is considerable public opposition to the arrangement that makes its future rather uncertain. This opposition mainly stems from the lack of public knowledge about key parameters—e.g., the true value of the leased facility and the optimal lease term—coupled with fear of loss of control over public infrastructure.

NOTES TO CHAPTER 11

1. A major equity issue is the impact of infrastructure development on poverty in underdeveloped countries (e.g., Ifzal and Pernia, 2003). The literature shows positive growth elasticity with respect to road construction, which implies that increased road investment in these countries results in increased wages and employment. This subject is not dealt with in this chapter.

2. A case in point is the fierce debate on the equity implications of Pennsylvania's proposed plan to toll the entire currently free I-80, a 311-mile long Interstate highway (turnpike). I-80 has remained toll-free so far in part due to federal government regulations, liable to change under a new federal program, which disallows tolls on highways paid for with federal money. To comply with this restriction, the toll plan's objective is to raise revenues to pay for necessary highway and bridge maintenance as well as supplement mass transit subsidies, which are expected to decline. Yet, the toll might negatively affect the travel costs for rural populations and dampen firm proclivities to (re)locate in remote rural areas. No wonder that the program, promoted as benefiting Pennsylvania's entire population but particularly urban residents, is strongly opposed by rural communities (Hamill, 2007).

3. A more effective analysis of this issue should have examined transportation expenditures as a percentage of household *income*. Unfortunately, the income data available are quite unreliable, with accurate income data very difficult to obtain.

4. In units of Purchase Power Parity (PPP), a measure commonly used to compare income levels between countries.

5. In 1990, over 65% of the population in the South Bronx earned less than $20,000 annually while over 45% earned less than $10,000 annually (in 1990 prices).

6. Also used were travel time and cost matrices, calculated from actual bus and subway data relative to headways, in-vehicle time, and average walk time to/from the nearest stations.

7. The weights $w_{ij}^m = (L_{ij}^m)/(L_{ij})$, where L_{ij}^m is the number of people using mode m for home-to-work travel between i and j; and L_{ij} the total number of people traveling between i and j.

8. Conduct of a route and mode choice analysis requires an individual choice database, which is largely unavailable.

9. To measure accessibility by location requires the coding and routine updating of the highway and transit networks. In large metropolitan areas these are formidable tasks.

NOTES TO CHAPTER 12

1. For example, during the planning of New York's West Street project (Route 9A), which needed restoration after the events of September 11, 2001, especially in the area adjacent to the World Trade Center site, New York State's governor expressed his preference for a bypass tunnel, into which four traffic lanes would be depressed, together with creation of a local street at grade and pedestrian crossings. The capital costs of this option were estimated at $860 million (in 2004 prices). Other suggestions included a grade option ($175 million) and a no-action. While an EIS was conducted, no formal project evaluation process, which would have considered all relevant impacts, was performed.

2. In the context of environmental externalities, these are also called *anthropogenic* effects, meaning processes, objects, or materials derived from human activities, as opposed to those occurring naturally, free of human interference.

3. In 2005, over two-thirds of total US petroleum use was consumed by transportation in all its modes (US DOT *Transportation Statistics Annual Report*, 2006).

4. These figures are taken from data compiled by the World Resources Institute (*Navigating the Numbers*, 2005) and from a presentation given by Shigenori Hiraoka of the Japan International Transport Institute at the "Seminar on CO_2 Emission Reduction from Aircraft," October 9, 2007, Washington, DC. (http://www.japantransport.com/conferences/2007/10/pr_Hiraoka.pdf). See also *National Surface Transportation Policy and Revenues Study Commission, Final Report*, 2007, Washington DC. (http://www.transportationfortomorrow .org/).

5. Noise is measured in *decibels* (dB), along a logarithmic scale. A 10 dB increase represents a doubling in noise level. *Decibel A-weighted* dB(A) units stress the human ear's sensitivity to frequencies and correlate well with subjective impressions of loudness. Common noise levels range from 30 to 90 dB(A). For further explanantions see VTPI (2002).

6. "Leq" represents the equivalent continuous sound level in dB(A) for a specific time period (e.g., 8 hours).

7. Several studies have found that a traffic volume increase of only a few hundred motor vehicles per day reduces adjacent residential property values by 5%–25% (Bagby, 1980; Hughes and Sirmans, 1992). Based on these figures and assuming 150 residences per mile of urban residential street, with average value of $100,000 per residence, VTPI (2002) has computed the value decline as 18¢/VMT.

8. In the context of railway pollution at peak and off-peak periods, Rietveld (2002) argues that policies based on average environmental costs lead to erroneous results.

9. Information and a list of sources on traffic safety in the US can be found in the NHTSA National Highway Traffic Safety Administration website (http:// www.nhtsa.dot.gov/); for a Canadian source center see: http://www.sfu.ca/ traffic-safety/resources.html.

10. For a study of road factors and their impact on accidents see Blum and Gaudry (2001).

11. Speed differentials resulting from highway improvements are known to contribute to traffic accidents. Stop and go travel, especially in rural areas, is therefore a major cause of fatal traffic accidents.
12. For a comprehensive database see the US DOT National Highway Safety Administration website (http://www.nhtsa.dotgov).
13. The marginal costs for providing security to an additional user, together with free riders, are close to zero.
14. In Canada, major emitters of Green House Gases (GHG) are electric power plants. In 2004, there were 321 facilities that emitted approximately 279 million tons of GHG. This amount equals about 37% of the country's total emissions and exceeds the combined total of GHG from cars, trucks, planes, and trains (Source: PollutionWatch, (http://www.pollutionwatch.org/)).
15. These costs are much lower, of course, on a per passenger basis. But for estimating the FMC from an investment (e.g., the impact of noise on housing value), it is correct to use VKM as the output measure.
16. For *internalized* accident costs (including fixed, variable, and time costs), they report long-run AC, which exceeds long-run MC ($0.3458/VKM vs. $0.2986/VKM). This result probably reflects the fact that marginal accident costs decline with increases in traffic volumes and thus lower speeds.
17. Federal Highway Cost Allocation Study, *Summary Report, 1997*, US Department of Transportation, Federal Highway Administration (www.fhwa.dot.gov/policy/hcas/summary/index.htm).
18. For comparison, a 2000 study by the National Highway Traffic Safety Administration, which used the human capital method, reports *average* accident costs of 8.6¢ per VM (http://www-nrd.nhtsa.dot.gov/Pubs/809446.PDF).
19. $7.60/H represents 50% of the median wage rate for all NJ occupations in 2000.
20. The study further computed FMC assuming VOT of $32.30/hour, which represents 75% of the median wage rate in management occupations in New Jersey (in 2000). As can be expected, the results were much higher than those shown in Table 12.4.
21. Source: the Port of New York and New Jersey (PNYNJ) website, http://www.panynj.gov/.
22. Private car equivalent (PCE) ratios are 3–4 cars per truck.
23. See Chapter 6, Appendix A, for the derivation of δ.
24. OMB assumes an annual income per capita growth of 1.5%–2% and marginal elasticity of utility from income of 1.5. For the definitions used by OMB see: http://www.whitehouse.gov/omb/circulars/a094/a094.pdf.
25. Arrow (2007) points out that simple calculations show that for $\delta < 8.5\%$, the PV of benefits from environmental improvements exceeds the PV of the corresponding costs.
26. Empirically, actual average insurance premiums were estimated to be about 30%–40% below the optimal premiums, defined as those necessary to internalize *all* accident marginal costs (Vickrey, 1968).

NOTES TO CHAPTER 13

1. The word "infrastructure" seems to have originated in 19th century France. Throughout the first half of the 20th century it was used to refer primarily to military installations. The term came into prominence in the US in the 1980s following publication of the Choate and Walter (1981) report, which initiated a public debate over the nation's "infrastructure crisis," purportedly caused by

decades of inadequate investment and poor maintenance (http://en.wikipedia.org/wiki/Infrastructure).

2. *The New York Tribune*, September 18, 1868 (quoted in Ambrose, 2000).

3. Following the civil war, US federal and state governments vigorously supported the development of transcontinental railroads, whose stated objective was to tie the nation together. By granting huge amounts of land to railroad companies, benefits were also expected to accrue from anticipated increases in property values (Cain, 1997).

4. See for example Fogel's (1964) challenge of the accepted view on the impact of railroad construction on the American economy.

5. In a recent expert forum organized by the Great Vancouver Regional District (GVRD) in Canada, with participants drawn mainly from industry, it was bluntly stated that the region's economic future directly depended on expanding its transportation infrastructure, including the highway network, the port, and other key facilities (*The Vancouver Sun*, "Gateway Viewed as Economic Key," September 26, 2006, B7).

6. In Japan, in the early 1990s, the economy remained stagnant despite the enormous resources invested in transportation infrastructure.

7. The test is defined in terms of the degree to which a series U can improve prediction of another series, V. Thus, U is regarded as causing V if the prediction of V on the basis of its previous observations can be improved using U's previous values.

8. Some studies have employed a cost function model. For lack of quality data on factor prices, this approach has not been more widely adopted. See for example Nadiri and Mamuneas (1996); Morrison and Schwartz (1996).

9. As a result, the error term does not exhibit the regular statistical properties of a normal distribution with a zero mean, constant variance, and zero spatial covariance. For further discussion see Kelejian and Robinson (1992). Most studies test for first-order autocorrelation, namely, spillovers to adjacent localities. Yet, second- or higher-order spillovers are quite likely (Cohen and Morrison, 2004). Ports and airports in particular are known to generate economic impacts well beyond their immediate geographic region.

10. That is: $\Delta Q / \Delta H = 0.045 \cdot 633692/85235 = 0.34$.

11. Historical records seem to confirm this result. For example, it has been reported that US railroad investments in the late 19th and early 20th century yielded $33,000–$200,000 NPV of revenues per mile for the first 500 miles but only $3.5–$25,000 per mile for the second 500 miles (Caine, 1997).

12. Munnell (1990) has concluded that public highway capital creates positive cross-state spillovers. Holtz-Eakin and Schwartz (1995), on the other hand, have rejected the hypothesis that highway capital has positive output spillovers. Boarnet (1997) has concluded that the redistribution of economic activity subsequent to a transportation investment and the subsequent spillover effects were equal in magnitude but with opposing signs.

13. These benefit categories are also labeled "static" and "dynamic" (Cain, 1997).

14. A case in point is the as yet unfulfilled expectations for extensive economic development on the Belgian side of the Channel Tunnel.

15. This tunnel is the cornerstone of the project entitled: "Access to the Region's Core (ARC)." See Berechman and Passwell (2005) for a review.

16. We should note here that multiplier effects are not sustainable because once the project is completed investment funds will no longer be available to fuel the local economy. A case in a point is the Lotschberg train tunnel project in the Swiss Alps. The capital costs of constructing the 22-mile tunnel (along with another 20 miles of maintenance and emergency tunnel) came to $3.5 billion. The immediate impact of this huge investment was prosperity for the

town of Fruitgen, located near the tunnel's entrance, where about 1,200 workers spent their money on items including lodging, food, retail, and entertainment. But once construction ended, these revenues—short-term multiplier benefits—all but disappeared. Yet, the same project freed warm underground water deposits that the town intends to use for a warm water fishery—a result representing a long-term economic growth effect (*The New York Times*, September 19, 2007).

17. For an application of the multiplier effect in airport development see Batey et al. (1993).
18. For a theoretical analysis see Baumol and Wolff (1994).
19. An example is the Regional Input/Output Modeling System (RIMS-II), used by the US Bureau of Economic Analysis.
20. Many of the evaluation methodologies reported in the literature contain similar components (see for example NCHRP, 1991; Weisbrod and Weisbrod, 1997). However, by and large, they fail to establish proper causal linkages between the primary transportation effects and the economic growth effects. As a result, these methodologies include ample double-counting of benefits and tend to overestimate the investment's true social welfare gains.
21. They are most likely correct. The public, which cannot comprehend the intricacy of a transportation benefits analysis, easily grasps the notion of increased employment in its immediate region.
22. See recent EEA report, *Urban Sprawl*, http://reports.eea.europa.eu/eea_report _2006_10/en/index_html
23. The proposed project included construction of a major transportation center and major capital improvements to rail, subway, and bus transit in the area.
24. To simplify the analysis, each of these variables was expressed as a linear function of its determinants. The supply function was assumed to be upward-rising throughout with respect to its relevant variables. It represents participation decisions in the wage-travel costs space. Hence, variables (a) and (b) are, in fact, single-choice variables.
25. The 2SLS procedure is an instrumental-variable approach to producing consistent estimates, using Generalized Least Squares (Wacziarg 2001; Zellner and Theil, 1962).
26. Main job categories: executive, administrative, and management; transportation; construction; sales; general services; manufacturing.
27. For example, communications and other public utilities, wholesale and retail trade finance, real estate, and insurance.
28. The generality of these findings needs to be examined against Portland's unique geographical situation. The city is located at a key intersection of major cross-continental highways and rail routes. Owing to the gateway status of its marine and airports, these facilities crucially depend on truck transportation, which is particularly vulnerable to congestion.
29. Examples are Amsterdam's "Schiphol," with 58,000 workers within the airport city; Hong Kong's "Skycity," with 45,000 workers; Dubai's Jebel All Airport city and Subic Bay in the Philippines (FedEx's Asia hub). In 2004, the Dallas-Ft. Worth Airport generated $7.5 billion in wholesale transactions.
30. On average, about two-thirds; in some places, like NY, this reaches about 80%.
31. For example, the growing trade imbalance between Western countries and the Far East, mainly China, has resulted in many empty containers moving from west to east, with full containers moving in the other direction. As this imbalance escalates, so do freight hauling unit costs.
32. Historically, this approach is consistent with the concept of "land value taxation" proposed by the American political economist Henry George

(1839–1897), who advocated the use of a single tax on land rent as the main source of government revenues.

33. See for example Al-Mosaind et al. (1994).

34. For a review of the empirical literature, residential and commercial, see Vessali (1996). For a case study of the effect of LRT on commercial properties, see Weinberger (2001).

35. Unfortunately, planning realities in many metropolitan areas make use of a GELUT model unlikely; estimated changes in real estate values from transportation improvement therefore tend to be quite problematic.

36. Notable examples are de La Barra (1989), MEPLAN (Echenique et al., 1990), PROPOLIS (Spiekermann and Wegener, 2004), DELTA/START (Simmonds and Still, 1998), and UrbanSim (Wadell, 2000). For a review see Wilson (1998).

37. To use ILUT models, various elasticity parameters—such as the elasticity of demand for housing with respect to travel costs and income—are required as input. These are often obtained from a separate statistical analysis.

38. For more on the analytical properties of GE models see Mas-Colell et al., (1995). Weisbrod and Treyz (1998) have reported attempts to use COBA within a GE model.

39. In their seminal work, Dixit and Stiglitz (1977) incorporated scale economies into a general equilibrium model assuming a monopolistically competitive market structure. See also Venables (2007).

40. Brown and Anderson (1999) have studied trade flows between Canada and the US. They found that trade between contiguous regions such as Ontario and Michigan tended to be intra-industry rather than interindustry trade.

41. Lowered transportation costs act to increase the *range* of goods available to consumers in the trading countries (Fujita et al., 1999).

42. In this formulation we did not include unobserved individual heterogeneity variables, assumed to be controlled by the time-invariant regional-specific effects.

NOTES TO CHAPTER 14

1. The majority of small-scale projects, especially those in rural areas, are never subjected to COBA, let alone to a formal project selection process. Commonly, the key criterion for project selection is safety. As pointed out throughout this book, large-scale or mega-projects are, by and large, required to undergo some form of COBA although the process is often initiated too early in the project, when data, mainly on demand and costs, are incomplete or unreliable.

2. All too often, political interests and distributional aspects are the key considerations in project decision making. Given the normative thesis that underlies this book, the discussion focuses on formal project selection processes.

3. Janic and Reggiani (2002, Appendix A) also mention the entropy method for weight assignment. Entropy is, in essence, a measure of uncertainty of a discrete probability density function. The highest level of uncertainty (maximum entropy) is obtained when all probabilities have equal weights. For further discussions see Hwang and Yoon (1981), and Straja (2000).

4. Appendix A provides the formulation for this example.

5. If, for example, criteria 5 and 6 cannot be assessed, the following formula is used to compute the weights of the four "new" criteria:

$$W_i = \frac{w_i}{\left(\sum_1^4 w_i\right)},$$

where w_i and W_i are the "old" and the "new" weights, respectively.

6. Another possible approach is to divide by the sum of scores and then multiply by 100.

7. Still another approach is to regard delays as conferring negative utility on users. Hence, each delay score receives a negative sign, and each score is then divided by the absolute value of the "best" (lowest) score.

8. An example of an operational scoring method is the one used by the Houston-Galveston Area Council (H-GAC), which is the Metropolitan Planning Organization (MPO) for this region. This MPO is responsible for developing the long-range transportation plan and for implementing federal funding decisions for transportation. The method involves assigning a total of "N" points (e.g., $N = 250$) to the overall system of M multiple criteria (e.g., $M = 10$). Based on an assessment of performance, each criterion receives a number of points on an ordinal scale, n_i (e.g., $n_1 = 50$; $n_2 = 25 \ldots$), provided that $\sum_{i=1}^{M} n_i = N$. Each criterion is further assigned a weight that reflects its importance in the opinion of H-GAC. The criteria are: congestion relief, safety, transit choice, economic development, goods movement, environmental justice, regional significance (spatial coverage), and the proximity of each alternative project to evacuation route and maintenance costs. As is usually the case, the critical issue for this MCA procedure is the generation of the weight assigned to each separate criterion.

9. For further reviews see Hwang and Yoon (1981), Williams and Giardina (1993, Chapter 3), and Vreeker et al. (2001).

10. See, for example, Korhonen et al. (1992); Wang (2000); Zionts (1997), as well as numerous articles in the *Journal of Multicriteria Decision Analysis*.

11. For more on this model see Nijkamp and Ouwersloot (1998).

12. Specifically, they used a GAM type method (i.e., the SAW method), a technique for order preference by similarity to the ideal solution (TOPSIS) method, and a hierarchy method (Analytic Hierarchy Process-AHP).

13. See also article in: http://www.socialresearchmethods.net/kb/scalthur.php.

14. Transport Analysis Guidance (*TAG Unit 1.1*), 2004b (http://www.webtag.org. uk/webdocuments/1_Overview/1_Introduction_to_Transport_analysis/index. htm).

15. For a thorough discussion of these and other issues see Glaister (1999), Vickerman (2000), and Sayer et al. (2003).

16. Thus, the weight for Transportation Benefits is 36.232%, for Other Transportation it is 9.058%, and for Construction Period 4.71%. Numerically, the weights were computed as follows: $[(50/50 + 12.5 + 6.5) + (12.5/50 + 12.5 + 6.5) + (6.5/50 + 12.5 + 6.5)] \times W$, where W is the total weight of the Direct Transportation Benefits ($W = 50/100$).

17. See also EURET 2002 (European Research on Transport); http://cordis. europa.eu/transport.

18. In the Gulf Island National Seashore, off the coast of the Florida Panhandle, County Road 399 has been destroyed by successive hurricanes and then repaired, until totally destroyed by hurricane Katrina in 2005. A lively debate has developed over whether to rebuild the road, which is the only one leading to an important tourist site (Fort Pickens), or leave it as it is, thereby preserving the seashore and beaches (Dean, 2005).

19. In West Vancouver, a plan to build a 2.4-kilometer stretch of new highway from Caulfield to Horseshoe Bay (known as the Eagle Ridge Plan) has been fervently opposed by residents of the local community. The road is part of the comprehensive Sky Highway improvements begun in preparation for the 2010 Winter Olympics. A key argument against the building of this road is its potential major damage to the area's sensitive ecosystem. The groups opposing the road also cited highway safety concerns (Hansen, 2005).

20. It is defined as a matrix of "1"s on the main diagonal and "0"s elsewhere.

NOTES TO CHAPTER 15

1. It should be noted that many of these projects were sponsored by different agencies; in that sense, a project sponsored by one agency would not be seen as "competing" with that of another agency. Each project was in effect treated by the decision makers as unique—not part of a network of new or complementary transportation improvements.
2. New Israeli Shekels (NIS).
3. During Phase 1, service will operate along Second Avenue from 96th Street to 63rd Street, where it will divert westward along the existing 63rd Street segment, stopping at the Lexington Avenue/63rd Street Station, where riders will be able to transfer to the F Line.
4. In the opinion of this author, these figures are highly inflated. The job figures are based on national averages; they ignore shortages of skilled construction labor and do not account for jobs lost due to interruptions caused by construction. Note that the SDEIS has estimated only 22,500 direct construction-related jobs. The time savings figures are based on unsubstantiated assumptions of actual time saved by SAS users and from overcrowding on parallel subway lines.
5. According to the SDEIS, the East Side will produce additional 30,000 residential units and 18.4 million SQF of office space by 2020. Even if correct, the extent to which the SAS is responsible for these figures remains cloudy.
6. The most pronounced changes would be in the North East part of the region, outside the City of Vancouver, and south of the Fraser River. See Greater Vancouver Transportation Authority (GVTA), Strategic Planning Department (2006).
7. See: http://www.spec.bc.ca/article/article.php?articleID=404.

References

American Association of State Highway and Transportation Officials (AASHTO), 2003. *Manual of User Benefit Analysis for Highways, 2nd Edition*.

Abdel-Aty, M., Kitamura, R., and Jovanis, P., 1997. "Using Stated Preference Data for Studying the Effect of Advanced Traffic Information on Drivers' Route Choice," *Transportation Research Part C*, 5(1), 39–50.

Adler N., and Berechman, J., 2001. "Evaluating Optimal Multi-hub Networks in a Deregulated Aviation Market with Application to Western Europe," *Transportation Research A*, 35(5), 1–18.

Akcelik R., 1991. "Travel Time Functions for Transport Planning Purposes: Davidson's Function, its Time-dependent Form and an Alternative Travel Time Function," *Australian Road Research* 21(3), 49–59.

Akcelik R., 1996. "Relating Flow, Density, Speed and Travel Time Models for Uninterrupted and Interrupted Traffic," *Traffic Engineering and Control* 37(9), 511–516.

Akintoye A., and MacLeod M. 1997. "Risk Analysis and Management in Construction," *International Journal of Project Management*, 15(1), 31–38.

Al-Mosaind M., Dueker K., and Stratham J., 1994, "Light-Rail Transit Stations and Property Values: A Hedonic Price Approach," *Transportation Research Record No. 1400, Planning and Programming, Land Use, Public Participation, and Computer Technology in Transportation*, 90–94.

Alsnih R., and Stopher P., 2003. "Environmental Justice Applications in Transport: The International Perspective." In D. A. Hensher and K. J. Button (Eds.), *Handbook of Transport and the Environment*. Amsterdam: Elsevier, 565–584.

Altshuler A., 1965. *The City Planning Process: A Political Analysis*. Ithaca, NY: Cornell University Press.

Altshuler A., and Luberoff, D., 2003, *Mega-Projects: The Changing Politics of Urban Public Investment*. Washington DC: Brookings Institution Press.

Ambrose S., 2000. *Nothing Like It in the World: The Men Who Built the Transcontinental Railroad, 1863–1869*. New York: Simon & Schuster Adult Publishing Group.

American Automobile Manufacturers Association, 1996. *Motor Vehicle 1996 Facts and Figures*. Washington DC: AAMA.

Anas A., 1983a. "Discrete Choice Theory, Information theory and the Multinomial Logit and Gravity Models," *Transportation Research B—Methodological*, 17(1), 13–23.

Anas A., 1983b. "The Effects of Transportation on the Tax Base and Development of Cities." In Report Number DOT/OST/P-30/85/005. Washington, DC: US Department of Transportation.

Anas A., 1995. "Capitalization of Urban Travel Improvements into Residential and Commercial Real Estate: Simulations with a Unified Model of Housing, Travel Mode and Shopping Choices," *Journal of Regional Science* 35, 351–375.

Armstrong R., and Rodriguez D., 2006 "An Evaluation of the Accessibility Benefits of Commuter Rail in Eastern Massachusetts Using Spatial Hedonic Price Functions," *Transportation*, 33(1), 21–43.

Arnold J., 1988. *The Evolution of the 1936 Flood Control Act*. Fort Belvoir, VA: Office of History, United States Army Corp of Engineers.

Arnott R., and Yan A., 2000. "The Two-mode Problem: Second-Best Pricing and Capacity," *Review of Urban and Regional Development Studies*, 12(3), 171–198.

Arrow K., 1963. "Uncertainty and the Welfare Economics of Medical Care," *American Economic Review*, 53(5), 941–973.

Arrow K., 1996. "The Theory of Risk-Bearing: Small and Great Risks," *Journal of Risk and Uncertainty*, 12, 103–111.

Arrow K., 2007. "Global Climate Change: A Challenge to Policy," *Economic Voice*, 4(3), Article 2. (http://www.bepress.com/ev). September 2007.

Arrow K., and Kurz M., 1970. *Public Investment, the Rate of Return and Optimal Fiscal Policy*. Baltimore MD: John Hopkins University Press.

Arrow K., and Lind R., 1970. "Uncertainty and the Evaluation of Public Investment Decisions," *American Economic Review*, 60, 364–378.

Aschauer D., 1989. "Is Public Expenditure Productive?" *Journal of Monetary Economics*, 23, 177–200.

Ashok K., and Ben-Akiva M., 2000. "Alternative Approaches for Real-Time Estimation and Prediction of Time-Dependent Origin-Destination Flows," *Transportation Science*, 34(1), 21–36.

Atkins S., 1983. "The Value of Travel Time: An Empirical Study Using Route Choice," PTRC Summer Annual Meeting, University of Sussex, UK.

Auerbach A., 1986. "The Theory of Excess Burden and Optimal Taxation." In A. Auerbach and M. Feldstein (Eds.), *Handbook of Public Economics*, Vol. 1. New York, NY: Elsevier.

Ayyub B., 2003. *Risk Analysis in Engineering and Economics*. Boca Raton, FL: Chapman & Hall/CRC.

Bagby G., 1980. "Effects of Traffic Flow on Residential Property Values," *Journal of the American Planning Association*, 46(1), 88–94.

Banister D., 1994. "Equity and Acceptability Questions in Internalising the Social Costs of Transport." In OECD/ECMT (Hrsg.), *Internalising the Social Costs of Transport* (S. 153–175). Paris: OECD Publications.

Banister D., 1997. "Reducing the Need to Travel," *Environment and Planning B*, 24(3), 437–449.

Banister D., and Berechman J., 2000. *Transportation Investment and Economic Development*. London: University College London Press.

Banister D., and Edwards M., 1995. *Measuring the Development and Social Impacts from Transport Infrastructure Investment: The Case of the Jubilee Line Extension in London*. Available from the authors at The Bartlett School of Planning, UCL, Wates House, 22 Gordon Street, London WC1H 0QB.

Bates J., Polak, J., Jones P., and Cook A., 2001. "The Valuation of Reliability for Personal Travel," *Transportation Research E, 37(2–3), April/July, pp. 191–229*.

Bates J., and Roberts M., 1986. "Value of time Research: Summary of Methodology and Findings," 14 PTRC Summer Annual Meeting, University of Sussex, 14–18 July, Brighton.

Batey P., Madden M., and Scholefield G., 1993. "Socio-Economic Impact Assessment of Large Scale Projects Using Input-Output Analysis: A Case Study of an Airport," *Regional Studies*, 27(3), 179–192.

Batty M., 1976. *Urban Modeling.* Cambridge UK: Cambridge University Press.

Baumol W., 1968. "On the Social Rate of Discount," *American Economic Review*, 58, 788–802.

Baumol W., 1970. "On the Discount Rate for Public Projects." In R. Haveman and J. Margolis (Eds.), *Public Expenditure and Policy Analysis.* Chicago: Markham, 273–290.

Baumol W., and Wolff E., 1994. "A Key Role for Input-Output Analysis in Policy Design," *Regional Science and Urban Economics*, 24, 93–113.

Becker G., 1965. "A Theory of the Allocation of Time," *Economic Journal*, 75(299), 493–517.

Beesley M., 1965. "The Value of Time Spent Travelling: Some New Evidence," *Economica*, 32, 174–185.

Beggs S., Cardell N., and Hausman J., 1981. "Assessing the Potential Demand for Electric Cars," *Journal of Econometrics*, 16, 1–9.

Beimborn E., & Puentes R., 2003. *Highways and Transit: Leveling the Playing Field in Federal Transportation Policy.* Washington DC: Brookings Institute. Available: http://www.brookings.edu.

Belson, K. "Toll Road Offers New Jersey a Fiscal Test Drive," *New York Times*, April 13, 2008.

Ben-Akiva, M., and Lerman, S., 1985. *Discrete Choice Analysis: Theory and Application to Travel Demand.* Cambridge: The MIT Press.

Berechman J., 1976, "Interfacing the Urban Land Use Activity System and the Transportation System," *Journal of Regional Science*, 16(2), 183–194.

Berechman J., 1993. *Public Transit Economics and Deregulation Policy.* North-Holland, Amsterdam.

Berechman J., 1995. "Transport Infrastructure Investment and Economic Development: A Review of Key Analytical and Empirical Issues." In D. Banister (Ed.), *Transport and Urban Development.* London: Chapman and Hall.

Berechman J., 2001. "Generator or Supporter: Transport Investment and Economic Growth," *New York Transportation Journal*, 5, 14–20.

Berechman J., 2006. "How Should Risks be Shared? The Challenge of Risk Allocation in Public Private Partnerships." Paper Presented at the New York State Department of Transportation Conference on Transportation Development Partnership, March 8, 2006, Albany, New York.

Berechman J., 2007. "Societal Full Marginal Costs of Port Expansion: The Case of NY." Paper delivered at the International Conference on Gateways and Corridors, Vancouver, Canada, May 2–4, (www.gateway-corridor.com).

Berechman J., and Chen L., 2008. *Incorporating Risk of Cost Overruns into Transportation Capital Projects Decision-Making.* Working Paper. New York: The City College of New York, University Transportation Research Center.

Berechman J., and Giuliano G. 1985. "Economies of Scale in Bus Transit: A Review of Concepts and Evidence," *Transportation*, 12(4), 313–332.

Berechman J., Kohno H., Button K., and Nijkamp P., 1996. *Transport and Land Use.* London, UK: Edward Elgar Publishing Ltd.

Berechman J., Ozmen-Ertekin D., and Ozbay K., 2006. "Empirical Analysis of Transportation Investment and Economic Development at State, County and Municipality Levels," *Transportation*, 33(6), 537–551.

Berechman J., and Paaswell R. 1983. "Rail Rapid Transit Investment and CBD Revitalization: Methodology and Results," *Urban Studies*, 20(4), 471–486.

Berechman J., and Paaswell R. 1997. "The Implications of Travel Profiles for Transportation Investment: The Bronx Center Project," *Transportation*, 24(1), 51–77.

Berechman J., and Paaswell R., 2001. "Accessibility Improvement and Local Employment: An Empirical Analysis," *Journal of Transportation and Statistics*, 4(2/3), 49–66.

Berechman J., and Paaswell R., 2005. "Evaluation, Prioritization and Selection of Transportation Investment Projects in New York City," *Transportation*, 32(3), 223–249.

Berechman J., and Pines, D., 1991. "Financing Road Capacity and Returns to Scale Under Marginal Cost Pricing," *Journal of Transport Economics and Policy*, 25(2), 177–181.

Berechman J., and Small K., 1988. "Modeling Land Use and Transportation: An Interpretive Review for Growth Areas," *Environment and Planning A*, 20(10), 1285–1310.

Blinder A., and Krueger A., 2004. "What Does the Public Know about Economic Policy, and How Does It Know It?" *Brookings Papers on Economic Activity*, 35(1), 327–397. Washington DC: The Brookings Institution.

Blum, U., 1998. "Positive Externalities and the Public Provision of Transportation Infrastructure," *Journal of Transportation Statistics*, 1(3), 81–88.

Blum U., Gaudry M., 2001. "The SNUS 2.5 Model for Germany." In M. Gaudry and S. Lassarre (Eds.), *Structural Road Accident Models: The International DRAG Family*. Elsevier, 67–96.

Blumenberg E., 2003. "Transportation Costs and Economic Opportunity Among the Poor," *Access*, 23, 40–41.

BMVBW, 2002. *Federal Transport Infrastructure Plan, 2003: Basic Features of Macroeconomic Evaluation Methodology*. Berlin: Federal Ministry of Transport, Building and Housing. (http://www.unece.org/trans/doc/transsitdocs/Germany-Transportinfrastructureplan.pdf).

Boardman A., and Greenberg D., 1996. *Cost-benefit Analysis: Concepts and Practice*. Upper Saddle River, NJ: Prentice Hall.

Boardman A., Greenberg D., Vining A., and Weimer D., 2001. *Cost-benefit Analysis*. Upper Saddle River, NJ: Prentice Hall.

Boarnet M., 1997. "Infrastructure Services and the Productivity of Public Capital: The Case of Streets and Highways," *National Tax Journal*, 50(1), 39–57, March 1997.

Boei, William. "RAV Line Gets Final Approval, Construction to Start in 2005," *Vancouver Sun*, December 2, 2004, p. A1. (http://www.spec.bc.ca/article/article.php?articleID=404.).

Boiteux, M., 2000. *Transports: choix des investissements et prise en compte des nuisances*. Commissariat General du Plan. Paris: La Documentation Francaise.

Booz, A. H., 2004. *Managing Capital Costs of Major Federally Funded Public Transportation Interim Report*. FTA, McClean.

Bradford D., and Hildebrandt G., 1977. "Observable Preferences for Public Goods," *Journal of Public Economics*, 8(2), 111–131.

Bradford N., 2000. "The Policy Influence of Economic Ideas." In M. Burke, C. Moors, and J. Shields (Eds.), *Restructuring and Resistance: Canadian Public Policy in an Age of Global Capitalism*. Halifax: Fernwood Publishing.

Bridge M. "RAV Cost Pushes Past $2-Billion Mark: Official Says the Apparent Increase Reflects Adjustments for Inflation," *The Vancouver Sun*, March 4, 2006., p. B1.

Brown M., and Anderson W., 1999. "The Influence of Industrial and Spatial Structure on Canada–U.S. Regional Trade," *Growth and Change*, 30(1), 23–47.

Brownstone D., and Small K., 2005. "Valuing Time and Reliability: Assessing the Evidence from Road Pricing Demonstrations," *Transportation Research Part A*, 39, 279–293.

Brueckner J., and Selod H., 2006. "The Political Economy of Urban Transport-System Choice," *Journal of Public Economics*, 90, 983–1005.

Bruzelius N., 1979. *The Value of Travel Time*. London: Croom Helm.

Bruzelius N., Flyvbjerg B., and Rothengatter W., 2002. "Big Decisions, Big Risks: Improving Accountability in Mega Projects," *Transport Policy*, 9(2), 143–154.

Bureau of Labor Statistics (BLS). 2001. *Consumer Expenditure Survey*. (http://www.bls.gov).

Bureau of Transport and Communications Economics (BTCE). 1996. *Traffic Congestion and Road User Charges in Australian Capital Cities*. Report 92, Canberra: Australian Government Publishing Service.

CAA (Civil Aviation Authority). 2001. *Cost of Capital—Position Paper*. June 2001. London: Civil Aviation Authority House.

Cain L., 1997. "Historical Perspective on Infrastructure and US Economic Development," *Regional Science and Urban Economics*, 27(2), 117–138.

Calfee J., and Winston C., 1998. "The Value of Automobile Travel Time: Implications for Congestion Policy," *Journal of Public Economics*, 69: 83–102.

Carroll D., Jr., and Bevis R., 1957. "Predicting Local Travel in Urban Regions," Papers of the Regional Science Association, Vol. 3.

Cederbaum G., Arbocz J., Newman, P., and Kenworthy J., 1996. "The Land Use-Transport Connection: An Overview," *Land Use Policy*, 13(1), 1–23.

Cervero R., 2003. "Road Expansion, Urban growth, and Induced Demand," *American Planning Association Journal*, 69(2), 145–163.

Cervero R., and Duncan M., 2002. "Benefits of Proximity to Rail on Housing Markets: Experience in Santa Clara County," *Journal of Public Transportation*, 5(1), 1–18.

Cervero R., and Hansen M., 2002, "Induced Travel Demand and Induced Road Investment: A Simultaneous-Equation Analysis," *Journal of Transport Economics and Policy*, 36(3), 469–490.

Cervero R., and Landis J., 1995. "Development Impacts of Urban Transport: A US Perspective." In D. Banister (Ed.), *Transport and Urban Development*. London: Chapman and Hall.

Chen Y., and Florian M., 1996. "O-D Demand Adjustment Problem with Congestion: Part I. Model Analysis and Optimality Conditions." In L. Bianco and P. Toth (Eds.), *Advanced Methods in Transportation Analysis*. Berlin: Springer-Verlag, 1–22.

Cho C., 1999. "The Economic-Energy-Environmental Policy Problem: An Application of the Interactive Multiobjective Decision Method for Chungbuk Province," *Journal of Environmental Management*, 56(2), 119–131.

Choate P., and Walter S., 1981. *America in Ruins: Beyond the Public Works Pork Barrel*. Washington DC: Council of State Planning Agencies.

Chu L., Kim H., Liu H., and Recker W., 2005. "Evaluation of Traffic Delay Reduction from Automatic Workzone Information Systems Using Micro-Simulation." Paper Presented at the 84th Annual Meeting of the Transportation Research Board, Publication # 05-2751.

Chu X., and Polzin S., 1998. "The Value of Having a Public Transit Travel Choice," *Journal of Public Transportation*, 2(1), 91–116.

Chui M., and McFarland W., 1987. "The Value of Travel Time: New Elements Developed Using a Speed Choice Model," *Transportation Research Record 1116*, TRB, National Research Council, Washington, DC, 15–21.

Cirillo C., and Axhausen K., 2006. "Evidence on the Distribution of Values of Travel Time Savings from a Six-Week Diary," *Transportation Research A*, 40, 447–457.

Cochrane R.,1975. "A Possible Economic Basis for the Gravity Model," *Journal of Transport Economics and Policy*, 34–49.

Cogan J., 1980. "Labour Supply with Costs of Labour Market Entry." In J. P. Smith (Ed.) *Female Labour Supply: Theory and Estimation*. Princeton University Press, 327–364.

Cohen J., and Morrison C., 2004. "Public Infrastructure Investment, Inter-State Spatial Spillovers, and Manufacturing Costs," *Review of Economics and Statistics*, 86(2), 551–560.

Cohen H., and Southworth F., 1999. "On the Measurement and Valuation of Travel Time Variability Due to Incidence on Freeways," *Journal of Transportation and Statistics*, 2(2), 123–131. Washington DC: Bureau of Transportation Statistics.

Cohen A., and Einav L., 2003. "The Effect of Mandatory Seatbelt Laws on Driving Behavior and Traffic Fatalities," *Review of Economics and Statistics*, 85(4), 828–843.

Cole, Sherman Inc., 1990. "Attitudinal Survey: Tradeoff Analysis." Excerpt from Draft Report, Prepared for VIA Rail, Canada.

Coleman B., and Smetters K., 1999. "Discounting Inside the Washington D.C. Beltway," *Journal of Economic Perspectives*, 13(4): 213–228.

Colonna P., and Fonzone A., 2004. *New Ways of Viewing the Relationship between Transport and Development*, Conference Paper, Portland, OR. (http://www.njrati.org/files/technology%20transfer/conferences/portland/updatedPDFs/Portland_Colonna&Fonzone.pdf).

Cooper D., and Chapman, C., 1987. *Risk Analysis for Large Projects: Models, Methods and Cases*. Hoboken, NJ: John Wiley & Sons.

Crousillat E., and Martzoukos S., 1991. *Decision Making Under Uncertainty—An Option Valuation Approach to Power Planning*, PRE Energy Series 39. Washington, DC: The World Bank.

Dafermos S., and Nagurney A., 1984a. "Sensitivity Analysis for Asymmetric Network Equilibrium Problem," *Mathematical Programming*, 28, 174–184.

Dafermos S., and Nagurney A., 1984b. "Sensitivity Analysis for the General Spatial Economic Equilibrium Problem," *Operations Research*, 32, 1069–1086.

Dargay J., and Hanly M., 1999. "Bus Fare Elasticities," ESRC Transport Studies Unit, London: University College London, (www.ucl.ac.uk/~ucetmah).

Da Silva Costa, J., Ellson, R., and Martin, R., 1987. "Public Capital, Regional Output, and Development: Some Empirical Evidence," *Journal of Regional Science*, 27, 419–437.

Davis L., 2008. "The Effect of Driving Restrictions on Air Quality in Mexico City," *Journal of Political Economy*, 116, 38–81.

Deacon R., and Sonstelie J., 1985. "Rationing by Waiting and the Value of Time: Results from a Natural Experiment," *Journal of Political Economy*, 93(4), 627–648.

Dean C. "When the Sea Destroys a Road, the Question Arises: Is It Worth Saving?" *New York Times*, December 13, 2005.

De Borger B., and Proost S., 1997. *Mobiliteit: De Juiste Prijs*. Garant, Leuven-Apeldoorn.

de Corla-Souza, P., and Cohen, H., 1999. "Estimating Induced Travel for Evaluation of Metropolitan Highway Expansion," *Transportation*, 26, 249–262.

de Jong G., Daly A., Pieters M., and van der Hoorn, T., 2007. "The Logsum as an Evaluation Measure: Review of the Literature and New Results," *Transportation Research A*, 41, 874–889.

de Jong G., and Gunn H., 2001. "Recent Evidence on Car Cost and Time Elasticities of Travel Demand in Europe," *Journal of Transport Economics and Policy*, 35(2): 137–160.

de la Barra T., 1989. *Integrated Land Use and Transport Modeling: Decision Chains and Hierarchies*. Cambridge: Cambridge University Press.

Delucchi M., 1998. *The Annualized Social Cost of Motor Vehicle Use in the United States, Based on 1990–1991 Data*, UCD-ITS-RR-96-3. Davis, CA: University of California, Institute of Transportation Studies.

Delucchi M., 2000. "Environmental Externalities of Motor-Vehicle Use in the US," *Journal of Transport Economics and Policy*, 34, 135–168.

Delucchi M., and Hsu Shi-Ling, 1998. "External Damage Cost of Noise Emitted from Motor Vehicles," *Journal of Transportation and Statistics*, 1(3), 1–24.

de Palma A., and Marchal F., 2000. "Dynamic Traffic Analysis with Static Data: Some Guidelines with an Application to Paris," THEMA Working Papers 2000-55, THEMA (THéorie Economique, Modélisation et Applications), Université de Cergy-Pontoise.

de Palma A., and Rochat R., 1997. "Impact of Adverse Weather Conditions on Travel Decisions: Experience from a Behavioral Survey in Geneva," *International Journal of Transport Economics*, 24(2), 307–325.

DeSerpa A., 1971. "A Theory of the Economics of Time," *The Economic Journal*, 81(324), 828–846

DeSerpa A., 1973. "Microeconomic theory and the valuation of travel time: some clarifications," *Regional Urban Economics*, 2, 401–410.

Dixit A., and Pindyck R.,1994. *Investment under Uncertainty*. Princeton, NJ: Princeton University Press.

Dixit A., and Stiglitz J., 1977. "Monopolistic Competition and Optimum Product Diversity," *American Economic Review*, 67(3), 297–308.

Downs A., 1957. *An Economic Theory of Democracy*. New York: Harper and Row.

Downs A., 2004. *Still Stuck in Traffic: Coping with Peak-Hour Traffic Congestion*. Washington DC: Brookings Institution Press.

Duffy-Deno K., and Eberts R., 1991. "Public Infrastructure and Regional Economic Development: A Simultaneous Equations Approach," *Journal of Urban Economics*, 30(3), 329–343.

Dunn Jr. J., 1998. *Driving Forces: The Automobile, Its Enemies, and the Politics of Mobility*. Washington, DC: The Brookings Institution.

Dupuit J., 1844. "De la mesure de l'utilité des travaux publics," *Annales de Ponts et Chaussées*, Second Series, Volume 8. Translated: Dupuit, J. (1952), "On the Measurement of Utility of Public Works," *International Economic Papers* 2, 83–110. English translation reprinted as pages 255–283 in K. J. Arrow and T.Scitovsky (1969), *Readings in Welfare Economics*. Homewood, Illinois: Richard D. Irwin.

Eberts R., 1986. "Estimating the Contribution of Urban Public Infrastructure to Regional Growth," Working Paper 8610, Federal Reserve Bank of Cleveland.

Echenique M., Flowerdew J., Hunt J., Mayo R., Skidmore I., and Simmonds D., 1990. "The MEPLAN Model of Bilbao, Leeds and Dortmund," *Transport Reviews*, 10, 309–322.

Economic Development Research Group. 2005. *The Cost of Congestion to the Portland Region, A Study Done for the Portland Business Alliance, Port of Portland, Metro and Oregon DOT*. (http://www.edrgroup.com).

ECONorthwest and PBQD. 2002. *Estimating the Benefits and Costs of Public Transit Projects*, TCRP Report 78, (http://gulliver.trb.org/publications/tcrp/tcrp78/index.htm), TRB (www.trb.org).

Edmonds G., 1983. *Rural Transport Policy in Developing Countries*. London: Thomas Telford Ltd.

Edwards M., and Mackett, R., 1996. "Developing New Urban Public Transport Systems: An Irrational Decision-Making Process," *Transport Policy*, 3(4), 225–239.

Elvik R., 1994. "The External Costs of Traffic Injury: Definition, Estimation and Possibilities for Internalization," *Crash Analysis and Prevention*, 26(6), 719–732.

Enoch M., Potter S., Ison S., and Humphreys I., 2004. "The Role of Hypothecation in Financing Transit: Lessons from the United Kingdom," *Transportation Research Record*, Journal of the US Transportation Research Board, Washington DC, No 1864, 31–37.

Eriksen K., 2000. "Calculating External Costs of Transportation in Norway," *European Journal of Transport and Infrastructure Research*, 9–25.

EURET, 1994. "Cost benefit and Multicriteria Analysis for New Road Construction: Final Report," Report to the Commission of the European Communities, Directorate General for Transport, Doc. EURET/385/94, Brussels.

EURET, 2002. "Transport RTD Programme Homepage." Transport RTD Programme. (http://cordis.europa.eu/transport/).

FHWA (Federal Highway Administration), 1996. *Conference on Benefit Cost Analysis.* US Department of Transportation, 17.

Federal Highway Cost Allocation Study, *Summary Report, 1997*, US Department of Transportation, Federal Highway Administration (www.fhwa.dot.gov/policy/hcas/summary/index.htm).

Feitelson E., 2002. "Introducing Environmental Equity Dimensions into the Sustainable Transport Discourse: Issues and Pitfalls," *Transportation Research D*, 7(2), 99–118.

Feldstein, M., 1999. "Tax Avoidance and the Deadweight Loss of the Income Tax," *Review of Economics and Statistics*, 81(4), 674–680.

Fielding G., 1987. *Managing Public Transportation Strategically: A Comprehensive Approach to Strengthening Service and Monitoring Performance.* San Francisco: Jossey-Bass Publishers.

Flyvbjerg B., 2003. "The Lying Game," *Eurobusiness*, 5(1), 60–62.

Flyvbjerg B., Bruzelius N., and Rothengatter W., 2003. *Megaprojects and Risk: An Anatomy of Ambition.* Cambridge: Cambridge University Press.

Flyvbjerg B., Holm M., and Buhl S., 2002. "Underestimating Costs in Public Works Projects," *Journal of the American Planning Association* 68(3), 279–295.

Flyvbjerg, B., Holm M., Buhl S., 2005. "How (In)accurate are demand Forecasts in Public Work Projects? The Case of Transportation," *Journal of the American Planning Association*, 71(2).

Flyvbjerg B., Skarmis M., and Buhl S., 2004. "What Causes Cost Overrun in Transport Infrastructure Projects?" *Transport Reviews*, 24(1), 3–18.

Fogel R., 1964. *Railroad and the American Economic Growth: Essays in Econometric History.* Baltimore: John Hopkins.

Foote J., 2006. *Analysis of the Public Policy Aspects of the Chicago Skyway Concession.* Unpublished Paper. Cambridge, MA: John F. Kennedy School of Government, Mossaver-Rahmani Center for Business and Government.

Forkenbrock D., and Foster, N., 1990. "Economic Benefits of a Corridor Highway Investment," *Transportation Research*, 24A, 303–312.

Forkenbrock D., Mathur S., and Schweitzer L., 2001. *Transportation Investment Policy and Urban Land Use.* Iowa City: University of Iowa, Public Policy Center.

Forsyth P., 1980. "The Value of Time in an Economy with Taxation," *Journal of Transport Economics and Policy*, 14(3), 337–362.

Fowkes A., 1986. "The UK Department of Transport Value of Time Project," *International Journal of Transport Economics*, 13, 197–207.

Frame J., 2003. *Managing Risk in Organizations: A Guide for Managers.* Hoboken, NJ: Jossey-Bass.

Friedman L., 1985. *Microeconomics Policy Analysis*, New York: McGraw-Hill.

Friedman M., 1949. "The Marshallian Demand Curve," *The Journal of Political Economy*, 57(6), 463–495.

Fujita M., Krugman P., and Venables A., 1999. *The Spatial Economy. Cities, Regions and International Trade.* Cambridge, MA: MIT Press.

Fulton L., Meszler D., Noland R., and Thomas J., 2000. "A Statistical Analysis of Induced Travel Effects in the US Mid-Atlantic Region," *Journal of Transportation and Statistics* 3(1), 1–14.

Garcia-Mila T., and McGuire T., 1992. "The Contribution of Publicly Provided Inputs to State's Economies," *Regional Science and Urban Economics*, 22(2), 229–242.

Ghosh D., Lees D., and Seal W., 1975. *Optimal Motorway Speed and Some Valuations of Time and Life*. Manchester UK: Manchester School of Economics and Social Studies.

Gihring T., 2001. "Applying Value Capture in the Seattle Region," *Journal of Planning Practice & Research*, 16(3–4), 307–320.

Giuliano G., 1996. "Transporting L.A." In M. Dear, G. Hise, and E. Schockman (Eds.) *Rethinking Los Angeles*. Beverly Hills, CA: Sage Publications.

Giuliano G., 2004. "Land Use Impacts of Transportation Investments: Highway and Transit." In S. Hanson and G. Giuliano (Eds.), *The Geography of Urban Transportation*. New York: Guilford Press, 237–273.

Goldberg L., 1996, "Local Government Highway Finance Trends," *Public Roads Magazine*, 60(1), Summer 1996.

Goldman T., and Wachs M., 2003. „A Quiet Revolution in Transportation Finance: The Rise of Local Option Transportation Taxes," *Transportation Quarterly*, 57(1), Winter 2003, 19–32.

Goodwin P., 1996. "Empirical Evidence on Induced Traffic, a Review and Synthesis," *Transportation*, 23, 35–54.

Gordon P., Lee B., and Richardson H., 2004. *Travel Trends in U.S. Cities: Explaining the 2000 Census Commuting Results*. Report No. 90089-0626. Los Angeles, CA: University of Southern California, Lusk Center for Real Estate.

Gordon P., and Richardson H., 1997. "Are Compact Cities a Desirable Planning Goal?" *Journal of the American Planning Association*, 63(1), 95–106.

Gramlich E., 1994. "Infrastructure Investment: A Review Essay," *Journal of Economic Literature*, 32(3), 1176–1196.

Gramlich E., 2000. *A Guide Benefit-Cost Analysis*, 2nd Edition. Englewood Cliffs, NJ: Prentice Hall.

Granger C., 1969. "Investigating Causal Relations by Econometric Models and Cross-Spectral Methods," *Econometrica*, 37(3), 424–438.

Greater Vancouver Gateway Council. 2003. *Economic Impact Analysis of Investment in a Major Commercial Transportation System for the Greater Vancouver Region*. Prepared by Delcan and Economic Development Research Group, July 2003.

Greene W., 2000. *Econometric Analysis*. Englewood Cliffs: Prentice Hall.

Grimsey D., and Lewis M., 2004. *Public Private Partnerships: The Worldwide Revolution in Infrastructure Provision and Project Finance*. Cheltenham, UK: Edward Elgar.

Grout P., 2003. "Public and Private Sector Discount Rates in Public-Private Partnerships," *Economic Journal*, 113(486), C62–C68.

Gunn C., 1991. *Reclaiming Capital: Democratic Initiatives and Community Development*. Ithaca, NY: Cornell University Press.

Hamburg J., Blair L., and Albright D., 1995. "Mobility as a Right," *Transportation Research Record*, 1499, 52–55.

Hamill, S. "Pennsylvania Political War Over Planned Tolls on I-80," *New York Times*. August 26, 2007.

Hanke S., Carver P., and Bugg P., 1975. "Project Evaluation during Inflation," *Water Resources Research*, 11(4), 511–514.

Hansen, D. "West Van rejects Eagle Ridge plan: Council Sees Pictures, Vote No to Province's Proposal for Sea to Sky near Caulfeild," *The Vancouver Sun*. December 13, 2005, p. B1.

Hansen M., 1998. "The Traffic Inducement Effect: Its Meaning and Measurement," *Transportation Research Circular*, 481, 7–15.

Harberger A., 1978, "On the Use of Distributional Weights in Social Cost-Benefit Analysis," *Journal of Political Economy*, 86(2), 87–120.

Harvey C., 1994. "The Reasonableness of Non-Constant Discounting," *Journal of Public Economics*, 53(1), 31–51.

Hatch Mott MacDonald, 2004. "Fixed Link between Labrador and Newfoundland. Pre-feasibility Study Final Report." Government of Newfoundland and Labrador, Canada. (http://www.gov.nf.ca/publicat/fixedlink/pdf/AppendixF.pdf).

Hauer E., 1994. "Can One Estimate the Value of Life or Is It Better To Be Dead than Stuck in Traffic?" *Transportation Research A*, 28(2), 109–118.

Hay A., and Trinder E., 1991. "Concept of Equity, Fairness, and Justice Expressed by Local Transport Policy Makers," *Environment and Planning C*, 9, 453–465.

Hensher D., 1997. "Value of Travel Time Savings in Personal and Commercial Automobile Travel." In D. Greene, D. Jones, and M. Delucci (Eds.), *The Full Social Costs and Benefits of Transportation*. Berlin: Springer-Verlag.

Hensher D., and Rose J., 2005. "Respondent Behavior in Discrete Choice Modeling with a Focus on the Valuation of Travel Time Savings," *Journal of Transportation and Statistics*, 8(2), 17–30.

Hensher D., and Truong T., 1985. "Valuation of Travel Time Savings—A Direct Experimental Approach," *Journal of Transport Economics and Policy*, 19(3), 237–261.

Hess B., and Almeida T., 2007. "Impact of Proximity to Light Rail Rapid Transit on Station-Area Property Values in Buffalo, New York," *Urban Studies*, 5/6, 1041–1068.

Hess S., Bierlaire M., and Polak J., 2005, "Estimation of Value of Travel-Time Savings Using Mixed Logit Models," *Transportation Research A*, 39(3), 221–236.

Hickling, Lewis, Brod, Inc. 1995. *Measuring the Relationship between Freight Transportation and Industry Productivity: FINAL REPORT*, NCHRP 2-17(4). Washington, DC: Transportation Research Board, National Research Council.

Hickling, Lewis, Brod, Inc. 1997, *Valuation of Travel-Time Savings and Predictability in Congested Conditions for Highway User-Cost Estimation*, A Report, Prepared for NCHRP. Washington, DC: Transportation Research Board, National Research Council.

Hicks J., 1940. "The Valuation of the Social Income," *Economica*, 7(26), 105–124.

Higginson M., 1999. "Alternative Sources of Funding," *Public Transport International*, 48(5), September, Copenhagen, Denmark.

Highway Capacity Manual (1965), Special Report, 87. Washington DC: TRB National Research Council, Chapter 7, 160–186.

Hill M., 1968. "A Goals-Achievement Matrix for Evaluating Alternative Plans," *Journal of the American Institute of Planners*, 34, 19–29.

Hine J., and Mitchell F., 2003. *Transport Disadvantage and Social Exclusion: Exclusionary Mechanisms in Transport in Urban Scotland (Transport and Society)*. London: Ashgate.

Hollander Y., 2006. "Direct Versus Indirect Models for the Effects of Unreliability. Transportation Research, Part A," *Policy and Practice*, 40(9), 699–711.

Holmes J., 1972. "An Ordinal Method of Evaluation," *Urban Studies*, 9(2), 179–191.

Holtz-Eakin D., Newey W., and Rosen H., 1988. "Estimating Vector Auto-regressions with Panel Data," *Econometrica*, 56(6), 1371–1395.

Holtz-Eakin D., and Schwartz A., 1995. "Spatial Productivity Spillovers from Public Infrastructure: Evidence from State Highways," *International Tax and Public Finance*, 2(3), 459–468.

Homburger W., Kell J., and Perkins D., 1992. *Fundamentals of Traffic Engineering*, 13th Edition. Berkeley: University of California, Institute of Transportation Studies.

Hoover G., and Burt M., 2006. *Build It and Will They Drive? Modeling Light-Duty Vehicle Travel Demand.* The Conference Board of Canada, (http://www.e-library.ca).

Huang W., 1995. *The Effects of Transportation Infrastructure on Nearby Property Values: A Review of the Literature.* Berkeley, CA: University of California, Institute of Urban and Regional Development.

Hughes W., and Sirmans C., 1992. "Traffic Externalities and Single-Family House Prices," *Journal of Regional Science,* 32(4), 487–500.

Hwang L., and Yoon K., 1981. *Multi Attribute Decision-Making: Methods and Applications,* Lecture Series in Economics and Mathematical Systems. Berlin: Springer-Verlag.

Ifzal A., and Pernia E., 2003. "Infrastructure and Poverty Reduction. What is the Connection?" ERD Policy Brief Series No. 13. Asian Development Bank, Economics and Research Department, 1–13, Manila, Philippines. (http://www.adb.org/Documents/EDRC/Policy_Briefs/PB013.pdf).

Ihlanfeldt K., and Sjoquist D., 1998. "The Spatial Mismatch Hypothesis: A Review of Recent Studies and Their Implications for Welfare Reform," *Housing Policy Debate,* 9(4), 849–892, Fannie Mae Foundation, Washington DC.

Imprint-Net Conference. October 16, 2007. Brussels, Belgium. (http://www.imprint-net.org/conferences/2/).

"Infrastructure," Wikipedia, The Free Encyclopedia (http://en.wikipedia.org/wiki/Infrastructure)

INFRAS/IWW. 2000. *External Costs of Transport: Accident, Environment and Congestion Costs of Transport in Western Europe.* Zurich / Karlsruhe. (http://themes.eea.europa.eu/Sectors_and_activities/transport/indicators/cost/TERM25%2C2002).

Jaafari A., 2001. "Management of Risk, Uncertainties and Opportunities on Projects: Time for a Fundamental Shift," *International Journal of Project Management,* 19, 89–101.

Jahren C., and Ashe, A., 1990. "Predictors of Cost Overruns Rates," *Journal of Construction Engineering and Management,* 116(3), 548–552.

Janic M., and Reggiani A., 2002. "An Application of the Multiple Criteria Decision Making (MCDM) Analysis to the Selection of a Hub Airport," *European Journal of Transport and Infrastructure Research,* 2(2), 113–141.

Jansson J., 1994. "Accident Externality Charges," *Journal of Transport Economics and Policy,* 28(1), 31–43.

Jara-Diaz, S., and Farah M., 1988. "Valuation of Users' Benefits in Transport Systems," *Transport Reviews,* 8(3), 197–218.

Jessop A., 1999. "Entropy in Multi-attribute Problems," *Journal of Multicriteria Decision Analysis,* 8(6), 61–70.

Jia W., and Wachs M. 1998. "Parking and Affordable Housing," *Access,* 13, 22–25 (http://socrates.berkeley.edu/~uctc/access.html).

Jianling L., and Wachs M., 2004. "The Effects of Federal Transit Subsidy Policy Investment Decisions: The Case of San Francisco's Geary Corridor," *Transportation,* 31(1), 43–67.

Jiang X., and Adeli H., 2003. "Freeway Work Zone Traffic Delay and Cost Optimization Model," *Journal of Transportation Engineering,* 129(3), 230–241.

Jiwattanakulpaisarn P., Noland R., Graham D., and Polak J., 2006. "Granger Causality Test of the Relationships between Highways and Economic Development: Which Came First?" Paper presented at the 53rd North American Meetings of the Regional Science Association, November 16–18, Toronto, Canada.

Johansson M., 1987. *The Economic Theory and Measurement of Environmental Benefits.* Cambridge: Cambridge Press.

Journal of Multi-Criteria Decision Analysis. New York, NY: Wiley Interscience.

Kahneman D., 2003. "Maps of Bounded Rationality: Psychology for Behavioral Economics," *American Economic Review*, 93(5), 1449–1475, December 2003.

Kahneman D., and Tversky A., 1979. "Prospect Theory: An Analysis of Decision Under Risk," *Econometrica*, 47, 263–291.

Kain J., 1968. "Housing Segregation, Negro Employment and Metropolitan Decentralization," *Quarterly Journal of Economics*, 82(2), 175–197.

Kain J., 1990. "Deception in Dallas: Strategic Misrepresentation in Rail Transit Promotion and Evaluation," *Journal of the American Planning Association*, 56, 184–196.

Kaldor N., 1939. "Welfare Propositions of Economics and Interpersonal Comparisons of Utility," *Economic Journal*, 49(195), 549–552.

Kasarda J., 2000. "Aerotropolis: Airport-Driven Urban Development." In The Future of Cities in the 21st Century. Washington, DC: Urban Land Institute, 32–41.

Keeler T., and Small K., 1977. "Optimal Peak Load Pricing, Investment and Service Levels on Urban Expressways," *Journal of Political Economy*, 85, 1–25.

Kelejian H., and Robinson D., 1992. "Spatial Autocorrelation: A New Computationally Simple Test with an Application to Per Capita County Policy Expenditures," *Regional Science and Urban Economics*, 22, 317–331.

Kidokoro Y., 2004. "Cost-Benefit Analysis for Transport Networks: Theory and Application," *Journal of Transport Economics and Policy*, 38, 275–307.

Kidokoro Y., 2006, "Benefit Estimation of Transport Projects—A Representative Consumer Approach," *Transportation Research B*, 40(7), 521–542.

Kleven H., and Kreiner C., 2003. *The Marginal Cost of Public Funds in OECD Countries: Hours of Work Versus Labor Force Participation*, CESifo Working Paper No. 935 (http://www.CESifo.de).

Knight F., 1921. "Risk, Uncertainty, and Profit," Hart, Schaffner, and Marx Prize Essays, no. 31. Boston and New York: Houghton Mifflin.

Korhonen P., Moskowitz H., and Wallenius J., 1992. „Multiple Criteria Decision Support—A Review," *European Journal of Operational Research*, 63(3), 361–376.

Kraus M., 1981. "Scale Economies Analysis for Urban Highway Networks," *Journal of Urban Economics*, 9, 1–22.

Krugman P., 1995. *Development, Geography and Economic Theory*. Cambridge, MA: MIT Press.

Krutilla K., 2005. "Using the Kaldor–Hicks Tableau for Cost-Benefit Analysis and Policy Evaluation," *Policy Analysis and Management*, 24(4), 864–875.

Lahiri K., and Yao W., 2004. "The Predictive Power of an Experimental Transportation Output Index," *Applied Economic Letters*, 11(3), 149–152.

Lakshmanan T., and Anderson W., 2002. *Transportation Infrastructure, Freight Services Sector and Economic Growth*, A White Paper prepared for the US Department of Transportation, Federal Highway Administration. Boston: Center for Transportation Studies, Boston University.

Lakshmanan T., and Chatterjee L., 2005. "Economic Consequences of Transportation Improvements," *Access*, 26, 28–33.

Lakshmanan T., Subramanian U., Anderson W., and Leautier F., 2001. *Integration of Transport and Trade Facilitation: Selected Regional Case Studies. Directions in Development Series. Washington, DC: World Bank*.

Lam T., and Small K., 2001. "The Value of Time Reliability: Measurement from a Value Pricing Experiment," *Transportation Research E*, 37, 231–251.

Lane B., 2008. "Significant Characteristics of Urban Rail Renaissance in the United States: A Discriminant Analysis," *Transportation Research A*, 42(2), 279–295.

Leclair R., 2004, "The O-Train: The Straight Facts," Report to Transportation and Transit Committee and Council, Ottawa Public Works and Services, Ottawa, (http://ottawa.ca/calendar/ottawa/citycouncil/trc/2004/07-21/ACS2004-TUP-TRN-0009.htm).

Lee D., Klein L., and Camus G., 1999. "Induced Traffic and Induced Demand," *Transportation Research Record*, 1659, 68–75.

Levinson D., Gillen D., Kanafani A., and Mathieu J., 1996. *The Full Cost of Intercity Transportation—A Comparison of High Speed Rail, Air and Highway Transportation in California*, Report No. UCB-ITS-RR-96-3. Berkeley: University of California, Institute of Transportation Studies.

Levinson D., and Gillen D., 1998. "The Full Cost of Intercity Highway Transportation," *Transportation Research 3D*, 207–223.

Levinson H., 1995. "Freeway Congestion Pricing: Another Look," *Transportation Research Record*, 1450, 8–12.

Likert R., 1932. "A Technique for the Measurement of Attitudes," Archives of Psychology, 140, 1–55.

Lind R., 1982. "A Primer on the Major Issues Relating to the Discount Rate for Evaluating National Energy Options." In R. Lind et al. (Eds.), *Discounting for Time and Risk in Energy Policy*, Washington DC: Resources for the Future.

Lindblom, C., 1959. "The Science of Muddling Through," *Public Administration Review*, 19(2), 79–88.

Litman T., 2002b. "Evaluating Transportation Equity," *World Transport Policy & Practice*, 8(2), 50–65. (http://ecoplan.org/wtpp/wt_index.htm).

Litman T., 2003. *Transportation Cost and Benefit Analysis: Techniques, Estimates and Implications*. Victoria, Canada: Victoria Transport Policy Institute.

Litman, T., 2004a. *Transit Price Elasticities and Cross-Elasticities*. Report prepared by the Victoria Transport Policy Institute (VTPI), (http://www.vtpi.org).

Litman T., 2004b. *Transport Cost Benefit Analysis—Congestion Costs*. Report prepared by the Victoria Transport Policy Institute (VTPI), (http://www.vtpi.org).

Litman T., 2007. "Evaluating Rail Transit Benefits: A Comment," Transport Policy, 14(1), 94–97.

Lootsma F., 1992. *The REMRANDT System for Multicriteria Decision-Analysis via Pairwise Comparison for Direct Rating*, No. 92–05. Delft: Delft University of Technology, Faculty of Technical Mathematics and Informatics.

López Suarez, and Monzón de Cáceres, A., 2006. "The Integration of User Benefits in Evaluation Frameworks: The Uncertainty Implications of Modeling Decision-Makers' Preferences. Paper presented at Transportation Research Board (TRB), Washington DC.

Lynde C., and Richmond J., 1992."The Role of Public Capital in Production," *The Review of Economics and Statistics*, MIT Press, 74(1), 37–44, February.

Maddison D., Johansson O., Pearce D., Calthrop E., Litman T., and Verhoef E., 1996. *The True Costs of Road Transport*. London: Earthscan.

Marshall A., 1920, *Principles of Economics*, Macmillan, London.

Marshall N., 2000. "Evidence of Induced Demand in the Texas Transportation Institute's Urban Roadway Congestion Study Data Set." Paper No. 00-0181, CD-ROM of the Annual Meeting of the Transportation Research Board, Washington, DC, January.

Martens K., 2005. "Grounding Transport Planning on Principles of Social Justice," *Berkeley Planning Journal*, 19, 1–17. (www-dcrp.ced.berkeley.edu/bpj).

Martinez F., and Araya C., 2000. "A Note on Trip Benefits in Spatial Interaction Models," *Journal of Regional Science*, 40(4), 789–796.

Mas-Colell A., Whinston M., and Green J., 1995. *Microeconomic Theory*. Oxford, UK: Oxford University Press.

Mayston D., 1993. "Public and Private Sector Project Appraisal: A Comparative Evaluation." In A. Williams and E. Giardina (Eds.), *Efficiency in the Public Sector*. Cambridge, UK: Edward Elgar, 3–25.

McCann P., 1998. *The Economics of Industrial Location: A Logistics-Costs Approach*. Heidelberg: Springer.

McFadden D., and Train K., 1978. "The Goods/Leisure Tradeoff and Disaggregate Work Trip Mode Choice Models," *Transportation Research*, 12, 349–353.

McKinnon A., and Woodburn A., 1996. "Logistical Restructuring and Road Freight Traffic Growth: An Empirical Assessment," *Transportation*, 23, 141–161.

McNally M., 2000. "The Four-Step Model." In D. Hensher and K. Button (Eds.), *Handbook of Transport Modelling*. New York: Pergamon.

Mera K., 1973. "Regional Production Functions and Social Overhead Capital: An Analysis of the Japanese Case," *Regional and Urban Economics*, 3(2), 157–186.

Metropolitan Transport Authority (MTA). *MTA Outstanding Debt*. March 14, 2006. (http://www.mta.info/mta/investor/pdf/mar06debt.pdf).

Metropolitan Transit Authority. *MTA Capital Construction—Second Avenue Subway Planning Study*. (http://www.mta.info/capconstr/sas/).

Meyers L., Guarino A., and Gamst G., 2005. Applied Multivariate Research: Design and Interpretation. Thousand Oaks, CA: Sage.

Midwest High Speed Rail Association. *Why Railroads: A Cleaner Environment*. Chicago, Illinois. (http://www.midwesthsr.org/youCanHelp.htm).

Miller T., 1991. *The Costs of Highway Crashes*. Publication # FHWA-RD-055. Washington, DC: Federal Highway Administration.

Mishan E., 1971. *Economics for Social Decisions*. New York: Praeger Publishers.

Mishan E., 1988. *Cost Benefit Analysis*. London: Routledge.

Modigliani F., and Miller M., 1958. "The Cost of Capital, Corporation Finance and the Theory of Investment," *American Economic Review*, 48(3), 261–297.

Mohring H., 1961. "Land Values and the Measurement of Highway Benefits," *Journal of Political Economy*, 69, 236–249.

Mohring, H., 1976. *Transportation Economics*. Cambridge: Ballinger Publishing Company.

Mohring H., 1993. Maximizing, Measuring and *Not* Double-Counting Transportation Improvement Benefits: A Primer on Closed- and Open-Economy Cost-Benefit Analysis," *Transportation Research*, 27B(6), 413–424.

Mohring H., and Williamson, 1969. "Scale and 'Industrial Reorganization' Economies of Transport Improvements," *Journal of Transport Economics and Policy*, 3, 251–271.

Mokhtarian P., and Salomon I., 2001. "How Derived is the Demand for Travel?, Some Conceptual and Measurement Considerations," *Transportation Research A* 35(8), 695–719.

Mokhtarian P., Samaniego F., Shumway R., and Willits N., 2002. "Revisiting the Notion of Induced Traffic through a Matched Pairs Study," *Transportation*, 29(2), 193–220.

Moomaw R., and Williams M., 1991. "Total Factor Productivity Growth in Manufacturing: Further Evidence from the States," *Journal of Regional Science*, 31, 17–24.

Morrison C., and Schwartz A., 1996. "State Infrastructure and Productive Performance," *American Economic Review*, 86(5), 1095–1111.

Mun S., 1994. "Traffic Jams and Congestion Tolls," *Transportation Research B*, 28(5), 365–375.

Munnell A., 1990. "Why Has Productivity Growth Declined? Productivity and Public Investment," *New England Economic Review*, January Issue, 4–22.

Munnell A., and Cook L., 1990. "How Does Public Infrastructure Affect Regional Economic Performance?" *New England Economic Review*, September/October, 11–32.

Myers D., Yen M., and Vidaurri L., 1996. "Transportation, Housing, and Urban Planning Implications of Immigration to Southern California," Research Report No. LCRI-96-04R, Lusk Center Research Institute, School of Urban Planning and Development, University of Southern California.

Nadiri I., and Mamuneas T., 1996. *Constitution of Highway Capital to Industry and National Productivity Groups.* Report prepared for FHWA. Washington DC: Office of Policy Development.

Nash C., 1993. "Cost-benefit Analysis of Transport Projects." In A. Williams and F. Giadina (Eds.), *Efficiency in the Public Sector, the Theory and Practice of Cost-Benefit Analysis.* London: Edward Elgar.

Nash C., Preston J., 1993. "Competition in Rail Transport: A New Opportunity for Railways?" Institute of Transport Studies, University of Leeds.

National Cooperative Highway Research Program (NCHRP). 1991. *Primer on Transportation, Productivity, and Economic Development*, Report No. 342. Washington, DC: NCHRP.

National Surface Transportation Policy and Revenues Study Commission, Final Report, 2007, Washington DC. (http://www.transportationfortomorrow.org/).

Nellthorp J., and Mackie P., 2000. "The UK Roads Review—A Hedonic Model of Decision Making," *Transport Policy*, 7(2), 127–138.

Nelson J., 1982. "Highway Noise and Property Values: A Survey of Recent Evidence," *Journal of Transport Economics and Policy*, 16(2), 117–138.

New Jersey Transit Authority, 2006. *Trans-Hudson Express Tunnel Project: Modeling and Analysis of the Link between Accessibility and Employment Growth.* New York, New York.

Newnan D., Lavalle J., and Eschenbach T., 2000. *Engineering Economic Analysis*, 8th Edition. Austin: Engineering Press.

Niemeier D., 1997. "Accessibility: An Evaluation Using Consumer Welfare," *Transportation*, 24(4), 377–396.

Nijkamp P., and Ouwersloot H., 1998. "A Decision Support System for Regional Sustainable Development: The Glag Model." In J.C.J.M. van den Bergh and M.W. Hofkes (Eds.), *Theory and Implementation of Sustainable Development Modeling.* Kluwer, Dordrecht, 255–273.

Nijkamp P., and Rietveld P., 1979. "Conflicting Social Priorities and Compromise Social Decision." In I. G. Cullen, (Ed.), *Analysis and Decision in Regional Policy.* London: Pion.

Nijkamp P., and van Delft A., 1977. *Multicriteria Analysis and Regional Decision-Making.* Leiden University: Martinus Nijhoff Social Sciences Division.

NIST/SEMATECH e-Handbook of Statistical Methods, http://www.itl.nist.gov/div898/handbook/.

Noland R., Small K., Koskenoja P., and Chu X., 1998. "Stimulating Travel Reliability," *Regional Science and Urban Economics*, 28, 535–564.

Noland R., and Cowart W., 2000. *Analysis of Metropolitan Highway Capacity and the Growth in Vehicle Miles of Travel.* Presented at the 79th Annual Meeting of the Transportation Research Board, Washington DC.

Noland R., 2001. "Relationship between Highway Capacity and Induced Vehicle Travel," *Transportation Research*, 35A(1), 47–72.

Noland R., and Polak J., 2002, "Travel Time Variability: A Review of Theoretical and Empirical Issues," *Transport Reviews*, 22(1), 39–54.

NTA—Metropolitan Mass Transit Authority. *About Neta: Company Profile.* 2005. (http://www.nta.co.il/site/en/neta.asp?pi=40).

OECD, 2008. Transport and Energy: The Challenge of Climate Change, International Transport Forum. http://www.internationaltransportforum.org.

Office of Management and Budget (OMB). 1992. *Guidelines and Discount Rates for Benefit-Cost Analysis of Federal Programs.* http://www.whitehouse.gov/omb/circulars/a094/a094.pdf.

Ong P., 2002. "Car Ownership and Welfare-to-Work," *Journal of Policy Analysis and Management*, 21(2), 239–259.

Ortuzar J., and Gonzales R., 2002. "Inter-Island Demand Response with Discrete Choice Models—Functional Form, Forecasts, and Elasticities," *Journal of Transport Economics and Policy*, 36, Part 1, 115–138.

Ortúzar J., and Willumsen L., 2001. *Modelling Transport*, 3rd Edition. West Sussex, England: John Wiley and Sons, Inc.

Oum T., and Zhang Y., 1990. "Airport Pricing: Congestion Tolls, Lumpy Investment and Cost Recovery," *Journal of Public Economics*, 43, 353–374, December 1990.

Oum T., Waters W., and Young., 1992. "Concepts of Price Elasticities of Transport Demand and Recent Empirical Estimates," *Journal of Transport Economics and Policy*, 26(2), 139–154.

Ozbay K., Bartin B., and Berechman J., 2000. *Full Costs of Highway Transportation in New Jersey*. New Jersey Department of Transportation Report.

Ozbay K., Bartin B., and Berechman J., 2001. "Estimation and Evaluation of Full Marginal Costs of Highway Transportation in New Jersey," *Journal of Transportation and Statistics*, 4(1), 81–104.

Ozbay K., Bartin B., and Berechman J., 2007. "Alternative Methods for Estimation Full Marginal Costs of Highway Transportation," *Transportation Research A*, 41(8), 768–786.

Ozbay K., Ozmen-Ertekin D., and Berechman J., 2006. „Modeling and Analysis of the Link between Accessibility and Employment Growth," *Journal of Transportation Engineering ASCE*, May, 132(2), 385–393.

Ozbay K., Ozmen-Ertekin D., and Berechman J., 2007. "Contribution of Transportation Investments to County Output," *Transport Policy*, 14(4), 317–329.

Paaswell R., and Berechman J., 1977. "The Impact of Car Availability on Urban Transportation Behavior," *Transportation*, 6(1), 121–134.

Paaswell R., and Berechman J., 2007. "Models and Realities: Choosing Transit Projects for New York City." In M. Van Geenhuizen, A. Reggiani, P. Rietveld, *Policy Analysis of Transportation Networks*. Ashgate, Surrey, UK: .

Paaswell R., Goldman T., and Peters J., 2004. *Impacts of Deferred Investment on Capital and Operating Budgets: Case Studies*. Draft Report. New York: City University of New York, University Transportation Research Center.

Paaswell R., and Recker W., 1977. *Problems of the Carless*. New York: Praeger.

Patriksson M., 1994. *The Traffic Assignment Problem: Models and Methods*. Utrecht, The Netherlands: VSP.

Peeta S., and Ziliaskopoulos A., 2002. "Fundamentals of Dynamic Traffic Assignment: The Past, the Present and the Future," *Networks and Spatial Economics*, 1(2), 201–230.

Pham L., and Linsalata J., 1991. "Effects of Fare Changes on Bus Ridership," American Public Transit Association, Washington DC (www.apta.com/info/online/elastic.htm).

Pickrell D., 1990. *Urban Transit Rail Projects: Forecast Versus Actual Ridership and Cost*. Washington, DC: US Department of Transportation.

Pickrell D., 1992. "A Desire Named Streetcar: Fantasy and Fact in Rail Transit Planning," *Journal of the American Planning Association*, 58(2), 158–176.

Pindyck R., 1991. "Irreversibility, Uncertainty and Investment," *Journal of Economic Literature*, 29(3), 1110–1148.

Pindyck R., 2000. "Irreversibilities and the Timing of Environmental Policy," *Resources and Energy Economics*, 22, 233–259.

Pouliquen L., 1970. *Risk Analysis in Project Appraisal*. World Bank Staff Occasional Papers, No. 11. Baltimore, MD: John Hopkins University Press.

Pred A., 1966. *The Spatial Dynamics of US Urban-Industrial Growth*. Cambridge, MA: MIT Press.

Proost S., de Palma A., Lindsey R., Balasko Y., Meunier D., Quinet E., Doll C., van der Hoofd M., and Pires E., 2004. *Theoretical Framework*, REVENUE Project, (Deliverable 2, Funded by 5th Framework RTD Programme), Rome: ISIS.

Public Financial Management, Inc. 1989. *Final Report Intergovernmental Financial Risks of New Rail Start Projects*. DTUM60-87-C-71343 Task 4. Urban Mass Transportation Administration. Washington DC.

Quinet E., 1997. "Full Social Cost of Transportation in Europe." In D. Greene, D. Jones, and M. Delucchi (Eds.), *The Full Costs and Benefits of Transportation Contributions to Theory, Method and Measurement*. Berlin: Springer, 69–111.

Quinet E., 1998. «Principes d'Economie des Transports," *Economica*, Paris, France, 419.

Quinet E., 2000. "Evaluation Methodologies of Transportation Projects in France," *Transport Policy*, 7(1), 27–34.

Quinet E., and Vickerman R., 2004. *Principles of Transport Economics*. Northhampton, MA: Edward Elgar.

Raiffa H., and Schlaifer R., 1968. *Applied Statistical Decision Theory*. Cambridge, MA: MIT Press.

Ramjerdi F., 1993. "Road Pricing in Urban Areas: A Means of Financing Investment in Transport Infrastructure or of Improving Resource Allocation: The Case of Oslo." Proceedings of the Sixth World Conference on Transport Research. Vol. 3. Lyon, France.

Ran B., and Boyce D., 1996. *Modeling Dynamic Transportation Networks*. New York: Springer-Verlag.

RAVCO, 2003. *Project Definition Report*. Vancouver, BC: RAVCO.

Recker W., 2001. "A Bridge between Travel Demand Modeling and Activity-Based Travel Analysis," *Transportation Research B*, 35(5), 481–506.

Redmond L., and Mokhtarian P., 2001. "The Positive Utility of the Commute: Modeling Ideal Commute Time and Relative Desired Compute Amount," *Transportation*, 28(2), 179–205.

Regional Plan Association. 2003. *The Economic Benefits of the Second Avenue Subway, A Report*. New York, NY: Regional Plan Association.

Regional Plan Association (RPA). 2004. "What We Know: Transit Investment Worth its Weight in Real Estate," *Spotlight on the Region*, 3(11).

Regnier E. 2005. "Activity Completion Times in PERT and Scheduling Network Simulation, Part II," *DRMI Newsletter 2005, Review of Economic Studies*, 9, 77–88.

Research Methods Knowledge Base. *Thurstone Scaling*. 2006. (http://www.social researchmethods.net/kb/scalthur.php).

Rietveld P., 2002. "Why Railways Passengers are More Polluting in the Peak than in the Off-Peak: Environmental Effects of Capacity Management by Railway Companies under Conditions of Fluctuating Demand," *Transportation Research Part D*, 7, 347–356.

Rindt C., Marca J., and McNally M., 2003. "Agent-based Activity Microsimulation Kernel Using a Negotiation Metaphor." Paper no. 03-4087 presented at the 82nd Annual Meeting of the Transportation Research Board, Washington, DC.

Rodier C., and Johnston R., 2002. "Uncertain Socioeconomic Projections Used in Travel Demand and Emissions Models: Could Plausible Errors Result in Air Quality Nonconformity?" *Transportation Research Part A*, 36(7), 613–631.

Rosenbloom S., and Altshuler A., 1977. "Equity Issues in Urban Transportation," *Policy Studies Journal*, 6(1), 29–40.

Saaty L., 1980. *The Analytic Hierarchy, Process: Planning, Priority Setting, Resource Allocation*. New York: McGraw Hill.

Samuelson P., 1947. *Foundations of Economic Analysis*, Cambridge, MA: Harvard University Press.

Sandmo A., and Dreze J., 1971. "Discount Rates for Public Investment in Closed and Open Economies," *Economica*, 38(152): 395–412.

Sawicki D., and Moody M., 2000. "Developing Transportation Alternatives for Welfare Recipients Moving to Work," *Journal of the American Planning Association*, 66(3), 306–320.

Sayers T., Jessop A., and Hills P., 2003. "Multicriteria Evaluation of Transport Plans—Flexible, Transparent and User-Friendly," *Journal of Transport Policy*, 10(2), 95–105.

Schelling T., 1968. "The Life You Save May be Your Own." In S. Chase (Ed.), *Problems in Public Expenditures Analysis*. Washington DC: The Brookings Institution.

Schmeidler D., 1989. "Subjective Probability and Expected Utility Without Additivity," *Econometrica*, 57, 571–587.

Schreyer C., Schneider C., Maibach M., Rothengatter W., Doll C., and Schmedding D., 2004. *External Costs of Transport Update Study, Final Report*, (http://www.infras.ch/e/).

Schweitzer L., and Valenzuela Jr. A., 2004. "Environmental Injustice and Transportation: The Claims and the Evidence," *Journal of Planning Literature*, 18(4), 383–398.

Scitovsky T., 1941. "A Note on Welfare Proposition in Economics," *Review of Economic Studies*, 9, November 1941, 77–88.

Seaman M., and de Cerreño A., 2003. *Dividing the Pie: Placing the Transportation Donor-Donee Debate in Perspective*. Rudin Center for Transportation Policy & Management, NYU Robert F. Wagner Graduate School of Public Service, May.

Seaman M., de Cerreño A., and English-Young S., 2004. *From Rescue to Renaissance: The Achievement of the MTA Capital Program 1982-2004*. December 2004. New York: New York University, Rudin Center for Transportation Policy & Management.

Sen A., 1992. *Inequality Re-examined*, Cambridge, MA: Harvard University Press.

Shapira, Z., 1994. *Risk Taking: A Managerial Perspective*, New York: Russell Sage Foundation.

Shidlovsky E., and Sarel M., 2005. *The True Costs of Motor Vehicle Use and Preferred Policy*. Jerusalem: Israeli Ministry of Finance, Economic & Research Department (in Hebrew) (http://www.mof.gov.il/research_e/mainpage.htm).

Shirley C., and Winston C., 2001. *An Econometric Model of the Effect of Highway Infrastructure Investment on Inventory Behavior, Project Status Report to the Federal Highway Administration (FHWA)*. Washington DC.

Shoup D., 2005. *The High Cost of Free Parking*. Chicago: APA Planners Press.

Siemiatycki M. 2006. *Mega-Projects in the Making: A Century of Transportation Infrastructure Investment in Vancouver, Canada*. Unpublished PhD Dissertation. Vancouver: University of British Columbia.

Simmonds D., and Still B., 1998. "DELTA/START: Adding Land Use Analysis to Integrated Transport Models." Paper no. 688. Cambridge, UK: David Simmonds Consultancy.

Simon H., 1957. *Models of Man*. New York: John Wiley and Sons.

Skamris M., and Flyvbjerg B., 1997. "Inaccuracy of Traffic Forecast and Costs Estimates on Large Transport Projects," *Transport Policy*, 4(3), 141–146.

Small K., 1982. "The Scheduling of Consumer Activities: Work Trips," *American Economic Review*, 72, 467–479.

Small K., 1992b. "Trip Scheduling in Urban Transportation Analysis," *American Economic Review, Papers and Proceedings*, 92(2), 482–486.

Small K., 1992a. *Urban Transportation Economics*. New York: Harwood.

Small K., 1999a. "Project Evaluation," Chapter 5 of *Essays in Transportation Economics and Policy: A Handbook in Honor of John R. Meyer*. Edited by José A.

Gómez-Ibáñez, William B. Tye, and Clifford Winston, Washington, DC: Brookings Institution, 137–177.

Small K., 1999b, "Economies of Scale and Self-Financing Rules with Non-Competitive Markets," *Journal of Public Economics*, 74, 431–450.

Small K., 2001. *Urban Transportation Economics*. UK: Routledge.

Small K., and Kazimi C., 1995. "On the Costs of Air Pollution from Motor Vehicles," *Journal of Transport Economics and Policy*, 29, 7–32.

Small K., Noland, R., Chu, X., Lewis, D., 1999. *Valuation of Travel-Time Savings and Predictability in Congested Conditions for Highway User Cost Estimation*, National Cooperative Highway Research Program Report 431. Washington DC: National Academy Press.

Small K., and Rosen H., 1981. "Applied Welfare Economics with Discrete Choice Models," *Econometrica*, 49(1), 105–130.

Small K., Winston C., and Evans C., 1989. *Road Work: A New Highway Pricing and Investment Policy*. Washington DC: The Brookings Institution.

Small, K., Winston C., and Yan J., 2005, "Uncovering the Distribution of Motorists' Preferences for Travel and Reliability," *Econometrica*, 73(4), 1367–1382.

Smith K., 1984. "A Bound for Option Value," Land Economics, 60(3), 292–296.

Smith J., and Gihring T., 2004. "Financing Transit Systems Through Value Capture: An Annotated Bibliography." Working Paper, Victoria Transport Policy Institute Victoria, BC, Canada. (http://www.vtpi.org/smith.htm).

"Son of the Bridge to Nowhere." Editorial, *New York Times*, April 23, 2006.

Spiekermann K., and Wegener M., 2004. "Evaluating Urban Sustainability Using Land-Use Transport Interaction Models," *European Journal of Transport and Infrastructure Research*, 4(3), 251–272.

Steimetz S., and Brownstone D., 2005. "Estimating Commuters 'Value of Time' with Noisy Data: A Multiple Imputation Approach," *Transportation Research B*, 39, 865–899.

Stern N., 2007. *The Economics of Climate Change—The Stern Review*. Cambridge, UK: Cambridge University Press. (http://www.hmtreasury.gov.uk/independent_reviews/stern_review_economics_climate_change/stern_review_report.cfm).

Stokey E., and Zeckhauser R., 1978. *A Primer for Policy Analysis*. New York: W.W. Norton & Company.

Stough R., and Haynes K., 2002. "Mega-Project Impact Assessment." In R. Stough, R. Vickerman, K. Button, and P. Nijkamp (Eds.), *Transport Infrastructure*. Cheltenham, UK: Edward Elgar, 452–466.

Straja S., 2000. *Application of Multiple Attribute Decision Making to the HOST Peer Review Program*. Columbia, MD: U.S. Department of Energy, Office for Science and Technology, Institute for Regulatory Sciences.

Strotz R., 1965. "Urban Transportation Parables." In J. Margolis, (Ed.), *The Public Economy of Urban Communities, Resources for the Future*. Washington, DC, 127–169.

Stuart D., 1997. "Goal-Setting and Performance Measurement in Transportation Planning and Programming," *Journal of Public Transportation*, 1(2), 49–72.

Sturk R., Olsson L., Johansson J., 1996. "Risk and Decision Analysis for Large Underground Projects, as Applied to the Stockholm Ring Road Tunnels," *Planning and Development*, 19–23.

Su C., Cheng M., and Lin K., 2002. "Data Preprocessing for Ranking of Projects—A Case Study of Rail Transportation Investment." In *Proceedings*, The 17th Conference of Transportation Association, ROC, Chiayi Taiwan, December 20–23, 2001.

Sudgen R., 2003. "Conceptual Foundations for Cost-Benefit Analysis: A Minimalist Account." In A. Pearman, P. Mackie P., and J. Nellthorp (Eds.), *Transport Projects, Programs and Policies: Evaluation Needs and Capabilities*. Ashgate, Aldershot.

Taylor B., 1995. "Public Perceptions, Fiscal Realities, and Freeway Planning: The California Case," *Journal of the American Planning Association* 61, 1, 43–56.

Taylor, B., 2002. "Rethinking Traffic Congestion," *Access*, Number 21, University of California Transportation Center (www.uctc.net), Fall 2002, 8–16.

TD Bank Financial Group. 2004. *Mind the Gap: Finding the Money to Upgrade Canada's Aging Public Infrastructure.* May 2004.

Texas Department of Transportation. *The Texas Transportation Challenge.* http://www.txdot.state.tx.us/txdotnews/trans_challenges.pdf.

The National Counsel for Public-Private Partnerships, Partnerships for Progress. http://www.ncppp.org/.

The Port Authority of New York and New Jersey. New York, New York. http://www.panynj.gov/.

The Texas Transportation Institute. 2001. *Traffic Congestion Trends: 1986–2001, Portland Congestion Increases Most, Only Houston Drops Among 75 Areas.* Texas A&M University, Texas Transportation Institute, College Station, Texas. http://www.publicpurpose.com/hwy-tti20011986.pdf.

The Traffic Safety Project, *Resources.* Simon Fraser University. Burnaby, British Columbia, Canada. (http://www.sfu.ca/traffic-safety/resources.html).

The World Bank, 1996. *The Economic Evaluation of Projects.* Washington DC: World Bank Publications.

Thurstone L., 1928. "Attitudes Can be Measured," *American Journal of Sociology*, 33, 529–554.

Tirole J., 1988. *The Theory of Industrial Organization.* Cambridge, MA: MIT Press.

TRACE. 1999. *Elasticity Handbook: Elasticities for Prototypical Contexts.* Paris/Brussels: The European Commission, Directorate-General for Transport, (www.hcg.nl/projects/trace/trace1.htm).

Translink—South Coast British Columbia Transportation Authority. *Canada Line Opening 2009.* (http://www.translink.bc.ca/Projects/Richmond_Airport/default.asp)

Transport Analysis Guidance, 2004a. Disruption During Construction and Routine Maintenance. Report prepared by the Department for Transport, London, England, (http://www.webtag.org.uk/webdocuments/3_Expert/9_Major_Scheme_Appraisal_in_LTPs/3.9.2.htm#5_2).

Transport Analysis Guidance, 2004b. *TAG Unit 1.1: Introduction to Transport Analysis.* Report prepared by the Department for Transport, London, England, (http://www.webtag.org.uk/webdocuments/1_Overview/1_Introduction_to_Transport_analysis/index.htm).

Transport Canada, 1999. "Final Report Highway Infrastructure and Opportunities for Reductions of GHG Emissions," http://www.tc.gc.ca/programs/environment/utsp/transitstudies/docs/Cost-Benefit.pdf.

Transport Canada, 1999. "Transport and Climate Change: Options for Action," http://www.tc.gc.ca/programs/environment/climatechange/subgroups1/Options_Paper/English/Trans_Final_OR-en.pdf).

Transportation Research Board, 1995. *Expanding Metropolitan Highways: Implications for Air Quality and Energy Use.* TRB Special Report #345. Washington, DC: National Academy Press, (http://www.trb.org).

Transportation Research Board, 2000. *Highway Capacity Manual. 3rd Edition.* Washington, DC: Transportation Research Board.

Transport Studies Group (TSG). 2005. *Measuring Accessibility as Experienced by Different Socially Disadvantaged Groups.* London, University of Westminster, Engineering and Physical Sciences Research Council (EPSRC). (http://www.wmin.ac.uk/transport/projects/samp.htm).

Truong P., and Hensher D., 1985. "Measurement of Travel Time Values and Opportunity Cost from a Discrete-Choice Model," *Economic Journal*, Royal Economic Society, 95(378), 438–451.

UK Ministry for Transport, 2004. "Values of Time and Operating Costs," London: Integrated Transport Economics and Appraisal (ITEA).

"Urban Sprawl in Europe—The Ignored Challenge Document Actions," *European Environment Agency*. EEA Report No 10/2006. Copenhagen, Denmark.

US Department of Transportation, Federal Highway Administration. August 1997. *Highway Cost Allocation Study*, Tables V-23. Washington DC. http://www.fhwa.dot.gov/policy/hcas/summary/index.htm.

US Department of Transportation, Federal Highway Administration. October 7, 2008. *Congestion: A National Issue*. Washington DC. http://www.ops.fhwa.dot.gov/aboutus/opstory.htm.

US Department of Transportation, 1991. *Cost of Owning and Operating Automobiles, Vans and Light Trucks*, Washington DC.

US Department of Transportation, 1997. *The Value of Travel Time: Departmental Guidance for Conducting Economic Evaluations*. Washington DC.

US Department of Transportation, 2000. *Transit Benefits 2000 Working Papers*, Office of Policy Development, Federal Transit Administration. Washington DC.

US Department of Transportation, Federal Highway Administration, 2001. *National Household Travel Survey*. Washington, DC. http://nhts.ornl.gov/publications.shtml

US Department of Transportation, 2001. "The Value of Travel Time: Departmental Guidance for Conducting Economic Evaluations." Washington DC.

US Department of Transportation, 2002a. Washington DC: Bureau of Transportation Statistics, http://www.ops.fhwa.dot.gov.

US Department of Transportation. 2002b. "Measuring Up: The Trend Towards Voter-Approved Transportation Funding," Surface Transportation Policy Project.

US Department of Transportion (DOT). 2006. *Transportation Statistics Annual Report*. Washington, DC: Author, Bureau of Transportation Statistics (http://www.bts.gov/publications/transportation_statistics_annual_report/20.06/html/chapter_02/table_k_03.html).

US Department of Transportation, National Highway Traffic Safety Administration website. Washington DC. (http://www.nhtsa.dot.gov/).

US Department of Transportation, 2003. *2002 Status of the Nation's Highways, Bridges and Transit: Conditions & Performance*, Report to Congress. Washington, DC.

US Department of Transportation Federal Highway Administration, Public Private Partnerships, http://www.fhwa.dot.gov/ppp/.

US Government Accountability Office, 2005. Highlights of an Expert Panel, "The Benefits and Costs of Highway and Transit Investments," GAO-05-423SP, Washington DC.

van Ommeren J., van den Berg G., and Gorter C., 2000. "Estimating the Marginal Willingness to Pay for Commuting," *Journal of Regional Science*, 40(3), 541–563.

Varaiya P., 2005, "What We've Learned about Highway Congestion," *Access*, 27, 2–9.

Varian H., 1992. *Microeconomic Analysis*, 3rd edition. New York: W. W. Norton.

Venables A., and Gasiorek M., 1999. *The Welfare Implications of Transport Improvements in the Presence of Market Failure*. Report to Standing Committee on Trunk Road Assessment (SACTRA). Department of Environment, Transport and Regions, London.

Venabels A., and Gasiorek M., 1996. "Evaluating Regional Infrastructure: A Computable Approach." Manuscript. London: London School of Economics.

Venables A., 2007. "Evaluating Urban Transport Improvements: Cost-Benefit Analysis in the Presence of Agglomeration and Income Taxation," *Journal of Transport Economics and Policy*, 41(2), 173–188.

Verhoef E., 1994. "External Effects and Social Costs of Road Transport," *Transportation Research A*, 28, 286.

Vessali K., 1996. "Land Use Impacts of Rapid Transit: A Review of Empirical Literature" *Berkeley Planning Journal*, 11, 71–105.

Vickerman R., 2000. "Evaluation Methodologies for Transport Projects in the United Kingdom," *Transport Policy*, 7(1), 7–16.

Vickrey W., 1960. "Utility, Strategy and Social Decision Rules," *Quarterly Journal of Economics*, 74, 507–535.

Vickrey W., 1968. "Automobile Accidents, Tort Law, Externalities, and Insurance: An Economist's Critique," *Law and Contemporary Problems*, 33, 464–487.

Victoria Transport Policy Institute (VTPI), 2002. *Transportation Cost and Benefit Analysis—Air Pollution Costs* (http://www.vtpi.org).

Vincent W., and Callaghan-Jerram L., 2006. "The Potential for Bus Rapid Transit to Reduce Transportation-Related CO2 Emissions," *Journal of Public Transportation*, 9(3), 219–238.

Vining A., and Boardman A., 2008, "Public-Private Partnerships in Canada: Theory and Evidence," forthcoming in *Canadian Public Administration*, 51(1), 9–44.

Visser B., and Swank O., 2007. "On Committees of Experts," *The Quarterly Journal of Economics*, 122(1), 337–372.

Von Wartburg M., and Waters, II, W., 2004. "Congestion Externalities and the Value of Travel Time Savings," Chapter 2. In A. Zhang, A. Boardman, D. Gillen, and W. Waters, II. *Towards Estimating the Social and Environmental Costs of Transport in Canada: A Report for Transport Canada*. Vancouver: University of British Columbia, Center for Transportation Studies.

Vreeker R., Nijkamp P., and Ter Welle C., 2001. *A Multicriteria Decision Support Methodology for Evaluating Airport Expansion Plans*, Discussion Paper, 9/01/01. Tinbergen: Tinbergen Institute.

VTPI (Victoria Transport Policy Institute), 1994. *Transport Cost Analysis: Techniques, Estimates and Implications, Victoria, British Columbia*, (http://www.vtpi.org).

VTPI (Victoria Transport Policy Institute), 2000. *Transportation Cost and Benefit Analysis—Roadway Costs, Victoria, British Columbia*, (http://www.vtpi.org).

VTPI (Victoria Transport Policy Institute), 2005. *TDM Encyclopedia*, (http://www.vtpi.org).

Wachs M., 1979. Transportation for the Elderly: Changing Lifestyles—Changing Needs. Berkeley: University of California Press.

Wachs M., 1989. *When Planners Lie With Numbers: An Exploration of Data, Analysis and Planning Ethics*. Los Angeles: University of California.

Wachs, M., 2003. "Improving Efficiency and Equity in Transportation Finance," Brookings Center on Urban and Metropolitan Policy Transportation Reform Series. Washington, DC: The Brookings Institution, 19 pages.

Wacziarg R., 2001. "Measuring the Dynamic Gains from Trade," *The World Bank Economic Review*, 15(3), 393–429.

Waddell P, 2000. "A Behavioural Simulation Model for Metropolitan Policy Analysis and Planning: Residential Location and Housing Market Components of Urban-Sim," *Environment and Planning B: Planning and Design*, 27(2), 247–263.

Wald, M. "Budget Gives Amtrak Carrots, but Wields Sticks as Well," *New York Times*, November 26, 2005.

Wang H., 2000. "Fuzzy Multicriteria Decision Making—An Overview," *Journal of Intelligent & Fuzzy Systems*, 9(1–2), 61–84.

Wardman M., 2001. "A Review of British Evidence on Time and Service Quality Valuations," *Transportation Research* E, 37, 107–128.

Waters II W., 1994. "The Value of Travel Time Savings and Link with Income: Implications for Public Project Evaluation," *International Journal of Transport Economics*, 12(3), 243–253.

Waters W., 2000. "The Elusive Link Between Transportation Infrastructure and Economic Growth: Testing for Causality Between Provincial Infrastructure Capital and Economic Activity." *Bridging the Gaps. Canadian Transportation Research Forum, Proceedings of the 35th Annual Conference*. University of Saskatchewan, Canada.

Weinberger R., 2001. "Light Rail Proximity Benefit or Detriment in the Case of Santa Clara County California," *Transportation Research Record*, 1747, 104–113.

Weisbrod B., 1964. "Collective Consumption Services of Individual Consumption Goods," *Quarterly Journal of Economics*, 78(3), 71–77.

Weisbrod G., and Weisbrod B., 1997. *Assessing the Economic Impact of Transportation Projects: How to Match the Appropriate Technique to Your Project*, Transportation Research Circular No. 477. Washington DC: National Academy Press.

Weisbrod G., and Treyz F., 1998. "Productivity and Accessibility: Bridging Project Specific and Macroeconomic Analysis of Transportation Investment," *Journal of Transportation Statistics*, 3, 65–79.

Weitzman M., 1994. "On the 'Environmental' Discount Rate," *Journal of Environmental and Management*, 26(2), 200–209.

Wheaton W., 1973. "Price Induced Distortions in Urban Highway Investment," *Bell Journal of Economics*, 9, 622–634.

Williams H., 1976. "Travel Demand Models, Duality Relations and User Benefits Analysis," *Journal of Regional Science*, 16, 147–166.

Williams H., 1977. "On the Formation of Travel Models and Economic Evaluation Measures of Users Benefits," *Environmental and Planning A*, 9, 285–344.

Williams A., and Giardina E., 1993. *Efficiency in the Public Sector, The Theory and Practice of Cost-Benefit Analysis*. London: Edward Elgar.

Williams H., Van Vliet D., Parathira C., and Kim K., 2001. "Highway Investment Benefits under Alternative Pricing Regimes," *Journal of Transport Economics and Policy*, 35(2), 257–284.

Williams H., and Yamashita Y., 1992. "Travel Demand Forecasts and the Evaluation of Highway Schemes Under Congested Conditions," *Journal of Transport Economics and Policy*, September, 261–282.

Willig R., 1976. "Consumer Surplus without Apology," *American Economic Review*, 66, 589–597.

Wilson A., 1998. "Land Use/Transport Interaction Models: Past and Future," *Journal of Transport Economics and Policy*, 32(1), 3–26.

Winston C., and Maheshri V., 2007. "On the Social Desirability of Urban Rail Transit Systems," *Journal of Urban Economics*, 62(2), 362–382.

Winston W., 1994. *Operational Research: Application and Algorithms*. Belmont, CA: Thompson International.

World Bank, 1994. *Infrastructure for Development*, World Development Report. Deception in Planning and Project Evaluation.

World Resources Institute, 2005. *Navigating the Numbers: Greenhouse Gas Data and International Climate Policy*. Montreal, Canada.

Yaari M., 1987. "The Dual Theory of Choice Under Risk," *Econometrica*, 55, 95–115.

Yang H., 1997. "Sensitivity Analysis for the Elastic-Demand Network Equilibrium Problem with Applications," *Transportation Research B*, 31(1), 55–70.

Zanakis S., Solomon A., Wishart N., and Dublish S., 1998. "Multi-Attribute Decision Making: A Simulation Comparison of Selected Methods," *European Journal of Operation Research*, 107(3), 507–529.

Zellner A., and Theil H., 1962. "Three-Stage Least Squares: Simultaneous Estimation of Simultaneous Equations," *Econometrica*, 30(1), 54–78.

Zionts S., 1997. "Bringing MCDM to the Forefront of Management Practice." In T. Stewart, Van-den-Honert, and C. Robin (Eds.), *Trends in Multicriteria Decision Making, Proceedings of the 13th International Conference on Multiple Criteria Decision Making*. Cape Town, South Africa, January 1997.

Zupan J., 2001. *Vehicle Miles Traveled in the United States: Do Recent Trends Signal More Fundamental Changes?* New York: Surdna Foundation, http://www.surdna.org.

Author Index

Subject Index